for Jim —
with many
help, and his

Frank.

C000176065

OIL POLITICS
A Modern History of Petroleum

OIL POLITICS
A Modern History of Petroleum

Francisco Parra

I.B. TAURIS
LONDON · NEW YORK

Published in 2004 by I.B. Tauris & Co. Ltd
6 Salem Road, London W2 4BU
175 Fifth Avenue, New York, NY 10010
www.ibtauris.com

In the United States of America and in Canada distributed by Palgrave
Macmillan, a division of St Martins Press, 175 Fifth Avenue, New York NY
10010

ISBN 1 86064 977 7

A full CIP record for this book is available from the British Library
A full CIP record for this book is available from the Library of Congress

Library of Congress catalog card: available

Printed and bound in Great Britain by MPG Books Ltd, Bodmin from
camera-ready copy supplied by the author

CONTENTS

ACKNOWLEDGMENTS

I am most grateful to those who took the time and had the patience to talk with me, some of them on several occasions, about the subject of this book. All of them have had great experience of the oil industry over many years. Many of them I have known for a long time, and I am fortunate to be able to count them among my friends:

Professor M. A. Adelman, Nordine Ait Laoussine, James Akins, Abdul Amir Al Anbari, James Bamberg, Elliot Cattarulla, Fadhil Al Chelabi, Manuchehr Farmanfarmaian, Sir Peter Holmes, Robert Mabro, Parviz Mina, Thomas D. Mullins, Farrokh Najmabadi, Fuad Rouhani, Ian Seymour, Ian Skeet, Sir David Steel, G. Campbell Watkins, Shaikh Ahmed Zaki Yamani.

My brother, Alirio A. Parra, gave me invaluable advice throughout.

I could not have written this book without hundreds of contacts over the past fifty years with others, friends and acquaintances, in oil companies, governments, international organizations, universities, and consultancies. Such merit as it has is due to them more than me.

Francisco R. Parra
FRParraM@aol.com
East Orleans, Mass.

ABBREVIATIONS

bd   barrels per day
kbd   thousand barrels per day
mbd   million barrels per day
MT   metric tons
LNG   liquefied natural gas
NGLs   natural gas liquids

ADPC   Abu Dhabi Petroleum Company
AGIP   Azienda Generale di Petrolio
AIOC   Anglo Iranian Oil Company
Aminoil   American Independent Oil Company
ANS   Alaska North Slope
ANWR   Arctic National Wildlife Refuge
AOC   Arabian Oil Company
API   American Petroleum Institute
Aramco   Arabian American Oil Company
BP   British Petroleum Company
BPC   Basra Petroleum Company
BNOC   British National Oil Corporation
CALTEX   California Texas Oil Company
CIEC   Conference on the International Economic Order
CFP   Compagnie Francaise des Petroles
CPE   Centrally Planned Economy
E&P   Exploration and Production (agreements)
EC   European Communities
ECA   Economic Cooperation Administration
ECE   Economic Commission for Europe (U.N.)
ECSC   European Coal and Steel Community
EEC   European Economic Community
ENI   Ente Nazionale Idrocarburi
ERAP   Entreprise de Recherches et d'Activités Pétrolières
FSU   Former Soviet Union
FTC   Federal Trade Commission
GATT   General Agreement on Trade and Tariffs
GAO   General Accounting Office

GCC	Gulf Cooperation Council
GSP	Government Selling Price (same as OSP)
ICJ	International Court of Justice
IEA	International Energy Agency
IPC	Iraq Petroleum Company
IPE	International Petroleum Exchange
IPEC	Independent Petroleum Exporting Countries
JNOC	Japan National Oil Corporation
JPDC	Japan Petroleum Development Corporation
JPTC	Japan Petroleum Trading Company
KOC	Kuwait Oil Company
LDC	Less Developed Country
MNC	Multinational Corporations
	The abbreviation is used to denote the Hearings and Report of the Subcommittee on Multinational Corporations of the US Senate's Committee on Foreign Relations.
MPC	Mosul Petroleum Company
MSA	Mutual Security Agency
NGO	Non-Governmental Organisation
NIOC	National Iranian Oil Company
NPC	National Petroleum Council
NYMEX	New York Mercantile Exchange
OCS	Outer Continental Shelf
OECD	Organisation for Economic Co-operation and Development
OPA	Office of Price Administration
OPEC	Organization of the Petroleum Exporting Countries
OSP	Official Selling Price
PDVSA	Petroleos de Venezuela S.A.
Pirinc	Petroleum Industry Research Inc.
PRT	Petroleum Revenue Tax
SAG	Saudi Arabian Government
SIRIP	Société Irano-Italienne des Pétroles
SNEA	Société Nationale Elf Aquitaine
SNPA	Société Nationale des Pétroles d'Aquitaine
SPR	Strategic Petroleum Reserve
STANVAC	Standard Vacuum Oil Company
TAPLINE	Trans Arabian Pipeline
TIPRO	Texas Independent Producers and Royalty Owners Assoc.
TPC	Turkish Petroleum Company
TPER	Total Primary Energy Requirements

TRC	Texas Railroad Commission
UAE	United Arab Emirates
UNCTAD	United Nations Conference for Trade and Development
UNIDO	United Nations Industrial Development Organisation
UNRRA	United Nations Refugee Relief Association
USMC	U.S. Maritime Commission
WSAG	Washington Special Action Group
WS	Worldscale
MEES	Middle East Economic Survey
OGJ	Oil & Gas Journal
PIW	Petroleum Intelligence Weekly
PE	Petroleum Economist
PPS	Petroleum Press Service

INTRODUCTION

Most of the oil consumed in the world today has moved from one country to another. It is by far the largest single commodity in international trade, and the oil industry is one of the largest and most international of all industries in the world. That is why it is important.

But that is not why, or not *just* why, it is interesting. There are several other reasons, and this book focuses on three of them.

The international petroleum industry was developed almost entirely by seven large companies (the "majors"), each with a colorful history of its own, though by 1950, where we take up the story, they were starting down the path to homogenization. As far as the "upstream" or crude oil producing end of the international business was concerned, the companies themselves were of exclusively US and Western European origin. But the crude oil was massively concentrated in a small number of backward (soon to be developing) countries in the Middle East and Latin America, and was owned by the governments of those countries. This made for a strange kind of relationship between investor and host country, and one imbued moreover with colonialistic overtones, since some of the countries had been colonies or protectorates of Britain, or were in some sense client countries of either Britain or the United States. In a narrow, legal sense, the relationship itself was embodied in concession agreements of extraordinary longevity which lay outside the jurisdiction of the host countries. But there were of course other dimensions to the relationship—political, commercial and cultural—that acquired increasing importance over time, especially during the Cold War years.

There were additional ingredients in this already explosive mixture. One was that the crude oil in these countries was incomparably cheaper than other sources of energy and, indeed, than other sources of crude oil—particularly in the United States. Whoever could control output was in a position to cash in on the huge economic rents to which this cost difference gave rise. Another, that oil was, and still is, perceived as a strategic material. Again, whoever could control output was in a position to starve his enemies of a vital resource, and occasionally did so.

Years of this uneasy relationship between foreign investor (the oil companies) and the host governments, intermingled with the strategic interests of the major industrial powers, mainly the United States and Britain, were punctuated by localized breakdowns, starting in the nineteen thirties with the cancellation of the Iranian concession in 1933, and the nationalizations in

1

Bolivia (1937), Mexico (1938) and Iran (1951). Despite the Iranian nationalization of 1951, the system continued to function quite well for a couple of decades, and the elements of fragility were not always plain to see. However, the strains on it were, in the end, too great, and it fell apart almost entirely in 1973. Its last vestiges disappeared in 1979, amidst turmoil that had dire economic consequences.

This triangular relationship between companies, host governments, and home-country governments, is at the heart of policies and politics in the international petroleum industry, and it is one of the three main focal points of this book.

The second is the painfully slow development of competition. The major oil companies were never, in the post-World War II period, a cartel that curtailed production in order to maintain price at levels substantially in excess of long-term supply costs. They didn't have to be. In all of the major Middle East concessions, in Indonesia, and (to a much smaller extent) in Venezuela, they were in partnership in varying combinations the precise composition of which owed more to historical accident than design. Nevertheless, there it was: a situation where there was no alternative to agreeing to investment programs (and therefore output levels) for almost all of the oil entering international trade. The result had to be a compromise between those that wanted to go fast, and those that wanted to go slow. Imbalances among companies' crude requirements were sorted out through purchases by the crude-short companies (companies with more of their own refining capacity than crude production) from the crude-long companies (companies with less of their own refining capacity than crude production). This was convenient. The majors were inclined, for reasons of self-interest and history, to cooperate rather than compete in the crucial upstream crude oil producing phase of the industry, and none of them was chomping at the bit for more cost-crude supplies with which to go into the market and cut the others' throats. Indeed, there were many occasions when substantial crude from solely-owned concessions in Venezuela (mainly those of Exxon and Shell), producible at very low incremental short-term cost, was shut in.

However, the system had just enough lee-way in it to allow for some competition among the majors. Moreover, the system was not a closed one. By the late nineteen fifties and early nineteen sixties, it was leaking all over the place. Exports from the Soviet Union became substantial and competitive production was developed by "independents" (mostly of US origin) in Venezuela, Libya, Algeria, offshore Iran, Kuwait and Saudi Arabia. So there was a distinct downward trend in crude prices over the years. But it was painfully slow.

The slowness of the process was exacerbated by other factors: the majors were vertically integrated—they owned most of the world's exportable crude oil production, most of the refineries running on imported crude, much of the world's marketing facilities, and much of the tanker and pipeline transportation facilities in between. Competition among them was thus largely confined to the products markets, where none of them had a clear cost advantage, and to the small independent refining sector. In fact, independent refineries, including State-owned ones, running on imported crude were few and far between in 1950 (though the sector was to grow rapidly), and true sales of crude oil—that is, arm's-length transactions between unrelated companies—correspondingly minor. In addition, world demand for oil was growing at such a fast rate, sustained over more than twenty years, that the companies were never under pressure from stagnating volume. There were even short periods when they had trouble keeping up with demand.

After the energy crises of 1973 and 1979, control over crude production in the Middle East and other OPEC countries passed to the governments, who promptly converted OPEC from a common-front organization designed to balance the common front presented by the seven major oil companies, into a cartel. The OPEC cartel started with the huge advantage of an initial price that had been driven up to astronomical heights by a series of political events affecting supply. But the essential link with major oil companies had been seriously weakened in 1973 and finally broken in 1979 and what had been in essence a system of international prorationing brokered by the companies, albeit subject to perpetual and conflicting pressures from various governments (including the United States), was transformed into a more familiar cartelistic situation, where cooperation (i.e., production restraint) in the service of high prices for all alternated with competition for volume in the service of each. Prices have in consequence drifted slowly though erratically down since 1981. These first two focal points run concurrently through the first two periods covered by this book, from 1950 to 1986, and then take a back seat to the third—the restructuring of the industry. This third period overlaps with the second period, and starts essentially in the mid nineteen seventies. Painful adjustments were made throughout the industry and an entirely different landscape emerged.

There are of course all kinds of interesting features of the international petroleum industry during the years since 1950 other than those which I mention above. For example, there is the pervasive impact of the growth of oil consumption on society, patterns of living and industrial development; the many issues that have arisen in recent years concerning the environment, a particularly sensitive one for the petroleum industry because oil pollutes so badly when it is spilt, and inevitably pollutes to some extent when it is burnt; the varied organization of national markets and the reactions of the governments of major importing countries to dependence for supplies on a small group of politically unstable developing countries, supplies which were channeled through a small number of foreign (except into the United States, Britain and the Netherlands) oil companies; the strategic aspects of supply, particularly during the Cold War; and oil's impact on the environment. I have touched on them briefly, but I have chosen to concentrate on the what, how and why of the relationship between companies, their home countries, and producing governments; on the growth of competition; and on the period of adjustment that followed the energy crises of the nineteen seventies. These are the three most international aspects of the industry and the areas where the policies of the different groupings and the politics of their interaction have been most critical.

* * *

It may seem perverse, or at least a bit odd, to put conclusions in an introduction, as I now propose to do, but it does have the advantage of allowing the reader to bear in mind where the book is going. After all, this is not a comprehensive history of the industry.

First, I believe that, during the period up to 1970, the system—a quasi-cartel subject to slowly increasing competition, operating in the context of concession agreements whose stringency ensured their ultimate and premature demise—was mostly beneficial. It allowed the rapid and orderly development of the world petroleum industry at prices that were higher than they needed to be, but not by any means excessive. It also had the great merit of being self-destructing in the long run. It fostered competition and the development of geographically diversified supplies. If it had not been killed abruptly by political events, it would have eventually fallen victim to increased competition. By 1970, it had outlived its usefulness.

The second period, from 1971 to 1986, is more difficult to judge. The price increases of 1973 and 1979-81 were extremely disruptive in the short- and medium-term not so much because of their size but because of the abruptness with which they were introduced, the economic disruption and inflation that followed, and the hardship wreaked on the forgotten peoples of the Third World. And yet, perhaps the world needed a large price increase to put an end to the breakneck speed at which consumption was growing. Certainly, it is counter-intuitive to think that we would have been better off without the vastly improved efficiency of fuel-burning equipment that the higher prices brought, from cars to refrigerators to home heating equipment and electricity generating plants; or that we would have been better off without the development of more geographically diversified sources of supply. OPEC on the other hand scored a Pyrrhic victory of ghastly proportions and its member countries are still suffering, and suffering severely, from its effects. They, who were to rule the roost in the world of energy, became, ironically, the chief victims of an almost universal delusion, that the cost and price of energy would continue to rise indefinitely.

The third period, after 1982-86, has been one of wrenching adjustments. Junking the misdirected investments of the years of delusion, such as shale oil, has been particularly painful. Scrapping surplus tankers, closing or scrapping surplus refineries and upgrading the rest, at great expense, has also been painful. But the industry has surely emerged into a healthier world, a more competitive one, a more cost-conscious one, a more technologically inspired one, and one free from the politically and now economically obnoxious concessionary system. But at least one part of the old puzzle persists: how do you reconcile vast quantities of extremely low-cost oil (in the Middle East), which would sweep the board in a truly competitive industry, with the strategic need for geographically diversified but higher-cost supplies? Part of the answer has become clear in recent years: advancing technology brings down the cost of the latter. But good arguments remain in favor of a price for Middle East oil significantly in excess of a truly competitive level.

There are of course other problems and opportunities, though of a substantially different nature from those of the past. Most recently, there has been the invasion and occupation of Iraq by the United States and its ally, Britain, with consequences for the petroleum industry that are yet to unfold fully. Above all, for the longer term, the countries of the former Soviet Union, plus China and India with their huge populations and vast distances, are forces that loom large on the horizons both of supply and demand. And who knows what new technologies will bring? No doubt the future will be just as interesting as the past.

Chapter 1
CORNERSTONE CONCESSIONS

The Concessionary System

The international oil industry expanded quickly after the Second World War, largely from the base of the low-cost oil reserves discovered in Venezuela and a handful of countries in the Middle East, by a handful of US and European companies, later dubbed "The Seven Sisters" by Enrico Mattei, head of Italy's national oil company, AGIP. The legal basis on which these reserves were to be developed had been established well before 1950 in the form of concession agreements, some dating back to the twenties and thirties. For the most part, they worked well until the mid-1970s, and then, within a period of a few years, were swept away in all the major producing countries.

To appreciate fully the long period of expansion and prosperity that was so summarily pushed aside, the basis for the concessionary system and the way it was implemented in the Middle East needs to be understood. Its consolidation and homogenization in the early 1950s were a major part of the story of the international petroleum industry during those years.

Outside the United States and parts of Canada, subsurface mineral rights are universally the property of the state. The government must either explore for and develop the minerals itself (in this case hydrocarbons) or make an agreement for a company to do so. And every producing country in the world has, at least initially, taken the latter route. Sometimes, state-owned companies subsist side by side with the private sector in exploration and production (E&P), as in a few industrialized countries; sometimes, the state has taken over and entirely nationalized the private sector companies, as in post-Tsarist Russia, Mexico and most OPEC countries; but at one time or another, all have been the way of the concession or E&P agreement, and a few, having nationalized, started returning to it in the early 1990s.

Until the 1970s, the important producers outside the Third World could be counted on the fingers of one hand: the US, Canada, the then Soviet Union and, stretching a point perhaps, China. A dozen others, notably Australia and West Germany, produced amounts which, though important domestically, were marginal on the international scale. After the big three of the industrial world, 95 percent of rest of world production in 1970 came from developing countries. Of these—around sixty of them—ten were pre-eminent: five in the Middle East (Iran, Iraq, Kuwait, Saudi Arabia and the United Arab Emirates— UAE), three in Africa (Algeria, Libya and Nigeria), plus Indonesia and Venezuela. None of the others was significant in terms of volume during the 1950-1970 period, and even the three African countries and the UAE were insignificant prior to 1960.

But in the 1950s, it was just the tiny group of six core developing countries—Indonesia, Iran, Iraq, Kuwait, Saudi Arabia and Venezuela—that provided much of the raw material base for the huge growth of the world petroleum industry in the 1950s, and the slightly larger group of ten that did so in the 1960s. They were poor, economically backward, and sparsely populated (except for Indonesia), had little infrastructure or capital that could contribute to the development of the industry, and few human resources. But they owned the oil in the ground.

Little wonder that the seven major companies undertaking the world expansion felt some insecurity about their raw material base. Five of the seven majors were American: Chevron, Exxon, Gulf, Mobil and Texaco. One was wholly British (British Petroleum), and one Anglo-Dutch, Royal Dutch/Shell.[1] They were joined in some of their Middle Eastern concessions by the French company, Compagnie Française des Pétroles (CFP). They had already lost, to nationalization, Mexico, Russia and Romania as sources of supply, and had been in danger of losing Iran in the 1930s. Nor is it surprising that those importing industrialized countries that were not a home base for the companies, felt uneasy about their double jeopardy: dependence on a few foreign companies, albeit from friendly countries, who were in turn dependent on the smooth functioning of oil concessions in a few politically unstable and not-so-friendly countries.

Relations among the seven major companies plus CFP fueled fears of their clearly oligopolistic potential. In the Middle East, in Indonesia and, to a much lesser extent, in Venezuela, producing operations were conducted by diverse groupings of partnerships between the companies. These mutated downwards into marketing and refining outside the producing areas. Except for Iran, where the Anglo Iranian Oil Company (AIOC, later BP) reigned supreme (though shortly to yield), the principal concessions in the Middle East were all held by various combinations of the seven majors in 1950. In addition, the minor concessions in Bahrein and Qatar were similarly held; and the "Red Line" agreement of 1928[2] among the Iraq Petroleum Company (IPC) partners—ninety-five percent majors—prevented any of them from seeking concessions independently of the others within the area of the former Ottoman Empire (meaning most of the Arabian Peninsula, including Saudi Arabia, but excluding Kuwait).

None of these partnerships had been formed primarily for the purpose of suppressing or restraining competition. Their historic origins were diverse and the web-like organizational structure that emerged to dominate the industry during the 1950s and 1960s almost fortuitous. The IPC group, operating in Iraq and elsewhere, emerged from the division of the spoils of the First World War among the victorious Allies as they dismembered the Turkish Ottoman Empire; the joint BP/Gulf concession in Kuwait, not part of the "Red Line" agreement, was the result of a shotgun wedding forced on the British by the Americans' "open-door" policy; and in Saudi Arabia, the Arabian American Oil Company (Aramco) partnership that eventually emerged among four US companies was a result, first, of the need for capital and markets of the original concessionaire, Standard of California (later Chevron), causing it to invite The Texas Company (later Texaco) in; then of the further need for capital, markets and political clout for these two to invite in Standard Oil of New Jersey (later Exxon) and Socony (later Mobil), both of whom promptly repudiated the "Red Line" agreement.

The partnerships had far-reaching though unintended consequences, not least in their effect on competition. In order to develop the concessions, the various partners had to agree on investment plans and targets, notably production targets, and these in turn depended on each company's individual requirements as well as its alternative sources of supply. Companies short of crude relative to their refineries' requirements wanted to develop production faster than those who were long on crude. The result was a compromise under which the crude-short companies purchased oil at a special price (e.g., half way, or a quarter way, between cost and the companies' publicly posted, or "shop-window", price) from the crude-long companies. Thus, no company could race aggressively ahead in the markets without paying the laggards off, and so making discounted sales less attractive for the laggards. The result was the restraint of supply in a manner that pre-empted the need for production quotas, price-fixing and other accoutrements of a formal cartel. It was far too clever to have been designed as one.

Concession Characteristics

The term *concession* is now and has for some years been considered politically incorrect because it smacks of rights reluctantly or corruptly granted by governments to foreign companies, under some kind of duress; or because the concessions stem from a time when now-independent states were mere colonies or protectorates. The term has been replaced by the more neutral one *exploration and production (E&P) agreements* which embraces the largely cosmetic nomenclature adopted in various countries, such as *production-sharing agreements, risk contracts, etc.,* that came later, though their financial and economic effects might not in principle be significantly different from the historically older concessions, however much their legal structure may differ.

Concessions (or E&P agreements) in developing countries vary vastly and significantly in content, but all of them have essential features in common:

– The government grants the company an *exclusive right* to carry out exploration, development and hydrocarbon production operations in a *defined area* for a *limited period of time*;

– The company *acquires title to the hydrocarbons* and is almost always free *to dispose of them* without further restriction;

– The company *bears the financial and commercial risks* associated with the undertaking;

– The company *agrees to make certain payments* (signature bonus, surface taxes, royalties, production taxes, etc.) to the government in return;

– The concessions are *contracts* with the state, though this does not in itself imply insulation from the state's general power to pass legislation overriding the terms of the contract.

In developing countries generally, and particularly in the Middle East and Africa (to a lesser extent in Venezuela), the contractual element was overwhelmingly preponderant during the period up to the early 1970s, to the point of excluding the legislative or regulatory element altogether as well as the jurisdiction of the local courts, leaving only the question concerning the validity of the concessionary contract as a matter for the national law of the host country.   In practice, there have been exceptions, notably some governments' prohibition of shipments of oil to Israel and, for brief periods, to other destinations. This prohibition was respected by the concessionaire companies and their affiliates, but its validity was never tested in the courts.

In industrial countries, exploration and production arrangements are usually called *licenses*, sometimes *leases*. They almost always have contractual as well as regulatory elements, but even when the contractual element and form appear to predominate (as in the United Kingdom), the licensee cannot always rely on the terms of his license to escape the application to him of the state's general legislative powers, despite these being possibly exercised in a manner inconsistent with the terms of the lease. In none of the licensing systems, predominantly contractual or not, is any provision made in industrial countries for international arbitration or for the choice of any law other than the municipal (national) law of the country concerned for resolving disputes arising out of the license terms. Such licenses are acceptable to the investing company in most industrial countries because the companies have sufficient confidence that they will be fairly treated within the national jurisdiction.

No such confidence exists for operations in developing countries where concessionary contracts or E&P agreements are the universal rule. These contracts are not in law *sui generis* (though attempts have sometimes been made to represent them as such). But, except in Venezuela and some other Latin

American countries, they almost always include two features which are unusual for run-of-the-mill commercial operations within a single domestic jurisdiction: a choice-of-law clause and an arbitration clause.

In a choice-of-law clause, the parties can (and in the case of E&P agreements almost always do) agree that their contract will be governed by a law other than the national law of the host country, or by a combination of that law and international law. The company is thus not exposed to changes in the host country's law, discriminatory or otherwise. A corollary of the choice-of-law clause is the arbitration clause: the law chosen by the parties must be applied to disputes arising out of the contract by a tribunal which cannot be a court of the host country if the company's objectives in the choice-of-law clause are to be realized. An arbitration clause is therefore included in the agreement and various devices are agreed to ensure the tribunal's impartiality.

Choice of law other than the national law of the host country, combined with arbitration, effectively lifted the Middle East (and other) concessions out of the jurisdiction of the host country and conferred a high degree of legal security on the concessionaire. There was no way that his concession could be legally modified without his consent (short of outright nationalization, which some of the concessions also sought to make illegal).

The concession agreements were of extraordinary longevity and size. As of 1950, their validity stretched to 1983-84 in Venezuela and 2020 in Kuwait, other countries in the Middle East being intermediate. They covered vast areas: three concessions, all owned by the same group of companies, covered the whole of Iraq; another single one took all of the southern half of Iran onshore; another one, all of Kuwait onshore; another, much of Saudi Arabia; and another single one, all of the emirates (Qatar, Abu Dhabi, etc.) onshore— each owned by a varying combination of the major companies. (See Appendix 1-1.) They were, in retrospect, grotesque—but brought undreamt of revenues to the host countries at the time.

The Specter of a Cartel

The major oil companies were not, however, immune to legal actions by their own governments. One of the lasting legacies of John D. Rockefeller and his Standard Oil Trust was to make large oil companies forever unpopular in the United States. The Trust was broken up in 1911 under the US antitrust laws, but its many progeny prospered. Three of them (Chevron, Exxon and Mobil) became major companies and, with Gulf Oil and Texaco, were the five US international majors. They soon ran afoul of the antitrust laws again and in 1952 were under investigation by the Federal Trade Commission (FTC). In mid-1952 antitrust proceedings were instituted by the Department of Justice, at President Harry S. Truman's behest, against the seven majors, including the two non-US ones. The case against them was based largely on the FTC's staff report, *The International Petroleum Cartel* .[3]

But in vain had the authors of the report searched high and low for a smoking gun in the form of current agreements among the majors to ration production and fix prices. It was a slightly comic spectacle, because the police knew they had their men but couldn't pin a crime on them – because none had been committed. The majors were simply reaping benefits which could hypothetically have been produced by the crime of which they were accused. Of course, they never offered the real explanation—the unavoidable requirement to agree on investment and production programs resulting from the joint-venture nature of their arrangements in the Middle East and Venezuela. How could they explain when they were so busy denying the arrangements' obvious results and advancing absurd claims about the highly competitive nature of the industry?

Connoisseurs will savor the multiple ironies involved in the achievement of Secretary of the Interior Harold Ickes's objectives (in the late 1930s and early 1940s) of working Saudi Arabia's huge reserves into world markets in an orderly manner (i.e., without competition) and maintaining secure access to them. At first, these objectives were to be realized by having the US government buy out the Standard of California concession; then (when that project fell through) by building or financing a pipeline to the Mediterranean; and finally by means of a petroleum agreement with Britain to impose order on the international petroleum industry. All these attempts foundered largely because of opposition from—of all sources—the US independent oil companies. In the event, the same goals were attained largely as a by-product of the joint ownership of Aramco and the other major concessions in the Middle East and, more particularly, of the joint investment arrangements that they necessarily implied. The crowning irony came of course when the Department of Justice brought its anti-trust suit against the majors for doing precisely what Ickes had wanted them to do—one of the first of many instances when the United States was to pursue simultaneously two diametrically opposed policies in the Middle East.

Securing the Base: The Concessions in 1950

The narrow geographic base on which the industry (in the form of the major oil companies) depended was the handful of concessions in the countries mentioned above. But the search for security involved much more than the arbitration and choice-of-law clauses embedded in the concession agreements. On the contractual level, it was essential that the governments' discretionary power to levy taxes should be made inapplicable to the concessionaire companies. It is a normal and universally recognized right of a government to impose taxes at its discretion, within constitutional limits and procedures, and providing that they are not confiscatory to the point where they become a disguised expropriation. Hence, a major threat to the security of the concessionaire companies was this power to tax which might have been exercised to the hilt, short of killing the goose that laid the golden egg. The oil industry (meaning in practice the sole concessionaire) was too big a part of the economy, too tempting a target, not just because of its size relative to the rest of the economy, but also because taxes on it imposed no pain on citizens of the country, the taxes being essentially on exports. This threat was eliminated by inclusion in the concession agreement of "fiscal stability" clauses under which the governments undertook not to increase taxes or tax rates of any kind during the life of the agreement. Venezuela never gave up that right; Iraq had it before revision of the original IPC agreement in 1931, but then surrendered it in return for a trifling additional one-time payment. By 1950, none of the four major producing countries of the Persian Gulf could increase taxes on the companies without breach of contract.

Iraq Netted

The original IPC concession provided that the company would be subject to non-discriminatory taxes imposed by the government of Iraq, in addition to the payments stipulated in the concession itself. Article 27 of the Convention of 14 March 1925, as revised by the Principal Agreement of 24 March 1931, read in part, "No other taxes, impositions, duties, fees or charges, whether Government or municipal or port, shall be imposed upon the Company, or upon its property or privileges or employees within Iraq, than those ordinarily imposed from time to time upon other industrial undertakings, or upon their property or privileges or employees . . . ". This of course left the door open for unlimited tax increases at any time, provided that they were generally applicable in Iraq and not discriminatory.

The door was promptly closed. A side letter dated 24 March 1931, addressed to IPC by the government and signed by Prime Minister Nuri Said, read in part, "In order to remove your doubts as to the liability of the Company in connection with Article 27 of the Convention . . . the Company shall be exempt from all taxation falling due on or after 1st April 1931, of whatever nature whether State or Municipal . . . " in return for certain additional but relatively minor payments on production. The revised Convention together with this side letter and others was agreed and ratified by the Iraqi Parliament. Iraq had truly sold its birthright for a mess of potage.

The 1931 revision actually went far beyond a change in the State's powers to tax: perhaps of greater importance was the area of the concession, which was in effect increased from 192 square miles which the company was to select and retain within 32 months of the 1925 agreement's effective date, to 32,000 square miles with no relinquishment provisions. This was a decisive step in shutting competition out of the Middle East: if the parcel system had been retained, many more companies would have come in and the history of the oil industry in the Middle East would have been quite different. Here is what the State Department's oil expert in the 1950s had to say about the 1931 revision:

> The companies were now only interested in breaking up the parcel agreement. So in 1931 they persuaded the Iraqi government to modify the original agreement. It was a great mistake that this was ever modified. Nuri-es Said . . . was the Prime Minister then, and he put his initials on what I certainly consider one of the worst oil deals that has ever been signed, and one that in my opinion has damaged the interests not only of Iraq but of the whole world. He gave up the favorable conditions which the Iraqis had won in the 1925 agreement . . . Nuri came in and sold out his country for 400,000 pounds. He needed cash, and in exchange he gave up the parcel system and he gave up a refinery which had to be built in Iraq before any oil was exported. He also gave up the drilling obligation which would have forced the company really to operate in Iraq, not drill one or two wells and forget the rest of the area. He gave up a pipeline convention which stated that pipelines had to be built within a certain time limit. He gave up a provision which indicated Iraq would get oil at the lowest cost sold to others. All these provisions he gave up or modified in the 1931 agreement.[4]

Eventually, the IPC group acquired the two other oil companies operating in the country, Basrah Petroleum Company (BPC) and Mosul Petroleum Company (MPC) which held concessions to nearly all of the remaining area of Iraq, and their terms were assimilated to the terms of the IPC concession.

These developments were a prime example of exploitation (in the pejorative sense of the word) of a country that was, as a national entity, a creation of the victorious First World War allies and a colony in all but name. The virtually unrequited revision of the original TPC concession agreement was all the worse for the fact that the giant Kirkuk field had already been discovered and no arm's-length government would ever have agreed to the modifications introduced, most particularly the substitution of the existing parcellation system for one large block blanketing half the country. From the companies' point of view, this was of enormous value because it shut out competition and held in reserve the exploration and development of some of the most geologically attractive acreage in the world, much of which remains virgin territory more than seventy years later. Law 80 of 1961 restored the *status quo ante* by unilaterally confining IPC to much the same acreage it held prior to the 1931 revision.

The early 1950s were to witness two events of major significance for the industry: the unification of tax payments in Middle Eastern concessions and the unequivocal defeat of Iran's attempted nationalization. But they started somewhere else: Venezuela kicked off with 50/50 in 1948.

Paying the Rent: 50/50 in Venezuela

The oil industry in Venezuela underwent a thorough reorganization in 1943, spurred on by a number of different factors of which pressure for higher taxes on the companies was an important one. For its part, the US government was anxious to ensure that there was no repetition of the Mexican nationalization of 1937, especially in view of Venezuelan oil's strategic importance during the war. Consequently it wished to see a speedy, stable structure emerge from the new deal proposed by the Venezuelan president, General Isaias Medina, and the whole reorganization was a peaceful process that became very much of a joint venture between Venezuela and the United States. Max Thornburg, a former employee of Standard Oil of California and, at the time, petroleum adviser to the US State Department, helped draft the 1943 Hydrocarbons Law, and the Venezuelan government retained the services of two US consultants. One of them was Herbert Hoover Jr., who was later to play an important role as petroleum adviser to Secretary of State John Foster Dulles, in the settlement of the Iranian oil nationalization dispute.

Venezuela's Hydrocarbons Law of 1943 consolidated previous legislation and, with the promise of a new round of concessions and an extension in the period of the older ones, the companies were persuaded to convert their older concessions voluntarily to the new regime, despite the increase in payments to the government that it entailed. One of the acknowledged objectives of the law, drawn up with US consultants in attendance, was to effect a 50/50 split of profits between the concessionaires and the government: it was thought that the minimum royalty rates specified by the law plus income and other taxes at the then going rates would be at least equal to company profits. There appears to have been no discussion of the basis in economics of 50/50. It just seemed to be fair, and was acceptable to both government and companies. But as a measure for the government to capture all of the economic rent associated with the production of low-cost oil, it was a non-starter; indeed, it was not even designed with that objective in mind.

In the event, mainly because of an increase in international oil prices, these expectations were frustrated and the 1943 law resulted in a profit split less favorable to the government than 50/50. In 1945, a new left-wing reformist party (Acción Democrática) came to power with a policy of ensuring that total oil revenues should amount to at least 50 percent of the companies' pre-tax profits, and the new government of President Rómulo Betancourt and his oil minister Juan Pablo Pérez Alfonzo imposed a special, one-off supplemental excess profits tax applicable to the year 1945, bringing payments for that year above the 50 percent level.

In 1947, a decree-law (no. 212) was approved by the National Assembly, raising income tax rates (applicable in addition to the payment of royalties and other specifically petroleum taxes) from a maximum of 9.5 percent to a maximum of 26 percent, and it was thought that this increase would ensure a total revenue to the government of at least 50 percent.   However, rising prices in 1946 and 1947 again resulted in a shortfall of payments below the 50 percent mark. These were made up by industry voluntary contributions to public works in the non-oil sectors of the economy. The government decided to remedy the situation once and for all, and the income tax law of 1942, which was then in effect, was amended in November 1948 to provide for an additional tax (Impuesto Adicional), to be set at whatever amount was needed to bring total tax payments by each company to a minimum of 50 percent of its pre-tax profits. There was no serious opposition to it by the companies who had already implicitly accepted the principle of 50/50 when they converted their concessions to the 1943 Hydrocarbons Law. In any event, the higher income taxes were financially painless for the US companies since they could be, and were, credited directly against US income taxes.

Although the 1943 Hydrocarbons Law was designed to produce a 50/50 split of profits, it was therefore not until 1948 that 50/50 became a legal reality. The historian Irvine H. Anderson, in a paper on the Saudi 50/50 agreement, says in reference to the early attempts to reach 50/50 in Venezuela " . . . in 1943, the Venezuelan government had enacted a complicated set of tax laws intended to divide profits equally with the oil companies . . . At the time, all parties clearly understood that under the United States Internal Revenue Act of 1918 the tax portion of these payments was deductible from corporate taxes normally due to the American government by Jersey and Gulf Oil."[5] Perhaps, but no one else seems to have remarked on it. This is curious because when it emerged that the same tax credits applied to Aramco in Saudi Arabia after the introduction of 50/50 there, they aroused considerable criticism. Rómulo Betancourt, whose party, Acción Democrática was in power when the Impuesto Adicional (the income tax amendment providing explicitly for a minimum 50 percent share for the government) was enacted into law on 12 November 1948, does not mention the tax credit in his book *Venezuela, Política y Petróleo;* indeed, Betancourt expresses his surprise at the lack of violent adverse reactions from the oil companies to the tax increases of 1946-1948 which, being a politician, he ends up attributing to the wise but firm government of his party. Neither Manuel Pérez Guerrero, who was finance minister in 1948 when the Impuesto Adicional was enacted, nor Pérez Alfonzo, who was minister of development (which included responsibility for the oil industry), ever alluded to this tax credit.

In any event, within a few days of passing the decree-law, the government was overthrown by a military coup and, although the 50/50 Impuesto Adicional was not repealed (why should it have been?), a new pricing formula for royalties, which were quite separate from income taxes, was eventually agreed and resulted in a reduction of the royalty on heavy crudes to reflect the collapse in the price of heavy fuel oil. Oil consultant Walter J. Levy, who with the State Department's Herbert Hoover Jr., was to play a part in the settlement of the Iranian 1951 nationalization dispute (as adviser to President Truman's special envoy Averell Harriman), was a consultant to the Venezuelan government on the royalty pricing formula.

It was widely believed in Venezuela that the oil companies had a hand in overturning the government of Acción Democrática in November 1948, but if so, they left no tracks. In any event, it seems highly unlikely: the tax increases were not contentious, and Creole (the Exxon subsidiary in Venezuela and the largest of the companies there) was in practice already paying about 50 percent to the government (50.9 percent in 1945 and 49.0 percent in 1946). The 1948 Impuesto Adicional was applied to 1948 income and, by agreement, an additional payment was made by Creole for the year 1947 to bring that year's payments up to the 50 percent minimum. Despite the tax increases, the companies continued making substantial profits: Creole realized a return of 42 percent on its net assets in 1948.

Moreover, the new tax structure was in effect an affirmation that the government did not intend to go down the road to nationalization, as Mexico had so recently done and from which the companies were still smarting. Nevertheless, Pérez Alfonzo believed that Creole had played a role in the military coup, and told me, much later—in the 1960s—that he had resolved at the time that he would make Creole pay for it one day.

In the latter half of 1949, the new military government despatched a three-man team to the Middle East, composed of Edmundo Luongo Cabello (shortly to head up a newly created Ministry of Mines and Hydrocarbons), Luis Emilio Monsanto and Ezequiel Monsalve Casado. Their mission was to explain 50/50 to the producing governments there and encourage them, for obvious competitive reasons, to raise their own taxes to parity with Venezuela.

They were decidedly not welcome. The Iranian Foreign Minister sent instructions to the Iranian Embassy in the United States, where the three had applied for visas, that they were to be refused. The instructions were ignored by the Iranian ambassador, who issued the visas and sent back a cable saying that the visit was in Iran's interests. Upon their arrival in Tehran (where the conflict with AIOC was already simmering), they were at first officially ignored (at the time, Venezuela had no diplomatic relations with Iran), and were hosted by Manucher Farmanfarmaian, at that time Director of Concessions in the Ministry of Finance that dealt with petroleum matters. They were later received by Finance Minister Golshayan and also paid a call on the Shah.

From Iran, they flew to Saudi Arabia, but were not even allowed off the plane, according to Farmanfarmaian. In Kuwait, they were received by the Emir but were accompanied on their visit by the British Political Agent (Kuwait was still a British Protectorate); and in Iraq, Luongo Cabello fell ill and the visit was apparently cut short.

50/50 in Saudi Arabia

Nevertheless, the introduction of 50/50 in the Middle East was only a question of time, and it came first in Saudi Arabia. But it came with a difference, as will be seen.

Crude oil production in Saudi Arabia and the Middle East generally was burgeoning. In 1947, the country's production rose by 50 percent over the previous year, then by 59 percent more in 1948 and a further 22 percent in 1949, to 174 thousand barrels per day (kbd), one-third of the Middle East's total production that year; and unit costs dropped rapidly, down to about $0.20 per barrel.

The large increases in production of 1947 and 1948 were partly offset by the decrease in price from $2.22 per barrel at the end of 1947, to $2.03 in May 1948, $1.88 in April 1949 and $1.75 in July 1949. These decreases were reflected in lower royalty payments, royalty being fixed at 12 percent of price. King Ibn Saud began to feel the pinch by 1949, as spending outstripped the growth in revenues. There were demands on Aramco for loans, contributions to a Saudi welfare fund, and more. These were accompanied by (probably not very serious) threats from Finance Minister Abdullah Suleiman to close down the whole Aramco operation if the government's demands were not met. Reluctantly, Aramco's four shareholding companies, all American, came to recognize that a substantial increase in payments to the government was becoming difficult to refuse. The State Department's concern was primarily over national security within the broader context of the Middle East generally, and it quickly concluded that higher payments were desirable and probably inevitable after the adoption of 50/50 in Venezuela. The outbreak of the Korean War in June 1950 reinforced these concerns, which were not so much fear of communism and Soviet penetration of the Middle East as the possible rise of hostile, nationalist regimes. Moreover, trouble was already brewing in Iran, where a new ("Supplemental") agreement had been negotiated by the British-owned Anglo-Iranian Oil Company (AIOC), sole concessionaire in Iran at the time, and signed by the government, but had failed to obtain the ratification of the Majlis, the Iranian Parliament.

By 1949, the Saudis were aware of the size of Aramco income tax payments in the United States, and were also aware that any Saudi income tax paid by Aramco could be credited against US income taxes. In a Department of State Memorandum of Conversation dated 20 July 1949, concerning a meeting attended by James Terry Duce (Aramco vice president), R. I. Brougham (Aramco vice president for finance), George McGhee (assistant secretary of state for Near Eastern Affairs) and others, Duce reported that the Saudi Arabian Finance Minister " . . . said he understood that Aramco could pay Saudi Arabia an income tax and deduct it from the company's US income tax, thus putting no increased burden on Aramco . . . ". Brougham said that " . . . the Saudis had asked George Eddy of the Treasury Department, when he was in Saudi Arabia, how to get more money out of oil, and Eddy mentioned various methods . . . It seems that Eddy told the Saudis that the sums paid by Aramco to Saudi Arabia in income tax would be deductible from US income taxes paid by that company."

The immediate problem for the Saudis was the tax exemption in the Aramco concession. Article 21 of the original concession of May 1933 reads in part that " . . . the Company and enterprise shall be exempt from all direct and indirect taxes, imposts, charges, fees and duties (including, of course, import and export duties), it being understood that this privilege shall not extend to the sale of products within the country, nor shall it extend to the personal requirements of the individual employees of the Company." However, having been told that a Saudi income tax would not materially affect Aramco, no strong opposition to such a tax was to be anticipated, and the King subsequently (with US legal advice) issued an income tax decree, towards the end of 1950, imposing an income tax of 20 percent on all companies within Saudi jurisdiction, including Aramco. Remarkably, at a meeting held at the State Department on 13 November 1950 between Fred A. Davies (executive vice president of Aramco), George McGhee (assistant secretary of state for Near Eastern Affairs), Gwin Follis (vice chairman of Socal), Orville Harden (executive vice president of SONJ), and Brewster Jennings (president of Mobil), " . . . there was general agreement . . . that despite the words in the concession agreement, no valid objection could be raised against the Saudi action because a sovereign cannot sign away his sovereign rights of taxation."[6]

The introduction of 50/50 into Saudi Arabia became a well-orchestrated joint undertaking of Aramco, its parent companies, the US State Department and the US Treasury, designed to offer to Saudi Arabia promptly and voluntarily what many recognized would sooner or later have to be conceded throughout the Middle East. Nothing was to be gained by resisting the inevitable and allowing conflicts to build up that could bring difficult political situations in their wake. As a place to start, Saudi Arabia was a natural choice—indeed the only feasible one. The United States had no say in Iran, where AIOC was the sole concessionaire; and British oil interests and political influence were pre-eminent in both Iraq and Kuwait.

Consequently, Aramco and its parent companies opened talks with the Saudis in 1950. The pattern bore a strong resemblance to the Venezuelan one, though compressed in time. On the advice of a US Treasury official and a Washington tax lawyer, King Ibn Saud issued a royal decree on 2 November 1950, imposing an income tax of up to 20 percent of net profits on corporations in the Kingdom. It was obvious that the proposed tax, together with royalties and other payments would not yield a 50/50 split (if that was the ostensible purpose), and a second royal decree was issued on 27 December 1950 imposing an additional income tax on companies engaging in the production of hydrocarbons in the Kingdom (Aramco was the only one), devised in such a manner that the total of all Aramco's income tax, royalty and other tax payments would amount to, but not exceed, 50 percent of the company's net profits. Three days later, Aramco agreed to submit voluntarily to both decrees.

This was the critical difference with the Venezuelan model: income tax in Venezuela was not a consensual matter, a subject of agreement between companies and government; it was no part of the concession agreements; it was a tax imposed at the government's discretion and could be changed at the government's discretion, just as income taxes normally are everywhere. The constraint on income tax rates on the oil industry in Venezuela was, rather, of an economic nature: excessive taxes would invite increased competition from the Middle East and a consequent decline in Venezuelan production. No comparable constraint existed for the low-cost producers of the Middle East, and it was therefore of the utmost importance for the oil companies to ensure that tax rates remained capped for the life of their concession agreements.

Apart from this fundamental difference, the whole process—the replication of the Venezuelan pattern in Saudi Arabia (basic income tax plus additional tax); the short time span between the first decree and the second; the virtually simultaneous promulgation of the second decree and the signing of the agreed amendment to the concession whereby Aramco "submitted" to the income taxes—was little more than a charade put on for the sole purpose of having the Saudi taxes qualify under the Internal Revenue Service (IRS) criteria as a credit against US income taxes, even though this was not at first taken for granted by the companies. Indeed, initially, the Saudi tax was payable on profits *after* the payment of taxes in the United States, while the companies were still uncertain that the Saudi tax would be allowed as a credit in the United States. By the end of 1951, Aramco had received formal confirmation from the IRS that the Saudi income tax payments would be eligible for treatment as tax credits, and a further supplemental agreement dated 13 February 1952 was signed eliminating the provision in the previous agreement for the prior deduction of US taxes in the calculation of 50/50. The net effect, of course, was that Aramco ended up paying essentially the same amount of tax—but to Saudi Arabia (where, after all, the profits arose) rather than to the United States. For the company and its parents, it was a painless way of satisfying the persistent demands of the host country.

Later, this arrangement was represented by some in the United States as a sleight of hand, an illegitimate exercise, a gift to Saudi Arabia of tax revenues properly belonging to the United States, a payment, almost, of foreign aid by the United States, and indeed this was the view of some members of the State Department itself. In fact of course the companies' taxable profits arose from the sale of oil f.o.b Saudi Arabia, and it was, and is, the universal rule for profits to be taxed in the first instance in the country where they arise, without prior deduction of foreign taxes. However, in justifying the "transfer" of these tax revenues from the US to Saudi Arabia, the companies chose to emphasize the danger they ran of cancellation of the concession if payments to the Saudis were not increased, and the consequent damage that might be done to US national security, given the fact that the United States had become a net importer of oil in 1948 and would in future be increasing its imports.

It was in fact difficult to see King Ibn Saud cancelling the American concession under practically any circumstances: no other major company would have taken it up, and it was too much, politically and economically, for any other company to handle. But it was hardly possible for the companies to point out that their profit margin per barrel was becoming so large throughout the Middle East that they had better move first with the precedent of an income tax within a strong contractual framework than wait for Iran or Iraq to explode with resentment. Here, the companies were tactically astute and strategically far-sighted, as events were already beginning to show in Iran.

Admittedly, at the Senate Hearings on Multinational Corporations in 1974, the companies were at some pains to exaggerate the pressure—virtual compulsion—they were subjected to before acceding to 50/50. Their dilemma was that they could not concede Saudi Arabia's right to set income taxes at whatever rate its government might deem appropriate; but they could not admit to the IRS that the Saudi income tax was a contractually and voluntarily agreed impost, like any royalty, because they would then not have been able to credit it fully against US income tax. Irvine H. Anderson goes on to say, "The only question remaining was whether Aramco's acquiescence in the Saudi decree, which negated the provision of the 1933 agreement exempting it from Saudi taxes, made the money an "agreed payment" equivalent to a royalty rather than a tax. The counter-argument was that a sovereign power cannot contract away its taxing power and the 1933 clause had been invalid in the first place."[7] But presumably the companies did not have the temerity to represent this as their position to the IRS. The opinion that "a sovereign power cannot contract away its taxing power" was certainly not shared by Aramco officers: neither Duce nor Brougham had any doubts about the validity of the concession's tax exemption, and in any event Saudi Arabia never appeared to question it.

50/50 Spreads

50/50 spread quickly. The companies offered essentially the same deal as the Aramco one to Kuwait and Iraq. Revised agreements were signed in Iraq by the Iraq Petroleum Company (IPC) and the government on 3 February 1952, ratified by Parliament and received the royal assent. In Kuwait, a similar agreement was signed and came into effect from 30 November 1951. Under pressure from the British companies (notably AIOC), the UK Treasury revised its tax rules to make the new producing country taxes deductible against UK income tax obligations.

The 50/50 deals doubled government revenues in the Middle East, from 30-40 cents per barrel to 65-75 cents, though at first they were not homogenous, being initially on a different pricing basis in each country. Indeed, it was not until 1955 that Saudi Arabia obtained posted prices as a basis for 50/50; Iraq's deal was on posted prices from the start, but Kuwait and Saudi Arabia were initially on lower, special long-term contract or inter-affiliate prices.[8]

The increased payments were offset by the companies against their tax payments to their home governments. The 50/50 agreements were to last almost twenty years and their durability was undoubtedly due in large measure to their perceived fairness; but in fact they did not yield a 50/50 split for very long. In Venezuela, the royalty-pricing formula got seriously out of line as the US crude prices on which it was principally based rose to substantially higher levels than market prices for Venezuelan crudes, and this had the effect of pushing total taxes (royalty, ordinary income tax and other taxes) well above 50 percent of company profits. In the Middle East, the companies' taxable income was computed on the basis of posted prices and the 50/50 split did not therefore take into account the lower prices for which some of the oil was actually being sold. OPEC was created only after the companies tried to redress this situation in 1959 and 1960 by actually lowering posted prices to reflect more closely the market value of the oil.

The 50/50 deals brought twenty years of relative peace in company-government relations, a peace which was greatly facilitated by sustained rapid growth in world demand and crude production. By 1954, the Iranian dispute (see below) had been settled; and the disputes with Iraq, though simmering for many years, did not boil over until after the passage of Law 80 in 1961, confining the companies to the proven producing areas of their concessions. Even then, the rupture with the companies was far from complete. The establishment of OPEC in 1960 did not unduly perturb company-government relations for another decade. 50/50 was a smash-hit, long-run success, and it did not much matter whether it had a basic economic rationale or not: it worked.

But not in Iran, at least not right away.

The Hostile Host: Iran Nationalizes

In October 1947, the Majlis (the Iranian Parliament—an upper house, the Senate, had not yet been created) passed a law rejecting a proposed Irano-Soviet oil venture in the north of the country and instructed the government to regain, by negotiation, "national rights" in the southern concession of the Anglo-Iranian Oil Company, which was owned 51 percent by the British government. Talks were initiated in 1948, and a Supplemental Agreement (supplemental to AIOC's 1933 Oil Concession Agreement) signed in mid-1949. It was not ratified by the Majlis and, after growing opposition, the government withdrew it in December 1950. In March 1951, Prime Minister Ali Razmara, an opponent of nationalization, which had been mooted in the

Oil Committee of the Majlis, was assassinated, and the following day, the principle of nationalization of the oil industry was passed into law. In May, a further law providing for the implementation of the principle was passed. In June 1951, all shipments of oil from Abadan ceased. AIOC took the case to arbitration and the British government filed a case with the International Court of Justice (ICJ). In October 1951, all British oil company staff were expelled from the country. The rest of 1951, all of 1952 and the first half of 1953 were spent in further rounds of negotiations, involving, variously, the company itself, the British government, the US government and the World Bank, interspersed with proceedings in the UN Security Council and the ICJ. In August 1953, the Iranian government under Prime Minister Mohamed Mossadegh (who had been the chief proponent and executor of nationalization) was overthrown, and a new government formed under Prime Minister Fazlollah Zahedi. Negotiations were resumed, but with a consortium of companies composed of the seven majors plus the Compagnie Française des Pétroles (CFP). In August 1954, agreement was reached on the resumption of oil operations in Iran.

It is a sorry tale, in which Iran, AIOC and Britain all emerged losing.

Iranian Grievances

When they sought renegotiation of the 1933 Agreement, the Iranians certainly had genuine grievances, some of which were not in principle contested by AIOC. The company was the sole holder of the southern concession, which covered an area of 100,000 square miles and had a duration of 60 years (until 1993). The 1933 Agreement provided for payments to the government of a flat royalty (four shillings per ton of oil exported or consumed in the country) plus a 20 percent share of the company's dividend distributions in excess of £671,000 attributable to profits from the Iranian operation, plus some other minor payments to local government. The royalty payment was subject to adjustment stemming from fluctuations in the gold value of sterling.

In Iran at the time, general attitudes towards the 1933 concession agreement can be summed up, variously, as follows: (a) the agreement was null and void because the then Finance Minister Takizadeh had signed it under duress; (b) Anglo-Iranian had illegally and systematically evaded certain payments or had fraudulently made under-payments; (c) the intent of the agreement had been frustrated by British government regulations concerning the distribution of dividends and the freezing of the price of gold in sterling terms; (d) payments should be increased and back payments made.

At an early stage in the negotiations, which started in 1947, the company was presented with a list of 25 grievances or points for discussion which had been drawn up by Dr. Pirnia, under secretary in the Ministry of Finance, and Manucher Farmanfarmaian, his Director of Oil Concessions. However, over the next year, negotiations (led by Finance Minister Golshayan and Prime

Minister Saeed for the government, and by Neville Gass and Sir William Fraser, director and chairman of the company, respectively) the issues were narrowed down to three: higher royalty payments, lower prices for products sold on the domestic market and increased employment for Iranians, especially at senior and middle-management level.

There were two major reasons to demand higher payments: first, Iran was obtaining no benefit from the rapid post-war escalation of international oil prices (indeed, it was adversely affected because prices on the domestic market were driven up); and the company was subject to UK government regulations restricting dividend distributions. The situation was aggravated by the fact that the company paid more in taxes to the British government on its profits from Iranian oil than its total royalty and dividend payments to the Iranian government. The second grievance, concerning the prices of products for the domestic market, which were set by reference to product prices in the US Gulf, was exacerbated by the rise in product prices world-wide. It should have been a simple and minor matter, but became contentious because of the totally different points of view of the two parties. Why, the Iranians asked, should they pay US prices for something that could be produced so much more cheaply in Iran from their own resources? Why, the company asked, should they sell products on the Iranian market so much more cheaply than they could get for them on the international market?

The third grievance, concerning the employment of Iranian staff, may or may not have been justified, but was certainly colored by the underlying British contempt for the "locals". A similar attitude had embittered and contributed to the Mexican nationalization of the industry in 1937, and was to surface again in the nationalization of the Suez Canal in 1956.

The Supplemental Agreement of 1949

The three grievances, and other, lesser ones, were, at the outset, clearly negotiable, especially given the company's and the British government's recognition of grounds in equity for an upward revision of payments, and the fact that the Iranian government's dissatisfaction was limited mainly to the then current level of payments and did not involve the basic terms of the 1933 Agreement. And negotiated they were, to the initial satisfaction of both parties. On 17 July 1949 a Supplemental Agreement was signed by AIOC and the Iranian government. Royalty payments were to be increased retroactive to 1948; preference was to be given to the employment of Iranians wherever qualified; and the prices of products sold in Iran for domestic consumption were to be reduced.

Both the government and the company underestimated the extent to which dislike and fear of the British had built up in the country and how it would affect the attitude of the members of the Majlis over the critical question of ratification of the Supplemental Agreement. But the political

environment in Iran was changing radically. The struggle for power between
the Majlis and the Shah had sharpened, and oil was to be its focal point. The
various nationalist groups of which Dr. Mohamed Mossadegh became leader,
and the pro-Communist Tudeh party were set against the pro-Shah
government of Prime Minister Ali Razmara.

On the other side, too, preoccupations were far from confined to the
purely commercial aspects of the dispute. The Korean War broke out in June
1950, and the United States, recently turned from net oil exporter to net
importer, placed greater emphasis on the strategic importance of the Middle
East and its oil reserves. Under Mossadegh, Iran appeared politically volatile
and possibly vulnerable to an extreme left-wing, pro-Soviet takeover. The
British for their part, chronically short of dollars, were greatly concerned by
the threat to an important source of sterling oil.

The Supplemental Agreement signed in mid-July 1949 by AIOC and the
Iranian government was submitted to the Majlis (by now, the lower house of
the Iranian Parliament—the upper house, the Senate, had been created in early
1949) in the form of a bill for enactment and ratification. But the bill was
opposed by Mossadegh and his followers in the National Front, and at the end
of July 1949 the Majlis adjourned without passing it. Elections for the new
Majlis centered around the oil issue. The National Front parties, which
opposed the agreement and, more generally, anything that could be interpreted
as subservience to foreign interests, made big electoral gains.

When the Majlis reconvened, the bill was submitted, in June 1950, for
study to a specially appointed Oil Committee of the Majlis, headed by
Mossadegh, and in December 1950 the committee reported back that it did
not favor the bill. The political temperature was rising rapidly and the
government decided to withdraw the bill at the end of the year. In January
1951, the Majlis asked the Oil Committee to consider what course the
government should now take, and to report back within two months. In the
meantime, Aramco's 50/50 deal of December 1950 had been reported in the
Iranian press, and AIOC told the Iranian government that it was ready to
conclude a similar one.

Things were now moving very quickly. On 19 February 1951, Mossadegh
put a formal proposal to the Oil Committee that the oil industry (meaning
AIOC in Iran) be nationalized; the committee in turn asked Prime Minister
Razmara's views. He referred the question to a panel of government experts
and on 3 March 1951 reported back that the experts did not believe the
proposal either practical or legal. Four days later, he was assassinated by a
member of the extremist religious nationalist party, the Feda'iyan-e Islam, and
the following day, the Oil Committee accepted the proposal that the industry
be nationalized, asking the Majlis for a period of two more months to study
ways and means of implementing the proposal.

Prime Minister Razmara was replaced by Hosain Ala, but the Shah's
choice was not sustainable, and shortly thereafter, Mossadegh became prime

minister at the head of a coalition of secular nationalist and religious parties.

Nationalization and Negotiation

On 15 March 1951, a single-article bill was passed in the Majlis, approving the principle of nationalization, and accepted five days later by the Senate. In short order, a nine-article bill providing for the implementation of the principle of nationalization was passed and on 1 May 1951, it received the royal assent. The deed was done; afterwards, it would be impossible to turn back.

It was an act of folly. Out of the window went the unusual, positive aspects of the 1933 Agreement, notably Iran's 20 percent share in AIOC's distributions to reserve and dividend; and the partial tax renegotiation clause (article 11) which would have permitted higher taxes to be introduced in 1963 —two features possessed by none of the other concessions in the Middle East. In the Majlis and its Oil Committee, discussions had not focused on the major fiscal merits or drawbacks of the Supplemental Agreement. In the Committee, "the technical and economic aspects of the agreement were rarely raised. The deputies were not well versed in oil and were interested in it only insofar as it related to politics. As a result the committee became an emotional jousting field . . . As a body that might find grounds for settlement, the committee had turned into a farce."[9]   Nevertheless, sensible or not, nationalization was a legal act carried out for deeply felt political motives, a fact which the British could not at first bring themselves to accept.

Turbulent negotiations followed nationalization. They were split into two main phases: during the first, AIOC and the British tried to get back into Iran with an offer equivalent to the 50/50 deal which was becoming the standard in the Middle East, retaining investment, management, operating and marketing control under cover of a face-saving device that would leave the industry nationalized in form only; during the second, AIOC accepted the reality of nationalization but demanded unacceptable levels of compensation, plus the right to purchase oil from Iran on a long-term basis. In addition, at an early stage, the British government instituted proceedings in the International Court of Justice against the Iranian government, but the court declared that it had no jurisdiction in the case.[10]

The Talks to Nowhere

The following two years, from June 1951 to July 1953, witnessed six separate rounds of negotiations and talks, with agreement sometimes seemingly within arm's reach, before the final debacle and overthrow of Mossadegh in August 1953.

It took the British some time to understand that when the Iranians said nationalization, they meant nationalization—ownership, management, operations, sales—the lot. Nor did they understand the objective, which was not to grab an economic and financial asset, but to rid the country of a major obstacle (as Mossadegh and the nationalists saw it) in the way of real political independence. Mossadegh and his group on the other hand understood quite well that nationalization would be difficult without the active cooperation, or at least total acquiescence, of the British, and were initially naive enough to expect it: Mossadegh wanted British staff to stay on as employees of the nationalized company; and a long-term sales contract with AIOC for the marketing of crude and products. Once disabused of the notion of AIOC cooperation, he came to believe he could manage without the British staff, and was only prepared to discuss the issue of compensation and the price of oil in a long-term sales contract.

Unfortunately for him, Mossadegh never understood until it was too late that time was *not* on his side. In this, he was at first encouraged by the United States, which took a more conciliatory approach than the British. The main US concern was not to salvage something for the company or even the British government, but only to find a *modus vivendi* which would preclude a Communist takeover in Iran. The reform-minded, popular Mossadegh looked like the best alternative to a feeble Shah on the one hand, or the Tudeh (communist party) on the other. And, after all, Mossadegh saw the British position (under US pressure) weaken considerably as the months went by. It took many months of US urging before the British finally accepted the reality of nationalization, rather than simply trying to get AIOC back in with a 50/50 deal and some cosmetics to preserve a facade of nationalization.

But time *was* against Mossadegh. Supply difficulties caused by the suspension of product shipments from Abadan and the extra demand for jet fuel and other fuels caused by the Korean War were easing; and Kuwaiti production, in which AIOC had a 50 percent interest, was being developed at a fast and furious pace: production increased by 63 percent in 1951 and a further 33 percent in 1952. Iraq, where AIOC had a 23.75 percent holding, also increased its output rapidly. Both countries by then had 50/50 agreements in place. Overall, during a period (1951-1953) when Iranian production dropped virtually to zero, Middle East production grew at an annual rate of 12 percent.

Towards the end of 1952, with Truman and Secretary of State Dean Acheson anxious to wrap up the affair before they left office (General Dwight D. Eisenhower had been elected President in November and was due to take office in January 1953), a new offer was prepared, jointly with Prime Minister Winston Churchill. By that time, all concerned—AIOC, the British government and the United States—had accepted the reality of nationalization, and the main issues were reduced to the matter of compensation and the international marketing of Iranian oil. The actual operation of the industry seems to have faded from the minds of both sides to the dispute. At the same time, in November 1952, the British approached the US Central Intelligence Agency (CIA) with suggestions for a coup to overthrow the Mossadegh regime. This eventually developed into an almost wholly CIA scheme, to be code-named AJAX, which was planned over the following months, but did not receive the final go-ahead (from Secretary of State John Foster Dulles and his brother, CIA Chief Allen Dulles) until late June 1953.

The gist of the Churchill-Truman proposals consisted in providing for compensation (including compensation for loss of future profits) by international arbitration; a long-term contract for the purchase of Iranian oil by AIOC and others; and $100 million in interim US aid. After some final negotiations during which Mossadegh sought to have a cap put on compensation, a final offer was put forward in February 1953 (by which time Eisenhower had succeeded Truman as president) that provided for compensation to be determined by the International Court of Justice, with cash payments to be limited in any case to 25 percent of the gross proceeds from the sale of Iranian oil over a period of twenty years, at the end of which any unpaid compensation would be settled by the delivery of free oil by Iran to AIOC.

The following month, towards the end of March 1953, Mossadegh rejected the proposals and put forward counter-proposals which were not far from the joint British-American position. It was too late: Mossadegh's political support in Iran was slipping away as the economic situation worsened, and, in American eyes, he appeared to be leaning on the support of the Tudeh party. He no longer looked like a good bet as an alternative to communism. And of course the Dulles brothers came in like a new broom, even more determined than Acheson to secure anti-communist regimes everywhere. Their fears were probably exaggerated: throughout the affair, the Soviet Union kept as quiet as a church mouse, perhaps preoccupied with Stalin's failing health and then death in March 1953. Finally, British insistence on a tough deal was straining relations with the United States. Iran was perhaps not worth the candle.

In any event, from March 1953, the door was closed to further negotiations. After some searching, a suitable candidate to lead the coup was found in the person of General Fazlollah Zahedi, and Operation AJAX was put in motion in mid-August 1953. It went through an initial comic-opera episode of delayed messages, mob demonstrations against the Shah, followed by the flight of the Shah to Baghdad and then Rome, further demonstrations, this time by a pro-Shah bazaari mob (rented for the occasion by the CIA whose operative-in-charge, Kim Roosevelt, seems to have been only marginally less amusing than Inspector Clouseau), and the help of the army. The pro-Mossadegh forces were routed and the Shah returned triumphantly to Tehran. Mossadegh was arrested on 20 August 1953 and later put on trial. General Zahedi was named prime minister. The path was at last open for a settlement on US/British terms.

Enter the Consortium

In October 1953, Herbert Hoover Jr., who had been appointed petroleum adviser to John Foster Dulles, was despatched to Iran to assess the situation concerning the resumption of oil talks. Iran resumed diplomatic relations with Britain in December 1953, and talks re-opened with AIOC and the British government. The situation remained delicate: Mossadegh was on trial and the new Iranian government could not risk reversing the still popular nationalization laws, nor bringing AIOC back to run the industry. AIOC made a last effort to regain its position in Iran, but under pressure from the British government and the United States, the company finally agreed to a solution suggested by Hoover to the new Iranian government—that negotiations should be initiated with a consortium of companies in which AIOC would have less than a majority share. A consortium was duly formed of AIOC together with the other major oil companies.

The US majors came apprehensively to the table: they demanded, and got, antitrust clearance; but some of them neither needed nor wanted access to more crude—they had more than they could handle in Saudi Arabia, Kuwait and Iraq, and undertaking to help Iran back into a world market that now had little room for it might cause problems in the other countries, all keen on further expansion. In the end, the consortium that was formed to negotiate with Iran consisted of AIOC with a 40 percent share, Royal Dutch-Shell with 14 percent, the five US majors (Chevron, Exxon, Gulf, Mobil and Texaco) with 8 percent each, and CFP with 6 percent. Later, each of the US companies turned over 1 percent to Iricon, a group of US independents, mainly as a sop to the Department of Justice, much concerned about antitrust issues (it still had a case pending against the five US majors).

In September 1954, the negotiations, which had been led by the Iranian Finance Minister Ali Amini and Exxon's Howard Page, ended in the signing of a new agreement between the Iranian government and NIOC on the one hand and the individual member companies of the Iranian Consortium on the other. An agreement between AIOC and Iran on compensation (mainly for one of the smaller producing fields and a refinery with which the National Iranian Oil Company (NIOC) would service the internal market) was also signed at the same time.

In December 1954, AIOC changed its name to the British Petroleum Company, which was now rapidly becoming a more geographically diversified and balanced company (though destined, ironically, to remain crude-long for many more years). In the end, AIOC Chairman Sir William Fraser's intransigence and stubbornness during the negotiations, which had antagonized the British government and just about everyone else, and had appeared at the time a great obstacle to an early solution to the problems that arose after the rejection of the Supplemental Agreement, were all that kept AIOC from being pushed out into the cold altogether, and salvaged for it a 40 percent interest in the consortium and a tidy little income on the side in the form of the sale of its original 60 percent share of the concession to the other members of the consortium.

The drafters of the new agreement went to great lengths to construct a form that catered to Iranian political sensibilities: the industry remained "nationalized", and the physical assets owned by NIOC but operated and managed by subsidiaries of the new consortium (Iranian Oil Participants Limited), along the lines of the solution mooted much earlier, in the negotiations with Mossadegh. But the substance of the agreement was a tightly worded 50/50 profit-sharing deal, by then standard in the Middle East, with provisions for fiscal stability (no increase in taxes, royalties or other payments) throughout the life of the agreement, which was to be for twenty-five years (to 1979), plus three five-year renewals at the option of the consortium, to take its duration to 1994. Disputes were to be settled by international arbitration, applying not Iranian law, but the general principles of international law. The companies committed themselves to increasing production over a number of years to reach at least 600 kbd by 1957. An important volume commitment of some kind, though not of any specific level, was taken for granted by all concerned—indeed, it was the main raison d'être for bringing in the international majors: they had the power to do it without wrecking prices, simply by cutting down on their production elsewhere. It was in fact an awesome display of the companies' oligopoly position, or "power of disposal", as noted petroleum consultant Paul Frankel called it, and it was not lost on the governments of other producing countries that the majors could and would respond to pressure by increasing production in one country at the expense of another. Not surprisingly, the pressure grew over the years *pari passu* with the growth in surplus producing capacity and potentials, the most intense pressure coming from Iran, the country that had most benefitted from the companies' power in the first place. The initial commitment was in the event exceeded as the level rose to 730 kbd, thanks in part at least to lower taxation on volumes in excess of the minimum commitments. This tax break was given in a side letter to the main agreement of 1954, and took the form of a discount of 5 percent of the posted price (the tax base) on the first 10 million cubic meters (172 kbd) of production above commitment, 7.5 percent on the second 10 million and 10 percent on the third 10 million. Five percent of the posted price amounted, in 1957, to a tax break of $0.05/per barrel on Iranian Light crude, equivalent to slightly more than 5 percent of the tax. Full advantage was not taken of these discounts, as commitments were exceeded by only about 1.6 mn cubic meters (28 kbd) in 1955, 3.8 mn (66 kbd) in 1956 and 7.4 mn (127 kbd) in 1957.

The restrictive clauses must have reached their apex in the 1954 agreement between Iran and the Iranian Consortium. The arbitration clause alone took up five and a half pages of the fifty-six page agreement and the choice-of-law clause sought to internationalize the agreement by making it subject to principles of international law.

This time, after cancelling the concession once (in 1932), and nationalizing the company another time, in 1951, Iran was gagged and bound hand and foot.

Conclusions

The outcome was not an unhappy one for the world of oil, which was in a general sense the winner. But there were losers. Iran, after three years of upheaval, got essentially what had been offered to Prime Minister Razmara shortly before his assassination (i.e., a 50/50 deal)—and lost its incipient way to democratic, constitutional rule. It was political disaster for a generation—to be followed by a second one. The US majors got a share in a concession they did not particularly want at the time, and the United States itself got an increasingly repressive government in Iran that they could and did support for 25 years. True, it was followed by a bitterly anti-American regime, but by then it didn't much matter (contemporaneous brouhaha notwithstanding), and mattered even less after the disintegration of the Soviet Union. AIOC lost 60 percent of its concession; born again as BP, it was an apparent loser, but perhaps better for the experience. The episode at least made the company more evenly balanced and diversified. Britain perhaps came off worst: it gained nothing and the whole episode probably encouraged Prime Minister Eden to adopt a tough, uncompromising and ultimately disastrous stand against Egypt when the Suez Canal was nationalized. Two things of major importance to the future of the oil industry had happened, neither of them particularly intended nor foreseen at the time. First, Iran suffered a crushing defeat, the lesson of which was not lost on other producing countries in the Middle East (and elsewhere). If 50/50 was the big carrot that kept the producing government more or less happy for twenty-odd years, the defeat of Iran was the big stick that threatened anyone who got too far out of line. The companies were wise enough to always allow a little slack in the reins, but the whip was there, and not even the most militant of anti-company governments—Iraq—dared overstep the limit. Its Law 80, promulgated in 1961, virtually confiscated the company's mostly idle acreage, but carefully refrained from taking away any of its current producing properties.

Second, a single company, AIOC, had been replaced by a partnership among the seven majors (plus CFP). Just as everywhere else in the Persian Gulf, a joint undertaking of the majors now held the dominant concession. From then on, no company could act entirely independently anywhere in the Gulf: nothing could be decided without at least a majority consensus of the companies involved in a given country; and nothing could be done in one country that did not affect all the majors' interests in the other countries. The most important areas concerned were of course investment, production and offtake, and negotiated tax increases. The fact that they were all in the same boat together forced all the majors to adopt a unified stand *vis-à-vis* the demands of the host countries.

With the conclusion of the new agreement, the base from which the majors and the world industry were to expand so rapidly for the next twenty years was secured. That base was comprised four countries: Iran, Iraq, Kuwait and Saudi Arabia, which among them could for all practical purposes provide unlimited amounts of crude oil producible at a derisory operating cost. Like Iran after 1954, Iraq, Kuwait and Saudi Arabia were securely tied down by long-term agreements which could not be revised, which regulated virtually every aspect of relations between the concessionaire companies and the government, including tax rates; which were taken out of the country's legal system by choice-of-law clauses and compulsory arbitration provisions; and in which the government had no say whatsoever on any matter of substance. The host governments were reduced to mere landlords and were not notably unhappy in that role, with the exception of Iraq after the overthrow of the monarchy in 1958, until the early 1970s. However, by the late 1960s, there was a considerable groundswell of opinion building up in favor of a more active role for governments.

In the meantime, total revenues were increasing rapidly as production rose and the governments were in any event blissfully unaware of what was going on in the world of oil outside (and to a large extent, inside) their own boundaries. They received only the most summary company accounts, were not permitted to audit them (they were given the external auditors' approval letters), did not know where their oil was being shipped to, had no idea of real market prices, did not know how much the companies were making, and did not even think in terms of competitive fuels. They had no operating or international marketing capability, and little contact either with each other or the oil world outside, at least until the formation of OPEC in 1960. They were well-paid eunuchs. Even OPEC's first ten years were largely confined to assisting in the negotiation of minor upward revisions in the tax base. But at least it was a beginning to an understanding of what they were involved in and at the heart of.

Appendix 1-1
PRINCIPAL CONCESSIONS IN THE MIDDLE EAST AS OF 1950

Country	Iran	Iraq	Kuwait	Saudi Arabia	Iran - 1954
Concessionaire	BP (AIOC)	IPC Group	KOC	Aramco	Consortium
Production in 1950, kbd	660	140	344	547	259
Area, Th. Sq. Kms.	259	443	16	932	259
Year of Expiry	1993	2005	2025	1993	1993
Duration, Years	60	75	92	60	60
Companies' Equity Share, Percent					
BP (AIOC)	100	23.75	50	-	40
CFP	-	23.75	-	-	6
Chevron	-	-	-	-	7
Exxon	-	11.875	**	30	7
Gulf	-	-	50	-	7
Mobil	-	11.875	-	10	7
Shell	-	23.75	**	-	14
Texaco	-	-	-	30	7
8 Companies	100	95	100	100	95
Others	-	5	-	-	5
Total All	100	100	100	100	100

** Exxon and Shell had special long-term large crude oil purchase arrangements at special prices with BP and Gulf, respectively.

32

Chapter 2
BIG BANG AND THE GROWTH OF THE MARKETS, 1950-1973

In 1950, the United States was the only country where the oil industry was well-developed. Between 1950 and 1973, the industry in the rest of the world grew ninefold—a rate of increase of 10 percent per year sustained, amazingly, over a period of twenty-three years. Two hundred new refineries were built outside the United States and some older ones expanded. About 1,750 tankers of ever-increasing size were launched. Over 2.5 billion new motor vehicles were put on the roads, more than half of them in the United States. Air travel replaced ocean liners and every other form of long-distance travel. In Western Europe and Japan, oil dethroned coal. Petrochemicals brought a wide range of entirely new products. World oil demand including the United States and the Centrally Planned Economies (CPEs) more than quintupled, growing from 11 million barrels per day (mbd) in 1950 to 57 mbd in 1970. Economies boomed; peace (more or less) prevailed; in the oil industry, the seven major oil companies reigned supreme.

It was the golden age of oil.

People's lives were transformed, and the transformation was possible on two counts.

First, the basic technology already existed. The internal combustion and diesel engines had been invented in the nineteenth century; the jet engine in the 1930s; the basic refining processes were well-established; and thermal cracking had been introduced in 1913, catalytic cracking in 1936.

Second, the oilfields of the Middle East provided the resource base for virtually unlimited, low-cost petroleum products across the board—fuels, lubricants, asphalt and petrochemical feedstocks.

It is not surprising that the profound transformation in people's lives, to which cheap energy would contribute so much, was but dimly perceived even as it was upon us in the late 1940s. Western Europe was struggling to recover from the devastation of World War II, fearful of a Soviet takeover and uncertain whether the future would bring another economic depression or growth and prosperity. Japan had been traumatized by the fire-bombing of its cities and the horrors of Hiroshima and Nagasaki. Even in the United States, relatively unscathed by war, the dark clouds of the Cold War were soon to gather. No one was in a mood to speculate about, dwell upon, or plan for

33

the coming comforts, delights and freedom of movement that cheap energy would help to bring. (And how much further from people's minds were the problems of congestion and pollution!)

The present chapter sets the scene for the period from 1950 to 1973, describing and discussing the sustained rapid growth of crude production and oil product demand—two sides of the same coin—upstream and downstream investments in different areas, the dominion of the seven major oil companies, and the penetration and reaction of markets. I have taken 1973 as a watershed, because it marks the loss of control over price by the major companies, the beginnings of the dis-integration of the industry and the tripling of oil prices imposed by OPEC.

The Middle East Emergent

The oil industry's "Big Bang" was the discovery and development of the super-giant fields of the Middle East. Enough of them had been discovered well before 1950, where we take up the story, to have made some countries and companies understand that they were on the brink of a new world of some kind for oil.

In Iran, the Masjid-e-Sulaiman field had been discovered as early as 1908, to be followed much later by Gach Saran (1928) and Agha Jari (1938), all giants. Though not fully proved up till later, BP (AIOC at the time) in fact had more reserves in these three fields than the combined reserves of the whole of the United States.

In north-central Iraq, the great Kirkuk field had been discovered in 1927 and a 12-inch pipeline to Haifa in Palestine and Tripoli in Lebanon completed by 1935, looped with a 16-inch line in 1950. Ain Zalah was discovered in 1939 and Zubair in 1948. A 30-32-inch line from Kirkuk to Banias in Syria was completed in 1952, and a 12-inch line from Zubair to Fao on the Persian Gulf in 1950.

In Kuwait, super-giant Burgan had been discovered in 1938. Despite the total lack of infrastructure where fields were discovered throughout the Middle East, all of them were cheap to produce because so prolific, but Kuwait was the cheapest of all. Near the coast, but at some elevation from it, oil flowed under great reservoir pressure to the surface, then downhill through the pipelines to the shipping terminal. By 1960, operating expenses were less than 5 cents per barrel; Kuwait oil sold for $1.50/B.

In Saudi Arabia, the Dammam field had been discovered in 1938, followed by Abqaiq and Abu Hadriya in 1940, Qatif in 1945 and Ghawar, the world's largest oilfield, in 1948. Other smaller fields had also been discovered in Bahrain (Awali in 1932) and Qatar (Dukhan in 1940).

It is not clear when it dawned on companies and governments (especially the US government) that Middle East reserves were of such a magnitude that they would become central to the development of the world petroleum industry and *ipso facto* of great strategic importance. The US, British and French governments had of course already been deeply involved in Middle East oil since the negotiations after the First World War for participation in the Iraq concessions. The British government had been involved even earlier in Iran, acquiring shares in BP, its main preoccupation being to own a source of fuel oil for its navy, then being converted from coal to oil. But it was perhaps not until the Burgan and Dammam discoveries in 1938 and Abqaiq in 1940 that the greater importance of the resources began to be perceived, with the realization that, as US reserves declined, the center of gravity for world crude oil production would shift to the Middle East. Certainly by 1943 the United States was evincing keen interest in the area, particularly in Saudi Arabia, and in 1943 dispatched a "Technical Oil Mission" to the Middle East, headed by Everette DeGolyer, an eminent geologist, to report on reserves in the area. The mission made a preliminary estimate of reserves of 14 billion barrels, but the State Department (presumably basing its judgment on DeGolyer's findings) thought that potential reserves were substantially in excess of this figure.

By 1944, Middle East proved reserves were put at the conservative figure of 16 billion barrels: though technically not perhaps "proved", the companies must have already known that the probable reserves behind the discoveries and first development wells were staggering. In 1948, the companies were talking, though rather guardedly, about "the world's most important crude oil reserve area, the Middle East".[1] By 1949, published estimates had more than doubled, to 33 billion barrels, and these again more than doubled by 1953 when reserves were put at 78 billion barrels—two and a half times the reserves of the United States—still much too conservative. In each of the succeeding four years, the Middle East's proved reserves increased by an average of 23 billion barrels, as though the world had annually gained new reserves equal to those of the world's largest producing country—the United States—with two differences: they would be far cheaper to produce than US fields; and they were all in the hands of fewer than ten companies. Much of the reserve increase was of course not as a result of new discoveries, but simply the upgrading of discoveries already made, as knowledge of their size increased with further drilling.

For company managements, the size of these reserves and the task of developing them that lay ahead must have been awesome. It is not surprising that the majors chose (assuming the alternative was ever seriously considered) cooperation over competition, for there were three powerful reasons favoring joint efforts:

First, the complementarity of the crude-short and crude-long companies made cooperation a "natural".

Second, time was short and resources for development limited: the governments of Middle Eastern countries were already beginning to press for higher revenues and there was an acute shortage of materials necessary for development, notably steel, especially large-diameter pipe.

Third, none of the companies wanted to break the existing price structure.

The complementarity of the crude-short and crude-long companies made cooperation rather than competition practically a foregone conclusion. Four companies had actual or potential substantial crude producing surpluses: BP in Iran and Kuwait, Gulf in Kuwait, Chevron and Texaco in Saudi Arabia. In order to go ahead with the large-scale development of crude producing capacity, they needed assured outlets which their own downstream refining capacity could not provide; nor did they have the time and resources to construct such facilities and build up the associated marketing networks. The four companies could not depend on arm's-length crude sales to independent refiners, since practically none existed outside the United States The only path realistically open to them was to come to some arrangement with the crude-short companies that could provide a solid base for expansion of crude production.

The first steps had already been taken when Chevron, which had the original concession in Saudi Arabia, teamed up with Texaco in 1936. Texaco, which had developed markets in the Far East, took a 50 percent interest in the Arabian American Oil Company (Aramco), holder of Chevron's Saudi concession. The two companies also formed another joint 50/50 subsidiary—Caltex—mainly to market East of Suez. Texaco contributed its established Far Eastern subsidiaries to the enterprise, and Chevron its concessions in the Netherlands East Indies (later Indonesia).

It was nowhere near enough, and in 1947 and 1948, arrangements were made for Exxon and Mobil to acquire 30 percent and 10 percent of Aramco, respectively, the agreement being finalized in December 1948 after Exxon and Mobil had managed to extricate themselves from the provisions of the Red Line Agreement that prohibited them from acquiring concessions anywhere in the former Ottoman Empire (which included Saudi Arabia). It was a perfect match and worked well over the years despite some severe initial friction between the old and the new partners.

BP and Gulf, the other two crude-long companies, took a different course, reaching long-term, high-volume crude sales agreements with Shell, Mobil and Exxon. In May 1947, Shell contracted to buy large quantities (at least 1.25 billion barrels) of Kuwait crude from Gulf over a period of twenty-two years at prices that were essentially a split of profits on a net-back basis. However, just to make sure that Gulf did not later decide to compete as well as cooperate, the agreement restricted Gulf's freedom in Shell markets downstream.

In September of the same year, 1947, Exxon and Mobil signed separate though similar agreements with BP for the long-term purchase of crude from Kuwait and Iran. Again, high volumes (1.3 billion barrels in aggregate over 20 years) and special prices were involved. In 1948, Mobil signed a second agreement along similar lines. These agreements were at first contingent on the construction of a pipeline from the Iranian fields to the Eastern Mediterranean. This Middle East Pipeline (MEPL) was to be constructed as a joint venture of seller and buyers. The project was later dropped.

Time was certainly short. This second element pushing the companies to cooperative efforts to develop the Middle East's reserves, consisted mainly of pressures from two sources:

First, from the markets, where, at the then prevailing prices, demand was insatiable and growing: indeed, the companies were taken aback at the strength of demand. In 1948, for example, Mobil was reporting that "the demand for oil, both at home and abroad, has increased beyond all expectations . . ."[1] However, by 1949, surpluses were beginning to appear. They would soon disappear once more, with the outbreak of the Korean War and then the Iranian nationalization.

In addition, the companies were beginning to face pressure from rulers and governments of the producing countries, who were stepping up their demands for increased revenues.

Finally, preservation of the existing price structure was a dominant interest for all of the major oil companies, who had large-scale production elsewhere, mainly in the United States and to a lesser extent in the Far East. It was of course of concern to BP which already had a substantial flow of oil from its Iranian fields and the Abadan refinery. Joint ventures in production upstream and marketing downstream, together with the quasi-partnerships of the long-term sales contracts made for rapid and "orderly" (buzz word for muted competition) development.

Indeed, "orderly" development was still, for a time, of concern to the US government, which viewed the Middle East's vast reserves as a matter of strategic importance. Much effort had been expended by Department of the Interior Secretary Harold Ickes trying to devise means to "accommodate" Middle East oil in the markets without breaking the price structure, and it was due to this concern that the US government almost became owner or part-owner of the Aramco concession and the Trans-Arabian Pipeline (Tapline). The US and British governments had in addition signed agreements, never ratified, that were in essence plans for Anglo-American cartel arrangements which, if they had been put into effect, would have made previous attempts to establish an international cartel fade into insignificance. The so-called Washington Agreement of 8 August 1944 called for the development of petroleum resources for international trade "in an orderly manner on a world-wide basis" (article I) and for making supplies available to all comers "at fair prices" (article I.1). After some trouble in the US Congress, a Revised Petroleum Agreement (the London Agreement) was concluded between the two governments on 24 September 1945, which again called for "orderly" development, though the reference to "fair prices" was dropped. The original and revised agreements both called for the conclusion of an International

Petroleum Agreement by "the governments of all interested producing and consuming countries" (article III.1) which would establish an International Petroleum Council. The Council would, *inter alia*, " . . . prepare periodic estimates of world demands and supplies available for meeting the demands, and to report as to the means by which such demands and supplies may be correlated so as to further the efficient and orderly conduct of the international petroleum trade". In other words, it was to be a Texas Railroad Commission (TRC) writ large, on the international stage, whose main purpose would be, like the TRC domestically, to maintain prices by constraining supply. (The TRC was a state regulatory body in charge of fixing an overall monthly "allowable" production for the state, and pro-rating it among the producing companies. It was created in the 1930s for conservation purposes, after over-production of many fields appeared to be resulting in damage to the reservoirs—and causing prices to collapse. Its significance was to maintain prices at a relatively high level. Because Texas was the major US producing state at the time, it also served to anchor prices for all other producing states.) The Agreement died of neglect after it became clear that it would never get through the US Senate in the face of industry opposition.[2]

US official attitudes were soon to change. The Economic Co-operation Administration (ECA), later the Mutual Security Agency (MSA), the administrator agency for the Marshall Plan, brought pressure to bear on US companies to lower the price of Middle East oil, and the Department of Justice brought an antitrust suit against the seven major oil companies in 1953. The suit seems in retrospect peculiarly short-sighted if not positively irresponsible in the international context, given the critical importance of the development of the Middle East's oil resources for the recovery of a war-torn world. The fastest route to development at the time was cooperation among the companies and the last thing needed was a series of legal impediments.

The suit started as separate criminal and civil antitrust actions brought against the seven majors. BP and Shell were dropped because the antitrust laws were deemed inapplicable to foreign corporations acting outside the United States. Then the criminal part of the action was dropped. The rest was whittled away over the next decade, until the only results were some consent decrees of relatively minor importance, including, however, the dissolution in 1960-62 of the Standard Vacuum Oil Company (Stanvac), a jointly owned subsidiary of Exxon and Mobil operating in South and Southeast Asia. Its component parts were split between new wholly-owned subsidiaries of Exxon and Mobil.

Underlying these developments was a constant tug of war between the Justice Department's enthusiastic team of trust-busters and the State Department's deep concern over the strategic importance of Middle East oil and the absolute necessity of developing it quickly and keeping it largely in the hands of US companies. In the end, the State Department won out, and "the enforcement of the Anti-Trust laws . . . [was] deemed secondary to the national security interest".[3] Perhaps in the end the suit did some good by keeping the companies on their toes and forestalling the collusion on prices that might otherwise have taken place.

What emerged in fact was not a cartel bent on pushing prices up to a point where revenues were maximized—they would never have gotten away with that—nor much in the way of real competition. It was something in between: reluctance to break the prevalent price structure side by side with competition among the majors within the confines of their offtake agreements (the agreements among the partners on how much oil they would take each year). On balance the somewhat greater pressure was for more competition among the majors and less price-maintenance, as witness the slowly declining price of crude oil, a trend that would undoubtedly have proceeded more rapidly had it not been for intermittent supply crises, in 1950 (the Korean War), 1951 (Iranian nationalization), and 1956-57 (the Suez crisis). The downward pressure, it should be noted, started and continued well before the independents got any significant crude production in Libya, Venezuela and the offshore Persian Gulf concessions. In any event, by 1963, BP (a leading price-cutter among the majors) was calling for restraint (on the part of others):

> The problem facing each responsible company with shut-in production—and here again I am referring to the world as a whole and not to the domestic US situation—is therefore this: How much oil can we sell annually without contributing to a fall in prices which would not render many of our own operations unprofitable, but— which is even more important—reduce the revenue of many of the principal exporting countries to a point which is politically insupportable?
> At the end of the day, it may well be that the answer must be looked for in the individual conscience and judgment of those of whatever nationality who find themselves in responsible positions.
> – Sir Maurice Bridgeman, Chairman of BP, in a speech to the American Petroleum Institute on World-wide Production: Its Prospects and Problems, November 1963.

Middle East Reserves

There are thousands of oilfields in production throughout the world today, but of the dozen largest, ten are in the Middle East. Of the next two dozen largest, fourteen are in the Middle East. In aggregate, they account for about two-thirds of the world's proved oil reserves. By oil industry standards, they are operated at the glacial speed of not much less than 1:100 production-to-reserves ratio, and have been running at a similar ratio for the past forty years, as upward revisions in reserve estimates offset production withdrawals.

That is half the story. The other half is that they are dirt-cheap to develop and produce. Certainly, many millions of high-risk dollars were initially invested to bring them onstream, but by 1960, when some of the largest were getting into their stride, out-of-pocket operating expenses were generally in the range of 5 to 20 cents per barrel f.o.b the port of export. By 1960, the combined net assets (including assets not related to production, such as refineries) of the major companies' joint producing subsidiaries in Iran, Iraq, Kuwait and Saudi Arabia, accounting for virtually the whole of the Middle East's crude production, only amounted to about $900 million. This was not much more than their net profits for the year—that is, a nearly 100 percent return on investment. During the twenty years from 1952 to 1973, the Middle East contributed 42 percent of the increase in world production (excluding communist countries) but accounted for less than 4 percent ($6 billion) of worldwide capital and exploration expenditures on crude oil production. For this, net additions to proved reserves of 270 billion barrels were made, and 65 billion barrels withdrawn as production. Manna from heaven.

Capital expenditures of the world petroleum industry are shown in on the charts in Appendices 2-1 and 2-2 which illustrate dramatically the relatively insignificant sums invested in the Middle East over the period 1952 to 1973.

The disparities were (and still are) massive. The United States accounted for two-thirds of the world's total capital expenditures on oil and gas production (about $91 billion out of a total of $137 billion from 1952 through 1973), with only meager results, despite the discovery of the giant Alaskan Prudhoe Bay field. By comparison, the sums spent in the Middle East amounted to a paltry $6 billion during the whole period. Similar disparities existed, and persist, between operating expenses in different areas.

The fact that the Persian Gulf is as distant from the great importing centers of the US Atlantic and Gulf Coasts, Northwestern Europe and Japan as it is possible to get by tanker (farther from the former two than the Antarctic) allowed some higher-cost fields closer at hand to be developed on the back of the transportation savings involved. Most of the rest would not be economically viable in a fully competitive oil economy, including the whole of the North Sea, much of Venezuela and most US fields—a fact that was to acquire enormous importance in the run-up to the 1970-1973 crude price increase.

Given these physical size and cost dimensions, the speed with which the Middle East was developed from the late 1940s to the early 1970s is not so surprising, breakneck though it was. Afterwards, OPEC brought growth to a halt (in 1973), but by that time, Big Bang had irrevocably taken place.

The growth of crude oil production and proved oil reserves is shown in the charts in Appendices 2-3 and 2-4.

The appendices show the growth of world production of crude and natural gas liquids (NGLs) from 1950 to 1973, and the growth in proved reserves over the same period. The main and obvious points are the decreasing relative importance of the United States and the growing size and importance of other areas, most especially the Middle East. But any reader with a passing knowledge of capital and operating expenses in different areas of the world would be struck by the disproportionate increases in output relative to reserves in the United States and in the Middle East. In the United States, though the production increase was modest in absolute terms, it was a much higher proportion of the increase in reserves than obtained for the Middle East.

The Markets

The bountiful supplies of the Middle East were of course not enough in themselves; the oil still had to be refined and brought to market, at capital costs, by comparison with which the investment required for the development of the Middle East was nugatory.

Throughout the period from 1950 to 1970, oil markets grew rapidly though, as might be expected, unevenly from country to country and area to area. Overall, as noted above, they more than quadrupled. The US market, already relatively well developed, more than doubled; Western Europe and the CPEs both grew ninefold; Japan, one hundredfold, increasing from virtually no consumption at all to become, with demand of 4 mbd, the world's second largest consumer of oil products, after the United States. The rest of the world, that is, the developing countries, increased their demand fourfold.

By the mid 1960s, such was the growth in demand, companies were having to reassure the public that there would be enough oil in the long term to supply the rising tide of consumption:

> Our petroleum supplies should remain adequate many years beyond 1975—at least another decade at approximately present costs. With some modest increases in energy costs, the Free World's oil supplies probably will be adequate for another decade or two beyond that.
> – Jerry McAfee, Vice President of Gulf Oil Corporation, in an address to the AIME Annual Meeting, February 1964.

A more emphatic affirmation of the adequacy of long-term supplies came from Shell:

> At all events there is no risk of shortage of either oil or gas in our 25-year forward look. . . . One thing is certain: there is absolutely no doubt that we shall be able to find, produce and put to use all the additional petroleum we shall need wherever it is.
> – J. H. Loudon, Senior Managing Director, Royal Dutch/Shell Group of Companies, in the Seventh Cadman Memorial Lecture, Institute of Petroleum, London, May 1965.

Similar messages were being heard from other major companies.

Market growth of this magnitude required large-scale, continuing investment because, while the latent demand was there in the form of customers willing and able to buy petroleum products, the facilities were not. The growth of crude oil production had to go hand in hand with growth in the construction of pipelines, shipping and receiving terminals, tankers, tank trucks and tank wagons, bulk storage plants, refineries and service stations—not to mention roads, cars, trucks and tractors, airports, planes, diesel locomotives, oil-fired space-heating facilities and oil-burning equipment for industrial plant and electricity generation; and of course a whole new petro-chemical industry.

The Organization of the Markets

We have seen how crude oil production, particularly outside the United States, was very largely in the hands of seven major oil companies, more often than not in partnerships that limited their ability or inclination to compete with each other, though it did not entirely suppress them. How about refining and the markets?

Joint Ventures Downstream

If you are in bed together upstream, with no one able to expand production faster than anyone else, there are strong arguments for staying in bed downstream, saving the cost of duplicating facilities and preserving the price structure by not competing in the products markets. But that wasn't quite the situation: the majors were tied together upstream in some countries, with varying degrees of ownership from country to country; but in others, they were on their own. Exxon and Shell, for example, produced in Venezuela for the most part through wholly owned subsidiaries, creating an internally competitive position with their jointly owned concessions of the Middle East. For example, was the additional barrel produced in Venezuela by Exxon's wholly owned subsidiary there more or less profitable than the additional "over-lift" barrel out of Saudi Arabia, purchased at a special price from its crude-long partners? Similarly, the different degrees of ownership in those concessions from country to country created conflicts of interest among the partners. For example, (other considerations, mainly political, apart) where should Mobil seek to take its additional barrel—in Iran, Iraq, Qatar or Saudi Arabia? It had an equity interest in all four concessions and it could overlift from one or more of them; or it could step up its long-term purchase volumes of Kuwait crude from BP. The system, then, was by no means rigid. To a certain point, one company could increase its crude availability faster than another with the right balance of choices, and it was this fact that drove competition among the majors—muted though it was.

This hybrid system extended into the downstream, but only to a limited extent, despite the industry's history of cartelistic division of markets. In refining and marketing, there were several joint ventures among the majors in certain areas and countries, though there were at the same time many more wholly owned refineries and marketing subsidiaries competing with each other in other markets. Moreover, the overall mix of downstream joint ventures bore little similarity to the upstream mix. Caltex (a fifty-fifty, mainly downstream, joint venture of Chevron and Texaco) was formed in 1936 and one of its main functions later became the provision of outlets for the two companies' Saudi output. It competed with Stanvac, similarly established, and fulfilling some of the same functions, by Exxon and Mobil. Neither Caltex nor Stanvac were by any means limited to refining Saudi crude and marketing the products obtained from it; indeed, both joint ventures had production in Indonesia, and both of them pre-dated the parent companies' interests in Saudi Arabia.

Apart from Stanvac and Caltex, joint ventures in refining and marketing by the majors were the exception rather than the rule and they probably were of little importance in themselves as a serious constraint on competition. Joint ventures with other non-major companies were not uncommon in some countries such as Japan, Italy and Germany; nor were joint ventures among groups of non-major companies, but these usually arose out of special circumstances and were in no way an outgrowth of the upstream partnerships in the major concessions in producing countries.

Vertical Integration

Nevertheless, the dominance of the major oil companies in refining and marketing, particularly outside the United States, was overwhelming in the 1950s, though diminishing slowly. This high degree of vertical integration was virtually inevitable, given the circumstances at the time. There was no large market for Middle East crude in the shape of independent refiners (outside the United States), so downstream refineries had to be built and the majors had the cash flow to do it. Nor could a strong independent refining sector emerge without government intervention, because few investors would be willing to put up a refinery without an assured source of crude oil on competitive terms —and all the low-cost crude was in the hands of the majors. As a result, it was not so much the partnerships in refining and marketing of the majors, where they existed, that constrained competition in many national markets, but the obstacles to entry. Competition was for the most part therefore limited to competition among the majors themselves, and indeed several of the independent refiners that came to exist in the larger markets were later bought out by the majors or by independents with newly developed crude sources. In the international oil industry at the time, vertical integration was the name of the game.

The Opposition

Middle East oil was not greeted with universal enthusiasm. In the United States, import restrictions were imposed in the name of national security but mainly at the instigation of the swarms of small, independent (and mostly high-cost) producers, and the coal industry. In several countries of Western Europe, the coal industry had to be heavily subsidized and state-owned electricity generating plants compelled to buy coal rather than switch to fuel oil. In both the United States and Western Europe, there was considerable concern over how security of supply could be assured, with attention being focused, particularly in the latter, on the diversification of supply sources.

In Venezuela, there was concern of a somewhat different kind. The Middle East represented a considerable new competitive threat, particularly as ocean transportation costs were dropping rapidly, thus eroding Venezuela's freight advantage to the United States and the rest of the Western Hemisphere.

US Import Restrictions

As soon as it became clear that the size and cost of Middle East oil reserves were such as to make imports into the United States highly profitable, and potentially unlimited, rumblings of alarm began to sound among the country's small domestic producers and land owners whose number was legion and whose political influence in the oil states of the South enormous. The majors, who were responsible for almost three-quarters of crude oil imports and virtually all heavy fuel oil imports into the East Coast of the United States during the decade from 1946 to 1955 (when voluntary import restrictions were formally introduced), soon started making reassuring noises.

It did not take very long for some of the implications of Middle East oil to sink into the US domestic producers. Production in the United States was not keeping up with demand and the United States became a net importer of oil for the first time in 1948. But that was not the problem. The problem was, first, that Middle East production was clearly so much cheaper than most US production that it could be easily imported, despite the long freight involved, and push the highest-cost US producers out of the business: i.e., a lot of small but rich and politically powerful individuals and companies. With free imports, it was thought that the price of oil in the United States might drop from over $3.00 per barrel to $2.00 per barrel within a few years.

The second part of the problem was that the major US companies producing oil in the Middle East were also large net buyers of oil from the small independents in the United States. If they chose to import rather than buy, as they were most likely to do, then the independents would be faced with both declining price and declining volume.

Throughout the period from 1949 to 1954, pressure was exerted on the majors to hold imports down, both by Congress and at the state level, especially by the Texas Railroad Commission (TRC) which, as noted above, set monthly production allowables for Texas, the largest producing state, which was, inevitably, the "swing" state, or the state that absorbed much of the seasonal and other swings in demand. Most of the producing states had bodies similar to the TRC, regulating production ostensibly to enforce good production and conservation practices, but with the practical effect of maintaining prices at levels high enough to support production from the higher cost wells, including the "stripper" wells pumping one or two barrels a day. The initial reason for the establishment of these regulatory bodies—to prevent the kind of wasteful production that occurred in the 1930s—was real enough, but as time went by, the conservation motive faded into the background and supporting price became the pre-eminent though officially unacknowledged goal. As always, everywhere, price supports created huge vested interests in the maintenance of a system whose ripple (or rather tidal wave) effects were to have massive consequences for the international industry. Imports threatened that system because to maintain price at any given level, allowables had to be reduced in order to accommodate them, a process that could only go so far. In the end, the lure of profits from lower-cost imported crude was too great to hold the line despite pressure on the importers from the TRC.

The Trade Agreements Extension Act of 1954 provided for increased restrictions on "imports threatening to impair the national security". The debate over imports then turned to greater emphasis on their effects on national security. The arguments, briefly, went as follows:

Against imports: Increasing imports would result in decreasing prices and the displacement of domestic production. Incentives for exploration would be reduced and producing capacity soon decline. In the event of an emergency reducing the country's access to imported oil, the United States would be caught short. Imports were therefore a threat to national security.

For imports: US reserves were limited and there was a danger of producing them at an excessive pace; imports would "supplement but not supplant" domestic production and prevent premature depletion. Hence, a reasonable volume of imports was in the national interest on security grounds, as well as for other reasons.

As far as heavy fuel oil imports were concerned, the coal industry weighed in with the argument that it had lost some ten to twenty million tons of output during the period from 1946 to 1954, that the low price of foreign oil constituted "unfair" competition, and that the declining producing capacity of the domestic coal industry would endanger national security.

The national security argument against imports may have had some, but not much, justification. It rang hollow at the time, as Mobil's president pointed out in 1950:

> Fears that oil imports might make us dependent on distant sources of
> supply that would be cut off in an emergency seemingly ignore many
> important strategic considerations.
> – Annual Report, 1949

In other words, as everyone knew, or should have known by 1955 when the national security argument ostensibly became pivotal in the issue, denial by a foreign power (meaning the Soviet Union at that time) of access to Middle East crude was a *casus belli.*

For the time being, however, with the cold war heating up and President Eisenhower and Secretary of State Dulles in charge, vested interests were able to successfully harness the national security argument to their ends. No doubt the Eisenhower administration gave careful consideration to the national security arguments, but they cut both ways and in the end it is difficult to think that anything would have been done had it not been for intense political pressure from the pro-import-restrictions lobby. In the event, a program of voluntary import restrictions was instituted in 1955 to hold imports to the 1954 ratio of imports to domestic production (slightly less than 10 percent).

The restrictions came at a bad time. The Iranian nationalization dispute had just been settled, in August 1954, and US companies had, with tacit US government approval, committed themselves to a schedule of increasing offtake from Iran to help it re-establish itself in the markets. Obviously, import restrictions were not at this juncture helpful, and Iran's return would have to be accommodated by even lower growth in other exporting countries.

Over time, the voluntary program broke down, and a Mandatory Oil Import Program was established by presidential proclamation with effect from April 1959. Crude and product imports into Districts I-IV (the Lower 48 minus District V, comprising the West Coast States plus Nevada, Arizona and Alaska) were to be restricted to approximately 9 percent of estimated demand. However, heavy fuel oil imports into I-IV were excluded from the general quota and limited to 1957 levels, and this limit was itself later stretched as fuel oil yields from domestic refineries continued their downward trend. Imports into District V were "limited" to the difference between District V production and estimated demand. Overland imports (from Canada and Mexico) were exempted from the restrictions on the grounds that they would be available even in a supply emergency. This was inconsistent with the main national security argument, which claimed that security would be impaired because imports would so weaken the domestic industry that it would not have enough developed reserves in case of an emergency—nothing to do with the security of oil availability from neighboring countries. But foreign policy considerations overrode logical consistency.

Crude oil quotas were distributed pro-rata to refining capacity, regardless of whether the refiner-recipients had ever imported any crude, or indeed physically could. Quotas (or tickets) were saleable; the windfall was worth about $1.00/B. The majors quietly dropped their opposition to imports controls, recognizing both the value of their import quotas and, perhaps more importantly, the value to them of maintaining a high price for crude in the United States; the US independents that had gone abroad to develop an overseas source of production objected mainly to the receipt by domestic refiners, without overseas production, of part of the benefits of import restrictions.

What were the international implications of the restrictions?

Venezuela

Outside of general trade policy and non-oil foreign policy considerations, there were two important consequences to the restrictions. First, relations with Venezuela were soured; second, the restrictions contributed further to the general weakening of international crude prices that had already been taking place.

Unlike Canada and Mexico, Venezuela was not granted an exemption from the import restrictions, ostensibly because it could not export overland to the United States and tankers would be vulnerable in the event of an armed conflict (with, presumably, the Soviet Union). To no avail did the State Department urge exemption for Venezuela: the pro-US right-wing military dictatorship of General Marcos Pérez Jiménez had been overthrown at the beginning of 1958 and, after an interim period, replaced in February 1959 by a left(ish), democratically elected government headed by President Rómulo Betancourt. Dr. Juan Pablo Pérez Alfonzo (soon to be one of the driving forces behind the establishment of OPEC) was Minister of Mines and Hydrocarbons. The direction Betancourt's government would take on oil policy, especially with Pérez Alfonzo at the wheel, was uncertain. New policies were being introduced and a tough line being taken on price and taxes with the companies. These changes included higher income taxes, the creation of a national oil company (Corporación Venezolana de Petróleo), greater emphasis on conservation, attempts to control export prices, and others. In the past, the United States had treated Venezuela with kid gloves, ever since the Mexican nationalization in 1938, and the last thing it wanted was another Mexico on its hands.

Nevertheless, the real reason for not including Venezuela in the exemptions was simply that it was too big an exporter. Mexico's exports were negligible; Canada's were not so small but wholly confined to the northern Midwest states. Venezuela on the other hand, supplied virtually all US imports of fuel oil, and almost half of its total crude oil imports (in 1958) of 950 thousand barrels per day (kbd). It was capable of considerable further expansion, especially from the crop of US independents that had been granted concessions in 1956-57 and whose production was now coming onstream.

Exemption for Venezuela was impossible without putting at risk the whole program of import restrictions.

Betancourt protested. Eisenhower replied that the Canadian exemption was necessary because otherwise Canada would build a pipeline from the Western producing provinces to Montreal, and Venezuelan oil (a large proportion of Eastern Canada's imports) would be shut out. The Canadian exemption was therefore in Venezuela's interest. The Mexican exemption was pro-forma, since imports from Mexico were, and would remain, negligible. Nevertheless, Eisenhower told Betancourt, the United States would continue to examine the situation in consultation with Venezuela, particularly with respect to some hemispheric arrangement. Nothing came of these discussions, nor of State Department proposals to mollify Venezuela by scrapping restrictions on fuel oil imports, though, in.the event, they were substantially relaxed. It was soon clear that Venezuela was not going to benefit from any sort of US price umbrella and that it would have to look elsewhere. US import restrictions were not a determining factor in pushing Venezuela to seek agreement with Middle East countries on price support, but they were certainly an additional spur.

The second main consequence of US import restrictions was their contribution to further weakening international crude oil prices under the pressure of increasing competition, to which we will return in a subsequent chapter.

European Coal

In 1950, Western Europe produced 450 million metric tons (MT) of hard coal (cf., US= 505 million), with Britain, Germany and France accounting for 88 percent of the total. This level of production was sustained until 1960, taking none of the vigorous growth in the overall energy market, but not losing in absolute terms. After 1960, European coal started its long decline, reaching 325 million MT in 1970, a drop of nearly 30 percent in ten years. Thereafter, decline continued during, ironically, a period of high oil prices, reaching 133 million MT in 1995, nearly all of it in the much-reduced mines of Germany and the United Kingdom. The Netherlands closed down its small industry altogether in the early 1970s and turned to its own natural gas reserves; Belgium closed down its industry somewhat later; and France all but closed down its coal industry when it turned increasingly to nuclear power for electricity generation in the late 1970s and 1980s.

With the advent of cheap oil from the Middle East, and the cheaper fuel oil made from it, European coal, mostly deep-mined, became hopelessly uneconomic. But it was everywhere a nationalized industry, and except to the extent that there is always a dichotomy between government *qua* government and the managers of its nationalized industries, who, like ambassadors to foreign countries, become spokesmen for the domain to which they have been

assigned, the real and most powerful defenders of Western Europe coal were
the trade unions, particularly militant in Britain. The Germans had less
trouble with their unions because much of their coal was mined by Turkish
gästarbeiter (guest workers) who, of course, had no political voice. Strikes for
more pay and strikes against reductions in the labor force became commonplace, culminating in Britain with the downfall of Prime Minister Edward
Heath's government, the election of a labor government, and rampant
inflation as it gave in time after time to wage demands (as though the OPEC
price increases of the early seventies were not enough). The unions in Britain
were finally quelled by Prime Minister Margaret Thatcher.

In the 1960s, there were about one million workers in the coal industries
of Western Europe (about 40 percent more than the number of employees,
worldwide, of the seven major internationals working in all phases of the
business). European coal was subsidized, its main competitor—fuel oil—was
taxed, and markets, such as the state-owned electricity sector, delivered to it
on a platter. The work was dangerous, nasty, polluting and often resulted in
"black lung" for the workers at the coal-face. European governments felt
justified in maintaining a clearly uneconomic industry mainly on the grounds
of national security, fearing that access to oil might be cut off for an extended
period, or that the major oil companies would favor their home countries in
the event of oil shortages and the need to ration whatever was available.
However, it was quite clear that they were just as concerned about the miners'
political clout as national security. Indeed, Professor M. A. Adelman, in 1967,
characterized European coal as "no longer an industry, but only a means of
social insurance, and therefore should be phased out."[4]   And, to a large
extent, phased out it was, very slowly. Everyone was well aware of the parlous
state and poor prospects for the coal industry. In 1962 and again in 1964, the
European Communities published joint studies of the long-term outlook for
energy in the Community area. Among their conclusions:

> The coal industry's competitive position will not improve over the
> long term . . . the amount of Community coal which would be
> competitive in the absence of all aid is only slightly higher than half
> of current production . . . taking into account security considerations,
> social and regional concerns, and the dangers weighing on a market
> exposed to such uncertain political factors, this justifies aid to coal to
> maintain production and sales at a level above its purely competitive
> position . . . [5]

Nevertheless, there was something pathetic, and touching, about the spectacle
of workers, above all in Britain, with their mystique of Welsh choirs and
Yorkshire colliery brass bands, clinging to the dirtiest and most arduous jobs
left in the industrialized world.

Security of Supply

Concerns over security of oil supplies had been ostensibly addressed in the United States by the imposition of import restrictions. (See above.) In Western Europe, it was largely addressed by propping up an uneconomic coal industry at vast expense. But the Europeans, with the exception of Britain and the Netherlands, which were the home countries of two of the international majors (BP and Royal Dutch/Shell), also felt vulnerable because they were dependent on the major (to them, foreign) oil companies, who were in turn dependent on a small number of politically volatile countries in the Middle East.

Diversification of supply sources became the aim, both with respect to supplier countries and supplier companies. In the face of little or no domestic production, it was generally thought that the ideal situation would be one where a domestic company, state-owned or not, would own or "control" oilfields in various countries from which oil imports would be wholly or largely drawn. After the watershed years of the early 1970s, this issue of upstream ownership and control of foreign crude sources died a natural death when the major oil companies were edged out of most of the OPEC countries and eventually evicted altogether. But for a while during the 1950s and 1960s, it played an important part in the establishment and motivation of state oil companies.

In 1950, Italy already had a state oil company, the Ente Nazionale Idrocarburi (ENI), a left-over from the pre-war Fascist regime, which Enrico Mattei resurrected on the back of Po Valley natural gas and transformed into a major industrial power in Italy. ENI and its oil subsidiary, the Azienda Generale di Petrolio (AGIP) successfully sought concessions in a number of countries abroad, offering host governments apparently more attractive terms than the majors, notably under a joint venture system, starting in Egypt and Iran in 1957. However, ENI's foreign production never amounted to anything significant (less than 25 kbd in Iran) during the two decades from 1950 to 1970.

In France, the government held a 35 percent interest in the Compagnie Française des Pétroles (CFP), which had been established in 1924. CFP in turn held a 23.75 percent interest in the Iraq Petroleum Company (IPC) group and so had substantial production. However, because of its minority shareholding, the government did not regard CFP as the appropriate instrument for its search for security of oil supplies. It had a larger shareholding in a number of different companies, notably SN Repal and CREPS in Algeria, and it later (in 1966) set up the wholly owned Entreprise de Recherches et d'Activités Petrolières (ERAP) to consolidate its holdings in the other companies in which it had an interest. For a few years in the 1960s, before and after Algerian independence in 1962, French companies, in most of which the French government had a large equity stake, accounted for a major share of Algeria's total production (68 percent—690 kbd—by 1970), but the arrangements under which the oil was produced had undergone important revisions since independence, at the expense of the companies. Worse was to come.

In 1971, most of the existing French interests in Algeria were nationalized; by 1972, they accounted for only 23 percent of the country's production. Within five years, the French government companies, by then consolidated in ERAP, withdrew altogether. CFP clung on for another five years.

Algeria must have in fact decided early on in the game to take over full control of its oil and gas industry, and the French, seeking in effect to emulate the position of the United States in the Middle East, to have their own "franc" oil, and to enjoy the "security" of overseas production controlled by French companies, ended up paying over the odds, in taxes, for a short-lived illusion, and paying a higher than market price for oil purchased from Algeria's national oil company.

Germany was the most free enterprise, market-oriented economy of Western Europe. It nevertheless had two wholly owned state oil companies plus an important minority interest in a third. Between them, the three companies controlled refining capacity of 1.6 mbd in Germany (mid-1960s), but little crude production, and none outside the country. Private-sector companies were active in exploration abroad, subsidized to some extent by the government, but they had come to the scene late in the day. By 1966, one of them (Gelsenberg) had a modest 40 kbd of crude production in Libya and another (Wintershall) 23 kbd in Canada. These two companies, along with five other German companies, agreed to pool their foreign exploration efforts in a new joint company, Deminex: they brought to the table exploration interests in Iran, Oman, Canada, Peru, Algeria, Spain, Morocco, Somalia, the Netherlands and the UK sector of the North Sea.

Deminex was not a state oil company, but was dominated by wholly- or partly-owned state companies and received important subsidies for foreign exploration. Subsidies necessarily imply non-commercial motives, and it is not entirely clear what these were in the case of a government dedicated to a market economy in other sectors. The long-standing involvement of government in the oil industry; a large state-owned refining capacity with no in-house crude supply; the decease, by foreign take-over, of some important German independents, such as Deutsche Erdöl (DEA), acquired by Texaco; a hangover of the image of oil as a strategic material, "vital" to national security; these all perhaps played a part in the German government's decision to encourage and participate indirectly in foreign exploration. It was, mercifully, too little too late, and (unlike France) Germany escaped the fate of being tied to high-cost and politically difficult sources of crude supply abroad. In the post-1970 world of oil, Deminex went on to commercial success on a limited scale, notably in the North Sea, the United States, Canada and Egypt. But by then it was a different company with a different motivation.

In Spain, the government also had a history of direct involvement in the industry, holding important equity interests in four companies engaged primarily in refining and marketing. None had any producing interests. In 1965, the government set up a wholly owned company, Hispánica de Petróleos SA (Hispanoil) for the express purpose of foreign exploration. They too were late on the scene and by 1970 had no foreign production; but like Deminex, the company acquired a life of its own, independent of original motivation, and continued its search and operations long after its original raison d'être had evaporated.

In addition to the Western European governments' efforts, Japan made a belated attempt to help its own companies develop production overseas. It came on the scene even later than Germany and Spain, setting up the Japan Petroleum Development Corporation in late 1967 (whose name was later changed to Japan National Oil Corporation—JNOC). The company's main function was to provide equity capital and loans to Japanese private sector companies for exploration and production abroad. It was too late to make any impact before the early 1970s, though Japanese private-sector companies did in fact develop significant amounts of production on their own in various countries, notably in the Neutral Zone through the Arabian Oil Company.

It was all a snare and a delusion. The state companies could not hope to emulate the seven majors; in any event, any "security" felt by the majors' home countries because of the "control" exercised by their companies over production was also soon to prove illusory. The state-owned companies of Western Europe, or their surrogates, for the most part found only insignificant amounts of oil in terms of their countries' import needs. In the one instance where they found more, France's various companies in Algeria, the home country ended up paying more in investment costs, production taxes and ultimately prices than they would have needed to shell out as simple purchasers of oil from other sources.

The 1970s opened with demand still booming, prices dropping, supplies plentiful, world proved reserves at an all-time high and new producing areas developed or being developed. The major oil companies were still dominant on the international scene though their position was being slowly eroded. In 1950, world (excluding CPEs) production of coal had been one-and-a-half times greater than crude oil production. By 1970, crude production was two-and-a-half times greater than coal production. Oil had swept the board.

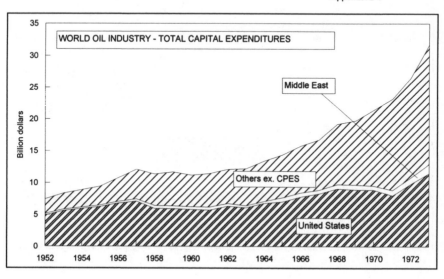

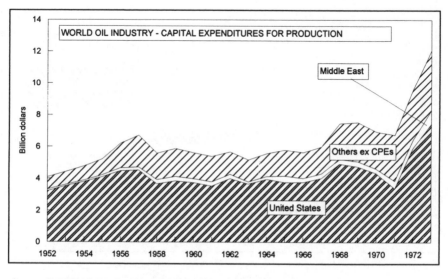

Source: Chase Manhattan Bank,'Capital Investments of the World Petroleum Industry'.

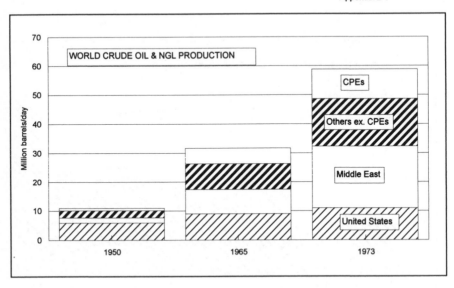

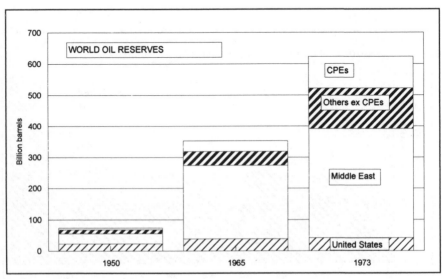

Chapter 3
FIXING THE CRUDE OIL PRICE STRUCTURE

People of the same trade seldom meet together, even for merriment and diversion,
but the conversation ends in a conspiracy against the public, or in some contrivance
to raise prices.
– Adam Smith, *The Wealth of Nations.*

The Late Forties and Early Fifties: the Majors Dispose

If the process by which crude oil prices came to be established in Venezuela
and the Middle East during the early post-war period can be called a decision,
then it was among the most important economic ones ever taken in the
international oil industry. The various formulae adopted had, as we shall see,
a specious economic justification that built a bonanza share of profit into
crude production—where the major oil companies' grip was tightest and the
rent the greatest. It was a "decision" that could not have been taken without
powerful constraints on competition in the upstream, and it allowed the
majors to harness some of oil's resource rent—the vast difference between
supply costs in the Middle East and Venezuela on the one hand, and all other
sources of energy on the other.

The majors used these rents to sustain and expand their dominant
position in world product markets and, along the way, transportation and
refining. However, they soon found it necessary or expedient to yield an
increasing share of the growing torrent of gold to the host governments so
that they could hang on to the rest. Not surprisingly, the governments
evolved and grew economically and politically until the inevitable happened:
they took over, with grave economic consequences for everyone concerned.
But that all came much later.

Here we look at how the price structure was established and some of its
immediate consequences. It must be borne in mind that the crude price being
set was, or rather was meant to be, the real market price, the price that non-
affiliated buyers would pay in arm's-length transactions, the price that
everyone would pay, and a price that was to be transparent, being published
or "posted". In fact, of course, its main application was to transfers between
affiliates because there were so few independent refiners around the world.

Also, the price determined international flows of oil money and, after the introduction of 50/50 into the Middle East, producing-government revenues.

In 1950, where we take up the story, nearly all of the crude oil trading across national borders moved between subsidiaries of the seven major oil companies. Whenever one subsidiary transfers oil to another subsidiary in a different country, a price must be imputed to the transaction. It is not an academic exercise: the country from which the export takes place wants to make sure that the exporting company is not selling at an artificially low price in order to decrease its taxable income. The country into which the oil is imported wants to make sure that the importing subsidiary is not paying an artificially high price for the same motive. So the problem of pricing could not simply be ignored, as if it were of no consequence except for the small fringe of non-affiliated transactions. In the case of products, the prices were more "real" in the sense that more non-affiliated buyers were concerned, some with considerable clout (notably the armed forces of the United States and Britain). And since the major oil companies also owned or leased most of the world tanker fleet, the tax inspector in the importing country also had to cope with the freight paid by the importing affiliate for ocean transportation. Was it a "fair" rate?

As far as crude oil is concerned, various pricing formulae were used during the period preceding the World War II and through the 1950s, all of which were based on some relationship to US domestic posted crude prices.[1] In oil industry literature, this is well-trodden ground, and only a brief recap is necessary here. They were, however, important because although they were, as prices, an economic fiction, they were an *operative* fiction, and had serious economic consequences that were felt long after the formulae themselves had vanished from the face of the earth: they were, as we shall see, formulae for the hors-d'oeuvres which gave the producing governments an appetite for monopoly rents.

International Oil Pricing Formulae

The companies started with a system firmly grounded in what can best be described as fig-leaf economics, an economic logic that never corresponded to reality but which at first was close enough to be invested with a measure of plausibility. In its several variants, it lasted a substantial period of time, providing a basis for real prices in the third-party market, as well as a tax device for companies and host governments. It was destined to break down entirely under the pressures of economic change and increasing competition. By that time, however, it would have cast an irrevocable spell on the upstream that has shaped much of the industry to this day.

Three pricing formulae adopted and used by the industry should concern us here. They were (a) the "Gulf-plus" basing point; (b) the London

Equalization point; and (c) the New York equalization point. Underlying all of them was the model of a competitive market where a new, small producer (the Middle East) enters a marketplace dominated by other suppliers (the United States) and sells at the going price, however arrived at. The new producer is a "price-taker"; he is too small to influence the price, upwards or downwards. The various pricing formulae, it was implied, were not "chosen" or "settled upon" by the Middle East producers, but were merely a description of the marketplace at a given time.

This market model may have had some relevance to the supply/demand situation existing (mainly for refined products) in the 1930s, but it was far removed from any post-World War II reality. US oil was not there in the market in unlimited quantities, setting a ceiling, or a floor, or anything else, to prices—on the contrary, it was rapidly disappearing from world markets, and in 1949, did so. From 1949, the relatively high US domestic price sucked in quantities of lower-cost oil from Venezuela and the Middle East, which had to be limited by constraints of various kinds (see Chapter 2), culminating in mandatory import controls in 1959 that lasted until 1971. By this time, 1971, international prices had risen to such an extent that it was no longer necessary to protect US domestic production from "cheap" foreign imports: there weren't any.

The question for the majors in the post-World War II world was how to price, mainly for inter-affiliate transfers, a vast quantity of newly found oil, cheaper than anyone could have imagined.

But there were constraints: (a) pressure, ultimately political, from real or surrogate buyers represented by the MSA/ECA (see below) and other governmental agencies concerned primarily with foreign exchange limitations in Western Europe; (b) in the US market, the domestic price structure, not to be broken lightly or without loss to the majors themselves (but which had in any event to be protected in the end from suppliers and buyers to whom its maintenance was not of great concern); and (c) the lack of any publicly acceptable reason for raising prices from their previous levels (or, more accurately, reference point).

The solution was more of the pre-war same, subject to suitable adjustments to a slightly modified rationalization. The "same" was a relationship to US prices, which was acceptable to, and became accepted by, the major importing countries. Independent, third-party crude purchasers would pay the same price (for a while), but they were too small to be a factor in influencing the choice.

In summary, the pricing formulae developed as follows:

Gulf-plus

Prior to World War II and for a few brief years thereafter, the United States was the world's major exporter of crude and products. It remained a net exporter of oil until 1948, and after that, was the largest intra-regional shipper of oil with large movements from the Texas Gulf Coast to the US Atlantic Coast. Within the United States, the major oil companies, while important, operated alongside a host of other "independent" producers, many of them very small producers indeed, others of medium and even quite large size. Their oil was bought at the well-head, mostly by non-affiliated refining companies, of which there were far fewer. It was an open market with prices published (or "posted") by the refiner/purchasers for each grade of oil in the field. It was also, incidentally, a highly stable market, because the volume of production was controlled in each of the main producing states by state conservation commissions (the most important of which was the Texas Railroad Commission), set up in the 1930s to eliminate technically wasteful production practices harmful to the reservoirs. It was not long before the conservation commissions started taking market demand into account when establishing the overall monthly production allowances. They thus became surrogate oligopolists, controlling supply at levels that yielded stable and remunerative prices for the producing companies. But the existence and functioning of these commissions were incidental to the companies' setting of international prices, and the fact that the US base prices were determined by supply controls does not affect the economic logic of the companies' international pricing, though it affected most fundamentally the basic price level itself.

The pricing system adopted by the major oil companies for oil produced outside the United States was simply the US Gulf Coast price plus freight to the buyer's terminal wherever located. This was the "Gulf basing-point system", or "Gulf-plus" (plus freight, that is). Thus, for example, a company in Italy, whether affiliated or not, would pay for Venezuelan or Middle Eastern crude or products, the US price f.o.b the Gulf of Mexico plus freight from the United States to Italy. The major company in the Middle East or Venezuela got that price, minus freight to Italy. In the absence of any serious competition among Venezuelan/Middle Eastern suppliers, the logic, of course, was that the buyer's only alternative was to actually buy U.S crude, which would not have produced any saving.

Non-US exporters reaped great profit from the system. First, they enjoyed a component of profit represented by the amount by which their producing costs were lower (they usually were) than those of Texas producers; then, if they were closer to the buyer, they also got the difference between actual freight and freight from the US Gulf (the so-called "phantom" freight, which seemed to arouse more moral indignation among those in hot pursuit of a phantom cartel than any other aspect of oil pricing).

Apart from the awkward but not unmanageable fact that the same c.i.f. price for every destination necessarily resulted in a different f.o.b. price for each one, there was an obvious inequity for the refiner close to the non-US source being obliged to pay the same price as the refiner more distant from it.

After the war, the system was modified so that f.o.b. crude prices in both Venezuela and the Middle East were set at the same level as US Gulf Coast prices, thus doing away with price differentials for different destinations. (In fact, most of the discussions revolved around product prices, especially products sold to the US and British navies. But the same principle applied to crude.)

London Equalization

Production in Venezuela and the Middle East was expanding rapidly and pushing US crude out of its export markets, entailing large exports to multiple destinations. So the economic logic was modified, and prices were set in accordance with a more or less imaginary competitive interface between US and Middle East crudes. London was chosen as an "equalization" point for US and non-US crudes. The reasoning was as follows:

Middle East and Venezuelan crudes were to be sold as far afield as Northwest Europe (London being an appropriately important single destination for the purpose). Therefore the price f.o.b. Middle Eastern export ports would be the f.o.b. US price plus freight to London, minus freight to the Middle East. Similarly, the price f.o.b. Venezuela would be the c.i.f. London price for US crude, minus freight from London back to Venezuela. All buyers, wherever located, were to be charged these prices.

New York Equalization

The London equalization point did not last long despite the efforts of the major companies with producing interests in the Middle East to prolong its lucrative life. In 1949, the United States became a net oil importing country, though close to 1 million barrels per day (mbd) of producing capacity had been shut in by the conservation commissions to maintain domestic prices. The majors had started moving Middle East crude to their US Atlantic Coast refineries on a substantial scale. They no longer needed to continue buying so much expensive Texas and other US crudes when they had growing supplies of their own (much lower-cost) crude in the Middle East.

Clearly, though, sales of Middle East crude to the United States could not be priced at the London equalization price; this would have resulted in a price c.i.f. the US Atlantic Coast higher than the price for US crude at the Gulf Coast plus freight. So the majors made an exception and absorbed the difference. But this obviously implied two-tier pricing f.o.b. the Middle East: one price to the United States, and another, higher price to all other destinations. This was not merely a matter of transfer pricing, because the transfer prices were reflected in the level of product prices in the markets, which is where the real money was made. But if the majors were to stick with a uniform f.o.b. price to all comers and still export to the United States, they would have to lower their price to a level that would accommodate the US Atlantic Coast market (that is, price equalization at New York), but lose them a slice of their profit margins on sales to Europe and other Eastern Hemisphere destinations.

And this is what happened, but not before a rearguard action was fought during which the companies had it both ways. For a year or so (1948-49), they continued to charge the London equalization price to Eastern Hemisphere buyers and the New York equalization price to Western Hemisphere buyers. There were objections (see below), but the majors stalled, claiming that their shipments of Middle East crude to the United States in 1948 were the result of extraordinary circumstances that would not recur and which did not justify fundamentally altering the existing structure on international crude prices, that is, the London equalization point. (Never mind that, with the disappearance of US exports, the last shred of an excuse for charging London equalization prices to anyone had vanished.) Anyway, it was not long before the majors accepted the inevitable consequence of large-scale shipments of Middle East crude to the United States and lowered their f.o.b. prices to everyone accordingly.

Once Texas crudes were displaced from Northwest Europe and then to a large extent from the US East Coast, which was quite soon, the remaining shreds of the economic "logic" of equalization-point pricing disappeared, but in the absence of serious competition among Middle East suppliers, the melody lingered on. The New York equalization price was to be the basis for the companies' posted prices for the next ten years, determining taxation levels regardless of the still small but growing arm's-length sales to independent refiners—at growing discounts off the postings.

The External Pressures: the ECA and Others

The establishment and development of crude prices described above did not, of course, happen in a vacuum. There is some case, though perhaps not a very strong one, for saying that Venezuelan crude prices were set by the market in the immediate post-war period, but there is really no case at all for saying that about Middle East prices. From the outset, they were the result of policy decisions taken by the companies involved. They did not go unquestioned.

The initial pricing system adopted for the Middle East—identical c.i.f. prices everywhere equal to c.i.f. Texas crude prices—had been adopted well before the World War II and was perfectly logical for new suppliers not yet needing to compete with each other, so long as they could simply nudge Texas crudes gradually aside, but it was unsustainable in the context of growing supplies in the Middle East and expanding markets.

The US Navy, a large purchaser of products and also the purchaser of crude oil for the United Nations Refugee Relief Agency (UNRRA) immediately after the war was the first to question the companies' prices (specifically, Aramco's). After a period of negotiation during which the Navy tried (unsuccessfully) to ascertain Aramco's producing costs, a price of $1.05/B. f.o.b. Ras Tanura for Arabian crude was agreed, for deliveries to Italy, and this in effect became a base price for a short period. It was essentially the same as the US Gulf Coast price.

US crude prices rose sharply after the lifting of wartime price controls by the Office of Price Administration (OPA). They were tracked by the companies in the Middle East, and led to very large price increases; at the same time, the decision was taken to establish uniform f.o.b. prices to all destinations. To accomplish this, London was chosen as an equalization point (see above) with crude oil shipped from Venezuela at the f.o.b. Venezuelan price, which was in turn linked to the US Gulf Coast price, equalized at New York, minus US import duty of $0.105/B. In late 1947, this worked out at $2.22/B. f.o.b. Ras Tanura, being the Venezuelan crude price c.i.f. London, minus freight from the Persian Gulf to London.

However, the freight used was based on the full USMC rates,[2] whereas actual rates had come down significantly, and the $2.22 price could no longer be justified. The Persian Gulf price was accordingly brought down to $2.03/B. in May 1948, using a freight rate of USMC minus 35.5 percent. This price was rapidly overtaken by events as exports from the Middle East to the United States expanded. Under pressure from the US Economic Cooperation Administration (ECA), the agency in charge of disbursing Marshall Aid funds for Europe including the financing of some of Europe's oil imports, the majors finally agreed to the price reductions necessary to equalize world crude prices at New York. (See above.) The $2.03 price was dropped to $1.88 in April 1949 and under continuing pressure from the ECA, to $1.75, in July 1949. The New York equalization point, and, consequently, the linkage to US crude prices was thereby implicitly accepted by the ECA. It was not to be seriously questioned again until 1955.

The Introduction of Posted Prices in the Middle East and Venezuela

Until the early 1950s, prices from Venezuela and the Middle East (insofar as there were any arm's-length prices) had been contract prices, with changes, usually at the discretion of the seller, simply being notified to buyers from time to time. This was, of course, quite different from the system in the United States, where buyers "posted" in the field the prices at which they were willing to buy oil from producers, at the wellhead.

However, with the new, New York-based pricing system to be consolidated and consecrated, and after the introduction of the 50/50 tax arrangements in the Middle East, there was an increasing need for open, uniform prices, available to all-comers. The most compelling argument for such a system was the taxation of oil under the new 50/50 regimes in the Middle East, described in Chapter 1. These provided for a 50/50 division of the companies' net profits, that is, of income after deducting costs, and though royalty was to be formally retained, the 50/50 split included it (a matter that was later to lead to one of the first serious disputes with OPEC). It was therefore necessary to establish, to the satisfaction of the governments involved, what the companies' income was, so that they could be assured that they really were receiving 50 percent of the net. It was also desirable to demonstrate to the growing arm's-length market of non-affiliated refiners that there was one price to all. The easiest and most convincing way was to publish, or "post," a selling price, applicable to all comers (subject to availability), and such posted prices were soon introduced throughout the Middle East. The first posting was made by Mobil for Iraqi Kirkuk crude in October 1950, followed by a posting of Arabian Light crude in November 1950, Venezuelan crudes in July 1952, Kuwait in April 1953, and Iran in October 1954 (after the settlement of the Iranian nationalization dispute). The companies were then able to say to the governments that no buyer would pay more than the posted price, and, if they should happen to pay less, government revenue, being based entirely on a calculation of company revenue at the posted price (as adjusted for volume discounts, etc.), would not be affected.

The posted price system was deeply flawed. Payments to the governments rapidly became, in substance though not in form, nothing but a royalty, though a royalty with a difference. As actual sales prices were increasingly discounted, the posted prices became a mere fiction, giving rise to a tax payment to the producing government no longer related to the market price. But previously, payments to the governments had been fixed in absolute terms, and could not be unilaterally reduced by the companies. Now, while the payments had more than doubled, they could quite legally be reduced by the companies at their discretion, by simply lowering the posted price. And in fact, as competition started to grow, the temptation to lower their payments to the governments was to prove too great: the companies accordingly lowered their posted prices.

I think on the whole that the companies did not act with the intention of, in effect, evading taxes. They all recognized that posted prices had no market reality, but there seems to have been a strong feeling among some of the company managements that postings ought to reflect, in some measure at least, the directional movement of the market. And if the market was going down, then they, the companies, were entitled to pay lower taxes.

The companies would in fact have been quite happy with a payment fixed in absolute terms like the old royalty. But they couldn't go this route without forfeiting the income tax credit in their home countries, which they were able to claim when 50/50 was introduced into Venezuela and the Middle East. (See Chapter 1.) They were locked into the fiction that posted prices were a proper basis for the calculation of taxable income and that producing-country taxes on this "income" were income taxes within the meaning defined by the US (and British) tax authorities.

But the producing governments had come to view the payments as what they in fact were—a royalty that should not be reduced "arbitrarily" by the companies. But they couldn't formally go this route either without foreclosing the potential benefits to be derived from a possibly rising market in the future. What they wanted was a floor that would ratchet up in good times and not come down in bad.

So, in accordance with the revised concessionary agreements (revised to accommodate the introduction of 50/50), the companies were free to modify their posted prices at their discretion, though the presumption was clearly that they would not make any change not justified by the market. In the Middle East, the governments thus remained in the role of *rentiers*, collecting their revenues and having very little influence on any of the industry's operations, investments or other plans; nor did they (with the exception of Iraq) in fact evince much interest in matters other than revenue, expressing this interest through constant nagging for increased production.

The situation in Venezuela was very different. The 50/50 provisions of the income tax law were a minimum, not a maximum; they had been introduced by government legislation with the tacit assent but not formal approval (which was not required) of the companies; and taxes were based on the prices at which sales of crude and products were actually made. In addition, the bulk of production was accounted for by companies not tied to each other through joint producing arrangements; the one joint arrangement that mattered (the Mene Grande Oil Company, owned jointly by Gulf, Shell and Exxon) was not an obstacle. Posted prices in Venezuela, introduced in July 1952, had no fiscal significance, and were initially put in place mainly to show that there was basically one price to all comers, or at least one maximum price.

Upstream Consequences

By tying their export prices in the Middle East and Venezuela to US price levels (subject to freight and quality adjustments), the companies chose to concentrate profits in the upstream where they were in virtually full control of all available supplies and competition could not easily penetrate.

I said above that the pricing structure chosen by companies in the early fifties would "cast an irrevocable spell on the upstream", even though largely applicable to transfer sales, and that the US companies' tax position in the United States would also have a profound effect. The two are linked.

The "irrevocable spell" was the creation and then consolidation of high and rising government revenues from taxation of the high upstream profits, but behind a barrier—which is what posted prices rapidly became—that effectively insulated them from market pressure on price unless and until the companies reduced their posted price in response. By the time the pressure came, with the slow growth of competition, income tax on "profits" had been virtually transformed into fixed per barrel payments from which the governments would soon brook no reduction. Posted prices went for long periods without change, regardless of what was happening in the markets. The governments had absolutely no exposure to market fluctuations, and they quite correctly believed that the companies never had a compelling market reason for reducing posted prices: tax payments effectively set a floor under market prices.

In the ten years following the introduction of posted prices, there were to be only four changes to the basic posted prices of oil in the Persian Gulf, and these tracked (though with no great precision) changes in US crude prices. At the end of the ten years, OPEC was to block any further change; but by then, indeed, discounting off the posted price level had become universal except for the most ignorant buyers.

The oil industry came to account for an overwhelming proportion of total government revenue, and the governments' stake in oil taxes based on the posted prices became a central national interest. Later, this was to give birth to OPEC and ultimately the wholesale nationalization of the industry, and a lot of other, more general economic consequences that are not part of this story. The economic development of the producing countries was fundamentally affected by the high level of revenues; the high price of oil (relative to cost) created balance-of-payments difficulties for many other countries; and competition from other sources was accelerated.

Prices: the Deafening Silence

Talk of international crude oil prices, or anything else to do with the economics of the industry, was strongly and quite effectively discouraged by the majors. They were halcyon days, the first half of the 1950s, when competition was nil, demand was booming, and the public discussion of prices taboo. Virtually nothing was published; prior to 1955, practically the only intelligible source was Dr Paul Frankel, a well-known consultant, in a number of articles published in British trade journals (see bibliography); a chapter on Price Determination in the International Petroleum Industry, in the US Federal Trade Commission (FTC) report (1952) on *The International Petroleum Cartel* (which itself drew heavily on Frankel's work); and a paper by Walter J. Levy called The Past, Present and Likely Future Price Structure for the International Oil Trade. This latter paper was presented to the World Petroleum Congress that was held in the Hague in 1951, and, while both detailed and original for its time (in fact, a bit of a landmark piece), was remarkable, first, for discussing the topic explicitly in the context of a quite imaginary degree of competition, and, second, for never mentioning the role of the major companies from beginning to end. The whole piece can be read without discovering whether there were two, twenty or 200 companies of any significance in the international oil trade. Perhaps this was part of the price of being allowed to present the paper at all to the Congress, which was dominated by the majors themselves, and was largely dedicated to the presentation and discussion of technical papers.

For several years thereafter, very little of note was published on the topic of oil prices. Then, in 1955, the United Nations Economic Commission for Europe (ECE) published a study it had prepared for its Coal Committee, entitled The Price of Oil in Western Europe. It caused a furor in the industry, mainly because it suggested that the then current price of oil could not be explained in terms of competition in the industry, and that the lack of competition was resulting in product prices in Western Europe that were higher than would otherwise be the case. Among the report's conclusions:

> The distribution of production and trade is not closely responsive to differences in underlying price/cost relationships in the major producing centers. In this more fundamental sense the market could scarcely be regarded as unified nor prices as resulting from the free play of competitive forces.

> The wide divorce which persists between prices and production costs in the Middle East suggests that, if this link were severed, the price charged on sales to European countries by the Middle East could be significantly lowered without adverse effects on the further development of its crude oil production.

This scarcely sounds like inflammatory stuff today, but at the time it seemed dangerous. The newspapers got advance notice of it, and sensationalized it (by the standards prevailing in those days) into anti-oil company matter. International oil, in the wake of the Iranian nationalization and the tensions of the Cold War, was deemed important to the West's national security, and both the US and British governments disavowed the report. More significantly, the ECE and the UN Secretariat generally were told not to meddle in international oil affairs again—and they never did.

The report is actually worded in cautious language, almost absurdly so, as though the authors knew they were treading on eggs. The Secretary General of the ECE, Gunnar Myrdal, must have known that it would provoke a sharp reaction, and it must have been for this reason that its publication was quickly rushed through, with the unusual, and unusually worded, imprimatur of the ECE's Coal Committee:

> The Coal Committee invites the Secretariat promptly to publish, on its own responsibility, simultaneously in New York and Geneva the

document 'The Price of Oil in Western Europe' in its present form.

Among the reactions, one of the sharpest came from Shell. Shell's chairman, Sir Frederick Godber, devoted nearly two pages of his eight-page statement in the company's 1954 Annual Report (published in May 1955) to its deprecation:

> This document [the ECE publication] set forth the results of a study made, on its own initiative, by the Secretariat of that Commission for its Coal Committee. ... The fact that on the authors' own admission the document had to be based on incomplete knowledge of relevant facts, and that its conclusions, as well as many of its statements, are accordingly erroneous and academic, makes it very questionable whether it ought to have been presented to the Committee as a contribution of value.

> Furthermore, on the accepted precept that a little learning is a dangerous thing, it is even more questionable whether it should, or even would, have been published in the ordinary course of events. However, the decision to publish it was undoubtedly influenced by the fact that ... leakages of its contents appear to have taken place, and the Press here as well as elsewhere gave much publicity to distorted versions.

Sir Frederick then goes on to defend the level of crude and product prices with reference to Shell's moderate profits (14 percent return on capital employed) and the oil industry's need to generate future investment funds internally:

> To the extent, therefore, that these future requirements must be financed out of earnings, it is a complete fallacy to regard such earnings as profits in the conventional sense. Moreover, should prices fall to a point where it became impossible for the Industry to make adequate provision for financing expansion, there would be a shortage of oil products, with the consequence that economics would eventually prevail. This would inevitably, after a period of dislocation, bring us back to where we are today, which shows clearly enough what is the influence which must govern prices in the Industry.

Indeed.

I have dwelt on this incident, the publication of the ECE report, at some length partly because it is, in retrospect, so amusing, but also, and more important, because it did not seem so amusing at the time. The suppression by the majors (with the connivance of their home governments) of discussion of an important economic issue was bad enough. A subservient trade press constantly presented the industry as highly competitive, and the subject of oil prices as too complex to be understood, let alone discussed, by outsiders. The truth was that the industry, particularly at the crude-producing end, didn't need to compete until the mid 1950s, and then but softly; and crude pricing, far from being complex, was extremely and delightfully simple—far removed from the complexities of today's spot and forward markets, and futures, and government prices with adjustment factors (all related to ill-defined markets), and OPEC production quotas.

Possibly more serious in economic terms, however, was the industry's ability, and avowed purpose, to finance its expansion out of current earnings (i.e., out of monopoly rents), giving it a huge advantage in the form of access to cost-free capital, including the absence of administrative costs. The consumer paid enough to give the majors an adequate return on their capital, plus fresh capital to finance expansion, all without making new equity issues or recourse to capital markets. However, competition was soon to rear its ugly head, and by 1955, when the ECE report was published, prices were already beginning to slip. Decline would be slow but erratic, punctuated by supply crises, until the moment arrived in the early 1970s when the companies would lose the final vestiges of influence over price. And, ironically, consumers and the world at large, would then find themselves faced with something so much worse than the company quasi-cartel that they could hardly have contemplated it as a possibility.

Chapter 4
THE GROWTH OF COMPETITION, 1950-1970

Senator Church: *You might even envisage a completely competitive situation, an open market in which these elaborate sharing arrangements and production formulas are not involved, and the oil is bid for by the various companies in a completely free, open and competitive way. That would be another way of doing it, would it not?*

Mr. Shafer (Vice President of Conoco): *Nothing is impossible, Senator. I have not participated in one of those yet.*
– Church Committee Hearings on Multinational Corporations, Part 7, p. 264. March 1974.

Background

Under the weight of increasing supplies of geographically diversified oil in the hands of the non-majors, competition grew fitfully during the two decades from 1950 to 1970, interrupted by one supply crisis after another. One would have thought, in an industry where world demand was rising at a sustained rate of 7 percent per year for twenty years, that there would have been plenty of room for all and sundry to come in and prosper. In fact, however, making inroads into the entrenched, overwhelmingly preponderant position occupied by the seven international major companies by 1950 was slow, painful and sometimes politically motivated. The seven were not, however, a monolithic bloc, or even an oligopoly colluding on price. Indeed, limited competition among the majors themselves was an important—perhaps the most important—factor in the growth of such competition as emerged.

The seven majors dominated the world petroleum industry, especially outside the United States, for the whole of the period from 1950 to 1973. At the outset, in 1950, they found themselves in a position to do so for the simple reason that, through a series of largely accidental historical circumstances, they happened to be there first with the most. Thereafter, their dominance was sustained by their almost exclusive access to low-cost oil in the Middle East, Venezuela and Indonesia; by prices propped up in the United States through state-administered constraints on supply and abroad by the constraints on supply resulting from their joint offtake agreements in Middle East concessions; and by favorable tax treatment, most notably in the form of the 27.5 percent depletion allowance (an income tax deduction) in the United States in effect at the time. The enormous cash flow resulting from this extraordinary congruence of unrelated elements gave no one else much chance to compete effectively with them. Opposition was confined to nibbling around the edges (of which there was quite a lot in the 1970s), and government-supported companies.

In the closely held world market for crude oil in the 1950s, competition crept in almost imperceptibly at first, gradually gaining enough strength to exert a long-term downward pressure on prices, punctuated by short-term supply crises. The process was extraordinarily slow. No international oil company ever went out of business during these years and the upstream everywhere remained highly profitable.

There was some intramural competition among the majors; if they had had untrammeled access to the unlimited supplies of the Middle East's low-cost crude, the infighting would indeed have been fierce. But they didn't, and in fact they were all tied together in partnerships in the four major producing countries of the Middle East as well as (to a lesser extent) in Venezuela and Indonesia. Investments were made pro-rata to each company's equity interest in each concession (except in Kuwait where other constraints on disposal existed), but total production was governed by the joint investment and production programs, or "offtake agreements", as they were known in the industry, among the partners.

Offtake agreements were a necessary feature of the joint equity ventures in production in the Middle East concessions because they were the mechanism by which the partners' shares in production were reconciled with their equity participation in investment. They were by far the most important source of constraint on competition among the majors during this period; but they also left room for some limited jostling over market position, meaning more or less discreet price-cutting.

The Offtake Agreements

The offtake agreements themselves were complex, varied substantially from country to country and affected different companies in different ways, depending on their alternative sources of integrated supply. They were, in addition, well-guarded secrets, and what the outsider has come to learn of them in detail is largely confined to what US congressional investigations into various aspects of the oil industry have winkled out. However, with the exception of Kuwait, they all had one feature in common, namely, an implicit restriction on output which in all cases was a compromise between the partners that wanted to develop more producing capacity quickly and those that didn't want to go as fast. The former ended up short of the crude required by their refineries and markets downstream, and the latter long. The differences were balanced by the crude-short companies taking, in return for an additional payment over and above tax-paid cost, the unwanted amounts of crude that were the share of the crude-long companies.

Three of the best-known economists who were close observers of the oil industry—Professor M. A. Adelman of MIT, Jack Hartshorn of *The Economist* and Professor Edith Penrose of London's School of Oriental and African Studies, all concluded that the companies' offtake agreements in the Middle East and elsewhere were a significant impediment to competition:

In discussing "The Competitive Effects of Joint Ventures" and the offtake agreements in the Middle East, Adelman concludes that "each of the Persian Gulf producing companies takes account of the actions of all others . . . each can be assured that nothing is contemplated to threaten an excess of supply and a threat to price. Each can hold back output in the almost certain knowledge that all others are doing the same. This may not explain the price level, but it does help to explain why the decline has been so slow." (*The World Petroleum Market,* p.88.)

Hartshorn says, "No cartel agreements survived to clamp conformity on to the business behavior of the major groups after the war. None was needed . . . But the joint operating companies did and do survive; . . . and clearly these partnerships . . . do serve generally to restrain severe internecine competition in terms of development . . . This does not wholly preclude effectively competitive behavior . . . Each partner within them has some room for maneuver, even where strict rules obtain." (*Oil Companies and Governments,* p. 161 et seq.)

Penrose concludes that "The discovery of much low-cost oil in the Middle East within a very short period caused a very great change in the conditions of supply. The potentially disruptive effects of this, it can plausibly be argued, were averted or at least delayed by the control over the development of oil which followed as a "natural" consequence of the combination of the joint ownership of crude-oil producing companies, the vertical integration of the major groups, and the restraint imposed on each group by the oligopolistic nature of the competition in the industry." (*The Large International Firm in Developing Countries - The International Petroleum Industry.* p.71.)

The offtake agreements and the special supply arrangements affected each company differently, and each company had its own internal order of supply priorities which depended on the profitability of each of its alternatives. Consider, for example, Exxon in the late 1950s. Outside the United States and Canada, Exxon's main sources of supply were substantial wholly owned production in Venezuela, most of which could be expanded without agreement with anyone else; a 30 percent interest in Saudi Arabia's Aramco; a 7 percent interest in the Iranian Consortium; an 11.875 percent interest in the Iraq Petroleum Company and its associates; a 50 percent interest in Stanvac's Indonesian production; and long-term, special-price purchases of

Iranian and Kuwaiti crude from BP. To some extent—a large one—Venezuelan crude was destined (via topping to heavy fuel oil) for the US East Coast market, and this part of its available crude was not directly competitive in Exxon's scheme of things with its Middle East supplies, at least in the short term. Each source of supply had a different cost, and the differences had to be measured not simply as producing costs but in terms of delivered costs to Exxon refineries worldwide.

By contrast, BP had no production in Venezuela, Indonesia or Saudi Arabia. It had a 40 percent stake in Iran; an elastic 50 percent stake in Kuwait; a 23.75 percent stake in the IPC group of companies; and a quite inadequate downstream refining and marketing network to cope with such bountiful supplies. In addition, BP collected $0.10/B. from everybody else's Iranian production, as part of the selling price of its 60 percent interest to the other companies in 1954. Obviously, its priorities were vastly different from Exxon's. The potential tug of war was resolved by Exxon's (and Mobil's) long-term, special price purchases from BP.

This conflict of priorities among the majors was one of the few things about arrangements in the Middle East that were wholly beneficial for the consumer. Complete identity of interests upstream would have eliminated such competition among the majors as developed.

However, the situation was in fact more complicated because of political pressures that in effect forced the companies to work together and in practice determine overall production increases from year to year in each country. It is impossible for an outsider to the process to know the details of how the companies responded precisely to the political pressures, in terms of determining each country's overall production. Obviously, they did not get together and set country quotas for one and all. But there were several notable examples, mainly concerning Iran, Saudi Arabia and Iraq, where the overall production of one country had to be set by agreement among the companies, and production from other countries adjusted accordingly. These decisions could not have been made on purely economic grounds: they were exclusively political, and the criterion consistently applied by the companies was whatever would cause less trouble. I do not mean to imply that the companies played a passive role in the process. They didn't, and there were several notable examples where the companies made it plain to governments that were being "difficult" that they, the companies, had the power to punish or reward by shifting offtake among countries.

The most prominent example of the system at work was the arrangement made for the settlement of the Iranian nationalization dispute of 1951-54. The 1954 Consortium Agreement in Iran provided for a minimum production schedule of 17.5 million cubic meters of crude (302 kbd) in 1955, rising to 608 kbd in 1957. However, by 1955, crude supplies were plentiful in the world market and Iranian oil was not needed, so it had to be "accommodated" by adjusting production in other countries. Price-cutting was not an option: the third-party independent refining sector available at any given time was insufficient to absorb these quantities; cutting price would have reduced the profitability of Iranian crude, would have been unlikely to increase overall demand by an amount sufficient to keep previous levels of production up elsewhere, and would have soon rebounded on the value of all crude via the product markets. The only sensible course was for the majors to adjust production elsewhere and thus slot Iranian production in gradually, in an "orderly" manner. Indeed, their ability to do this was the principal reason why they were called in.

The majors could, and did, jointly program offtake from other countries in accordance with the political requirements reflected in their contractual commitments in Iran, and the major purpose behind the programming was, obviously, to avoid adverse price effects—otherwise why bother? It was not a vastly different system in principle from the Texas Railroad Commission (TRC), where a total production allowable for a forward period was determined by the nominations of offtakers, and the total then pro-rated to each producer. The governments of the producing countries were not, however, privy to the process and could only make menacing noises from the sidelines when their share appeared to be unsatisfactory.

There were two other major instances (and many minor ones) when the total offtake from one country was determined in response to political pressures or events, with collateral effects on the offtake of another country or countries. First, there were the reductions in offtake from Iraq during periods of conflict with the government (most of the time) and the use of Iraq by the companies as swing producer; second, there was the size of some of the post-1957 increases in production in Iran, which were the direct result of pressure from the Shah, some of it via the State Department. These had little to do with the immediate profitability of the choices, and the "collateral effects"—reducing production elsewhere—had everything to do with avoiding the price consequences that they would otherwise have had.

It is difficult to imagine a real-life situation on this scale further removed from what an economist would describe as "competition" than the one that obtained in the Middle East from 1950 to 1973. The companies were not simply passive non-competitors locked into a system that had to reconcile their offtake requirements with their equity holdings. They actively pursued certain policy goals to favor one country (usually Iran) over another, or penalize one country (usually Iraq) in favor of the others, then used the system to suppress adverse price effects. But these were nevertheless defensive policies, however politically active the companies were at times in pursuing them. What they did *not* do was use the system to engineer price increases above current levels; I doubt if the possibility was ever even considered. The crude-short companies would never have put up with it, and in any case a key player, Exxon, was (and remains today) quite paranoid about anything to do with collusion on prices.

In my view, the offtake agreements and related arrangements became, quite unintentionally and without design, the most extraordinarily effective network ever set up in the industry, with pervasive effects on its shape during the whole of the two decades to 1970. Formally unconnected but closely interwoven by circumstance, they facilitated the expansion of Middle East oil into the markets in the "orderly" fashion so beloved of successive US administrations and the majors; they were clearly not in themselves agreements in restraint of trade and could not therefore be in themselves the focus of antitrust actions by the US Department of Justice; they allowed for just enough intramural competition to produce a gently declining price and, *ipso facto*, a sort of alibi for the quasi-cartel; and they kept the peace among the host governments of the Middle East. What more could you ask for?

Competition: the Crawling Peg

In 1954, Chevron bid for and won a large part of the crude supply contract put up for bids by Brazil's state-owned Petrobras for its new Cubatao refinery. Chevron was the low bidder for all of the refinery's requirements, but was awarded only two-thirds of the total volume, the other third going to Exxon supplies out of Venezuela, purportedly for security of supply reasons. Chevron quoted a delivered c.i.f. price, entailing a discount (lightly disguised as an unrealistically low freight rate) off the posted price for Arabian Light crude of $1.93/B. It was the beginning of competition among the majors, and in a way, a "natural". Chevron was long on crude in Saudi Arabia; tanker transportation costs were coming down, allowing Middle East crude to compete further afield; and Venezuela had limited supplies of the light crude required for the Brazilian market, whereas it formed the bulk of Saudi Arabia's production. Nevertheless, such an incursion into an area regarded as Venezuela's backyard came as something of a shock to the rest of the industry.

Thereafter and for the next fifteen years, competition as reflected in decreasing prices proceeded slowly and erratically. The publication by Petrobras of the price offers it had received set an example for other refiners, and thereafter the price details of public-bid crude supply contracts to state-owned refineries in Argentina, Uruguay and India as well as Brazil became highly visible markers for the value of crude oil in the arm's-length market. They were soon joined by Japan and Italy, both high-volume importers of crude without any important crude-producing interests. Taken together, this body of information constituted a kind of crawling peg that progressively showed the extent to which competition was eroding price, and in effect provided the starting point for negotiations on all subsequent contracts.

The outbreak of competition in 1954 was not fortuitous. The temporary shortages caused first by the outbreak of the Korean War in 1950 and then by the nationalization of Anglo-Iranian in 1951 were over, and now large new volumes of Iranian oil had to be shoe-horned into the market after the conclusion of the Consortium agreement in Iran. The slow but steady downward slide in prices was temporarily interrupted by the supply disruptions of 1956-57 during the Suez crisis and later, though to a lesser extent, after the Six-Day War of 1967. In the meantime, the independent refining sector was growing and with it the number of arm's-length sales.

Over the period from 1954 to 1970, after which prices began to rise again under the pressure of increasing taxes in producing countries, the price of crude oil (roughly adjusted to Arabian Light crude f.o.b. the Persian Gulf) dropped from $1.90 to $1.25/B, a total decrease of one-third or approximately 2 percent per year on the average. Why so slow, why so painful? A major reason was, of course, the effect of the offtake agreements noted above, but there were others:

First, demand was so buoyant during those years that those with an established position in the market (the majors) felt no urgent need to crush the upstarts by stepping up the pace. The majors were not facing any loss of market in absolute terms—indeed, they were themselves growing rapidly, though marginally less than would have been the case in the absence of the growth of production from new sources.

Second, a significant part of the competition manifesting itself in cut-price, arm's-length, publicly reported sales, was coming from among their own ranks, notably from the chronically crude-long companies such as BP. No doubt this was behavior unbecoming of a gentleman, but the crude-long companies could be counted on not to overdo it, at least with respect to volume, and in the final analysis, they could be partly neutralized by an increase in the "special arrangement" purchases by the crude-short companies.

Third, the total volumes of oil becoming available from the "new" competitive sources—the US independents and other companies in Venezuela, Libya, the Persian Gulf offshore; and Soviet exports—were relatively small and grew relatively slowly. And, to a limited extent, something could be done about some of them without resorting to increased price competition. The majors successfully allied themselves with the devil (in this case, the Libyan government) to force a tax increase on the Libyan independents, which cooled their competitive ardor; and of course had no trouble in convincing other governments, notably the British (the United States needed no urging) not to grant licenses for the import of oil from the Soviet Union. Let us look briefly at each of these "new" sources of competition, taking advantage along the way to examine and comment on aspects in their development other than the purely competitive ones.

The US Independents in Venezuela

In January 1956, Venezuela's Ministry of Mines and Hydrocarbons announced that new concessions would soon be awarded in Venezuela. The first awards were duly made in August and September of that year, and further concessions granted in two rounds in 1957, the last in October of that year. Much of the acreage was awarded to the three major oil companies (Exxon, Shell and Gulf) that already accounted for most of the country's production, but significant amounts of highly prospective areas were given to a score or so of mainly US independents.

By 1961, production by the non-majors from the new concessions was less than 300 kbd, 10 percent of total Venezuelan production. Over the next five years, it grew to 500 kbd, 15 percent of the total, but started declining soon thereafter.

Production from the US independents newly in Venezuela was not a serious competitive threat to the major companies. The Sun, Phillips and Sinclair groups accounted for almost three-quarters of the new oil, and the rest never developed any significant production. None of them had refineries or markets outside the United States and all of them had counted on exporting their production to their domestic plants, directly or through exchanges. Unfortunately for them, they had no sooner started developing production than the United States imposed mandatory import controls (in 1959) and they were reduced to disposing of the oil they produced in excess of their import quotas by buying import "tickets" from other domestic refiners. They made no serious attempt to sell crude in the limited arm's-length market outside the United States nor did they attempt to develop their own markets there. In the sparse information publicly available on the arm's-length crude market during the period, notably the public bids to supply the State-owned YPF refineries in Argentina and the ANCAP (also state-owned) refinery in Uruguay, bids from the Venezuelan independents nowhere appear.

In total, the non-majors in Venezuela accounted for only a small proportion of crude competing in international markets during these years: 2.9 percent in 1961, rising to 3.3 percent in 1963, then falling back to 2.5 percent in 1966. Their importance as a source of competition was further blunted by their almost total concentration on the US market, through their own import quotas and the purchase of import tickets for any production in excess of quotas.

The US Independents and Other Non-Majors in Libya

The US independents and other non-major producers in Libya presented more of a problem for the majors. Though fewer in number than the independents in Venezuela, they came to have far higher production, and given their proximity to Europe and their initially privileged tax position in Libya itself, they presented a greater competitive threat.

The first major discovery in Libya was made by Exxon in 1959, and a series of other discoveries by majors and independents followed hard on its heels. By 1965, production by the independents totaled 580 kbd (47 percent of total Libyan production), nearly all of it in the hands of the Oasis Group

(Continental, Marathon and Amerada). By 1968, it was up to 1.1 mbd, nearly all of it accounted for by the independents in the Oasis Group (in which Shell had by then taken a 16.7 percent interest), Occidental and Nelson Bunker Hunt.

Ten companies other than the majors were producing oil in Libya prior to the nationalizations that began in 1971. They were: Amerada, Continental and Marathon in the Oasis Group, Occidental, Gelsenberg (in partnership with Mobil), Bunker Hunt, W. R. Grace and Atlantic Richfield (in partnership with Esso Sirte), Phillips, and Amoco.

The Petroleum Law of 1955

Trouble was in the cards, foreseen by some[1] from the start. Preliminary geological surveys in the early 1950s had proven favorable, and the Libyan government began to draft petroleum legislation designed to attract foreign companies to explore and drill for oil. The Libyans received some extremely good and some extremely bad advice, key aspects of which were incorporated into the country's first petroleum legislation, the Petroleum Law which was promulgated in July 1955.

The good advice was to try to attract a diversity of companies, each holding a limited amount of acreage and subject to relinquishment schedules that would promote rapid exploration. Above all, the concession situation in the Middle East was not to be replicated: there, a single concessionaire, jointly owned by the major companies, held most of each country's prospective and producing acreage, and was—or appeared to be—too powerful. The 1955 Law consequently divided the areas up for concession grants into a number of relatively small parcels and restricted the granting of more than a limited number of them to any one company or group of companies.

The bad advice was to offer terms that were generous to the point of absurdity, far below standard terms in the Middle East. The terms included income tax of 50 percent, based on an undefined income (rather than on posted price, as in the Middle East); a depletion allowance of 25 percent of gross income (versus none in the Middle East); depreciation and amortization of capital at a rate of 20 percent per annum (instead of the standard 10 percent), and 12.5 percent royalty, which could be offset wholly against income tax, this last provision, however, being standard at the time. In additions, concessions were to be granted on a first-come first-served basis, a provision that would, if strictly interpreted, deprive the government of taking into account the quality of the applicant. Whoever tendered such advice[2] and whoever decided to accept it could not possibly have sat down and worked through a few elementary hypothetical examples of the fiscal consequences, without, at the very least, being guilty of criminal negligence. In fact, the terms would clearly work out to a government revenue equivalent to about $0.20/B. in the Middle East, whereas actual revenues were then around

$0.80/B. It was a case of impeachable fiscal irresponsibility (had such a criminal offense existed in Libyan law) or gross corruption on the part of the Libyan government of the day that accepted the advice, and/or downright swindle on the part of those tendering it.

Both the good advice and the bad advice were to affect, profoundly and adversely, relations between oil companies and governments, not just in Libya but throughout the Middle East. The results of the bad advice convinced the Libyans that they had been hoodwinked and swindled, their sense of outrage being heightened no doubt by embarrassment at having been so maladroit. Fortunately for them, the good advice meant that they could renegotiate terms company by company, rather than be faced with a single, solid block of companies jointly holding a single concession, as in the Middle East. But the next few years were a constant struggle by the government to renegotiate fiscal terms to at least get them on a par with the Middle East. It was complicated by the government's policy of granting more concessions and by the royalty-expensing issue in OPEC (which Libya joined in mid-1962). It was also the story of eliminating the huge competitive advantage the independents enjoyed in Libya by virtue of their low tax payments.

Petroleum Regulation No. 6 (1961)

In the first round of leasing under the new law, fifty-one concessions were handed out to seventeen companies in 1956, among them several US independents and other non-majors. But even before the first drop of oil was exported from Libya, the government had woken to the fact that it had given too much away. They turned for advice to Dr. Nadim Pachachi, an Iraqi who had been Minister of Oil in his own country, and an amendment to the 1955 law was introduced by Royal Decree (subject to parliamentary ratification) in July 1961, abolishing the depletion allowance, reducing depreciation and amortization rates and providing for taxes on income from exports to be based on a posted price which was to be arrived at by agreement between the company and the government, with rebates for marketing expenses limited to 2 percent. The companies with acreage already in Libya would not be eligible for the grant of new concession areas unless they converted their existing ones to the new law.

After a period of discussion, the government backed down on a major point, and in December 1961, issued Petroleum Regulation No. 6, which reaffirmed the validity of the companies' rights under the original concessions and allowed reasonable rebates to meet the competitive conditions of the market, to be deducted from the posted price for tax purposes. To all intents and purposes, this meant that Libya was back where it started on this point, that is, with tax payable on actual sales prices, rather than the posted ones. The amendment to the law was ratified in early 1962. Exxon and its partners in Esso Sirte, BP, Gulf and the German independents in the country converted to the new law promptly; others resisted for a while, but by the end of 1964 (almost three years after the regulation had been passed), all had converted. Some of the worst aspects of the 1955 law were set aside, notably the depletion allowance, but the definition of gross income still allowed for large discounts from the posted price in arriving at gross taxable income.

Exxon, however, felt strongly that a system allowing for the payment of income taxes on a basis other than posted prices was not viable in the long run. Income taxes based on arm's-length sales prices would place Libya too far out of line with the Middle East, and although by the terms of their concessions and the Libyan Petroleum Law and Regulations, Exxon was entitled to take the same deductions from gross revenue (namely, discounts off posted prices) as the independents did, they opted not to do so, in the interests of good relations with the government.

However, the temptation was too much for the independents whose right to pay tax on the basis of heavy discounts off posted prices had now been confirmed. The stage was set for them to sell at prices yielding revenues on which they paid less than $0.30/B. in total taxes to the Libyan government, compared with $0.90 paid by Exxon, based on revenue calculated at full posted prices. The Oasis Group's sales prices ranged generally between $1.35 and $1.65/B., averaging about $1.60/B. in 1964, compared with posted prices of between $2.17 and $2.23/B. It should be said, however, that the independents in the Oasis Group were not driving prices recklessly down—it would have been foolish for them to do so. Like everyone else, they were getting the best price obtainable at the time, and indeed prices of $1.55-$1.60/B. were not out of line with the then going prices of around $1.30/B. to $1.40/B. for light crudes f.o.b. the Persian Gulf at which the majors themselves were selling in arm's-length contracts. It is probably truer to say that the majors knew they could not compete on price grounds with the independents because the latter could, if pushed, go far lower than the majors; so the net effect was not so much on price as on backing major company Middle East crude out of the European market.

In any case and by any reckoning, Oasis and the other independents were making about $0.60/B. more in profit than Exxon—the difference between their tax payments. The majors, led by Exxon, reacted as best they could against all the new sources of competition, tailoring their response to the particular situation—in the case of the Libyan independents, by getting the playing field leveled, preferably before the Libyans handed out any more concessions.

During 1964, crude exports of the independents averaged about 350 kbd, rising to about 530 kbd in 1965, mostly on sales to independent (non-major) refineries in Europe. There was little alternative market: the United States was to a large extent closed off by import restrictions and the Oasis partners had little access to refining capacity outside the United States. Ease of entry, that hallmark of a truly competitive situation, was notably absent in refining and marketing in Western Europe.

Continental did, however, acquire a 40 percent interest in a refinery at Karlsruhe, West Germany, and started construction of a new 60 kbd grass-roots refinery in the United Kingdom. It also acquired several small marketing companies and outlets in Austria, Belgium, Germany and the U.K., and concluded processing agreements with other refiners, usually on a netback pricing basis.

Marathon acquired minority equity stakes in refineries in Spain (La Coruna) and Germany (Mannheim) plus processing deals in Italy and Switzerland, and a few service stations in Italy and Germany. But basically, like Continental, it remained largely unintegrated and dependent on low-price deals with independent refiners.

The third Oasis partner, Amerada, never attempted to even start the process of downward integration into the markets and simply sold the whole of its production, at first to Continental, then to Shell. In 1966, Shell acquired a 50 percent interest in Amerada's Libyan concession.

Exxon's Posted Price

Predictably, trouble was not long in coming. But it came, initially, from a totally unexpected source: Exxon. Exxon had seen from the beginning that tax payments to the Libyan government on any basis but par with the Middle East would cause untold trouble and would be quite unsustainable. Reactions in Libya might be strong enough to start the country down the road to nationalization; there might also be sharp reactions in the Persian Gulf where the producing countries would regard the majors' production in Libya as unfairly threatening their own levels of output. OPEC had just been created in the wake of posted price decreases in the Middle East in 1959 and 1960: it was no time to go out looking for trouble in exchange for a fast buck. Exxon therefore opted not to take advantage of the full provisions of Libya's over-generous petroleum law, but to pay taxes from the start on the basis of posted prices, as in the Middle East. Indeed, according to Bennett Wall, Exxon's official historian, Exxon was determined to play the good citizen in Libya from the start, and there is no particular reason to doubt him. Here was enlightened self-interest at work.

All the odder, then, that at this juncture, Exxon should make such an egregious blunder as to post a price that was clearly out of line with the postings for Kirkuk and Arabian Light crudes at Eastern Mediterranean ports. In July 1961, as noted above, a Royal Decree had amended the 1955 Law by, *inter alia,* providing for taxes to be based on posted prices. Exxon had indicated that it would convert its first-round concessions to the amended law (when ratified). Then, in August 1961, Exxon posted a price for Zelten (Brega) crude of $2.21/B. of 39 °API, clearly some way below the postings for competitive crudes at Eastern Mediterranean ports. It would save the company a few cents per barrel on taxes.

The Libyan government immediately protested that Exxon's price for Zelten was too low. Exxon's was a colossal mistake, an extraordinary act of shortsightedness. It was to focus attention and government grievances on prices, and not the same kind of price grievance that OPEC had over posted prices in 1960, where no one disputed the companies' right to reduce postings, but rather their failure to take into consideration the exporting countries' important economic interests. In Libya, on the other hand, Exxon had an obligation to post a price that, in good faith, would be consistent with prices posted in the Eastern Mediterranean, and indeed it tried later to justify its postings in these terms. But Exxon deliberately skewed the figures in order to decrease its tax base in Libya, and when the time came for a reckoning, this issue was high on the list. The reason that it was so important was that it revolved around the control of price, and when the Libyan government was later successful in forcing the companies to adjust their prices upward, attention in the Middle East turned from volume to price—with, in the end, disastrous results.

Exxon's posting, the company explained, was the average of the Persian Gulf and Eastern Mediterranean postings for Arabian Light, Iranian Light and Kirkuk, plus freight to Rotterdam, minus freight from Libya (Brega) to Rotterdam. The calculation was based on assumptions about the applicability of freight rates that implied a clear inconsistency between Persian Gulf and Eastern Mediterranean postings; no adjustment was made for gravity, sulfur or wax content; and the choice of freight rates was in any event contentious. Nevertheless, the government ill-advisedly chose not to go to arbitration, as provided for by the law, and Exxon stuck by its decision.

Exxon management later expressed disappointment that its efforts to be good citizens in Libya, do the right thing and pay taxes on posted prices instead of realizations, as the independents would do, met with no gratitude or recognition. Libyans saw no reason to be grateful for only being swindled a bit rather than a lot. The Libyans later had to swallow the Exxon posting, but it stuck in their craw and would be high on their "revenge" list when the time came.

The Royal Decree of 1965 and the Defeat of the Independents

Much more serious still was the trouble brewing with the independents. Libya joined OPEC in July 1962, at about the time the independents were starting to export and one year after Exxon had started. The modifications to the 1955 Petroleum Law introduced in 1961 provided for the payment of taxes on the basis of posted prices, subject to rebates that the companies needed to grant in order to be competitive in the markets. The rebates claimed by the independents took their taxable income base down to $1.60/B.

in 1964, as noted above, and with the other tax deductions to which they were entitled, their tax payments down to less than $0.30/B., compared with about $0.90 paid by Exxon. The Oasis Group's exports of its Sider blend crude to Italy were sold at an average f.o.b. price of $1.59/B. in 1964, compared with an average f.o.b. price of $2.20 for Exxon's exports of Zelten (Brega) crude. In 1965, Oasis' realizations on Sider blend to Italy dropped to an average of $1.53/B. All in all, Libya lost about $200 million during the three years from 1963 to 1965 on the difference between Exxon's and Oasis' per barrel taxes.

Not surprisingly, the government protested at the level of discounts or rebates being taken, but the Libyan independents stood on their rights and could not be legally forced to change their position. If ever there was an apt characterization of them at that time, it was British Prime Minister Edward Heath's phrase (used in an entirely different context), about "the unacceptable face of capitalism". The totally inexperienced Libyans didn't know enough to be able to distinguish good advice from bad, and the independents—not the majors—were taking rapacious advantage of the situation.

It took the Libyan government more than three years to do something after the independents had started exporting substantial quantities of crude in 1962. There were many cross-currents: development drilling and trunk pipeline construction were in full swing; arguments that the independents' discounts were necessary to the rapid expansion of Libyan exports; a desire to avoid unilateral action; the royalty-expensing negotiations that OPEC was carrying on with the companies and which achieved partial success in 1964; and the desire not to prejudice a second round of concessions that was being planned. The only lever the government legally had against the independents was to audit their discounts to ensure that they were reasonable within the meaning of Petroleum Regulation No. 6. This could have been a lengthy and awkward process for the independents, but scarcely critical: at worst, a few cents here and there of the discounts might have been disallowed.

In the end, it was the majors, particularly Exxon, that forced the Libyans' hand. The independents in the Oasis Group were increasing their production rapidly and there were others in the offing. By 1964, Mobil was producing and exporting and Amoseas (Chevron/Texaco) was developing important discoveries, but Exxon was by far the largest major producer and therefore took the lead to force Libya to level the playing field. It started selling discounted oil to non-affiliated refiners and using the discounted sales prices as part of its tax base, blaming such lower tax levels directly on the independents, so that the Libyan government was now faced with lower per barrel taxes all round. The majors then urged the government to introduce new, sweeping amendments to its petroleum legislation, to the effect that all tax payments should be made on the basis of posted prices without discounts and that royalty-expensing should be introduced on the basis of the majors' general offer to OPEC. Then, drawing on their Venezuelan experience of the 1940s, they suggested that, as an inducement to convert existing concessions to the new law, their duration should be extended to run their agreed period from the date of the conversion rather than from the original date. In addition, there should be a quit-claim on most outstanding issues, including of course the claim against Exxon's own posted price. Companies not converting to the new law would be barred from any further concessions in the next round. Finally, the arbitration provisions in the previous law, which gave primacy to Libyan law, would be altered to accord primacy to the principles of international law or the general rules of law, over Libyan law.

A royal decree was issued along these lines on 20 November 1965 and, incidentally, Exxon's posting was accepted. The decree was ratified by Parliament and the companies given until 15 December to indicate their acceptance. The majors (except Gulf) immediately offered to convert—but with an important proviso: *all* companies would have to accept before their own acceptance became effective. Among the independents, Amerada and Gelsenberg did so immediately; the rest missed the deadline, despite a forty-eight hour extension. In Vienna, the OPEC Conference passed a resolution that none of its member countries would thenceforth give concessions to any company which did not convert to the new Libyan law, and a special session of Libya's Parliament was convened to pass a law that would make compliance obligatory under pain of having exports suspended, followed possibly by nationalization. Except for Phillips and Gulf, all companies then converted. The decree was passed by Parliament on 5 January 1966, and on the following day it was announced that the last two hold outs had finally agreed.

There may have been some doubt about the legality of prohibiting shipments (if it had come to that) under the January decree, but there was no doubt about the legality of the nationalizations that would have followed. The government's "victory" was not clear-cut, however. It had, after all, been powerfully prodded by Exxon, and it paid a substantial price in the form of its quit-claim with Exxon, the extensions of the concession period and the unfavorable change in the choice-of-law clause in its arbitration provisions. Exxon et al. were criticized at the time by some industry observers, who predicted that no good would come of this pact with the devil. But in the event, more potent forces would work to change the balance of power between companies and governments than the Libyan precedent of 1965-66.

The Russians Are Coming

Until the mid-1950s, the Soviet bloc's exports of crude and products were negligible, not exceeding 100 kbd until 1956. But the discovery and development of large fields and the limited opening-up of the economy to international trade now set the Soviets on a course of export expansion. During the second half of the decade and extending through 1961, Soviet bloc exports increased very rapidly—at 40 percent per year—to reach nearly 700 kbd in 1961. Growth slowed down thereafter, but still proceeded at a healthy clip of almost 10 percent per year until 1967. Growth then virtually came to a stop before starting to decline in 1969 and 1970.

Most of the Soviet bloc exports came, naturally, from the Soviet Union, with somewhat more than 100 kbd from Romania during the period of the late 1950s and 1960s. Shipments were made to a variety of destinations, with Italy being the principal customer in Western Europe, though West Germany, Finland, France and Sweden also bought substantial amounts, as did Japan. Among developing countries, Egypt, India, Ceylon and Brazil were the most prominent buyers of Soviet oil.

The Russians, like any other trader, sought the best prices they could get, and the price data publicly available does not indicate any particularly intensive price-cutting. They shaded going prices in order to get into the markets, but not by much, and their exports to any one country were a relatively small proportion of the country's total demand. As with any additional supplies into markets, other things being equal, the overall effect was to push prices gently down, but there was no collapse and Soviet f.o.b. crude oil prices remained in the range of $1.20 to $1.30 to the most important customers, notably Italy, France and Japan, during the 1960s. Smaller, and less knowledgeable, buyers paid more.

The relative mildness of the price effects of Russian competition is not surprising. Between 1955 and 1968, when the Soviet export drive ran out of steam, world demand for oil (excluding the Soviet bloc itself) increased by a total of nearly 20 mbd; Soviet exports captured only 5 percent of that growth.

Nevertheless, the majors responded with alarm to the growth in Soviet exports, and for good reason. First, they didn't know when expansion would be reined in, if at all. Second, they were unable to fight the export drive with lower prices even if they had wanted to: there was no visible cost floor under Soviet sales, and in any event, most of the Soviet Union's sales were tied to trade agreements with the importing country. The only recourse the majors had to combat Soviet competition was by trying to influence governments to prohibit, or at least limit, imports from the Soviet Union. The United States needed no urging, and while there was no formal prohibition, imports from the Soviet Union remained essentially at zero. The United Kingdom, home to BP and Shell, did not impose any formal restriction either, but in fact licences to import oil from the Soviet Union were simply not granted. In the Common Market, M. Robert Marjolin, Vice President of the European Community's Commission, tried in 1961 to introduce a set of voluntary limits whereby members of the EEC would agree to limit imports of Soviet bloc oil to 10 percent of their requirements. The proposal was promptly vetoed by the Italians.

Arguments used to try to convince government to take some action to limit imports from the Soviet Union generally centered on national security. Typical enough was Exxon's comment, in its 1960 Annual Report (p.4):

Though the Soviet oil offensive is related to economic needs, the aim undoubtedly is also to weaken western alliances and disturb normal patterns of trade and investment.

The trade press, as usual more royalist than the queen, went further:

Apart from the obvious risk of security of supply owing to the unpredictable political relationships between East and West, large imports of low-priced Russian oil into Western Europe are apt to upset the international oil market, and so ultimately impede investment and the needed diversification of sources of supply.
– Petroleum Press Service, August 1961, p. 302.)

A bit far-fetched, but nicely worded. The "obvious risk of security of supply" (meaning, presumably, disruption of supplies from the Soviet Union) was not even a remote one. These were the years when the independents (and some other companies) appeared in some strength in Venezuela, Libya and the offshore Persian Gulf; when Abu Dhabi, Algeria and Nigeria emerged as important producers; and when OPEC was created to stem the decline in per barrel oil revenues. No one would have missed the Russians.

In fact, after the initial alarm, Soviet bloc exports became accepted as part of the scene. Towards the end of the 1960s, Soviet exports stopped growing and prices even firmed somewhat. On the whole, Russian oil contributed to holding oil prices down at relatively weak levels, and in doing this provided economic returns to the independent and state-owned refining sector in Western Europe, if not to the companies themselves, or at least to their home countries on a balance-of-payments basis: their oil import bill was probably lower than it otherwise would have been.

Persian Gulf Offshore

Competition, more dangerous in a sense, also appeared in the Persian Gulf offshore, where two E&P agreements were signed by Iran with non-majors in the late 1950s. The first was an agreement signed in 1957 with AGIP, a subsidiary of Italy's ENI, to set up a 50/50 joint venture company called the Société Irano-Italienne des Pétroles (SIRIP) between AGIP and the National Iranian Oil Company (NIOC) to explore for and produce oil in a sector of Iran's Persian Gulf offshore. It was the first such joint venture signed in an OPEC country, and was followed the next year, in 1958, by a similar agreement with Amoco to set up the Iran-Pan American Oil Company (IPAC). This time, the competitive danger was not so much the volume of oil that might be produced from these concessions, nor a privileged tax position for the concessionaires (as in Libya), but quite the reverse: the concessions appeared to be more favorable to the government, in three important respects:

first, they provided for a carried interest in favor of NIOC during the exploration period (i.e., NIOC's partner would bear all of the cost of exploration up until the discovery of oil in commercial quantities, and would only then be reimbursed for NIOC's share); second, the duration of the agreements was much shorter (a maximum of forty years from the start of commercial production) than for the majors' concessions; and, third, they incorporated stringent relinquishment provisions.

In 1957, Saudi Arabia signed an agreement with the Japan Petroleum Trading Company (JPTC) covering the Saudi 50 percent share in the Neutral Zone offshore area, providing for a 56 percent share for the government in the company's integrated net earnings, and an option for the government to acquire a 10 percent equity interest in the Japan Petroleum Development Corporation (JPDC) at par share value after the discovery of commercial production. The following year, Kuwait signed a similar agreement with the Arabian Oil Company (AOC) covering its 50 percent share of the offshore Neutral Zone. (The onshore Neutral Zone was covered by earlier agreements—between Saudi Arabia and Getty in 1949 for the Saudi share, and between Kuwait and the American Independent Oil Company (Aminoil) in 1948 for the Kuwaiti share; but these two earlier agreements did not incorporate terms significantly more favorable for the governments than the majors' concessions).

The obvious and natural consequence of these agreements was to increase host government pressure on the major oil companies for the revision of the existing concessions. This was a competitive threat of a different kind, because while it did involve additional volumes of oil in the hands of non-majors, the majors were more apprehensive about the discontent they engendered in the governments over existing terms—any upward revision of fiscal terms in favor of the government would erode the majors' competitive advantage.

Later on, in the late 1960s and early 1970s, there were to be a number of other offshore E&P agreements signed with non-majors, but by that time, fundamental changes in the majors' concessions had either taken place (with the Tehran Agreement of 1971), or they were in the air.

In the event, the amounts of oil produced under the terms of the Iranian offshore and the offshore and onshore Kuwait/Saudi Arabia Neutral Zone agreements with the non-majors grew to a respectable size over the years, increasing from 229 kbd in 1961 to 609 kbd in 1966 and 1,025 kbd in 1970.

The Majors' Shifting Supply Sources

At the same time as these developments were taking place, the bonds between the major oil companies were being loosened as they developed new sources of supply outside the Middle East and away from the constraints imposed by the offtake agreements there. These changes occurred mainly in the second half of the 1960s, and mainly in two countries—Libya and Nigeria.

In Libya, Exxon developed production from 100 percent-owned fields, reaching almost 500 kbd by 1965 and over 600 kbd by 1968, plus substantial other production in partnership with independents. Texaco and Chevron, in partnership, had developed nearly 250 kbd in Libya by 1968, and BP about 160 kbd. BP and Shell, in partnership, developed 240 kbd of production in Nigeria by 1965.

Three of the companies (BP, Texaco and Chevron) were already long on crude, but—especially BP—were far too heavily dependent on the Middle East, and diversification of supply sources was of some considerable importance to them. Exxon and Shell, not so dependent on the Middle East, were crude-short, but in any event welcomed the diversification of supply sources that Libya and Nigeria represented.

It is impossible to know precisely how these new supplies affected the level of (limited) intra-mural competition among the majors, or to what extent they disturbed the functioning of the offtake agreements in the Middle East, a balance that was in any event shifting as the majors, or some of them, developed Abu Dhabi, where production reached nearly 500 kbd in 1968. However, if the competitive effect of the new supplies cannot be easily seen, it can hardly have been entirely neutral and the presumption has to be that they contributed something in the way of increased competition.

Competition Downstream

So far, I have dealt exclusively with the growth of competition upstream—for good reason: that is where there was least of it, and that is where the majors had chosen to concentrate their profits. Competition certainly existed in other phases of the business, refining and marketing, but it was neither intense nor did it pose much of a threat to the majors. There was more competition in tanker transportation where there was a large and thriving group of entrepreneurial tanker owners, mostly Greek at first, with names that became household currency—Onassis, Niarchos, Latsis et al. But the majors tended to be net inward charterers, and competition among owners favored them. Indeed, the majors had been instrumental in creating these independently owned fleets by signing long-term charter agreements that allowed their owners to finance the fleet's construction in the first place.

As for refining, the independent sector grew with the rest of the industry. But as a competitive threat, it was not much of a danger. By far the largest component of cost for any refiner is the raw material—crude oil—and the majors had an inexhaustible supply of by far the cheapest crude in the world. The independents could either buy from the majors, and perhaps get a good price by buying from one that did not refine and market products in the independent's area, but not the kind of price that could drive a competing major from his market area; or the independent could buy from the Soviet Union and also get a good price, but there weren't many other competing sources so it was unlikely to get a margin that the majors could not meet if they wished to. In any event, the truly non-integrated independent refinery became a rarity outside the United States. As non-integrated producers came onstream, especially in Libya, the independent refiners were bought out; or they were bought out by crude-long majors pressed to find outlets.

State-owned refineries posed a different problem for the majors. They could not be displaced or bought out, and they could usually depend on some favorable treatment to make a profit. But at least they were confined geographically, being strong notably in France and Italy; in addition, there were limits on the extent to which they could sensibly expand. No one wanted a state monopoly in refining and marketing.

Developing countries too, many newly independent, wanted refineries that the majors did not want to build because the markets they would serve were either too small, or were already being served by one of their export refineries. These small developing countries paid a high price for their refineries because they inevitably got a high-cost (low thruput) unit, and then perhaps ended up paying a high price for the crude supply.

Larger developing countries, such as Brazil and India, also built state-owned refineries which, being larger, tended to get good prices from the majors competing among themselves. The majors did not, of course, much care for the publicity these countries gave to the bids they received for their crude-supply contracts, which tended to be at substantial discounts, but at least the markets were local and there was little spill-over effect.

Japan was a special case. Its market grew at a phenomenal rate, but most of its refineries were joint ventures between major oil companies and local large industrial groups. The crude supply, of course, was in the hands of the major oil company partner. Competition—such as it was—remained, in the final analysis, virtually limited to the majors.

Conclusions

By 1963, crude oil production in the hands of the non-majors in exporting countries, plus net exports from the Soviet bloc, totaled 2.4 mbd—a respectable amount of oil, perhaps as much as 10 percent of all oil entering primary international trade. It was still growing fast, and by 1968 had reached 5 mbd, about 15 percent of oil entering primary international trade, surely enough in the way of new supplies from new companies entering the market to trigger some sharp downward movement. And yet prices, though continuing their declining secular trend, showed no signs of collapsing. Why?

First, the world market was growing rapidly. True, the independents were eating into the majors' market share, but in absolute terms, the majors were still growing, and growing rapidly. Hence, the pressure they felt from these sources was not great enough for them to prefer a price war than to move over a bit.

Second, much of the new crude in the hands of the non-majors was not "homeless". It was being produced by companies that had a ready destination for it in their own refineries, usually in their home countries, or was, in the case of Algeria, sheltered by special arrangements. In Venezuela, as mentioned above, most of the US independents had ready outlets for their Venezuelan crude in their refineries in the United States, even if they had to purchase import tickets for some of it. The same is true of some of the non-majors in the Middle East, notably Amoco and AGIP, as well as some of the others.

This was a prime example of why vertical integration tends to suppress competition: it is not true, or was not true during this period, as is sometimes argued, that vertical integration simply shifts competition from the upstream crude market to the downstream products market. At the crude level, "homeless" crude can only move by a cut in price, which may or may not be met by the majors. But crude with a home in the refinery of an integrated independent moves to that refinery, and the major who was previously supplying that company simply moves over; he does not rush out to expand his own refinery (if he has one) in the market served by the independent's refinery, in order not to lose volume, and he certainly doesn't set about building a new one every time he loses a crude sale. And this is why the majors regarded Soviet bloc exports and much of the Libyan crude in independent hands with alarm: it was "homeless", and therefore a real threat to the existing level of crude prices everywhere. Much of the other crude was not.

In addition, some of the homeless crude in the hands of the independents was effectively neutered. For example, Amerada sold half of its equity share in the Oasis Group to Shell, as well as its remaining production.

Third, some of the new crude in the hands of the non-majors suffered from higher tax-paid costs than the majors' crude. This was notably the case in some of the Persian Gulf offshore concessions, as well as most of the crude produced by the US independents in Venezuela. And this was why the majors exerted themselves in Libya to prod the government into raising taxes on the independents.

It is not possible to measure the extent to which these factors mitigated competition, but it is clear that it was very considerable. Perhaps more than half the total volume involved was not exerting a direct pressure on prices.

Chapter 5
ENTER OPEC: THE EARLY YEARS, 1960-1968

OPEC's Roots

The history of the international petroleum industry is marked by attempts to restrict supply and maintain high prices. They include the Achnacarry ("As Is") Agreement; the abortive Anglo-US treaties towards the end of the World War II to set up an international petroleum council; and the system of allowables practiced, in the name of conservation, by various states in the United States, most notably in Texas, where the Texas Railroad Commission (TRC) was the lynchpin, setting monthly maximum allowable production levels which were then pro-rated among the producers. The TRC was hugely successful for a few years in the early 1950s on the US domestic scene, though the system soon had to be insulated from foreign competition by import restrictions. It produced high prices, which provided the basis for international crude pricing with a specious theoretical justification backed up by a self-policing system of partnership agreements in crude producing countries. OPEC therefore has a long and varied lineage, and indeed it was originally intended by two of its founders—Venezuela's Juan Pablo Pérez Alfonzo and Saudi Arabia's Abdullah Tariki—to play the same role as the TRC, but on the international stage.

The organization came into existence as a result of a number of circumstances, some of which were not in fact closely related. In 1958, two major political events occurred which brought to power nationalistic governments hostile, in different ways, to the status quo. The first occurred in January, when a revolution in Venezuela toppled the military dictatorship and brought to power an interim government which was soon followed, in February 1959, by the democratically elected government of Rómulo Betancourt and his *Acción Democrática* party. Pérez Alfonzo was appointed Minister of Mines and Hydrocarbons. In December 1958, with the encouragement of then President-elect Betancourt, the interim government of President Edgar Sanabria increased income tax rates applicable to the oil industry, effective 1 January 1958, to bring total government revenue from all oil industry taxes up to almost 70 percent of net profits. It was easy, in Venezuela, to increase tax rates on the industry—Venezuela had never surrendered its legislative prerogatives on taxation, and income taxes were not the subject of contractual agreement with the companies. But a serious problem remained: how to fight the weakening market.

The second important (for the creation of OPEC) political event of 1958 came in July when a revolution led by a group of senior army officers in Iraq put paid to the pro-Western Hashemite monarchy. The King, his family and his notoriously pro-Western Prime Minister Nuri al-Said were all murdered, and a Republic instituted. Under the monarchy, negotiations with Iraq Petroleum Company (IPC) had been proceeding, without great acrimony, on the relinquishment of acreage and future production levels, among other matters. Iraq had a number of justifiable grievances against the group of major companies that had been allocated concessions covering practically the whole country as part of the spoils of World War I and the dismemberment of the Ottoman Empire. After the revolution, and in the context of a military regime with only a shaky hold on the country (including other factions within the army), these feelings of grievance came to the fore and relations with IPC soon soured. Indeed relations were never again without major unresolved differences.

Radical governments were now in power in two major oil-exporting countries.

Coincidentally with these events, the market began to weaken seriously, after the Suez crisis of 1956-57 had been resolved and the Canal re-opened. In early 1959, a series of posted price reductions was made in the United States, Venezuela and the Middle East. They led directly to the creation of OPEC twenty months later.

But first, a brief look at the background of the two founders of OPEC sheds light on the organization's character. They were not extreme left-wing nationalist radicals; in fact, the new radical nationalist regime in Iraq played a minor supporting role in OPEC at the beginning—though the organization could not have been created under the *ancien régime*. On the contrary, Pérez Alfonzo and Tariki sought objectives that were indeed radical in terms of the oil industry structures of the time, but they sought to achieve them through a realistic common-front negotiation. The objectives were not unrealistic in themselves; it was the common front that could not be realized immediately.

The organization may well have come into being in some form or shape without Pérez Alfonzo or Tariki, but it is hard to imagine two men so coincidentally well-placed. Yet they were profoundly different in their aims, education, background and culture; apart from deep-rooted nationalism, they shared a curious trait: neither came anywhere near having the skills required for a competent politician. The former was a lawyer, an intellectual and an idealist with no stomach for the hurly-burly of political life but with the strong personal backing of Venezuelan President Betancourt; the latter was a geologist and activist whose rashness in accusing a member of the Saudi royal family of corruption in an oil deal was later to cost him his job and send him into years of exile. Pérez Alfonzo provided the rationalization; Tariki the fire.

Tariki was a powerful and charismatic speaker; Pérez Alfonzo a poor speaker but came to be revered in Venezuelan nationalist circles. Neither had much knowledge or understanding of economics, though they grasped the elementary proposition that if you restrict supply, prices rise. Their great merit was to see that the exporting countries needed a countervailing power to the multilateral bargaining position of the international majors, and then to bring one into being.

Juan Pablo Pérez Alfonzo

Pérez Alfonzo was born in Caracas in 1903, *de buena familia*, meaning white, upper middle-class and well-to-do. He graduated in law at the University of Caracas and was part of a young and honorable group that opposed the long dictatorship of General Juan Vicente Gómez, as nasty a piece of work as ever endowed a backward country with the dubious charms of political stability. In 1928, Pérez Alfonzo was jailed for his participation in student demonstrations.

After the death of Gómez, he entered politics and was elected to the Chamber of Deputies in 1939. In 1945, he was appointed Minister of Development (which at the time oversaw the oil sector) in the government of Rómulo Gallegos. One of his last acts before the government was toppled by a military coup in November 1948 was to shepherd through Congress the *Impuesto Adicional* (providing for a minimum 50 percent income tax), together with the then Minister of Finance, Manuel Pérez Guerrero, who was himself to become Minister of Mines and Hydrocarbons many years later (among several other prominent positions held by him in Venezuela and the United Nations). They were both jailed, then exiled after the November 1948 coup.

Pérez Alfonzo spent the 10 years from 1948 to 1958 in exile, in the United States and Mexico. As far as petroleum was concerned, his principal aim was to establish tighter national controls over the industry, and he almost certainly regretted the political impossibility of following Mexico's example in nationalizing the foreign oil companies.

When Betancourt's *Acción Democrática* party returned to power in 1959, Pérez Alfonzo was appointed Minister of Mines and Hydrocarbons, and rapidly introduced a number of regulatory measures as well as establishing a national oil company. Abroad, as he saw it, what the country needed in order to safeguard its interests was a sort of international Texas Railroad Commission composed of Venezuela and the major exporters of the Middle East; indeed, from beginning to end, this was his sole objective in OPEC. The idea had germinated during his exile, nurtured in discussions with Betancourt and Pérez Guerrero.

It must be said that Pérez Alfonzo was not primarily motivated by a desire to maximize revenue for the country; what he wanted was to brake depletion and obtain a "fair" price for what he termed the "intrinsic value" of the oil, a confused notion that nevertheless held a wide appeal for those many people who regarded mining as something more than simply another economic activity.

The idea of an association with the Middle East exporters was therefore for Pérez Alfonzo a means of introducing an international system of pro-rationing that would raise prices to a fair level, taking into account oil's intrinsic value, by restricting supply to the level of market demand at that (undefined) price and thus conserving Venezuela's resources and revenues from oil for a more orderly development. Trading volume for price may have been a good idea in moderation, though Pérez Alfonzo was always driven more by unrealistic fears of premature depletion than by economic logic.

However, when OPEC came into being, as we shall see, it was far from being an Organization committed to restricting supply in exchange for higher prices. In fact, the Middle Eastern producers were wedded to volume and (in effect) flat royalties. In any event, with the exception of Iraq, none was yet prepared for a confrontation with the companies involving the breaking of concession agreements.

It is a sad comment that when, many years later, OPEC did indeed adopt production restrictions, the resulting price increases brought such an orgy of consumption, waste and corruption that Pérez Alfonzo, ascete and conservationist to the bone, was prompted to say that he wished he had never heard of OPEC. His last book, *The Disaster*, dealt among other things with the consequences for Venezuela and Venezuelan society of oil prices that had risen to levels far above anything he could have seriously contemplated.

Abdullah Tariki

Tariki was as different from Pérez Alfonzo as chalk from cheese. A much younger man (he was born in 1919), more passionate though possibly shallower in his nationalism than Pérez Alfonzo, he took a degree in geology at the University of Cairo in 1945, and then took a specialized course in petroleum geology at the University of Texas. He acquired an American wife and some practical experience in the industry working in the United States before returning to Saudi Arabia in 1948. Nasserist in his political outlook, he was appointed director general of Petroleum and Mineral Affairs in 1957, and promoted to minister in December 1960 by King Saud.

Tariki did a great deal of damage during his tenure, arriving, for the sake of some misguided principles, at agreements with Aramco that went quite against the country's financial interests and had later to be cleared up through negotiation by Sheikh Ahmed Zaki Yamani, who was appointed Minister of Petroleum and Mineral Resources in April 1962 under the prime ministership of then Crown Prince Faisal.

Although he fell under the spell of Pérez Alfonzo and supported Pérez Alfonzo's pro-rationing objectives, Tariki's aims were not clear in any strategic sense. He was certainly not focused, like Pérez Alfonzo, simply on higher prices and slower development through production restrictions. What he apparently wanted above all was a hand in the direction and management of the industry, but some of his moves consisted largely of extravagant financial claims based on tortured economic reasoning.

In his efforts to gain scope for administrative and regulatory powers over the industry—meaning Aramco in Saudi Arabia—he brought in an American lawyer, Franck Hendryx, who set alarm bells ringing when he presented a paper at the First Arab Petroleum Congress held in Cairo in 1959 (see below), entitled A Sovereign Nation's Legal Ability to Make and Abide by a Petroleum Concession Contract, a paper obviously and clearly endorsed by Tariki. Hendryx's argument was not that the legal principle of *pacta sunt servanda* should be qualified by the principle of *rebus sic stantibus*. What he contended was that an "oil producing nation by the law of civilized nations may clearly, in a proper case, modify or eliminate provisions of an existing petroleum concession which have become contrary to the best interests of its citizens".

His arguments, more complex than we have room to consider here, were intellectually and legally respectable, though if tested in a neutral and objective court, would probably only have carried the day in a case involving extreme circumstances. Nevertheless, it was the most dangerous kind of challenge for the oil companies—a reasoned legal argument couched, actually, in relatively cautious terms and appealing to precedent in the US, British and French legal systems. Hendryx was much reviled and there was a great deal of indignant froth and more ritual appeals to the "sanctity" of contracts. But the paper's real importance was that, unlike other disputes between government and concessionary companies in the Middle East, which had always been specific to a particular situation, it set out a *generalized* challenge, based on legal arguments, to the concept of the unalterable nature of concession contracts. Once admitted, it would, in the companies' view (probably correct) have in practice opened the floodgates for arbitrary, unilateral changes going well beyond the scope of the limitations on such powers spelled out in the Hendryx paper.

The First Arab Petroleum Congress and the Mehdi Pact, April 1959

The first official contacts between Venezuela and the Middle East took place in 1949 with a three-man mission from Venezuela touring the Middle East to spread the good news about 50/50 (see Chapter 1). The second came ten years later, in April 1959, during the First Arab Petroleum Congress, though apart from it, and resulted in the so-called Mehdi Pact that was signed by representatives of Iran, Kuwait, Saudi Arabia, the United Arab Republic

(Egypt and Syria's short-lived union), Venezuela and the head of the Arab League's Petroleum Committee, an Iraqi.

Venezuela's prestige was running high. At the time (1959), the country was producing more oil than the two largest producers in the Middle East (Kuwait and Saudi Arabia) combined. Venezuelan income tax rates had been unilaterally increased in December 1958 resulting in an overall tax rate of almost 70 percent on industry profits. H. W. Haight, president of Creole (the Exxon subsidiary in Venezuela and the world's largest crude producing company at the time), issued a statement as he was leaving the country for consultations in New York, claiming that the government had reneged on its verbal assurances; he was not permitted back into the country. Legislating tax increases and chucking out the president of the country's largest producing company were barely conceivable in the Middle East of 1959; Venezuela's pre-eminent position and leadership among nationalist circles in oil-exporting countries was not questioned. Pérez Alfonzo was something of a hero.

It is worth taking some time to examine the Mehdi Pact because it was the first joint formulation of producer country aspirations and it also conveys the flavor of the times, far removed from today.

The substance of the pact was little more than a (rather modest) wish list, committing nobody to anything: the share (tax revenues) of petroleum producing countries should be increased; the current (posted) price structure should be maintained and no changes made by the companies without prior consultation with the host governments; refining capacity in producing countries should be increased; national oil companies should be established; each country should establish units to co-ordinate the production and conservation of hydrocarbons. The only obligation mentioned in the pact was that the signatories should bring to the attention of their governments the idea of establishing a joint consultative petroleum commission that would meet once a year to discuss common problems. Indeed, most of the "substance" of the pact echoed the resolutions of the Congress itself. Of course, for Venezuela, the key provision of the pact concerned the proposal for a consultative commission, which was to be the first step towards international pro-rationing.

The pact had no legal standing. Of the six signatories, only two—Pérez Alfonzo and Tariki—represented their governments, and it is not even clear that Tariki would have received prior authority to sign. The Kuwaiti, Ahmed Sayyid Omar, had no authority to represent his country on any matter involving foreign relations, which were still within the exclusive purview of the British Political Resident in Kuwait. (Omar still traveled at that time on a British passport—full independence from Britain was still two years in the future.) The Iraqi, Mohamed Salman, though presumed to have influence with the Iraqi government, held no official position in Iraq but was simply the head of the Arab League's Petroleum Committee, and he was most certainly not representing the Arab League when he signed. The Iranian, Manucher

Farmanfarmaian, was present at the conference only as an observer on behalf of the National Iranian Oil Company, of which he was a director. He had no authority to commit the company (let alone the Iranian government) to anything. The UAR representative, Saleh Nesim, appears to have been invited only out of courtesy, as the delegate of the host country to the Congress, though perhaps he was helpful in getting parallel recommendations adopted by the Congress itself. In any event, to forestall the misgivings of some of the signatories, a clause was inserted into the pact to the effect that all of the signatories were signing only in their "personal capacities". In legal terms, this was virtually meaningless; in political terms, however, it was the thin end of the wedge, intended to pave the way through influential intermediaries to formal consultations among the governments on petroleum policy matters.

No publicity was later given to the pact.

Prior to the meeting of the Congress, the oil companies, led by BP, had (in February 1959) reduced their posted prices by $0.18/B. (for the major grades of Middle East crudes), citing competitive pressures. The move brought postings down below the levels existing prior to the increases that had occurred during the Suez crisis of 1956-57; but by 1959, postings had lost their market significance, and were nothing more than a starting point for the computation of taxes in the Middle East. The companies' price move did nothing immediate to reduce real prices, but did effect a cut of about $0.09/B. in their taxes (a reduction of over 10 percent). Venezuelan postings, though they did not directly affect government revenue, were also reduced.

The reaction was strong enough to cause concern among the companies, but the governments nevertheless accepted the *fait accompli* complaining only that they had not been consulted. The Congress adopted a number of recommendations among which was one to the effect that "Any changes in the prices [of petroleum and its byproducts] should take place only after the subject has been discussed with the governments of petroleum-exporting countries."

The tone of the Congress itself may have betrayed a current of deep and strong feelings against the oil companies, but it was clear that the reaction among those in responsible positions or close to them was far more cautious and wary. They were clearly a long way from putting the tenets of Hendryx's paper into practice.

There was then a period of about one year during which very little happened that can be said to have contributed much to the later creation of OPEC, except that, in general terms, oil prices continued to deteriorate. There were other distractions in the only three countries (Iraq, Saudi Arabia and Venezuela) that could or would have pushed to keep up the momentum of international contacts among the oil-exporting countries, but even without them, such contacts were hardly a priority. Iraq was by then embroiled in drawn-out and acrimonious negotiations with the Iraq Petroleum Company group, which accounted for all of the country's production; negotiations broke down in October 1959 and an assassination attempt on President Qassem left him hospitalized for two months. Any bold new initiatives from Saudi Arabia were ruled out by the continuing struggle for power between King Saud and Crown Prince Feisal, but again neither of them would have accorded priority to the formation of the Consultative Commission proposed in the Mehdi Pact. And in Venezuela, extreme left-wing and pro-Castro disturbances were rife.

Then in May 1960, with the continued deterioration of crude oil prices, Pérez Alfonzo again turned his attention to the Middle East. During that month, he visited the United States and gave a talk in Dallas to the Texas Independent Producers and Royalty Owners Association (TIPRO) in which he advocated international pro-rationing as a means of keeping prices up. He was accompanied on that occasion by Tariki, who then went on to visit Venezuela. In July 1960, Mohamed Salman, director of the Arab League's Petroleum Department, also visited Venezuela.

On 9 August 1960, the Venezuelan government ordered a halt to all crude sales at price-discounts in excess of "normal commercial limits".

On the same day, Exxon announced posted price reductions for Middle East crudes. Other companies followed suit, but with lesser amounts, and the reductions, after some shuffling around, settled out at $0.10/B. for the major grades.

The reaction was immediate. A meeting of the major exporting countries was convened, and on 14 September, representatives of Iran, Iraq, Kuwait, Saudi Arabia and Venezuela met in Iraq and set up the Organization of the Petroleum Exporting Countries (OPEC).

The Posted Price Reductions of August 1960

After the posted price reductions of February 1959 and the sharp reactions they elicited from the Shah of Iran, from the Venezuelan government, from the governments of other petroleum exporting countries and in the First Arab Petroleum Congress, most of the major companies would have been content to let matters rest, at least for the time being, and make no further cuts regardless of market conditions. There was, however, a problem: competition was increasing and with it, so were the discounts being granted off posted prices. The postings had become disconnected from the market and, as noted above, were now nothing but the starting point for the calculation of taxable income in the Middle East. As long as they remained unchanged, the discounts granted by the companies in their sales to third parties would reduce their net profits, penny for penny. Government taxes, based on posted prices, would not be affected. To many in the oil industry, this seemed unreasonable; if per barrel income went down, then so should per barrel income taxes. If per barrel income tax remained unchanged while per barrel income declined, then this would be tantamount to an increase in the tax rate.

Exxon's chairman of the board, Monroe (Jack) Rathbone, decided some time during the first half of 1960 to reduce posted prices again, in spite of considerable opposition from some of his own directors, notably Howard Page, who thought such a move was not worth the risk of the strong reactions it would provoke among Middle Eastern governments, with unpredictable consequences.

BP was either consulted on the matter, simply told of the decision, or learnt of it indirectly through its contacts with Exxon. According to Bamberg, BP's official historian, "Harold Snow, one of BP's two deputy chairmen, told ... Rathbone ... in the spring of 1960 that 'I did not want to see at this time a reduction in Middle East posted prices which I felt would cause a great deal of trouble.' Snow ... repeated his concerns to Standard in July." Exxon's official historian, Bennett Wall, gives a confused account[1] of the process by which the decision was reached, saying that Howard Page sounded out Middle East government officials to see how they would react if the companies agreed to pick up half of the cost of the reduction in revenues (no reaction reported); that he sounded out the other major companies on picking up three-quarters of the cost (he was turned down flat); and that he proposed to the Exxon board that half of the cost be absorbed (proposal not accepted). Wall is uncertain of the precise timing of these contacts, but thinks the final decision may have been taken at a board meeting in July 1960. In any event, the decision was steam-rollered through by Rathbone, riding roughshod over the opposition, and a reduction of $0.14/B. on major crudes was announced by Exxon on 9 August 1960. Other companies, notably BP, followed suit after a few days with lesser amounts. Neither BP nor Shell appear to have seriously considered refusing to follow the Exxon lead—to let one of the seven majors go down to ignominious defeat was apparently too much to contemplate, and in the end, the average reduction settled out at $0.10/B. on the major crudes.

Within six weeks, OPEC, an organization that was a decade or so later to become the world's most powerful cartel ever, had been set up. Rathbone was jocularly dubbed "Father of OPEC" by some wag on the Exxon board (probably Howard Page), long before the title was conferred, with less irony, on Pérez Alfonzo.

But put yourself in Rathbone's shoes. BP was clearly not going to initiate another cut. Shell was not a price-leader in the Middle East, and the other majors certainly weren't. That left Exxon. So Exxon could either acquiesce in the *de facto* freezing of posted prices and per barrel tax payments, or it could try to continue BP's move of the previous year and make the producing countries bear at least part of the cost of declining market prices. Exxon itself was feeling a boost from the discovery of the large Zelten (Brega) field in Libya in 1959 which was being rapidly developed; but by the same token, more competition was in the wind from other Libyan producers and further market price-erosion could come with it. Now was the time to in effect reaffirm the principle that profit-sharing meant profit-sharing, on the downside as on the upside. Moreover, companies, as well as the governments of the United Kingdom and the United States thought it unlikely that concerted action by the main exporting countries would materialize, according to studies carried out in 1958. It is not clear at this point whether the companies were aware of the contents of Mehdi Pact. If so, they certainly did not take it seriously. In the event, the reaction was swifter and sharper than anyone had expected. Whatever its status, the Mehdi Pact and the subsequent contacts between Pérez Alfonzo, Tariki and Salman had worked brilliantly. The companies and their home governments were given no time to subvert the Baghdad meeting. But its effectiveness turned out in fact to be small. For ten years, OPEC accomplished nothing fiscally except, first, the freezing of posted prices, which the companies would have had to accept anyway, but at a higher level, had it not been for Rathbone's move; and, second, minor tax increases on the royalty-expensing issue, which the companies tossed the producing countries from time to time to give them something to gnaw on.

It is even possible, if you enjoy speculation, to wonder whether the companies were not better off *with* OPEC during the 1960s than they would have been without it. Perhaps OPEC member countries traveled more slowly together than they might have done individually. Certainly the companies used, or bribed, Iran to put the brakes on in OPEC. Was Rathbone right after all, and the others excessively fearful?

OPEC Organizes

The meeting called for in the wake of the August 1960 price reductions convened in Baghdad on 10 September for five days, adopting a number of resolutions, which were published on 24 September. Delegates from five countries attended.

Iran was represented by Fuad Rouhani, a deputy chairman of NIOC. Rouhani was a lawyer by training, spoke perfect French and English, and had been a supporter of Mossadegh's nationalization though not a supporter of Mossadegh against the Shah. His entire professional life had been spent with Anglo-Iranian and NIOC. Other members of the Iranian delegation included Fatollah Naficy and Manucher Farmanfarmaian, both of them directors of NIOC. Rouhani came with instructions as he later[2] said, from the Shah "that Iran could not associate itself with any emotional action which was not based on dispassionate study and appreciation of the point of view of all parties concerned. My directive from the Shah was to agree to any decision which members of that meeting would take which would look forward to a rational, logical investigation of the situation, as a result of which we would enter into negotiations with the companies." Rouhani knew what this meant: it did not include production restrictions and pro-rationing, or any other immediate confrontation with the companies.

The Kuwait representative was Ahmed Sayyid Omar, an under secretary at the Ministry of Finance (Kuwait, like Iran, had no Ministry of Oil at the time) who had been one of the signatories of the Mehdi Pact. He was accompanied by Feisal al Mazidi, also of the Ministry of Finance. Omar, a pleasant person—far from a firebrand—was no doubt told to go along with any unanimous decision on the part of the others, try not to look like a British stooge, and preferably not rock the boat.

The Iraqi representative was Ta'alat Al Shaibani, the Minister of Planning, but he seems to have played a small role in the proceedings. (Mohamed Salman had not yet been appointed Minister of Oil.)

Saudi Arabia was, of course, represented by Abdullah Tariki and he came accompanied by Franck Hendryx, who took an active part in the organizational side of proceedings, as well as Farouk Husseini, an official of the Ministry who was to render long and valuable service in the Ministry and, for a time, with OPEC, until his retirement.

Pérez Alfonzo came for Venezuela, but arrived too late for the inaugural meeting and his place there was taken by the Venezuelan Ambassador, Antonio Martín Araujo.

Tariki and Pérez Alfonzo both wanted immediate action on a tax increase and production restrictions, but Iran would certainly not go so far so soon, and Iraq, in the absence of Salman, was not really quite with it—Qassem was too deeply involved in the negotiations with IPC.

The Baghdad meeting became OPEC's First Conference. It had to satisfy itself with the adoption of three resolutions of which the salient substantive points were that:

Member countries should:

– endeavor to get August posted price reductions rescinded and ensure that no further price changes be made without prior consultation;
– study a system for the stabilization of prices through the regulation of production;
– set up a permanent organization to be called the Organization of the Petroleum Exporting Countries, which was to have a permanent secretariat and meet twice a year.

The tone of the resolutions was pitiful. The united needle-workers' trade unions of greater Manchester would have produced something with more red blood in it. The defeat of Iran by the major companies, the CIA and Britain in 1953 had cast a long shadow.

The next year and a half were spent in organizing the secretariat and carrying out studies, some of them commissioned from outside consultants, notably Arthur D. Little, Inc., and ENI. During this period, Iraq, under President Qassem, laid claim to Kuwait, declaring it a mere province and appointing the Ruler of Kuwait as its first Governor. The Ruler declined the honor and called in a few battalions of British troops to defend his country, whereupon the Iraqis withdrew from the positions they had taken up on the border, and the matter was forgotten for a few years.

OPEC Gets a Job: Royalty-Expensing

The Fourth Conference was scheduled for April 1962. In the meantime the studies commissioned had been completed. One of them was carried out by the United States consulting firm of Arthur D. Little (ADL), where I was by then working, and I went to Geneva in early 1962 and presented it to Rouhani. The gist of its conclusions were that:

(a) Return on net book worth (net assets) of the companies operating in OPEC member countries in the Middle East (excluding Kuwait, for which no data was available to ADL) during the years 1956-60 averaged approximately 66 percent per year. In Venezuela, it averaged 37 percent.

(b) There was no logical economic basis for posted crude prices, and the old "structure" used by the companies had irretrievably broken down. Government revenues could, however, be protected by opting for a system of fixed payments or royalties indexed to a measure of international inflation.

(c) International pro-rationing as a mechanism for stabilizing prices, at their 1960 levels, or their end-1957 levels, was a "fair long-term risk" though it would inevitably lead to some loss of markets.

(d) The determination of international crude prices by relating them to US price levels no longer corresponded to any economic realities. It would be necessary to pick an arbitrary figure reasonably acceptable to both producers and consumers that took freight differentials into account and could, like the fixed payment in (b), be indexed.

The study was well-received by OPEC and, I believe, helpful in providing some greater understanding of the issues.

The Fourth Conference was held in two sessions, the first in April 1962 and the second in July of that year. The first session marked a turning point for OPEC. Pérez Alfonzo pushed hard for an agreement and some action on pro-rationing, at least in principle, but even he must have known at this point that it was not to be. In the event, no agreement could be reached at the acrimonious meeting, and decisions were postponed to the second session.

Pérez Alfonzo had seen pro-rationing work, and work well, for producers in the United States, given its objectives. In a purely technical sense, it was not entirely unreasonable for him to think that the system could be transposed to the international arena. But in practical terms, it was an absurdly unrealistic policy. Pérez Alfonzo adopted it without any study of how it could be applied on the international scene. He had little understanding of the problems involved or of the political situation in the Middle East and the relationship between governments and companies in the region. There were many circumstances, some related to each other, but each of them sufficient in itself to rule out effective pro-rationing at the time:

– Pro-rationing could not possibly have worked without the cooperation of the companies, and they would have fought it tooth and nail—and been backed up by US political pressure on Middle East governments. The United States never cared very much what the level of taxes was on the companies in the Middle East; but it cared very much indeed about who controlled the flow of oil. To have overall allowables set by the governments would have been intolerable at that time. And of course the companies would have called for arbitration in accordance with the terms of their concession contracts; but that would have been the least of it;

– Iran never had the slightest intention of agreeing to a pro-rationing scheme. For many reasons, historical and political, the Shah was not about to abandon his more or less successful efforts to squeeze the Consortium for higher and higher volumes of production. He was backed up by the majority of NIOC Directors, particularly Dr. Reza Fallah, who never made any secret of his hostility to OPEC;

– In Saudi Arabia, Tariki had been replaced as minister by Sheikh Ahmed Zaki Yamani in 1962, and Crown Prince Faisal was now in virtual control of the government. Yamani was a superb politician with a fine grasp on the art of the possible; he knew that without Iran nothing could be done. But this was probably not the decisive factor for him. There was plenty for him to do at home. The idea of plunging into uncharted waters in a major confrontation with the companies was simply not in the cards. It would have embroiled the whole government in conflict and would have become the principal focus of political activity when there were plenty of other (non-oil) issues, foreign and domestic, that needed attention. Even if Yamani had wanted to go ahead, Faisal would not have permitted it.

– In addition, the timing could scarcely have been worse: Abu Dhabi, Libya, Algeria and Nigeria were all waiting in the wings, and they would have been used as further arguments to deter OPEC from production restrictions.

At the second session of the Fourth Conference, held in Geneva in early June 1962, Indonesia and Libya were admitted as members. Then followed three substantive resolutions, each one calling for negotiations with the companies on three separate issues:

– to restore posted prices to their pre-August 1960 levels (worth about $0.05/B. in increased taxes);

– to treat royalties as a deductible expense for income tax purposes, instead of a credit against the 50 percent tax obligation (the net effect of this would be to increase taxes by half of the royalty payments or about $0.11/B.); and

– to eliminate the marketing expenses which the companies were entitled to deduct from gross income in computing their income tax liabilities (worth about $0.015/B. in increased taxes).

OPEC's demands added up to $0.18/B. in increased taxes (somewhat over 20 percent) or roughly $350 million per year, based on 1962 production rates in the five Gulf countries to which the resolutions applied. This was equivalent to about 12 percent of the combined net earnings of the seven majors in 1962.

None of the three issues affected Venezuela directly: in Venezuela, taxes were not computed on the basis of posted prices as they were in the Middle East; royalties always had been treated as an expense rather than a credit against income tax; and the companies were not permitted to deduct marketing expenses (or indeed expenses of any kind incurred outside the country).

Venezuela was fobbed off at the Conference with a resolution recommending that each country establish a conservation commission similar to the Venezuelan Co-ordinating Commission for the Conservation and Commerce of Hydrocarbons. And a deal was done: Middle Eastern member countries would concentrate first on the royalty-expensing and marketing allowance issues. Once these were disposed of satisfactorily, all would turn their attention to prices and production controls as a means of stabilizing them.

A brief at last, after two years! Admittedly, two of the issues were entirely new and had had nothing to do with the establishment of OPEC. Gone was Tariki's call for an immediate increase in the income tax rate in the Middle East, and gone, or in abeyance, was Pérez Alfonzo's call for immediate pro-rationing. However, a job is a job, and better than none.

Royalty-Expensing Negotiations, 1962-1964

OPEC faced four serious problems in its negotiations with the companies.

The first was that it had nothing to offer. "Negotiation" usually means a process whereby each of the parties gives up something to, and gains something from, the other in any eventual agreement. No *quid pro quo* was offered by OPEC, so the companies had no incentive to give an inch.

The second problem was legal. There was no way that member countries could impose royalty-expensing on the companies without unilaterally breaking their concession agreements, and that was something neither Iran, nor Kuwait, nor Saudi Arabia were willing to do except as a last resort. The normal option of bringing gently increasing pressure to bear on the companies was not open to the governments concerned: it was all or nothing, and the memory of the defeat inflicted on Iran over the 1951 nationalization was painfully recent. None of the three countries had the stomach for a fight in which they would almost certainly be shown to be on the wrong side of the law, Hendryx or no Hendryx.

The third was political. Iran had clearly chosen, as a matter of policy, to look for increases in production as a means of boosting its revenues. In this, the Shah could, and did, appeal to the United States to put pressure on the companies to increase their offtake from Iran, his argument being essentially that as a bulwark against communism in the Middle East, he needed additional revenue to buy arms. The advantages of this approach were that it needed no renegotiation of concession terms and, though it might place the companies in an awkward position vis-à-vis Saudi Arabia, it didn't cost them a penny. They simply increased offtake from Iran and reduced it from other countries. The benefit was, of course, obvious to Saudi Arabia, which had to defend itself as best it could—and this precluded confrontation with the companies, since that would simply have provided them with further justification for the increase in offtake from Iran.

A further element of political weakness was Iraq's refusal to attend OPEC meetings after its claim to Kuwait had been repulsed, in 1961. Iraq did not resume attending OPEC meetings until April 1963.

The fourth was tactical. During the course of the royalty-expensing negotiations, unilateral action was in fact threatened (though not very convincingly) by the countries concerned, including Iran. The companies were kept well-informed of the extent to which pressure was building up by Reza Fallah , deputy managing director of NIOC, who during these years accompanied Behnia, and later Hoveyda, (the Iranian ministers of finance) to the OPEC conferences and consultative meetings. Fallah was a likable person. A gruff, outspoken, no-nonsense man, he made no secret of his anti-OPEC inclinations. Among the non-Iranians in the Secretariat, he was known jokingly as the "BP Delegate to OPEC". We didn't realize at the time quite how true it was. Indeed, he was in touch with the companies during the conferences themselves and was able to provide them with a blow-by-blow account of proceedings. This was not helpful to OPEC.

And finally, it should be said, the issue was simply not all that important to the individual member countries (as distinct from OPEC as an effective collective instrument to counter-balance the collective power of the companies). True, royalty-expensing would represent an increase of about 20 percent in government per barrel revenues —not to be sneezed at—but no one imagined that the companies would simply roll over and concede this the moment the first shot was fired. Moreover, the issue had to be seen in the context of other negotiations underway with the companies on a purely national level, notably in Saudi Arabia and Iraq. For example, Yamani negotiated and eventually signed three separate agreements in 1963: with the

Trans-Arabian Pipe Line Company (TAPLINE) on transit fees and other matters; with Aramco on relinquishment of acreage; and with Aramco on crude oil sales to Lebanon. In August 1966, an agreement was reached with Aramco on the issue of discounts (outstanding since 1961) on crude and product sales to third parties.

During the five years that followed the July 1962 Conference, a pattern was established: meeting followed meeting, with OPEC conferences and consultative meetings at ministerial level. Negotiations with the companies were held in between. OPEC would issue dire threats that carried no credibility. The companies would occasionally throw out a small bone—which would usually divide OPEC further rather than pacify it—until at last the principle of royalty-expensing was recognized by the companies, subject to a discount that would be phased out over the years to 1972.

There was only one brief moment when it seemed the Shah might go along with unilateral action against the companies, and that was in mid-1963.

Rouhani was told by the Shah that Iran would go along with unilateral measures if a satisfactory solution to royalty-expensing had not emerged by the time of the next OPEC Conference, and he in turn had let other member countries know this. In October 1962, the Shah had been ready to pull out of OPEC altogether, having been reassured by BP chairman Maurice Bridgman, that many of his demands would be met outside of OPEC. The companies and the British and US governments both encouraged the Shah to stay in, however, as a moderating influence. He agreed. Around mid-1963, he again swung back against the companies and started to back unilateral measures against them. The reason for this is not clear, but the year 1963 was intensely troubled politically in Iran. The Shah had launched his "White Revolution", termed by the government the Revolution of the Shah and the People, and dubbed the Revolution of the Shah Against the People by the opposition. Troubles came to a head in June when a little-known cleric, the Ayatollah Khomeini, delivered a strongly anti-Shah speech in Qum in early June. He was arrested and taken to Tehran, and the following day massive riots erupted in Tehran and many other locations in the country. The demonstrations were put down brutally, at the cost of thousands of lives in the streets of Tehran. Following this and continued unrest, it is possible that the Shah thought that taking a tough anti-company line would rally some popular support around him (though admittedly there is no hard evidence for this). By November, the Shah was once more in firm control, and the need for a popular foreign diversion against the companies had faded away; indeed, it may have begun to seem positively dangerous, and the companies no doubt pointed out to him that, once embarked on this course, he might not be able to control it. The companies added some financial inducements to sweeten his path. He then backed away from unilateral measures.

At the end of 1964, after an acrimonious meeting in Jakarta, some OPEC members signed supplemental agreements with the companies accepting an offer of partial royalty-expensing, subject to a phase-out of the discounts proposed by the companies; others refused it. In any event, the issue was off the table until 1966, when the phase-out provisions were to be reviewed.

Interlude: the First OPEC Production Programming Agreement, 1965

Venezuela now decided to push ahead with plans for a production program. It was almost five years after the establishment of OPEC. Pérez Alfonzo retired from the scene and left the task to Pérez Guerrero, a man of wide experience in the United Nations and in ministerial posts in Venezuela. He was a skilled and quiet-spoken negotiator, had been minister of Finance in Venezuela when 50/50 was introduced in 1948, and had returned to government in the Betancourt administration in 1959 as minister of Planning; he helped establish the UN Conference on Trade and Development (UNCTAD) and was to serve later as its secretary general. Like Rouhani, he spoke perfect French and English, as well as some Arabic.

In April 1965, OPEC held its Eighth Conference, approved the Statute of the Economic Commission (created at the Jakarta conference the previous November) and heard its first report. But Pérez Guerrero used the occasion to propose that the ground be laid for the adoption of a production program at the next conference. He accordingly saw each of the delegates privately and in turn, discussing with them the quotas that would be acceptable to them. The Economic Commission had come up with an estimate of the total increase in demand (10 percent) that would accrue to OPEC during the year the production program was to be put into effect (mid-1965 to mid-1966), and this was tentatively shared out among member countries.

Later that year, in July 1965, the OPEC Conference convened in Tripoli. It was a farce. Iran, at its insistence, was allocated a 17.5 percent increase in production, which was more than it expected the consortium to produce.

For Iran, the production program was merely a stick to beat the consortium with in order to get even higher production than was planned, and there was never any question of Iran actually accepting a ceiling to its production.

Saudi Arabia made it clear that it would only accept the program for the first six months of its period, which of course rendered it meaningless since the quota was based on a twelve-month period: Saudi Arabia's allocated increase was 12.0 percent for the year—it hardly stood any danger of exceeding its increase in the first six months, since that would imply an increase of 24 percent in its production.

Fuad Kabazi, the Libyan oil minister, saw no problem in signing up and declaring within a few days that he did not consider the program applicable to Libya.

Abdul Aziz al-Wattari, the Iraqi oil minister, dismissed the whole exercise as the farce that it was.

And of course there was no plan or provision for enforcement, either for the countries to observe their quotas or for them to compel the companies to observe them. There was no meaningful follow-up. In practice, Venezuela simply gave up on production programming and went its own way.

Royalty-Expensing Negotiations, 1966-1968

The royalty-expensing Supplemental Agreements of 1964 provided for a review, in 1966, of the allowable discounts applicable to posted prices after 1966, in the light of "the competitive, economic and market outlook" at the time. Consequently, OPEC's Eleventh Conference, held in Vienna from 25 to 28 April 1966, recommended that each member country concerned should seek the complete elimination of the discounts. More negotiations followed, and finally, a few days before another OPEC Conference was to convene, in Beirut on 10 January 1968, the companies came up with an offer that was promptly accepted by Iran, Kuwait and Saudi Arabia, to be followed later by Qatar and Abu Dhabi (which had been admitted to the organization in December 1967). Under the new agreement, the discount of 6.5 percent was to be retained for 1967, then progressively phased out entirely by 1972; but all this would be partly offset by increases in the light crude gravity allowances which would be phased out from 1973 to 1975. In the event, all this was swept aside in 1971 when the Tehran Agreement simply did away with the discounts altogether and royalties were from then on fully expensed. The royalty-expensing issue had kept OPEC alive, just.

OPEC's Early Years: Success or Failure?

During its early years, OPEC had a number of small achievements to its credit, but in one very fundamental sense, it was a resounding failure: it never managed to cross that fateful line between unilateral action and negotiation, and it never managed to strengthen its own negotiating position with credible threats of unilateral action. Such threats as were on several occasions made were easily deflected by the companies with pathetically small concessions. The truth was that most of the member countries, especially Iran and Saudi Arabia, had no stomach for a confrontation with the companies, and by 1968, the organization seemed to have been well and truly emasculated.

What of OPEC's achievements during these years?

The most important one was the development of a sense of commonality among its members. To be sure, it was and would always be an uneasy partnership because member countries inevitably had competitive or conflicting interests in many areas (not confined to oil), but when the time for serious action came, the ministers all knew each other very well and their sense of commonality allowed them to act quickly and effectively. It must also be said that OPEC had the extraordinary good fortune to have in some of its member countries outstanding and effective ministers at the helm who were at the same time both the creators and the product of this sense of commonality, notably Jamshid Amuzegar for Iran, Sheikh Ali Al-Sabah for Kuwait, Sheikh Ahmed Zaki Yamani for Saudi Arabia, and Manuel Pérez Guerrero for Venezuela. And it must be remembered too that this was a time of great ferment in the relations between developed and developing countries; OPEC was part of this. These were the days of the creation of UNCTAD and the UN Industrial Development Organisation (UNIDO), both of them organizations directed towards the needs of Third World countries. When the time came to stand up and be counted, after the 1973 price increases, no one among the greatest victims of the price rise—the developing countries—would side against OPEC.

OPEC's second most important achievement was its contribution to the growing knowledge of the industry in member countries, and awareness of their crucial role in an industry that was so important to the economic growth of the world and especially of the industrialized countries. Many currents contributed to this flow—the national oil companies, the Arab Petroleum Congresses and a stream of seminars and conferences as well as the generalized international preoccupation with the development of Third World countries. Anyone who was familiar with OPEC member countries during this period would attest to the vast difference in their knowledge and expertise between 1959 and 1969.

OPEC's third most important achievement, I believe, was its remarkable capacity to stay out of other political issues. In this, the membership of Iran and Venezuela was invaluable. The Six-Day War of 1967, for example, simply washed over OPEC as though nothing had happened (apart from the slight postponement of one of its conferences). If OPEC had allowed itself to be dragged into the Arab-Israeli conflict, or other political issues in the Middle East, it would not have been long before it would have split apart.

On the financial and fiscal side, OPEC accomplished little during its early years. Most important, it put a definitive halt to any further cuts in posted prices. Royalty expensing, phased in slowly though it was, brought in several hundreds of millions of dollars over the years. Not bad, for an expenditure of a few million dollars in a secretariat and occasional conferences and consultative meetings. The trouble was, it didn't *feel* good. The protracted negotiations and the tiny concessions, tea spooned out by the companies, cent by cent, did not smack of victory to the member countries. No one at this point was proud of OPEC. Venezuela, of course, was bitterly disappointed. The companies had skillfully manipulated Iran to subvert OPEC, and Saudi Arabia had, quite sensibly, made sure that nothing would be done without Iran being fully committed.

One has to conclude, I believe, that OPEC's weakness during its early years contributed to ten years or so of relative peace in relations between the companies and governments; that financially it made small but significant gains for its members; but that its perceived defeat at the hands of the companies, combined with its growing sense of commonality and knowledge of the industry, helped, to some extent, pave the way for the devastating economic storms of the seventies and early eighties.

The Companies: Clever but not Intelligent?

What of the companies? They were no doubt feeling pleased with themselves by the end of 1967. However, the question has to be asked, looking back at what was soon to follow, had they been too clever by half? Was their behavior largely responsible for what followed? Should they not have taken advantage of the creation of OPEC to pave the way for a healthier long-term relationship with the producing countries?

Most unlikely. At the time it was widely thought, even in OPEC member countries, that OPEC would fade into insignificance and become no more influential than other duds such as the Arab League's Petroleum Committee. When it survived for a couple of years, it was easily subverted, and at minimal cost. OPEC was a minor irritant, and the companies' tactics brought ten years of relative peace. The Tehran Agreement of 1971 and the seizure of power by OPEC in 1973 had their roots elsewhere, not in the frustration of OPEC, though OPEC's frustration no doubt contributed to the enthusiasm with which member countries pressed home their advantage when the time came. But it is equally possible to argue that these things would have occurred sooner if OPEC's demands had been met promptly, or if some entirely new deal had been put forward by the companies, for the unfortunate truth is that power is not easily divisible between antagonists.

Perhaps one of the most curious aspects of this period, however, was the mutual fear the companies and governments had of each other. In retrospect, the companies appear to have dreaded collective unilateral action on the part of the governments, and to have believed that they would have little chance of withstanding it should it come to that, regardless of the guarantees and arbitration clauses in their agreements. Nor did they seem to think that their home governments would come to their rescue if it were a question only of an increased fiscal burden. On the contrary, the home governments would probably have urged the companies to settle, as they were to do later.

But the OPEC governments for their part had no inkling yet of how easy it would have been to impose their will unilaterally on the companies. The Shah was too fearful of a repeat of the 1951 nationalization, which almost cost him his throne; Saudi Arabia was busy much of the time with its own internal power struggle between King Saud and his brother, Crown Prince—later King—Faisal, and in any event would scarcely move without Iran; Kuwait would inevitably side with Saudi Arabia; and Iraq virtually removed itself from the OPEC scene for a crucial year. But in any event, there simply wasn't enough trust among the key players in OPEC to permit coordinated action against the oil companies.

If it was all a bit of a bluff, the companies won hands down.

Chapter 6
THE TEHRAN AND TRIPOLI AGREEMENTS, 1971

The existing concession pattern is, I believe, a triangle standing on its point; it is bound to topple over unless changes continually take place. There can be no lasting "holding the line", particularly the financial line. A fixed and rigid position out there is in my opinion a fatal position. It is only by changing with changing circumstances can stability exist in the dynamic Middle East if we are to hold the oil, the area and the people.
– Richard Funkhouser in a talk entitled The Problem of Near East Oil, to the US National War College, 4 December 1953.

This chapter and the following three deal largely with the momentous changes in the petroleum industry during the years from 1970 through 1973 that culminated in the virtually total takeover of the companies' interests in the OPEC area by the governments. They were years when the international aspects of the industry (one of the focal points of this book) erupted onto the larger world scene; they were also years when the growth of competition (another focal point), or its suppression, was reshaped. These developments did not take place in an economic and political vacuum, and I shall return in the course of their analysis to the economic and political backdrop against which they were played out.

A Fresh Start: OPEC's Declaratory Statement of Petroleum Policy

In January 1968, OPEC's Fifteenth Conference met in Beirut and accepted a company offer on the royalty-expensing issue that in effect terminated the dispute. I had been appointed Secretary General the previous year, but due to illness was unable to attend any but the first session of the conference. When I returned, it was to a secretariat without a remit. OPEC was out of work again.

In December 1967, the OPEC Conference had instructed the Economic Commission to undertake a further study for a production program—a

110

resolution which, like so many others, was passed with the sole intention of placating one of the member countries, in this case, Venezuela. I could safely ignore it. I also concluded that the year ahead might profitably be spent in a pause for thought.

After some reflection, I decided that Resolution V.41 of 1963, providing for the compilation of a code of uniform petroleum laws for member countries, was a suitable excuse to work on a set of basic policy principles which, with the help of the head of the legal department, Dr. Hasan Zakariya (an Iraqi Harvard-trained lawyer), I drafted up in the first few months of the year. We then went on a tour of the most important member countries to brief them before the next conference, which was to be held in Vienna of that year.

The result was the adoption by the OPEC, in June 1968, of a Declaratory Statement of Petroleum Policy in Member Countries, incorporating nine basic principles. Three of them were to play an important role in subsequent developments. The first of these concerned participation and stipulated that, "Where provision for Governmental participation in the ownership of the existing concession-holding company under any of the present petroleum contracts has not been made, the Government may acquire a reasonable participation, on the grounds of the principle of changing circumstances."

The second provided for the government itself to establish the posted or reference prices on which income taxes would be based.

The third provided for governments to draw up detailed conservation rules to be followed by operators to fulfill their obligations with respect to the employment of the best conservation practices.

Others concerned the relinquishment of acreage, periodic renegotiation, and the settlement of disputes.

After this, the next step was to set about working toward the implementation of one of the principles adopted. I chose the one concerning conservation, and, with the help of Dr José Cirigliano, Chief of the Conservation Division of the Venezuelan Ministry of Mines and Hydrocarbons' Conservation Department, we drafted a Pro-Forma Regulation for the Conservation of Petroleum Resources, which was adopted by OPEC's Seventeenth Conference held in Baghdad in November 1968, resolving that member countries should implement the regulation as soon as possible. The Pro-Forma Regulation drew on various sources, including the Venezuelan Law of Hydrocarbons and its regulations, the US Interstate Oil Compact Commission's A Suggested Form of General Rules and Regulations for the Conservation of Oil and Gas, and the Province of Alberta's Oil and Gas Conservation Act and its Regulations.

The importance of the Pro-Forma Regulation was that it gave sweeping powers to the government to supervise and regulate many detailed aspects of exploration, production, gas utilization and other operations, for all of which the relevant ministry's consent was required. Although no detailed study was made of the matter, the regulation did not appear to conflict in any way with the existing concession agreements in member countries, which generally included an obligation for the companies to carry out operations in accordance with the best conservation practices in use in other producing countries. The question of who should define such practices in detail was left unresolved, but in normal circumstances it was clearly a regulatory function of government.

It was genuinely meant to assist member countries to exercise proper control over the operation of their oilfields. But of course, and more importantly, it was also meant to provide the government with powerful pressure points to apply to companies that might prove recalcitrant in complying with government objectives in other matters, rather like an extended income tax audit of politically awkward individuals in some other countries. Venezuela and Libya adopted it immediately, though this only required modest changes in Venezuela's existing regulations. But the Libyan minister of oil, Khalifa Musa, immediately recognized its potential and it became Regulation No. 8 of Libya's Petroleum Law, and was destined to be used later, extensively and rather harshly, to justify imposing cutbacks on the companies. The applicability to them of certain provisions of the regulation was questioned by some of the companies on the grounds that they contravened their concession agreements but the matter was never tested in the courts. In any event, the Libyan government then added, on 26 April 1971, an article to Petroleum Law No. 25 of 1955, providing for penalties for the violation of provisions of Regulation No. 8.

The implementation of the principles in the Declaratory Statement would of course transfer control over most key aspects of the concession-holding companies to the governments of the host countries. The Declaratory Statement was later seen as a fundamental turning point in OPEC and in the policies of its member countries.   Ian Skeet, in his book *OPEC: Twenty-Five Years of Prices and Politics,* said "These two documents constituted the basic formulation and justification for OPEC tactics for the next five years. OPEC was never to repeat this achievement." Ali Jaidah, as Secretary General of the organization in 1977-78 said in his Anniversary Recollections (OPEC press release 5-78), the "Declaratory Statement of Petroleum Policy in Member Countries [was] perhaps the most significant act by OPEC in its first decade and one which set the stage for the Organization's later actions." The Declaratory Statement was subsequently referred to on numerous occasions as a reference policy point in justification of later resolutions adopted by the OPEC, as well as in ministerial speeches and papers. But at the time, it went largely unnoticed. The outside world was inured to a series of empty OPEC resolutions. Indeed, with two notable exceptions, member countries did not for the time being take the policy objectives very seriously themselves, at least as priority items. But the two exceptions were important: Saudi Arabia's Yamani was dead serious about seeking participation in the companies and in fact was mainly responsible for inserting the participation principle into the Statement; and, as for the Conservation Regulation, Khalifa Musa, the Libyan oil minister, knew a blunt instrument when he saw one.

As far as relations between the OPEC governments and the companies were concerned, 1968 and 1969 were quiet years. There was a good deal of anti-company noise in the press in the form of official statements (some of them threatening), seminar papers, interviews and, above all, an incessant stream of critical articles. They were unaccompanied by concrete measures, which perhaps lulled the companies into a state of passive indifference, all the more so because behind the scenes deals were being made which indicated something less than loyalty to OPEC.

The Question

Then, in the fifteen months from January 1970 to April 1971, OPEC member countries accomplished far more in negotiations with the companies than they had been able to in the previous nine years.

On 1 September 1969, the Libyan monarchy was overthrown by a group of army officers, and a republic established in its place. The new regime called for price-adjustment negotiations in January 1970. By the end of October 1970, it had achieved its initial goal of a $0.30 increase in posted prices, and other, more momentous changes had been set in motion, culminating in the broad company/government agreements, the Tehran and Tripoli agreements signed in February and April of 1971, respectively, providing for much larger increases in per barrel oil revenues. Within another twenty months, OPEC member countries had, through negotiation, acquired a 25 percent ownership (or its financial equivalent) in the concession-holding companies and were set to acquire up to 51 percent in the following ten years. Along the way, a host of other modifications in the relationship between OPEC governments and the oil companies occurred, leading up to the debacle of 1973 when the companies were stripped of any remaining power to negotiate their tax payments, and lost much of their other powers in lesser matters.

The industry was shaken to its foundations by these events. Nevertheless, the companies still had the power to invest or not to invest, to lift more or less crude, depending on their requirements. However, in October 1973, OPEC member countries acquired the power, untested by the market or serious consumer government opposition, to control the supply of oil into world markets and set its price. They had become an economic menace to the rest of the world.

Why, and how, did this sudden reversal of fortunes take place? How did the relative bargaining strengths of the companies on the one hand and the OPEC governments on the other change so dramatically in so short a time? After all, at the beginning of 1968, the governments were meekly accepting, in settlement of the royalty-expensing issue (which had already dragged on for six years), a phase-in that, on the average, yielded a mere 1 cent per barrel per year for them over the next seven years.

There are subsidiary questions to be answered along the way. Did the United States initially encourage OPEC to raise prices? Did the companies welcome, or at least not ardently resist, an overall increase in taxes that was bound to push prices up? When did it finally dawn on OPEC member governments that the major oil companies were paper tigers? When did the companies wake up to the danger they were in? And why did they not come up with some imaginative "New Deal" that could perhaps have saved the underlying partnership between companies and governments? Why did the United States and Britain, as home countries to the major oil companies, not react anywhere near adequately in defense of the companies when unilateral action was taken against them by the host governments? And why did they, along with European governments generally, not react more forcefully to the economic threat that OPEC posed?

I shall return to these questions during the course of this chapter. But first, let us look in a bit more detail at what *did* happen that requires so much explaining.

The Long-Term Outlook for Supply and Demand

The first and by far the most important thing that happened was not a specific event but a sharp change in perceptions of future supply and demand for oil. Demand was growing faster than had been anticipated and although some slowdown was expected, growth in absolute terms would continue to be large, whereas the supply of energy was now growing more slowly. Notably, the expansion of nuclear energy was disappointingly slow. Serious declines in oil production were anticipated for the United States and the Soviet Union (making the latter a net importer). And spare capacity was fast disappearing everywhere. Shortage loomed.

This view, which first took hold during the period from 1969 to 1971 and held its grip for many years thereafter, colored everything that occurred during the next decade. Its importance is difficult to overstate, and it is impossible to understand the events in the industry during the 1970s and early 1980s without bearing constantly in mind that virtually everyone expected an acute "shortage" of energy some time in the near future. Underlying so many of the policies formulated and decisions taken during the 1970s was this newly rediscovered fear that the world was running out of oil, or that insufficient reserves would be discovered outside the Middle East, or that Middle Eastern producers might not consent to produce at the rates necessary to sustain growing demand, or some other fear that supply would be constrained and that therefore prices were irretrievably set to rise indefinitely. It was a view that was virtually universal in government and industry circles, in both producing and importing countries, and was to persist throughout the 1970s and into the early 1980s. It may not have been quite on the same scale as some of the more devastating economic ideologies that have gripped the minds of men in the past, but it was certainly the most damaging error of judgment about the future supply of a commodity that has ever been made. It was also the most important single factor in the radically altered bargaining position of the major oil companies and the OPEC governments. Somehow, the industry would have to come up with massive increases in production over the next ten to fifteen years, and the Middle East would have to contribute most of it. To the companies, it appeared that a huge expansion in the Middle East would be essential, and fear of losing the privileged access they enjoyed (through their concessions) to Middle East oil, drove them to appease producer government demands. Having demonstrated that they wouldn't fight when push came to shove, the companies were, step by step, shoved aside altogether.

It is not clear precisely when the major oil companies first became seriously concerned about their ability to supply the volumes of demand that might materialize. Certainly, prior to 1968, there was no indication that they thought there would be a long-term problem; in the short term, they were still fighting off the Shah's persistent efforts to force them to increase production in Iran, and indeed they were anticipating "a growing world-wide surplus of oil production over the next five years."[1] They certainly never tried to keep the Shah at bay by suggesting to him that the time was just around the corner when Iran's production would be pushed to its ultimate capacity, as their later forecasts were to suggest.

True, US spare producing capacity had just about vanished by the end of 1968, but there was ample spare capacity in the Middle East (close to one million bd in Aramco alone). In any event, concern for future supply began to surface in 1969, and was then increasingly reiterated in 1970. By mid-1970, the whole situation had been radically reversed and the companies were now looking at an increase in world demand of 20 to 30 mbd by 1980. Alaska and the North Sea would provide some of this, but most of it would undoubtedly have to come from the Middle East.

The first worried expressions surfaced in 1969. In July of that year, an article appeared in the *Petroleum Press Service* (PPS)[2] entitled "Areas of Growth" , which said, in part, "The suggestion has been made that oil consumption in the free world as a whole may nearly double [from 34 mbd to 68 mbd] once again, between 1968 and 1980 ... the petroleum industry is faced with the task of finding large new reserves ..." It may have been just a straw in the wind, but a moment's reflection is enough to understand how daunting a task appeared to lie ahead—developing more than 2 mbd of new capacity each year for the next twelve years. Nevertheless, no panic buttons were yet being pressed.

Over the next two years, prior to and after the Tehran/Tripoli Agreements, the alarming forecasts multiplied. Despite the fact that nearly all of them looked to a deceleration in the growth of demand, the cumulative increase still implied the massive development of new producing capacity. It was also widely thought at the time that in addition to burgeoning US oil imports, the Soviet Union would become a net importer: PPS wrote "The virtual certainty that both the United States and (to a lesser extent) the Soviet bloc will be drawing increasingly on imported supplies means that the annual production increase in the free world outside the United States will have to be larger than the consumption increase in the same area."

In June 1970, PPS reported the views of (unidentified) oil company economists to the effect that world "crude oil production would have to grow by 1989 to two and a half times last year's level, namely to 5 1/4 billion tons." That was equivalent to 105 mbd, an increase of over 63 mbd, slightly more than 3 mbd each year.

In July 1970, PPS was reporting that "Some industry experts have forecast [demand growth rates] as low as 5 percent. Even so, demand would still rise to 60 million barrels daily in 1980, compared with 35 million b/d last year."

In September 1970, PPS reported on a speech by a senior vice-president of Mobil forecasting an increase in free world production to 98 mbd by 1990, from 36 mbd in 1969.

In April 1971, Shell published a forecast of world demand (excluding communist countries)for petroleum fuels (excluding non-fuel uses) rising by 23 mbd by 1980.[3]

In the same month, April 1971, PPS was reporting on a pessimistic speech by H. P. Warman, BP's chief geologist, and saying that, "It is a daunting thought that the international oil industry has set itself the task of finding another 900,000 million barrels of oil by 1985." At the time, total world proved reserves stood at 620,000 million barrels.

By August 1971, PPS was advocating higher oil prices, in addition to the increases induced by the Tehran/Tripoli tax increases: "Oil, which is still a relatively cheap fuel despite recent price increases, will have to become more expensive—exclusive of taxes—if adequate supplies for the future are to be forthcoming." This, from a journal that was regarded as an industry mouthpiece, could only be interpreted by OPEC as an invitation to raise taxes even more, which would of course have the desired result of raising crude prices outside the OPEC area as well.

In September 1971, PPS reported that the US National Petroleum Council (NPC) estimated that US imports of oil would rise fourfold by 1985, to 14.8 mbd. NPC expected Free World demand to rise from 37 mbd in 1970 to 92 mbd by 1985.

By December 1971, estimated oil imports into the United States in 1985 were put at 18.2 mbd by the Chase Manhattan's energy economist, John Emerson.

All these were a mere hors d'oeuvre to the positive deluge of forecasts in the years immediately following, all of them predicting increases in demand over the next ten to twenty years that, it seemed, would inevitably bring oil supplies under extreme pressure. The seeds of the idea that an energy "gap" was developing were being sown. Supply would be inadequate to meet demand. Prices would have to rise to choke off demand and stimulate the development of energy supplies, oil and other. Almost everyone concurred: the US State Department was still quietly encouraging OPEC countries to seek higher taxes (and, with pass-through provisions now in place for most contracts, higher prices); OPEC of course wanted higher prices from the market, which would allow them to increase taxes; the financial community wanted higher oil prices; and the companies obviously had an interest in higher prices, though they did not want them brought about by OPEC-imposed taxes, especially unilaterally-imposed taxes.

In 1972, the US Interior Department's Office of Oil and Gas was forecasting an increase in US imports of 4.6 mbd by 1980 (up 135 percent from 1970); Walter Levy, a well-known oil consultant, thought that world demand would increase by 35 mbd by 1980 (up 80 percent over 1970); Shell put US imports at 19 mbd for 1985, and US demand at 29 mbd; an unidentified major oil company was reported to estimate Middle East production in 1985 at 43 mbd, an increase of 29 mbd over its level of 1970; Texaco put Free World oil demand at 70 mbd by 1980 (up 30 mbd from 1970); Shell put world oil demand at 79 mbd by 1985 (up 39 mbd from 1970). And so on, for the next ten years.

Apart from the massive increases anticipated for oil demand, virtually all of the forecasts shared one other feature in common: most of the increase would have to come from the OPEC area, and most of that would have to come from the Middle East. An average of 26 forecasts[4] published between mid-1974 and mid-1978 put OPEC production in 1985 at 40 mbd, up 17 mbd from 1970 (actual production in 1985 was 16.8 mbd, well under half the predicted figure). The alarming forecasts lasted right through the 1970s and until after the price increases that accompanied and followed the Iranian Revolution of 1979. As late as 1978, Exxon, for example, was forecasting OPEC production in 1985 at 40 mbd, and 1990 production at 44 mbd. (World Energy Outlook, Exxon Corp., April 1978.) Actual production was 25 mbd in 1990, after massive price increases had done their work.

By 1971, the companies had begun to draw up plans for a huge expansion of producing capacity in the Middle East: to over 20 mbd in Saudi Arabia by 1983; to 8 mbd in Iran by late 1976; to 5 mbd in Kuwait; and the government of Iraq announced that it would raise capacity to 5 mbd by 1980. The companies promptly ran into trouble in Kuwait where the government, alarmed at the prospect of premature depletion, slapped a production ceiling of 3 mbd on Kuwait Oil Company, the sole producer. Its legality went unquestioned.

Plans were also being laid to produce oil from the oil shales of Colorado, and a huge expansion of production from the Canadian tar sands, as well as other alternative sources of energy.

Such were the beliefs of companies and governments alike as they entered round after round of negotiations on various issues—tax rates, indexation, participation, applicable currency exchange rates—during the 1970s. There was no question in the companies' minds: they *had* to have Middle East oil, and in ever-increasing quantities. Bereft of any significant support from their home governments, and with the legal safeguards written into the concession agreements rapidly sinking into irrelevance, it is difficult to imagine them in a weaker bargaining position.

With the then prevailing outlook in mind, let us go back and briefly trace the actual events that led up to the Tehran and Tripoli Agreements and beyond.

The Storm Signals of 1969

Although, as far as the companies were concerned, all was quiet on the OPEC front during 1969, much was happening in individual member countries:

Iran

In Iran, four issues loomed large between the government and the consortium (the group of mainly major oil companies responsible for nearly all of the country's production):

The most immediate and pressing was the one of current revenues. In the biannual talks between the consortium and NIOC that took place in February and March of 1969, the Shah demanded a level of production and payments for the following fiscal year of more than the consortium thought it could give. He pressed for a commitment on increased production for the following five-years and, along the way, in April, publicly threatened to legislate a 50 percent participation for Iran in the consortium's oilfields if Iran's demands were not met. In May, the consortium conceded most of what the Shah wanted in increased production and revenue.

The second issue was a general increase in the level of taxation to put the consortium agreement on a par with the other new agreements that Iran had been signing with such companies as AGIP and Amoco, which did indeed provide for a 50 percent participation by the government.

A third issue was the management of reservoirs. NIOC, the national oil company, believed that gas reinjection would prolong the life of the reservoirs and increase ultimate recovery. But this was expensive, and the benefits of such investment would only show up well after the consortium's concession had expired, so naturally it was reluctant to undertake them.

Finally, a fourth big issue was the fate of the non-associated gas fields, of which there were several very substantial ones. The consortium would not develop them because there was no market for the gas; so NIOC, not unreasonably, wanted to take them over. The consortium, however, was unwilling to part with an asset that might turn out to be valuable at some time in the future, and in any case had no inducement to part with the fields since it could scarcely expect any compensation for something that it did not plan to develop.

Saudi Arabia

In Saudi Arabia, the burning issue was participation by the government in the equity of Aramco, and the Saudi oil minister, Ahmed Zaki Yamani, was turning up the heat.

Pressure for the nationalization of the companies was mounting in the Middle East, largely as a result of the defeat of the Arab countries in the Six-Day War of 1967. How else could the Arabs retaliate against US support of Israel?

Yamani saw participation as a way to deflect nationalization, which he regarded as a potential disaster. In May 1969, he again gave a talk (the second on the subject) at the American University of Beirut, entitled Participation Versus Nationalization—A Better Means to Survive. This time, he made it crystal clear that he was seeking participation both upstream and downstream. Indeed, he said, "Our main target is the downstream operations, because these are the key to the stability of prices in world markets."

In July 1969, OPEC's Eighteenth Conference directed the secretariat to establish a technical committee to make a study of all aspects of participation, and the committee's preliminary report was presented to the next conference at the end of November 1969. On upstream participation, the committee recommended an initial starting point of 20 percent, rising over a period of years to 51 percent. Acquisition of the government's share would be at net book value, in line with the Algerian government's acquisition of participation in Getty Oil Company, and other precedents. Some of the participation-oil (the government's share) would initially have to be sold back to the companies at uniform prices.

About half of the report dealt with downstream participation, and was essentially confined to the many practical difficulties that would be involved, particularly "the question as to whether downstream participation should extend to all or only to some of the phases subsequent to production, and also whether participation should take a diffuse or a concentrated form."[5]

Participation downstream never found favor with all of the Saudi cabinet, and Yamani was in the end defeated on this issue, which was quietly dropped; but that came a good deal later. Instead, some member countries, including Saudi Arabia, adopted a policy of limited downstream integration into the markets on their own.

Libya

On 1 September 1969 the monarchy of King Idris I in Libya was overthrown by a group of young army officers who established a Revolutionary Council of which Captain Muammar Qadhafi, who was 27 years old, emerged as the dominant figure. He was promoted to Colonel, appointed President of the Revolutionary Council and commander-in-chief of the armed forces. A republic was proclaimed and a new prime minister, Mahmud Sulaiman al-Maghribi, named. Assurances were rapidly given that Libya would respect all international agreements. There was to be no "spectacular" change in oil policy, though the interests of the Libyan people would be safeguarded by more effective control over operations. And that was that for the time being, though no one thought the contentious issues that had been on the table before, particularly over the level of posted prices, would be shelved.

Algeria

In the meantime, Algeria was warming up to face the companies in a confrontation that was intended in the long run, interim agreements to the contrary notwithstanding, to lead to total government control. In July 1969, Algeria was admitted into OPEC. In October 1969, it requested the opening of talks with France for an upward revision of tax-reference prices applicable to the French companies operating in Algeria, to take account of the Suez premium granted on Libyan and Eastern Mediterranean crudes. But by this time, Algeria already had a history of differences and negotiations with the companies, both French and non-French, stretching back to 1962, and was soon to embark on a series of nationalizations.

Iraq

Iraq remained as intransigent as ever. Things went from bad to worse as far as any accommodation with the companies was concerned, and the government prepared to cut the Gordian knot by actively developing the confiscated southern areas. In 1969, it signed an agreement with the Soviet Union for the development of the proven North Rumaila field and other semi-proven fields in South Iraq that lay in the concession area of the IPC group and from which IPC had been excluded by the (contested) Law 80 of 1961.

From Libya's Revolution to the Tehran/Tripoli Agreements

Despite the menacing events in different countries, however, there was nothing to suggest, at the end of 1969, that within one year, the whole of the existing system would be on the verge of fundamental change, much less that within four years it would have collapsed entirely.

The successive upheavals which led to the radical restructuring of the international petroleum industry in the post-1973 period began in 1969 with the Libyan Revolution. Along the way were the Libyan agreements of September-October 1970, with various companies, the Tehran/Tripoli accords of 1971, the Geneva I and Geneva II dollar exchange rate agreements of 1972 and 1973, the General Agreement on Participation of 1972, the Algerian, Libyan and Iraqi nationalizations of various companies in the early years of the 1970s, and the Arab-Israeli war of 1973, complete with embargo, and the repudiation of the recently signed agreements.

I do not propose to give here a blow-by-blow description of the tortured negotiations that led up to the various short-lived agreements that were made during the period. These have been amply and well described by others.[6] Instead, I shall try to recapitulate the main events of the period, in chronological form, and then turn to an analysis of why and how they happened.

On 6 January 1970, Algerian President Houari Boumedienne called for a fundamental revision of the 1965 Franco-Algerian oil agreement. Two weeks later, Libya's oil minister, Izz al-Din al-Mabruk, in a speech to oil company executives in the country, called for the resolution of outstanding issues between them, particularly on posted prices. During the following three months, neither side budged, but the governments took no unilateral action that might breach their agreements. However, cooperation between the two countries was close.

On 28 January, a joint communiqué was issued by the Libyan Ministry of Oil and Minerals, and an Algerian delegation headed by Nordine Ait Laoussine of Sonatrach, stressing their determination to cooperate and coordinate their efforts vis-à-vis their respective demands for an increase in their tax-reference/posted prices. On 5 February, Libya initiated negotiations with the oil companies on the posted price issue.

In early April, Exxon and Occidental made separate offers to increase their posted prices. These were deemed far below the required level, and the offers were rejected. Libyan oil minister Mabruk then visited Algiers to hold talks with Algeria's Minister of Industry and Energy, Belaid Abdessalam, on oil co-ordination measures. Later, in May, the oil ministers of Algeria

(Abdessalam), Iraq (Sa'adun Hamadi) and Libya (Mabruk) met in Algiers and issued a joint communiqué agreeing on a unified stand in their negotiations with the oil companies. (Iraq had already entered into negotiations with the companies on the level of posted prices for its crude at Eastern Mediterranean ports, which were of course directly related to prices f.o.b. Libya and Algeria.) They agreed to set a time limit to the negotiations, implement their demands by legislation if necessary and set up a joint cooperative fund for reciprocal support in the event of economic damage resulting from any confrontation with the companies.

In early May 1970, the Trans Arabian Pipeline (Tapline) from the Saudi Arabian oilfields to the Eastern Mediterranean port of Sidon was shut down after being ruptured in Syrian territory by a bulldozer which was supposedly engaged in laying telephone cable. Syria then denied repair crews access to restore the line, and Saudi Arabia accused Syria of "planned sabotage". Libya's (and Algeria's) negotiating position was of course greatly enhanced by the closure, and crude prices in the Mediterranean shot up.

Some part of the lost availability of oil at the Eastern Mediterranean was replaced by increased throughput via the 42-inch transit Israeli pipeline from Eilat on the Gulf of Aqaba to Ashkelon on the Mediterranean, the capacity of which was to be expanded from the its initial 400 kbd to 800 kbd. The line had come onstream in February 1970, transporting Iranian crude both to Israel and for export from Israeli ports. Iran had a small equity interest in the line.

In early June, the Libyan government ordered Occidental to cut back its production by approximately 300 kbd (from 800 kbd) on the grounds that the company had been overproducing and thus contravening Petroleum Regulation No. 8 (based on OPEC's Pro-Forma Regulation for the Conservation of Petroleum Resources). The cutback aggravated the shortage of Mediterranean crude availability after the 500 kbd drop caused by the closure of Tapline. The Libyan government also questioned Exxon's proposed price for its exports of liquefied natural gas (LNG) from its brand-new Brega plant, and initial exports were held up. These were the first unilateral measures taken by Libya and it should by now have been clear, if it was not already, that the new government was not going to put up with endless delays on the part of the companies. Later in the month, on June 15, Libya ordered Amoseas (Texaco/Chevron) to cut back its production by 100 kbd (from about 384 kbd). Further cutbacks were ordered—on July 9, it was the turn of the Oasis group (Continental, Marathon, Amerada-Hess and Shell), which was told to cut back by 150 kbd, to 895 kbd by August 1; on August 4, Mobil was ordered to cut back production by 40 kbd, to 222 kbd by August 15; and a week later, Occidental was ordered to cut back production by a further 60 kbd, down to about 440 kbd. Armand Hammer, president of Occidental, flew to New York, in July 1970, and asked Exxon Chairman James K. Jamieson to sell him oil at cost so that he could stand firm in Libya and not accede to Libya's price demands.   Jamieson refused, apparently out of hand—a move that was to have dire consequences, and when the companies finally got around to constructing some kind of "safety net", it was too late.

The Libyan Agreements of 1970

Hammer threw in the towel, and on 2 September, Occidental reached a settlement with Libya whereby it agreed to raise the posted price of its crude by $0.30/B., to $2.53/B., and by a further $0.02 each year for the following five years. The company also agreed to a higher rate of income tax, up to 58 percent, in lieu of retroactivity, and to make an additional payment of $15 million per year for agricultural development schemes in the Kufra oasis (it had undertaken to allocate 5 percent of its profits in Libya to the scheme when it obtained its original concession.)

Two days later, it was Exxon's turn. The company was ordered to cut back its production by 110 kbd by 5 September. The order applied to Exxon's wholly-owned Zelten field and to the Raguba field owned by Exxon (50 percent) and Libyan American Oil Co. (Arco and Grace).

All of the companies complied meekly enough with the production cuts, knowing that the balance would be blocked if they did not do so. The cuts totaled about 760 kbd by the end of September, about 20 percent of Libya's total production.

On 18 September, Continental, Marathon and Amerada-Hess, all members of the Oasis group, agreed to raise their posted prices by $0.30/B., in line with Occidental's earlier agreement. They also agreed to an increase in income tax rates from 50 percent to 54 percent (in lieu of retroactivity on the price increase). Shell, also a partner in the Oasis group, refused to agree, and it was thereupon prohibited from lifting its share of the group's production.

Thoroughly alarmed by now, the heads of the major oil companies met in New York on 25 and 26 September 1970 to discuss the situation, but it was clear that the fight had gone out of Texaco and Chevron, and that they were about to settle on Libya's terms, as they did within days of the meeting. David Barran, chairman of Shell and Eric Drake, chairman of BP, were the chief advocates of some collective banding together to resist further Libyan demands. They received no encouragement in their consultations with Alec Douglas-Home, the British Foreign Secretary, who happened to be in New York at the time, but knew that his European counterparts had no stomach for a struggle.   Nor was the State Department any more encouraging: confrontation was not seen as a feasible path, especially if it required US backing, since the United States felt it had no leverage on Libya.   It was the end of the road in this round, and, as it turned out, in any further attempt to make a firm stand or any other serious consideration of confrontation with the Libyan government, or any other OPEC member country. During those days in September 1970, the war was won and lost, though fighting would continue for a while longer.

On 28 September, Exxon and BP announced increases in their posted prices of Libyan crudes of $0.30/B., effective 1 September. The two companies also announced increases in their postings for crude f.o.b. Eastern Mediterranean ports.

On 30 September, Texaco and Chevron announced they had reached a settlement with the Libyan government providing for an increase of $0.30/B. in its posted price and an increase from 50 to 55 percent in its income tax rate, again in lieu of retroactivity.

By mid-October, all the companies operating in Libya had agreed to increase their posted prices by $0.30/B., with small further increases each year to 1975. In addition, varying increased tax rates were agreed in lieu of retroactivity: Occidental 58 percent; Mobil/Gelsenberg 55.5 percent; Exxon, Texaco, Chevron, BP, Bunker Hunt and Atlantic/Richfield 55 percent; Continental, Marathon, Amerada-Hess and Grace 54 percent. Shell finally agreed on October 16 and the remaining minor companies (ELF-Aquitaine, Hispanoil and Murphy) fell into line, but Phillips relinquished its concessions.

Except for most of Occidental's reductions, however, the production cuts were not restored when the companies agreed to Libya's demands. The cuts only served to demonstrate Libya's determination to act and to make credible the threats to nationalize if compliance was not forthcoming. By effecting a considerable reduction in the availability of short-haul crude, they also served to strengthen prices considerably.

In the space of a few months, Libya had achieved considerably more than OPEC had in over five years. Indeed, the other OPEC members sat by watching incredulously as Libya and Algeria made all the running. The Shah, upstaged by a 28-year old Arab army captain (as Qadhafi had been till he promoted himself to colonel), could barely bring himself to utter the man's name.

Exxon paid dearly for its reckless initial posting of Zelten (now renamed Brega) crude well below parity with Eastern Mediterranean crudes—in the arm's-length market, Brega sold for around $0.25/B. more than the lower-quality Kirkuk—and the other companies paid equally dearly for following Exxon's example. Even when Exxon caved in and gave way on the posted price, it made a weak, almost ridiculous, pretense of increasing its price without reference to the government, as though cutting a deal with the government would have established some kind of undesirable precedent. By then, nothing could have mattered less. Nor did the companies get a sympathetic hearing at the US State Department, since James Akins, head of its Office of Fuels and Energy, told the Church Committee's MNC Hearings that he had thought the Libyan initial demand for an increase of over $0.40/B. in the postings was about right, and he stated that he had shown his department's calculations to executives of most of the companies operating in Libya without encountering any serious dissent.

Meanwhile, in Algeria, the government nationalized the Algerian producing interests of Shell, Phillips, Elwerath and Ausonia Mineraria on 15 June. The four companies accounted for approximately 100 kbd of crude production between them. All four had been placed under government sequestration in 1967. Then, in July, the government unilaterally set the tax-reference price applicable to French oil companies at $2.85/B., up from $2.08/B. Subsequently, it was agreed that talks with France would be renewed on the revision of the 1965 agreement and a range of other issues.

On 27 October 1970, the Iraq News Agency announced that the IPC group had raised its posted prices f.o.b. Banias and Tripoli by $0.20/B. effective 1 September 1970, that an additional $0.06/B. on exports of oil from the Northern fields via Eastern Mediterranean ports would be paid as, in effect, part of royalty-expensing, and an additional $0.07/B. on exports from the Southern fields for the same concept, effective 1 January 1971; and that there would be a large increase (about 330 kbd) in production during 1971. However, the government's claims for retroactivity on royalty-expensing, and the companies' claims on the concession areas taken from them under Law 80 remained unsettled.

Income Taxes Increased to 55 Percent

The major oil companies, whose main interests lay after all in the Gulf, were now in an extremely difficult position. They could argue, with some justification, that the posted price increase in Libya was only, or mainly, intended to represent the freight advantage over the Gulf that came with higher freight rates, particularly after the closing of Tapline; but then that did not explain the increase in income tax rates that was supposed to be in lieu of retro-activity on Libya's claim that prices had been under-posted from the beginning. Even less did it explain the reason why such increased rates should be permanent. It was simply an inconsistent mess. Logically, the only way the companies could now resist a demand for increased payments in the Gulf would have been to make a lump sum payment to Libya for retroactivity, admit that the increase in postings was due to prior under-posting, plus a temporary element of freight advantage. But it probably would not have mattered much: logic now had little to do with it. The Gulf producers had seen the results of strong-arm methods applied to the majors and had drawn the obvious conclusions. Besides, the markets were strong; product prices had risen substantially, particularly in Europe, without any corresponding increase in crude prices, and the companies were thought to be reaping windfall profits. So the fat was in the fire, the floodgates breached, the dam burst and the Shah unstoppable. The "avalanche of fresh demands" that Shell's chairman David

Barran had predicted when the companies had been trying to get their act together the previous month had come without a pause for breath.

The Shah demanded an immediate increase in the income tax rate to 55 percent and an increase in posted prices, threatening to nationalize part of the consortium's proven acreage if he did not get his way. On 14 November, the Iranian Consortium agreed to an increase in the income tax rate in Iran from 50 to 55 percent, and to an increase in the price of Iranian Heavy crude from $1.63 to $1.72/B., both effective 14 November. For the time being, however, the posted price of light crudes was left unchanged. Similar terms for Kuwait were announced on 24 November. Elsewhere in the Gulf, the OPEC member countries' position was that the income taxes should be raised to 55 percent, and that light crude prices should also be increased substantially.

On 7 December 1970, Venezuela increased income taxes on the oil companies from a graduated rate rising to 52 percent, up to a flat rate of 60 percent effective 1 January 1970. The law, which was ratified on 17 December, also provided for the unilateral establishment of tax-reference prices by the government.

The market was still very tight, with spot prices exceeding even the new postings in the Mediterranean. Freight rates remained high. The companies were clearly in disarray and there were no signs of resistance from the United States or other consuming countries. So far, OPEC member countries had taken no collective action, apart from some cooperative efforts between Algeria and Libya, and consultations with Iraq and Saudi Arabia. The organization now took the bit between its teeth.

OPEC's Twenty-first Conference, held in Caracas from 9 to 12 December 1970, adopted a resolution incorporating several objectives: to establish a minimum 55 percent income tax rate in all countries; to establish a general increase in posted/tax-reference prices in all member countries; to eliminate the remaining OPEC allowances (royalty-expensing and marketing) provided for in the January 1968 agreement with the companies; to eliminate existing disparities between posted/tax-reference prices on the basis of the highest price existing in member countries; and to modify the existing gravity differential system from $0.02 to $0.015/°API from a 40 °API crude downwards. The Conference also appointed a special committee of the representatives of Iran, Iraq and Saudi Arabia to negotiate these demands on behalf of all Gulf countries, with negotiations to begin in Tehran within 31 days of the end of the Conference, and to convene an extraordinary meeting of the Conference to consider the results of such negotiations. It was also envisaged that a second negotiating group would cover short-haul crudes, the group to be comprised of Algeria, Libya, Iraq and Saudi Arabia. A third group—Indonesia and Venezuela—was also provided for, though exactly what they were to negotiate was not clear. For the companies, it was an inauspicious prelude to the New Year; for OPEC, a new dawn.

At this point, on 29 December, Saudi Arabia rather slyly slipped one in by legislating by Royal Ordinance the 5 percent increase in the income tax rate that had been offered by the companies in November, when it had been agreed in Iran. Ostensibly, this followed the pattern originally set when 50/50 was introduced in 1951: at that time, the companies had arranged that they would "submit" to the new tax. This time, they were not asked to "submit", and there is no public record of them having explicitly done so. A point was presumably being made by the Saudi government about unilateral legislation. But it was no time to quibble.

Libya Demands 60 Percent

Success had no doubt gone to Libya's head, and the government could not wait for the Gulf countries to act. On 3 January, the deputy prime minister, Major Abdessallem Jallud, called in the company representatives and notified them of Libya's demand for a 5 percent increase in the income tax rate, a further increase of $0.69 in the posted price as a short-haul premium, as per one of the Caracas OPEC Resolutions, of which $0.39 would be permanent and retroactive to the closure of the Suez Canal in June 1967, and the remainder temporary. (The Libyan government claimed that the $0.30 adjustment in postings was entirely due to the previous underposting of Libyan crude as compared with Eastern Mediterranean postings, and consisted of $0.10 freight and $0.20 low-sulfur premium.) In addition, adjustments would have to be made to take into account any adjustments in payments to Gulf countries as a result of the negotiations stemming from the OPEC Caracas Conference Resolution XXII.120. Finally, Libya demanded reinvestment in the country of $0.25/B. of all oil produced by the companies.

Given the premises, the tax increase demand was of course perfectly justified: the income tax increases on the companies in September and October had been agreed with the companies to be in lieu of retroactivity for the underpostings (and the companies had rashly signed official papers to that effect); but the tax increases in the Gulf had no such justification. The re-establishment of tax parity obviously required another 5 percent increase in the Libyan tax rate.

Some demand had been expected by the companies, though perhaps not quite as quickly as it came, and certainly not as large. The companies immediately dubbed it "leap-frogging", but the demand for a further increase in the income tax rate at least was the logical outcome of their own short-sightedness in disguising retroactivity as an income tax (which, incidentally, helped them with their home country taxes), and then agreeing to an unrelated tax increase in Iran and the rest of the Gulf. As for the $0.69/B. premium, it was certainly debatable, particularly in the light of current substantial sales in the spot market at well above posted price. (The Libyan government was selling over 200 kbd royalty oil in the spot market at well above the posted price.)

On 10 January 1971, Abu Dhabi Petroleum Company (ADPC) and Abu Dhabi Marine Areas (ADMA) agreed to an increase in the income tax rate to 55 percent effective 14 November 1970. Aramco parent companies raised the posted prices of Arabian Medium and Arabian Heavy crudes f.o.b. Ras Tanura by $0.09/B.

In the wake of OPEC's Caracas Conference and the new Libyan demands, the companies were freshly imbued with a sense of urgency and the desperate need to dam the cascade of demands that threatened to swamp them, alternating between the Gulf and the Mediterranean exporters.

They were, however, hamstrung, partly by the fear of antitrust action, partly by their inexperience in putting together a coalition that included independents with markedly different interests from those of the majors, and partly, perhaps mainly, by the lack of vigorous support from the US , British and European governments. With the exception of the Netherlands, the Europeans didn't want to know; all they wanted was for the companies to settle on terms that were reasonably affordable. The British and Dutch didn't feel that they could move without the rest of the Europeans. The Americans, who could have done something about it, with or without the Europeans, likewise did not want confrontation, especially with the Shah, and their support of the companies went only so far as to urge "moderation" on OPEC.

Nevertheless, the companies managed to put together a coalition of sorts, and even obtained the blessing of the US Justice Department (which in effect gave them antitrust clearance in a Business Review Letter), and the State Department. In all this, John J. McCloy, an eminent lawyer firmly wired into successive Washington Administrations and retained by most of the top oil companies, was instrumental. A group had been set up under his chairmanship in 1962, with the knowledge and consent of the Justice Department's Antitrust Division, initially to face the threat of the Soviet Union's oil offensive (seen as partly politically motivated) but soon to transfer its attention to oil in the Middle East and OPEC. Under his guidance, the companies devised a strategy of sorts—they would put up a united front to negotiate only with the whole of OPEC, Gulf and Mediterranean producers/exporters together, to reach a leapfrog-proof agreement of some duration. A group of top executives from sixteen companies, all of the seven majors plus CFP and eight independents, was formed—the so-called London Policy Group—to meet in London and help guide the negotiations that were to take place in Tehran. In addition to the seven majors and CFP, Marathon, Continental, Nelson Bunker Hunt, Occidental, Amerada-Hess, Atlantic-Richfield, Grace Petroleum and Gelsenberg signed up. Others that associated themselves later with the Message to OPEC (see below) were Petrofina, Elwerath, Hispanoil and the Japanese company, Arabian Oil Company (AOC). Elf/ERAP, the French state oil company, and ENI, the Italian State oil company, both declined. A Safety Net agreement was set up providing for the sale by all the other companies of crude oil at tax-paid cost to any company singled out for mistreatment by the Libyan government.

A Message to OPEC

The companies then went on to draw up a Message to OPEC, setting out, in a letter that was delivered to OPEC and all of its member countries on 16 January 1971, the framework for a simultaneous settlement of the OPEC claims with all member countries. In other words, what the companies wanted was a single negotiation leading up to a simultaneous settlement with all OPEC member countries on terms that were designed to represent fiscal parity for each country, a concept that of course took into account differences in geographical location (which gave rise to freight differentials) and differences in crude quality, both of which were normally reflected in the postings. The companies seem to have simply brushed aside, without a passing reference, the framework for regional negotiations, set up by the Caracas Conference. They did not in fact have, and were not entitled to, any say in the matter. The legal relationship between governments and companies was embodied in the concession agreements, and neither party had any obligation to negotiate except directly, and singly, with each other. In OPEC's early days, the companies had insisted on such separate negotiations in order to avoid contributing to OPEC cohesion, but, in practice, the Consortium's negotiations in Iran (where all the major companies and some others were represented) meant that anything agreed in Iran would have to be conceded to other countries—though this could not extend to agreements on offtake volumes. However, collective negotiations did not now suit OPEC member countries; but regional ones did. If pushed, they could insist on country-by-country negotiations, so the companies had no leverage they could use to insist on a single overall negotiation. This was one of the reasons they tried to enlist State Department help. The Algerians and the Libyans, however, always insisted on company-by-company talks in their own countries, where the concessions were held individually by companies, or small partnerships of companies.

The substance of the companies' proposals provided for (a) an (unspecified) revision of crude oil prices in all member countries, to be adjusted annually in accordance with worldwide inflation; and (b) a further, temporary freight rate adjustment for Libyan and other short-haul crudes. The settlement would be for a five year period, after which it would be open to review. But there would be no further increase in income tax rates above the then current levels, no retroactive payments to be made and no obligatory reinvestment.

But it was a plan without a strategy, without alternative scenarios, without fall-back positions, and without the recognition of new realities. How could it have been anything else? It was put together under extreme pressure of time among a disparate group of companies, some of which had no experience of dealing with each other, and it was highly expedient if not absolutely necessary for it to be cleared with the US State Department and the British and Dutch governments. Indeed, a team of company officials (J. Addison of the Consortium, Elliot Cattarulla of Exxon, and John Sutcliffe of BP) went to Tehran on January 13 essentially to gain a few days' time; after preliminary talks, it became clear that they were not empowered to negotiate and the talks were broken off.

The companies did, however, discuss the upcoming negotiations and their plan with the State Department, and it was agreed, they thought, that a State Department representative would visit key countries in the Middle East (Iran, Kuwait and Saudi Arabia) to urge moderation in their price demands and to press the case for a single, OPEC-wide negotiation. Accordingly, on 16 January, Under Secretary of State John N. Irwin and James Akins, Director of the Office of Fuels and Energy, were dispatched by Secretary of State William Rogers to Iran, Kuwait and Saudi Arabia. He reported back to the White House on 25 January. The objectives of the mission, as Irwin understood it, were "(a) to prevent an imminent impasse in discussions between the oil-producing countries and oil companies from resulting in an interruption of oil supplies; (b) to explain the reasons why the US government had taken steps to make it possible under American antitrust laws for the oil companies to negotiate jointly; and (c) to seek assurances from the Gulf producers to continue to supply oil at reasonable prices to the free world."[7].

Irwin got assurances on moderation (no numbers were mentioned), but he and Ambassador to Iran Douglas MacArthur II were easily convinced by the Shah not to support OPEC-wide negotiations where Iran and the moderates in OPEC would, according to the Shah, be dragged into immoderate demands by the OPEC hawks. As a result, Iran would have to impose "Venezuelan conditions", meaning a much more onerous 16.7 percent royalty, plus 60 percent income tax on posted prices fixed by the government. Later, in the MNC hearings, Irwin was to stress that his real mission had been to deflect any possibility that oil supplies would be cut off[8].

The Tehran Agreement, February 1971

By the time the top company negotiating team (headed up by BP's Lord Strathalmond and Exxon's George Piercy) arrived in Iran, it was to find that they had been cut off at the knees by Irwin, or so they thought, and the Under Secretary of State was telling them, the companies, that they "would be well-advised" to negotiate separately with the Gulf producers, and conduct parallel negotiations with Libya. But in fact the idea of a single, OPEC-wide negotiation was a non-starter anyway; on this score, the Irwin mission would have made no difference, because the Persian Gulf bloc would have probably, and the Libyans certainly, refused the collective negotiations; but it must nevertheless have been demoralizing for the company negotiators to find that they could not count on their own government for support, even on an important procedural issue. They must surely have concluded that when the chips were down, and if they tried to resist, their own governments would have pushed them into an agreement (just about any agreement) rather than risk a closing-down of supplies from the Gulf. The real damage that the Irwin mission did was to make this plain to the OPEC governments.

On 24 January 1971, the Shah warned the companies that they must reach a *regional* price agreement with the Gulf countries. Within a few days, the companies complied and talks started in earnest between the company representatives and the Gulf countries, represented by the Iranian Finance Minister, Jamshid Amuzegar, the Saudi Oil Minister Sheikh Ahmed Zaki Yamani and the Iraqi Oil Minister Sa'adun Hamadi. The company team was split in two, and one group left Tehran for Tripoli where it was to undertake "separate though necessarily connected" talks with the Libyan government. To no avail: the Libyans refused to discuss anything with the companies until the Tehran talks had been concluded.

On 29 January, Tapline was repaired and the oil flow resumed to the Eastern Mediterranean. Syria's transit fees were almost doubled, but it was too late to affect the negotiations.

OPEC's Twenty-second Conference, meeting in Tehran on 11 February, resolved that the six Gulf member countries would issue legislation by 15 February to put their minimum terms for higher oil prices into effect if the companies did not indicate their willingness to meet those terms by that date. The Conference also threatened to embargo shipments for any company that did not comply with the legislative measures within seven days of coming into effect, though later, Yamani said that if OPEC member countries were obliged to embargo oil deliveries to the companies, consuming nations would still be able to maintain their oil supplies provided they bought the oil directly from the national oil companies at the new price.

Within a few days, it was all over and on 14 February 1971, the OPEC Gulf member countries signed a five-year agreement, the Tehran Agreement, with the oil companies which provided for (a) an increase of $0.35/B. in the posted prices of Gulf crudes; (b) the elimination of the OPEC allowances agreed in January 1968, effective 1 January 1971; (c) an annual increase of $0.05/B. in the postings and a further annual increase of 2.5 percent to compensate for inflation and the fall in the purchasing power of the dollar; and (d) guarantees for the companies against "leap-frogging" in financial terms or embargo action. The increase in income tax rates to 55 percent was already in effect in Iran and the other Gulf countries, and so was not an issue.

The effect of the Tehran Agreement on government oil revenues in the Gulf member countries was an increase of approximately $0.35 to $0.40/B., depending on the type of crude, and averaging about $0.38/B. This included the effect (about $0.10/B.) of the income tax increases from 50 percent to 55 percent, put into effect first in Iran in November 1970 and other countries shortly thereafter. The increases were promptly passed on to the consumer, through the companies, in the form of crude and product price increases.

In March, as a consequence of the Tehran agreement, Venezuela raised its tax-reference prices by an average of about $0.58/B. The increase in its revenue per barrel was about $0.60/B., including the income tax increase of 1970.

The Tripoli Agreement, April 1971

The rest followed quickly. Libya soon made it clear that it intended to do better than the Gulf countries, and talks with the companies began again amid an atmosphere of threats of closure and nationalization. On 23 February 1971, oil ministers from four OPEC member countries—Algeria, Iraq, Libya and Saudi Arabia—met in Tripoli and delegated Libya to negotiate on prices on their behalf. Along the way, on 24 February, Algerian President Boumedienne announced that Algeria would take over a majority holding of 51 percent in all French oil interests in Algeria and would nationalize all hydrocarbon transportation and gas resources. On 15 March, the four ministers met again in Tripoli, agreed on minimum postings to be demanded and threatened that "the flow of [oil] will be halted if the companies fail to agree to and apply such minimum prices by a date to be fixed by the Libyan Government".

After various company offers had been rejected and a compromise reached, the talks in Libya ended on 2 April, when the government and the oil companies reached a five-year agreement (the Tripoli Agreement), effective 20 March 1971, providing for (a) an increase of $0.90/B., to $3.45/B., in the posted price of 40°API crude f.o.b. Libyan ports, of which $0.25 were temporary freight and Suez Canal closure premiums; (b) an annual increase of $0.05/B. in the postings and a further annual increase of 2.5 percent to compensate for inflation and the fall in the purchasing power of the dollar; (c) a rise in the income tax rate generally to 55 percent and the payment of a surcharge in lieu of retroactivity (meaning that the previous increases in income tax rates which had been in lieu of retroactivity were rescinded and replaced by lump-sum or other forms of payment); and (d) a general commitment by the companies to maintain certain levels of exploration expenditure. The total increase in revenue to Libya was about $0.90/B., including the increases of August-September 1970. Algeria benefited by a similar amount, and Nigeria by about $0.79/B.

During the next three months, from April to June 1971, there was a rapid-fire succession of related developments:

Algeria raised its tax-reference price to $3.60/B. and fixed compensation of the nationalized companies at $100 million. It also introduced OPEC fiscal terms (12.5 percent expensed royalty and 55 percent income tax), then unilaterally set new tax-reference prices, with partly retroactive effect, for the period 1969-75. And its state oil company, Sonatrach, and CFP reached an agreement settling the terms for CFP's oil operations in Algeria over a ten-year period.

Libya issued a Law on the conservation of petroleum and hydrocarbon resources, to make sure that there would be no question in the future as to its applicability to the companies. But it lifted the ban on LNG exports to Italy following a price agreement for Exxon's gas exports.

Nigeria, not yet a member of OPEC, signed an agreement with the operating companies along the lines of the Tripoli Agreement.

Iraq and the IPC group reached agreement on posted prices f.o.b. the Eastern Mediterranean ports of Banias and Tripoli. The agreement provided for (a) an increase of $0.801/B. in the posted price, to $3.211/B., including a variable Suez element; (b) an annual increase of $0.05/B. in the postings and a further annual increase of 2.5 percent to compensate for inflation and the fall in the purchasing power of the dollar; (c) a lump-sum payment in settlement of financial issues outstanding since 1955; (d) an increase in production; (e) the elimination of the OPEC allowances agreed in January 1968, effective 1 January 1971; and (f) an increase in the income tax rate to 55 percent, effective 14 November 1970.

Saudi Arabia and Aramco agreed to an increase of $0.811/B. in the posted price of Arabian Light crude, to $3.181/B. f.o.b. Sidon, effective 20 March 1971. This price also included a variable Suez element.

Everything had changed: the companies were in effect simply doing as they were told, agreeing to just about anything for the sake of peace and not questioning the validity of new legislation.

But What Did the Agreements Mean?

At the time, there was a tremendous hullabaloo in the press over the events leading up to the Tehran Agreement. Belligerent statements of the Shah and OPEC ministers were duly reported in the press, and alarm spread about the possibility of a general cutting off of supplies from the Middle East. The naturally more measured statements of the companies were also reported and commented on, mostly favorably by the American and European press. There was too, for those aware of it, an air of melodrama about the London Policy Group, high-ranking executives from the seven largest oil companies in the world, plus another nine internationals, sitting in an improvised war room in

BP's London headquarters and guiding fateful negotiations with Middle Eastern potentates in Tehran and Tripoli.

The international oil companies, and the industry generally, were shaken to the core. OPEC member countries were jubilant. And, for the first time since the Iranian nationalization of 1951, the governments of major consuming countries became concerned about the industry's operations in the principal exporting countries. Their concern was primarily focused on the Libyan cutbacks and, more importantly, on the threats coming from the Middle East to shut down all production if the companies did not comply with their demands. These threats were perhaps not intended seriously, but they were certainly taken seriously in some quarters. Indeed, according to Irwin's testimony in the MNC Hearings, the prime concern of the United States in sending him in, January 1971, on a visit to three "friendly" countries in the Middle East—Iran, Kuwait and Saudi Arabia—was to discourage plans to close down all production in member countries in the event of non-compliance by the companies (an apparently retrospective thought, since this was not a concern expressed at the time). Apart from that, no government took any concrete measure.

And there was some reason for that. As it turned out, the world economy was not seriously affected, and economic growth (GDP) in the OECD Area in real terms was above 3 percent in 1970 and 1971. Nor were the companies' profits seriously affected: net after-tax earnings of the seven majors rose in 1970 by 1 percent over 1969, then shot up in 1971 by another 11 percent. True, per barrel oil revenues of OPEC member governments rose by about 40 percent in Gulf countries (more in the Mediterranean), but this should be seen in the context of no significant increase since the 1950s.

Nor was there any sign of demand dropping off as a result of the higher prices: OPEC production rose 8 percent in 1971 over 1970, 7 percent in 1972 and then a startling 15 percent in 1973.

Financially, the whole thing had been a storm in a teacup. The US administration and the European governments could now relax; the issue had been settled for five years, and the cost was not inordinate. After all, the Gulf producers had gained 38 cents per barrel in additional tax revenues, and the price of oil, which had been around \$1.30/B in 1969, would now rise, if the tax increase was passed through in its entirety, to about \$1.70/B., which was slightly below where it had been in the mid-1950s—in nominal terms—in real terms, considerably less. It was also still far below the domestic price of crude in the United States, where a major crude such as West Texas Sour was selling for \$3.27/B. at the wellhead during the first half of 1971.

But if the financial impact of the Tehran and Tripoli agreements was relatively small on prices and company profits, the psychological impact on the industry and on OPEC governments was enormous; it was much less, but still noteworthy, on the governments of OECD countries. This was the first time that the companies had yielded promptly to a major demand from any producing country on an important fiscal question. It was also the first time that the governments had jointly made threats that were taken seriously about cutting off production. In Libya, the resistance lasted a few months; in the Gulf, a few weeks. Clearly, it paid to talk loudly and carry a big stick.

The companies, to their dismay, and the OPEC governments, to their delight, realized that the companies' home governments would not give them effective support in disputes of this kind, even though the companies were negotiating pretty much under the gun. From a strictly legal standpoint, it is not unequivocally clear that the concession agreements in force at the time were breached: the production cutbacks ordered in Libya were made ostensibly for conservation reasons and in accordance with a Libyan regulation, the validity of which was questioned by the companies but not tested in the courts. The Libyan government made it plain that it would not submit to arbitration, which would have been a breach of the concession agreement—but in the event none of the companies formally requested arbitration, and arbitration could have gone ahead with or without Libya's consent (and in fact did so after the Libyan nationalization of BP in 1972). The Libyan government also threatened nationalization, but that in itself was not a breach of the concession agreement. It should also be remarked that the production cuts ordered by Libya for conservation reasons were never restored, except for one part of Occidental's, so it can scarcely be argued that the cuts were entirely bogus and merely a means of exerting pressure on the companies.

Nor were the concession agreements in the Gulf breached, though Gulf member countries did in fact threaten an embargo, which most certainly would have been a breach. But it never came to that.

In any event, the support of the home governments was not conditioned on the legal technicalities. Politically, the United States and Britain (and other European governments) wanted a settlement, not a confrontation, whether on legal grounds or not. Nor was it necessary for there to have been a flagrant violation of the agreements for them to have given the companies vigorous support if they had been so minded. But they weren't and they didn't, and that left the companies without much recourse except to make as good a deal as they could in the circumstances. However, perhaps the most damaging aspect of the agreements from the company and consumer country point of view was the companies' commitment to raise tax payments by small but not insignificant increments every year over the following five years. This time, the companies did not even hint that the market might put a constraint on what they could pay in additional taxes, as they had so stoutly maintained on previous occasions; it was simply taken for granted that they would be able to pass the increased costs on to the consumer, and indeed they did, and said openly that they would have to. Contracts were renegotiated to provide for this kind of tax increase to be passed through to the buyer. In other words, tax increases of this sort of magnitude had little, and possibly no, effect on supplies from elsewhere, or on demand.   So, if the companies could demonstrably promise annual increases of specific amounts over a five-year period, producing governments naturally began to wonder, though without any great urgency at this point, precisely where the limits were to the companies' ability to pass through increased tax payments to the consumer.

All Change!

To repeat, one has to ask the question: How was it possible that the producing countries in OPEC could do so easily and rapidly during the few years that followed 1969 what they had been unable to make an inch of progress towards during the previous ten years—namely push taxes and prices sharply up?

On the surface of it, the companies were forced into it by the selective squeezing the Libyans engaged in, combined with a temporary shortage of short-haul crude in the Mediterranean during 1970. This was indeed the immediate and proximate cause of the first price hike ever engineered by an OPEC member country. But the price increase might not have been possible and certainly would not have stuck if it had been resolutely opposed—as it surely would have been only a few years earlier.

The year 1970 marked the beginning of serious conflict on a broad front between the governments of the principal oil-exporting countries and the major oil companies. The succession of power-plays, squeezes, tactical and strategic calculations and miscalculations on all sides, confused and confusing policies, agreements made and almost immediately renegotiated or broken, is all fascinating stuff, and has been told and retold in various versions, colorful and not so, with no doubt differing degrees of accuracy, bias and relish.

But the wretchedly weak bargaining position of the companies is not the whole explanation, not by a long mark. For despite this, the companies had, on paper, an impregnably strong legal position. They were under no legal compulsion to agree to *any* increase in tax payments, in Libya or anywhere else in the OPEC area (except Venezuela). Legally, they would have been fully within their rights to dig their heels in and refuse even to negotiate seriously. Indeed, the chairman of Shell, David Barran and the chairman of BP, Eric Drake, had advocated forming a common front to oppose the demands of the Libyans, but the US companies did not have the stomach for it and the British could not do it alone. So they chose not to stand on their rights, not to go to arbitration to settle any disputes with the governments, not to stall and play for time, but to negotiate—with the weakest of hands.

Why?

Everything had changed, and I doubt if the companies could have done otherwise. They had become the conduit for a large and essential part of the world's energy supplies and they could not possibly have coped with a show-down with OPEC governments without firm support from public opinion in the major consuming countries. They didn't have it and certainly wouldn't get it. Not even their own governments were disposed to countenance a confrontation. It was a far cry from Iran in 1951. Moreover, they were facing, or so they thought, a growth in demand that would, over the next decade and more, require the development of massive new producing capacity in the Middle East: they *had* to have a settlement, a new deal, that would allow them to get on with the job.

In the Middle East, the political situation had changed radically from the days when Iran could be confronted and eventually forced to back down. It was no longer possible for the major companies to stand on their rights and insist that their concessionary contracts be carried out to the letter. It was not a conflict they could win.

These circumstances—the economic importance of oil to the industrialized world, the key role the Middle East would have in satisfying the still-burgeoning demand for oil, and the political environment—are enough of an explanation.

But in fact there was much more. There was a realignment of interests: low prices were no longer so clearly in the long-term interests of the consumer.

The Importance of Oil in the World's Economies

Sometime during the period following the end of the Second World War, two fundamental changes in the nature of the international petroleum industry occurred. Rather like the incoming tide, slow and barely perceptible from moment to moment, they affected different parts of the industry at different times, but covered them all in the end.

First, the development and growth of the world economy became vitally dependent on imported oil rather than domestically produced coal. Oil became much more than a minor fuel confined largely to the smallish number of motorists and motorized transport existing outside the United States; now it was an essential industrial fuel, displacing coal on the railways, in industry and the generation of electricity, in a process that was irreversible in the short or even medium term. The consuming countries wanted assured supplies of oil at "reasonable" (i.e., low) prices, and said so. But the emphasis was on "assured" not price. Within limits, price, largely determined by the level of tax payments, was secondary. At every stage, accommodation (i.e., higher taxes) with the producing governments seemed preferable to confrontation, and this was true from the beginnings of 50/50 in 1948 in Venezuela (following the traumatic nationalization of the industry in Mexico in 1938). Indeed, we have seen in Chapter 1 how the United States helped engineer the introduction of 50/50 in Venezuela, in Saudi Arabia in 1950 and in the rest of the Middle East.

Second, in the major producing countries, oil revenues were no longer simply an agreeable and effort-free supplement to the income of the national treasury and the pockets of the countries' rulers, but became the engine of economic development and reform in Venezuela, Iran and Iraq, as well as the life-blood of the super-welfare states of Kuwait and Saudi Arabia. The producers wanted "control" over their producing industry, with assured markets for their oil at "reasonable" (i.e., high) prices. The governments could no longer tolerate a situation where the price and volume of their oil exports (and therefore their revenues) were determined arbitrarily by foreign oil companies with conflicting interests.

And all the companies wanted was a "reasonable" (i.e., high) return on their investments—a goal not necessarily incompatible with the aims of either the consuming countries or the producing countries.

The critical interests in the international oil industry that thus developed—critical for the consumer and critical for the producer—were much too important to pretend that they could be adequately encompassed by the simple commercial instruments that were the concession agreements, however appropriate these might be to more run-of-the-mill situations. But in the absence of a reasonably competitive market, the concession agreements, which only defined the rights and obligations of the producing companies, could not possibly accommodate the conflicting goals of consumer and producer . The companies were mere middle-men and hence they would, as circumstances dictated, primarily serve either the interests of one or the other. It was no use tinkering with the concession agreements.

The Political Environment

At the same time, a number of critical political developments and considerations had a substantial impact on the attitudes and actions of OPEC member countries in the Middle East and the Mediterranean.

The United States and Iran

In 1970, Britain announced that it would withdraw from the Middle East by the end of 1971. The United States could not, of course, take its place in any formal sense, but it found, or thought it had found, a good surrogate policeman for the Gulf in the shape of Iran. The Shah could have asked for no better present. He owed his throne to US action in 1953; now the United States would lean heavily on Iran as a good ally in the Middle East, a stalwart opponent of the Soviet Union and relatively friendly toward Israel. The Shah, who cultivated his relations with the United States assiduously, could now be confident that the United States would not want to antagonize him over a few cents per barrel and which, in any case, Europe and Japan would pay most of.

Indeed, the United States encouraged Iran to seek more revenue per barrel (which would have to be reflected in higher prices), both before and after the Tehran and Tripoli agreements because this was the easiest and politically best way to get the money to the Iranian government that was needed for the purchase of the arms necessary for Iran to play its assigned role. The Nixon Administration did not have to go to Congress to get the money, and the Japanese and Europeans would end up paying most of the cost, since they were the largest purchasers of Middle East oil. The Irwin mission left a clear impression with the Shah that, provided the proposed price (tax) increases were reasonable, price was not an issue.

Arab Frustration

Following the Six-Day War in 1967, the Arab-Israeli confrontation appeared to be stalemated. Nothing seemed to be moving, and as time wore on, Arab opinion, already simmering, threatened to boil over in frustration and resentment, much of it directed at the United States because of its consistently strong support for Israel. There were persistent calls for nationalization of the US companies. (Indeed, this was the genesis of Yamani's call for "participation", intended as a substitute for nationalization.) There were also intermittent calls for the use of the "oil weapon", meaning embargo. It was not possible in these circumstances for even the most moderate, or pro-American Arab country to stand aside. King Faisal's strong stance against the companies, in early 1971 and later, particularly on participation, reflected this situation.

The United States: A Reluctant Player

In the United States, energy was predominantly a domestic policy issue, not one of foreign policy. At the time, the key political question as far as oil was concerned, was how to deal with imports—i.e., how to reconcile the interests of the domestic (high-cost) producers with the interests of the consumer in low prices (attainable only through low-cost imports). But the United States did have a longer history of foreign policy involvement in energy, and it was deeply influenced by the trauma of the Mexican nationalization of US oil interests in 1938. Thereafter, the United States in practice tended to encourage the companies to accede to whatever demands the producing country might put on them for increased revenue—quickly if necessary, slowly if possible—provided of course that the demands could be accommodated within a reasonable consensual framework. Nobody in the US government or in US politics, not even the State Department, wanted to appear to be on chummy terms with the big international oil companies, which should just be told to get along somehow with the host governments and do their job of producing oil.

The State Department saw US interests in the Middle East as primarily strategic, meaning that it wanted US control over, or at least access to, the countries' oil resources, through the American and other oil companies from the OECD area. Support for Israel, viewed to a large extent as inevitable (given the widespread sympathy for Israel in the United States and the large and influential Jewish population in certain parts of the country), should therefore be as limited as politically possible. Otherwise, it was argued, the US companies would be swept away in the Arab countries, and US control and access with them.

It was the swan-song of this particular strand of thought in successive US administrations that, to put it at its most extreme, saw oil as by far the most important US interest in the Middle East, and Israel as an unfortunate and disruptive influence that threatened it. On this issue, in 1948, when Israel was about to declare itself an independent state and the United States had to decide whether to recognize and support it, Secretary of State George C. Marshall very nearly resigned. As it turned out, those who saw the inevitable Arab-Israel conflict as a menace that would lead to the ejection of US companies from Arab countries were right, and, as it turned out, it didn't much matter: "control" had always been a chimera (exclusion of the Soviets from the Middle East was the real and important goal), and as for "access", US interests were and are probably better served by having the US companies as independent buyers rather than hostage investors.

In the specific case of the events leading up to the Tehran and Tripoli agreements, the United States appears to have played no significant part at all except for the messy Irwin mission. The State Department was not formally asked by the companies to support them in their negotiations with the Libyan government in 1970, and did not protest the Libyan government's orders to different companies at different times to reduce production. On the question of prices, the State Department, in the person of Akins, was positively sympathetic to Libya. This would change shortly after the Agreements, and State Department policy would veer first in the direction of supporting further price hikes, then, in the run-up to October 1973 and the Yom Kippur War, in favor of restraining OPEC from excessive increases.

In considering the United States' relative lack of interest at this time in the negotiations between oil companies and host governments, it must be added in all fairness that the administration was preoccupied at the time with matters much weightier (such as extricating itself from Vietnam without loss of too much face) than a squabble over taxes between oil companies and a small desert country in North Africa. Besides, while perhaps the Gulf countries needed to be told to cool it a bit (the function of the Irwin mission), they nevertheless had to be kept sweet, especially Iran and Saudi Arabia.

The Climate of World Opinion

After Suez in 1956-57, it was clear that world opinion would no longer put up with gun-boat diplomacy, or even the kind of tactics to which Iran had been subjected after the 1951 nationalization. There was no longer any question of being able to use physical force in a dispute that was essentially between a foreign private investor, no matter how large, and the government of a country that was mistreating it. At best (or worst), measures would have to be restrained and confined to diplomatic pressures and, if pushed, graduated economic reprisals.

A Realignment of Interests

Apart from the various influences described above that were shaping the actions of the main players, something else very important was happening. Throughout the 1950s and most of the 1960s, everyone except the governments of the net exporting countries had a clear and unambiguous interest in low crude oil prices. Even in the United States, with a high-cost domestic industry to protect, no one wished to donate the difference between cheap imports and high domestic prices (propped up by restricted production and import controls) to the foreign producers; it was, instead, divvied up among domestic US refiners.

All of this was due to change. There were important reasons why the higher prices that were to result from the Tehran/Tripoli agreements should not be entirely unwelcome to the industry and to the governments of the major consuming countries.

Import Dependence

In Western Europe, the coal industry was being wiped out by imported oil and dependence on the Middle East was growing; in the United States, domestic producers were unable to keep pace with growing demand, and despite import controls, dependence on imports was also growing rapidly. There were intermittent calls, notably from the European Economic Community (EEC) as the European Union was then known, for the diversification of supply sources, but this went little further than wishful thinking. As previously noted, Spain set up a State-owned oil company, Hispánica de Petróleos (Hispanoil) to search for oil abroad; the German government sponsored a grouping of mainly private enterprise companies (Deminex) to do the same; Italy already had its national oil company, ENI, doing just that; France pinned its hopes on Algeria; the Japanese also set up a state-sponsored group (JNPC) to diversify the search for oil abroad. None of them came up with much of anything except the French in Algeria, and they were not destined to keep what they found there for very long.

Nuclear energy was a new source that, it seemed, held much promise at the time, but plants took years to construct and the price of fuel oil was coming down while the costs of construction were going up. It was clearly not the alternative to oil that some had hoped for when construction of the first commercial plant started in1964, at Oyster Creek in New Jersey.

Of course, one way to lessen import dependence was to dampen demand by increasing prices, and this was clearly perceived in certain parts of the US administration. However, doing it by raising excise taxes would have been extremely unpopular and the United States was already at something of a competitive disadvantage on energy costs vis-à-vis its competitors in international trade, notably Japan and Western Europe. European governments, blessed with a meeker public than the United States, had no such inhibitions about excise taxes, at least on gasoline, which were already much higher than US levels, but they did not wish to impose a heavy burden on industry by high excise taxes on industrial fuels (unless everyone else did, which they wouldn't) since this might render them less competitive in international markets.

High-Cost Discoveries

In 1968, oil was discovered by Phillips in the Norwegian sector of the North Sea. In the same year, oil was discovered in Alaska's North Slope. The price of oil in the Middle East was $1.30/B. Freight to northwest Europe from the Middle East was about $1.50/B., for a laid-down price of $2.80/B. At that price, not much was going to be developed in the deep and stormy waters of the North Sea. North Slope oil was somewhat better placed in that its price would be pitched at the level of US domestic crude prices, considerably above import parity. But even so, the economics of a trans-Alaska pipeline from the North Slope to Valdez (or any of the alternative means of getting North Slope crude to the market that were being mooted at the time) did not look good. Indeed, why the companies were drilling at all in those areas would be something of a mystery if they had not expected, sometime down the road, substantial price increases. Even so, they were not overly optimistic, and both the North Slope and the Ekofisk discovery wells would have been the last to be authorized if they had turned out to be dry.

The forecasts of the day, however, were showing massive increases in demand over the next two decades and plans were being laid for expansion in the Middle East that would create a storm of protest in some countries and be welcomed in others. Sooner or later, the forecasts seemed to say, there had to be a price increase. But none was visible on the horizon.

It might have been possible to develop North Sea and North Slope oil behind a high tariff barrier, but North Sea oil was Norwegian and British, and the rest of Europe was not keen on forgoing cheap Middle East oil in order to pour money into Norwegian and British pockets. As for the United States, it already had high enough energy prices without raising the cost of everything again in order to develop one (albeit very large) field. In any event, there was no serious discussion at the time of high tariffs. The price increase had to come from somewhere else. Without one, there was little enthusiasm for serious exploration and development of the North Sea's oil potential. (Gas, in the shallower waters of the southern sectors of the North Sea, where it was cheaper to operate, was a different story.)

Growing dependence on oil imports from the OPEC area and the high-cost oil discoveries close to home were both powerful reasons for the United States and Britain to see much that was positive about price increases.

It was also suggested at the time that the United States might welcome an increase in the price of oil as advantageous because it would increase the energy costs of Japan and other competitors in international trade. This is possibly true, but it certainly was not a decisive factor in any moves made by the United States to encourage OPEC to raise prices. The US economy was not at the time (and is not now) heavily dependent on foreign trade, and in any case, an increase of the size envisaged at the time by the United States would probably have had only a minor impact on the competitive position of Japanese and other countries' exports.

Conclusion

The reaction of the major consuming countries was, on the whole, one of relief. The supply disruptions repeatedly threatened by OPEC member countries had been averted, and all could now look forward to peace in our time. Professor M. A. Adelman thought otherwise. The OPEC governments would soon be back for another slice of the "wide margin" still available: "The Genie is out of the bottle," he said. People didn't take much notice of him at the time. But then they weren't given much time either.

The United States had reason to welcome the price increases, small though they were. Demand, especially import demand in the United States, was racing ahead. There were the perennial fears that world oil reserves would, in a few years, be insufficient to cope. Worse, the bulk of the world's reserves were concentrated in the wrong place—the Middle East; a price rise was needed to stimulate exploration elsewhere, as well as development of other sources of energy.

The companies didn't like being forced to pay higher taxes, but they were able to pass the tax increases on to the consumer in the form of higher prices, and they benefited hugely from the general rise that followed in prices for their oil and gas from the non-OPEC area. The Tehran Agreement was signed in February 1971 and the Tripoli one in April. The net earnings of the five US majors during the whole of 1971 rose by 12 percent over 1970, on an increase in their crude production of less than 7 percent. The companies were pleased that they had averted (by the skin of the teeth) the unilateral legislation that had been repeatedly threatened and that would no doubt have followed upon a breakdown in negotiations. However, unlike the public in major consuming countries and some of their governments, they probably did not take the threat of a production shut-down in the Gulf seriously, particularly since these threats did not emerge repeatedly until it had been made plain to the OPEC countries that that was what consumer countries feared the most.

There is no doubt that the companies needed a price increase to develop the North Sea and Alaska, and to help finance the enormous expansion that was being forecast. It has been suggested, consequently, that they saw a large increase in OPEC country taxes as the way to get it: they knew they would be able to pass the higher taxes on to the consumer, resulting, inevitably, in higher prices in Europe, and also producing higher profits on their production of oil and gas outside the OPEC area, at least until taxes were raised there as well. It has further been suggested that the companies therefore engineered the tax increases, putting up a tremendous show of reluctance in order to make sure that the fault would be placed fairly and squarely on OPEC's shoulders, and that OPEC and the Middle Eastern governments in particular would be blamed by consumers and the governments of importing countries. However, if such a conspiracy existed among the companies, there is no evidence to support it. It was scarcely necessary: OPEC needed no urging.

In any event, OPEC had tasted blood. Member countries began to perceive too that some countries, notably the United States, as well as the oil companies were no longer adamantly opposed to higher taxes that resulted in higher prices; that they even thought them necessary and desirable, though the companies intensely disliked the loss of control and the prospect of ever-escalating demands that a "victory" for OPEC would entail. It also became very plain for all to see that the companies and their home governments did not see eye to eye. Both may have been glad enough of the price increases, but the governments wanted to avoid confrontation at all costs, while the companies wanted to avoid unilateral OPEC country action at all costs.

The tax and price increases were small enough. The increase in tax, which would be fully reflected in prices, was about $0.38/B. in the Gulf, more in the Mediterranean, with another $0.25 to be phased in by small increments over the next four years. In magnitude, this was less than fluctuations in freight rates from the Gulf to northwest Europe or the United States

The most dispiriting aspect of the whole episode was the huge amount of ancillary bluster and threats. When a change in taxation, averaging about 3 cents per barrel per year since the decreases of 1959 (which had sparked the creation of OPEC) , can only be introduced on the back of threats (widely credited though barely credible) to shut down production entirely and cause untold damage to the world economy, then there is something terribly wrong with the system. That flaw was not addressed in the Tehran/Tripoli agreements, because the *kind* of relationship that existed in the consumer-company-producer triangle was not perceived as the central problem at the time. And the important things that happened during the period we have been discussing were not to do with money but with the underlying changes in this relationship. They were soon to bear fruit.

Chapter 7
THE STRUGGLE FOR CONTROL, 1971-1973

In the three years from 1971 to 1973, control over the oil industry in OPEC member countries passed from the major oil companies to the governments, in Algeria, Iraq and Libya by nationalization; elsewhere by "participation" or the simple abrogation of some of the companies' key contractual rights. By the end of 1973, the companies had for all practical purposes lost control over pricing, production levels and much of the investment decision. In urgent need of current and greatly increased future oil supplies, and lacking adequate political backing from their home governments, the companies submitted to the inevitable, salvaging what they could. The governments at last had what they wanted—control. Deeply cherished national aspirations were served.

Why Control?

The almost three years from the signature of the Tehran Agreement in February 1971 to the outbreak of war between Israel and the Arab states in October 1973 were marked by OPEC member countries' struggle for control over the industry. Not price, not revenue, not primarily money at all, but control. The means (participation, nationalization) for gaining control were made clear, but the fundamental objectives were never well-articulated, not fully understood by the countries themselves, and barely understood at all by others.

All of the countries of the Middle East and North Africa had until recently been, in one form or another, dominated by the British, the Americans or the French, and it was not possible for independence to *feel* complete, regardless of outward forms, when the companies hailing from these erstwhile colonial or semi-colonial powers could dominate their economies and take decisions in which the interests of the countries themselves were of quite secondary importance.

It was an intolerable affront, felt as keenly in Iran as in the Arab countries of OPEC. Mossadegh knew it and felt it and said so, frequently. The Shah knew it and felt it, and didn't say so, preferring to manipulate the United States and the West as best he could, but, at heart, he was as nationalist and anti-Western as Mossadegh (both, incidentally, educated partly in Switzerland). In the Arab world, the situation was complicated because the companies came from countries that were the "friends of my enemy", Israel, but that was not by a long mark the determining factor. And when Sheikh Abdullah Tariki (by then *former* Saudi oil minster) spoke of taking control of the industry, his economics may have been faulty, but the whole of the Arab world listened and applauded.

Worlds Apart

OPEC member countries had indeed tasted blood. After the Tehran and Tripoli agreements of 1971, which a couple of years earlier would probably have surprised them as much as they surprised the rest of the world, they knew two things of key importance: first, the major oil companies could be shoved around; second, the United States, Western Europe and Japan didn't much care, provided there were no supply disruptions. In fact, supply disruptions seemed to be the *only* thing they cared about, and therefore became the preferred threat of the producers.

In Iran, the Shah believed that he had been given a green light on prices (taxes) by Under Secretary of State John Irwin in 1971, as indeed he had, though that was not explicit. At this point, the United States did not appear to have any well-defined policy on oil prices: in the wake of Tehran and Tripoli, they were higher than they had been, but they were still low—well below domestic US crude prices.

There was a reason to worry—not about high prices but about low ones. In Washington, in various parts of the administration, a consensus was beginning to form that even higher oil prices were desirable, on a number of grounds, but it could hardly be described as official US policy at that point. US imports were increasing very rapidly: crude imports were up 36 percent in 1971 over 1970, and jumped a further 32 percent in 1972. A price increase would stimulate exploration at home, and give a fillip to the development of North Slope and North Sea crude. Moreover, the looming demand for investment funds looked ominous in the absence of a price increase. Consequently, the message that OPEC countries were getting was that, on the whole, further price increases would not be unwelcome, and the message was made virtually explicit when James Akins, Director of the Office of Fuels and Energy in the State Department, gave a talk at the Arab Oil Congress in Algiers in June 1972 in which he said that some OPEC countries were thinking of raising the price of crude to $5/B. by 1980 (they weren't). He was later reported to have revised the "target" year to 1977 and the "target" price to $7/B.

It is difficult to believe that these were innocent forecasts (Akins's protestations to the contrary notwithstanding). They were an invitation to OPEC to have a go. It wasn't that they couldn't do the simple calculations themselves to know their crude was vastly under-priced compared with alternative sources of energy; but Akins's statements were indicative of, at the least, consumer acquiescence—and that was important.

At the time, however, price was not even an issue in OPEC: the burning issues were participation (on which negotiations were proceeding) and nationalization (Iraq nationalized the Iraq Petroleum Company (IPC) the day before Akins's speech, and Algeria had recently nationalized 51 percent of French oil interests in the country). In any event, apart from adjustments consequent on dollar devaluation, the question of price increases *per se* (or tax-induced price increases, to be more precise) was to lie dormant for another fifteen months, during which the dominant concern in OPEC countries—the struggle for government control over the industry—unfolded along two separate but ultimately converging paths: participation and nationalization. In importing countries, on the other hand, and particularly in the United States, the dominant concern was, increasingly, anxiety over the energy supply crunch that was clearly coming, or so it seemed. Indeed, for the United States, Akins was undoubtedly right: the country was headed for a massive growth in oil imports which would incrementally have to come from the Middle East. The only way to head it off was a large price increase which would stimulate supplies from other areas (including the United States itself). It was a thesis that suited both sides. But never before or since had the basic preoccupations of the two groups been so widely separated; they were worlds apart—an energy crisis for one, control over resources for the other.

A Frenzy of Development

The struggle for control took place against the background of frenetic development worldwide in the downstream phases of the industry—in refinery and pipeline construction, the building of tankers and downstream marketing facilities and in exploration, development and production upstream, mostly in the OPEC countries themselves that were simultaneously the center of conflict! World demand was burgeoning and most forecasts spelled "energy shortage" in capital letters.

The weakness of the companies' bargaining position had to be seen in this light. Spare producing capacity in the United States had entirely evaporated, and it looked as though exports from the Soviet Union might dry up, that the Soviet bloc countries might indeed become net importers of oil. The companies had to have the oil, and they had to have it without delay. There was no room for maneuver; there was no way the shut-down of production from a major producing country (such as the shut-down of Iran in 1951-54) could be accommodated. Virtually all increases in world demand had to be met from the Middle East. A major supply disruption spelled disaster, and was to be avoided at all costs.

They were heady years. From 1970 to 1973, world demand (excluding CPEs) shot up by more than 20 percent. But production in the Middle East rose by 52 percent, and in Saudi Arabia and the UAE, it doubled. On volume, the Shah was happy at last, and could now turn his attention to control and, later, price.

World investments in the petroleum industry were going ahead at a breakneck pace: from 1970 to 1973, they increased by almost 50 percent (14 percent per year), double the rate of the previous ten years, which had themselves been boom years. And that was just the beginning: during the following eight years, from 1973 to 1981, world investments would keep rising at an average pace of more than 20 percent per year. Though somewhat exaggerated because they are not corrected for inflation, these are still growth rates unparalleled anywhere in a large industry that was after all well-established and mature by 1970, and they reflect the complete lack of short-term alternative sources of energy to satisfy the growth in demand. A few more figures: as of late 1970, there were over 70 projects for new grass-roots refineries around the world, plus 120 expansions, to add about 11 mbd of refining capacity, nearly all due for completion before 1974. Within less than six months, projects for another 7 mbd of capacity were announced. Together, these projects represented a 47 percent increase in world refining capacity. In the event, some of the projects fell by the wayside, but in fact, by the end of 1975, an additional capacity of 13 mbd (rather than the 18 mbd previously projected) had been installed, still an impressive increase in world refining capacity of 30 percent.

At the end of 1971, 37 million dwt of new tanker capacity was on order, a projected expansion of about 22 percent to existing world fleet capacity. Three LNG projects were being talked up in the Persian Gulf, another for Siberian gas for export (none of them materialized), and others for Brunei and Australia. Syncrude from the Canadian tar sands was to be greatly expanded. As it turned out, all of these were a mere appetizer for the flood of projects that came to the table after the price explosion of 1973.

As far as crude oil production was concerned, the main areas of development activity outside the OPEC area were the Norwegian and UK sectors of the North Sea and Nigeria. At the time, there didn't seem to be anywhere else to go for the kind of massive increases in production that would, it seemed, be necessary over the next decade. (Alaska was mired down in environmental problems impeding the construction of the Prudhoe Bay-Valdez pipeline.) Mexico's remarkable surge in production that took it from being merely self-sufficient to an important position as a major exporter, did not really get under way until 1975. Hence the apparently crucial importance in the early 1970s of retaining access to OPEC oil on practically any terms.

It is impossible to convey with a mere recitation of statistics the sense of urgency the industry felt, almost bafflement as to how they would meet the demands placed on them, and the helter-skelter expansion required. US engineering and construction contractors to the industry were expressing concern not over the capital requirements of the industry in the future, but

the sheer number of design engineers that would be needed. This, some
thought, would be the real bottleneck.

The Issues – Nationalization

There were three major nationalizations during the years 1970 to 1973, in
Algeria, Libya and Iraq. The circumstances and consequences of each of them
were very different, but they were all except for the nationalization of BP in
Libya, which was a mere act of misdirected revenge, seen as the path to
control.

Algeria's Nationalization of French Companies

Having picked off and nationalized the non-French companies in the late
1960s, Algeria now turned its attention to the French companies themselves,
which accounted for a much larger share of the country's production. Here
the situation was more complicated because French oil interests in Algeria had
to be considered in the context of the country's overall relationship with
France, which involved a whole series of other matters, especially preferential
trade conditions.

The main points of conflict concerned the low levels of investment by the
French companies, and various tax issues, mainly related to market prices.
Negotiations started in 1970, were broken off, then taken up again. But
following the Tehran Agreement of February 1971, President Boumedienne
announced that Algeria would take majority control of all French producing
interests in the country. Nationalization of the requisite shares of the French
companies followed promptly, on 1 March 1971.

The Algerians were planners with a strong socialist bent. Strategic
planning and responsibility for the oil and gas sector were entrusted to Belaid
Abdesselam, minister of Energy and Industry, who had occupied that post
from independence in 1965. But the Algerians had planned for post-
independence long before and, with considerable foresight, had started
training and forming cadres of professionals. Sid Ahmed Ghozali, later
president of Sonatrach and minister of Energy, and Nordine Ait Laoussine,
later executive vice president of Sonatrach and also a minister of Energy, were
sent abroad to study prior to independence. Both of them played prominent
roles in the events and negotiations leading up to the nationalization of French
interests in 1971 and in the settlements with CFP and ERAP that followed.
Abdesselam himself had set his eyes on effective control of the industry from
the beginning and knew that, over time, the Evian Agreements of 1965, with
the privileged position that they accorded the French, would have to be
radically altered. Within six years, he had accomplished that goal (subject to
some jostling along the way with Foreign Minister Bouteflika), employing
some pretty rough negotiating tactics and sailing close to the legal wind.

Ait Laoussine, when executive vice president of Sonatrach, had been in charge of negotiations with the French companies. Much later (in October 1985), he admitted: "It is clear that the Algerian government knew very well where it wanted to go. It had already taken a certain number of nationalization measures, and it was known that oil would not escape the rule. It would not be incorrect to say that if there had been the desire on the French side, not just to save the furniture, but to undertake broad operations of a nature to prove to Algeria that the French were there for development and improvement of the industry, and not just to recover their sunk investments, well then, I believe the outcome [nationalization] would have been postponed." (The quote is from the Elf/ERAP company history.) To which ERAP commented, "How can you imagine a company investing heavily with the expectation of only postponing nationalization?"

Algeria and Venezuela were the two outstanding examples where "control" over the industry was a prime motivating force, possibly as important as the money. Was it worth it? No doubt current revenue from the French companies was pushed to the limit, but the road to control via majority ownership in joint ventures was a sure recipe for inhibiting foreign investment. And so it turned out in Algeria. In the end, a tough fiscal policy had to be tempered to provide incentive with reasonable security, and indeed when Ait Laoussine, after several years' absence from the scene, came back as Energy minister in 1990, he took some steps to redress the balance.

Iraq and the Nationalization of IPC, June 1972

Iraq's relations with the IPC group of companies (Basrah Petroleum Company, Mosul Petroleum Company and IPC itself, all with the same ownership) had been deteriorating since shortly after the 1958 revolution that ousted the pro-Western Hashemite monarchy in a bloody coup. By 1972, the relationship was virtually irreparable.

Iraq had been grossly swindled in its dealings with IPC in the 1920s. In a passage quoted in Chapter 1, Richard Funkhouser of the US State Department characterized it as "one of the worst oil deals that has ever been signed ... [Iraqi Prime Minister] Nuri came in and sold out his country."

Nevertheless, that was the real world that post-1958 Iraqi governments had to deal with, and none of them was politically strong enough to deal with it in an intelligent manner. They blundered from one rash act to another, and when, seventeen years later, in 1965, they finally concluded a sensible agreement with IPC, negotiated for Iraq by a level-headed and skilled oil minister, Abdul Aziz al-Wattari, a petroleum engineer and oilman all his life, the government of the day was too weak to ratify it and the whole deal fell to the ground. Iraq was back, mired in stalemate and mutual recriminations.

For some time, no Iraqi government understood what Wattari saw quite clearly, that the companies could not possibly make an agreement that they were not prepared to see spread to the rest of the Middle East, and there was therefore no point in trying to negotiate one, regardless of past injustices. Little wonder that the concessions' days were numbered: the Iraqis saw that past wrongs could not be righted; that negotiations could not be pursued on the merits of an individual country's situation; that the companies would not explore and develop large tracts of geologically attractive acreage held under concession, but would not surrender it for others to develop; and so on. These were the majors at their most unattractive.

By 1972, there were innumerable issues on the table. The most important ones were the resolution of differences arising out of Law 80 of 1961 which took over virtually all of the companies' idle acreage, including some (North Rumaila) with proved reserves; the OPEC royalty-expensing issue, accepted by other OPEC members but rejected by Iraq; participation, on which IPC informed Iraq in March 1972 that it accepted the principle of 20 percent participation, in line with its acceptance in other OPEC member countries. The issue was, however, complicated in Iraq, because Iraq already claimed 20 percent participation as being due to it under the San Remo 1925 agreements that were the basis of the original IPC concession, but whose provisions had been, with some legal sleight-of-hand, circumvented by the company; and, critically, the export of oil, starting in April 1972, from North Rumaila, which Iraq had developed itself with the help of Soviet technicians. North Rumaila was in the concession area of the Basrah Petroleum Company (BPC), an IPC affiliate, and BPC not unnaturally protested and prepared to take legal action against purchasers. At the same time, IPC, taking full advantage of a temporary easing of the supply situation at Mediterranean ports, appeared to be retaliating by cutting production further, starting in March (mainly the northern fields of Kirkuk), by over 40 percent, a cut which IPC claimed was due to Mediterranean crude now being overpriced in comparison with Gulf crude, due to a sharp fall in freight rates that had severely lessened its freight advantage. Iraq responded by issuing an ultimatum in mid-May 1972 demanding that IPC increase its production, and then proceeded to nationalize the company the following month.

The immediate psychological effect was electric. The government got the political popularity it was after; the action was acclaimed by other OPEC members, some in rather guarded terms. The political motive having been achieved, Iraq set about limiting the financial damage it might entail. In the end, Iraq had gained little and had had to agree to compensation at several times the net book value that was later to become the rule in the Middle East.

Libya and the Nationalizations of Mid-1973

By mid-1973, everything was falling apart again as markets tightened rapidly and prices rose unexpectedly. Prices were soon too high for the Tehran and Tripoli agreements to survive because the agreements in effect provided for fixed tax payments per barrel regardless of the real market price. The companies were now raking in undreamt-of profits, and events were to prove once again that the penalty for badly structured agreements is death. In addition, politically, the Middle East was boiling over as the Arab-Israel dispute came to a head again; there was incessant talk of using oil as a political weapon (meaning constraining supplies even further) to offset US support for Israel in the worsening situation. Even Saudi Arabia and Kuwait were making guarded noises about restricting supply.

At the end of April 1973, Libya had demanded 100 percent control of all the companies involved in the London Policy Group, and talks had been initiated with some of them. For the time being, with the so-called Libyan safety net now in place, none was prepared to go any further than the financial equivalent of participation in the Gulf countries.

Libya had not signed the participation agreements, and it clearly needed to move on this front but was in a sense stymied. Algeria had nationalized 51 percent of the companies there, and there was already talk of revising the Middle East participation agreements.

On 11 June 1973, the issue was resolved by the nationalization of Bunker Hunt's interest in the Sarir field in a highly political context: President Qadhafi announced the nationalization in a speech on the third anniversary of the evacuation of the US Wheelus air base, and called the nationalization "a good, hard slap on its [the United States'] insolent face." Other Arab leaders, including President Anwar Sadat of Egypt, approved: opinion was universal in the Middle East that if the United States did not modify its stance towards Israel, US investments in the Middle East would be endangered and probably lost. The use of oil as a political weapon was daily becoming a hotter issue and there is no doubt that a tidal wave in favor of its use was forming and threatening to sweep away even the mildest dissent from Kuwait and Saudi Arabia. King Faisal and several of his ministers gave successive warnings to the effect that Aramco's expansion program, designed to boost producing capacity from its current level of about 8 mbd to as much as 20 mbd by 1980, might not be allowed to continue at the same pace.

At the same time, market prices continued to increase, fears of shortage were widespread, and customers were scrambling for crude oil and, in particular , to establish long-term ties with the producing governments that now had increasing supplies of "participation" oil at their disposal.

Two days after Libya's nationalization of Bunker Hunt, Kuwait formally asked Gulf Oil for the revision of its Participation Agreement (which had not even been ratified by the Kuwaiti Parliament). To everyone's surprise and the consternation of consumers, participation crude oil was being sold at prices in excess of the postings, and talk began about how to halt the increases. In fact, by July 1973, crude oil prices in the Middle East were still below where US domestic crude prices had been for the previous fifteen years. No one had any idea of what was in store just around the corner.

Once again, Occidental led the way to collapse. On 11 August 1973, the Libyan government issued a decree nationalizing 51 percent of the company's Libyan interests. It had obviously been cooking behind the scenes because the following day, Occidental signed an agreement with the government signaling its acquiescence in the decree.

The major oil companies had been caucusing in New York to come up with a common front towards Libya. But Libya now had the assurance of substantial production and the corresponding revenues from Occidental and most of the Oasis group (which had also agreed to the nationalization), and on 1 September 1973, it abruptly nationalized 51 percent of all the other companies' assets in the country and began to block shipments of oil by companies that did not conform. The companies involved (Liamco – an Arco subsidiary, Exxon, Mobil, Shell, Chevron and Texaco) objected vigorously and called for arbitration. It was pretty much last-ditch stuff and it only remained for Libya to wipe up the remaining pockets of resistance.

The majors, which still after all had substantial assets in the country, decided not to press for arbitration, for fear of losing them as well to nationalization. In April 1974, Exxon and Mobil accepted the 51 percent nationalization and compensation on the basis of net book value. Liamco, however, went through with the arbitration, and had its remaining 49 percent nationalized in March 1974.

The issues of nationalization and participation were now inextricably linked. There could be no further question of viewing participation as some kind of alternative to nationalization. They were, for all practical purposes, one and the same thing. But let us go back and trace something of the development of this other strand in the drive towards control.

The Issues – Participation

Nothing in the history of relations between companies and governments could be more ironic than the issue of participation. Here was an idea conceived and negotiated as an alternative to nationalization rapidly ending up itself as a short-cut to it.

The concept of participation was not new in the Middle East. There was a sort of participation in the original D'Arcy concession in Iran, and in Iraq there was a provision for participation by the government of up to 20 percent in any new capital subscriptions for IPC, later a matter of much contention.

The architect and chief proponent of participation in the existing concessions of the major oil companies in the Middle East was Saudi Arabia's oil minister Ahmed Zaki Yamani. He first raised the matter privately with Aramco in 1964, at the time talks were going on in Iraq for the settlement of a broad range of issues, including the one on participation. After the companies' offer to the government of participation in the exploration of unexplored areas in Iraq in 1965, he knew they could eventually be persuaded to adopt it everywhere, but the issue lay dormant until 1968. It should be recalled, however, that by then, there were nine new or recent joint venture agreements in the Gulf area, of which five were in offshore Iran. At this point, however, none included a major oil company.

Yamani had given two talks, in 1968 and 1969, at the American University of Beirut in which he floated the idea of participation in existing concessions and outlined its objectives and rationale. Yamani saw early on that the Middle East was headed for nationalization. He also understood that the most important thing about the major oil companies, as far as the producing countries were concerned, was that through their grip on the market and their worldwide vertically and horizontally integrated networks, they could provide market stability. They would continue to grow downstream; upstream, they would pay taxes at progressively higher rates until some sort of competitive limit with the outside world was reached.

But, Yamani thought, if that link with the majors were broken through wholesale nationalizations, the producing governments themselves would have to sell into the market, would end up competing with each other, and prices would drop. On tax, on the other hand, there was, for good political reasons, no competing: no government could be seen letting the companies "get away with" lower taxes—indeed, preventing that was what OPEC was originally about.

Participation was Yamani's alternative to nationalization: the governments could be part owners, and market their share of the oil by selling it back to the majors, or by selling directly to the non-major refiners, independents and State companies, or by integrating downwards themselves into refining and marketing in the industrial countries and in the Third-World importing countries.

So participation is what Yamani set his sights on. But before battle on the issue could be seriously joined, other events occurred. At the end of May 1969, Tapline was sabotaged by the Syrians, basically over a dispute concerning transit fees. In September came the Libyan coup under Qadhafi, and, by the end of the month, demands for an increase in the posted price. Events gathered momentum, and the issue of participation was swept aside until after the conclusion of the Tehran and Tripoli agreements of February and April 1971, and after 23 June 1971 when Saudi Arabia and Aramco signed an agreement on a new posted price for Arabian crude f.o.b Sidon, Lebanon. Finally, in July 1971, OPEC's Twenty-fourth Conference decided to "take immediate steps towards the effective implementation of the principle of Participation in the existing oil concessions" and set up a ministerial committee of Iran, Iraq, Kuwait, Libya and Saudi Arabia to formulate recommendations and submit them to an Extraordinary Conference of the Organization within a couple of months (Resolution XXIV.135). The Extraordinary Conference met in Beirut in late September 1971 and the committee's report was considered. The Conference then decided that all the member countries concerned should establish negotiations with the companies "either individually or in groups, with a view to achieving effective participation on the bases proposed by the [OPEC] Ministerial Committee". These bases were that participation in the existing concessions should be paid for at net book value, with provisions for the companies to buy back all or part of the governments' share of crude for an interim period. The percent participation was not at this point fixed, but it was understood that an initial 20 percent would constitute a minimum, and that this should rise over time to 51 percent.

Yamani was empowered to negotiate on behalf of the Gulf countries (Iran, Iraq, Kuwait, Qatar, Abu Dhabi and, of course, Saudi Arabia).

In the meantime, as though to underscore existing trends, NIOC announced on 27 July, the signing of three 50/50 joint venture agreements for offshore and onshore acreage. One of them, significantly enough, was with a major oil company, Mobil.

In October 1971, the companies started to gear up for another mammoth round of negotiations, obtained antitrust clearance from the US Department of Justice and set about reconstituting the London Policy Group. By this time, it seemed that participation in some form and to some degree was a foregone conclusion. Burning issues were how much participation, how much would be paid for it, and how much of the government's share would have to be marketed by the companies and on what financial conditions.

The initial reaction from the major oil companies was varied. Exxon took a hard line and a senior vice president, George Piercy, referring to the Tehran and Tripoli agreements concluded a few months before and the new demands—for participation and for currency-related re-adjustments to the Tehran Agreement—said in a speech to the Independent Natural Gas Association of America in San Francisco in October 1971:

> You can understand our dismay when these governments now confront us with two new demands ... We regard both demands as contrary to the word and the spirit of the five-year agreements so recently signed.

But the reaction of other companies was not quite as unequivocal. What is surprising is that they were surprised at all. Shortly after the conclusion of the Tripoli Agreement in April 1971, the secretary general of the Organization of Arab Petroleum Exporting Countries (OAPEC), Suhail Sadawi, and the deputy governor of Saudi Arabia's Petromin, Mohamed Joukhdar, both said publicly that they expected the Tehran and Tripoli Agreements to pave the way for participation. OPEC Secretary General Nadim Pachachi had twice warned that effective dollar devaluation would have to lead to an adjustment of posted prices. Perhaps years of ineffective posturing by producer-country officials had inured the companies to a new situation.

In any event, negotiations then opened by the group of countries concerned, with the talks being conducted by Yamani on behalf of Saudi Arabia with the Aramco companies in a series of different meetings, it being understood of course that anything agreed with Aramco would apply *mutatis mutandis* to the other countries. Little progress was made initially.

At about the same time, negotiations were started to readjust the posted prices set in the Tehran Agreement, to compensate for the loss of value of the dollar as a result of the currency's delinking from gold in August 1971. They soon took on a familiar pattern of escalating threats. At this point, neither set of talks amounted to much more than preliminary sparring. OPEC's Twenty-sixth Conference, held in Abu Dhabi on 7 December 1971, then rather brusquely called for final negotiations on participation and the dollar's loss of value. A date was set for discussions: 10 January 1972 for dollar loss and 20 January for participation. The threat was made explicit in a Conference Resolution: "In case such negotiations fail to achieve their purpose, an extraordinary meeting of the Conference shall be called to determine such concerted action as necessary ..."

The threats were taken seriously; but without wholehearted and tough-minded backing from the governments of consuming countries, particularly the United States and Britain, there was no contest. The United States, or at least part of the administration, still wanted higher prices, and the British didn't want any trouble. Not surprisingly, the fight had gone out of the companies, and the negotiations, brief enough, ended in their almost total capitulation. On 21 January 1972, OPEC and the companies announced that they had agreed on an increase in posted prices of 8.49 percent as compensation for dollar devaluation.

Attention then shifted back to participation. Nothing conclusive came out of the January 1972 talks, but the companies did not present OPEC with a flat no, which, Yamani had warned, would trigger some kind of concerted action on the part of OPEC. In mid-February, as a new round of talks between Yamani and the major oil companies was ending, King Faisal sent the companies a message, saying that participation was imperative and threatening to "take measures in order to put into effect the implementation of participation." This produced the desired effect, and on 10 March, the eve of the next conference, Aramco delivered a letter to Yamani accepting the principle of 20 percent participation in the existing concessions.

It was all over bar the shouting. But, as it turned out, there was quite a lot of shouting to be done. The matter of compensation was contentious and the positions of the parties far apart. OPEC was aiming at net book value and the companies asking for loss-of-profits or something similar. The buy-back provisions—provisions for the companies to buy back part of the share of production that would accrue to the governments as their participation—were also of great financial importance. Resolving these and other, lesser matters took several more months. Last but not least was the timing of the increase in participation, till the official goal of 51 percent was reached.

More talks took place in a kind of global road show with meetings held in Saudi Arabia, Beirut, Geneva, London and New York, and more threats issued. The companies finally bent to the inevitable, threw in the towel and both sides initialed a draft General Agreement on Participation on 5 October 1972. But it was not until December 20 that Saudi Arabia and Abu Dhabi signed the definitive General Agreement, followed by Kuwait and Qatar in early January 1973.

Broadly, the terms of the agreement were as follows:

– Government Participation

An initial 25 percent, effective 1 January 1973, to increase by 5 percent each year for four years starting in 1978, with a final tranche of 6 percent on 1 January 1982, taking total government participation to 51 percent.

– Buy-back of Government's Share of Production

At the time, it was thought that the governments involved would not be able to sell their share of the oil immediately and that the companies would not want to part with that much of their own equity oil. The government share was therefore split into three parts the proportions of which would change over time: (a) "bridging" oil, to be bought back by the companies at a price approximating the going market price was designed to allow the companies to meet their then current contractual obligations; (b) "phase-in" oil, to be bought back by the companies if the government so required, at a discount off the going market price; and (c) oil to be marketed by the government itself, directly.

– Compensation

Payment for the government's share to be based on "updated net book value", that is, net book value adjusted for inflation. This was, in effect, something approaching replacement value of fixed assets, and worked out at about four to six times net book value (depending on when the original investments were made). Compensation for the 25 percent was fixed as follows: Saudi Arabia (Aramco) $500m; Kuwait (KOC) $150m; Iraq (BPC only) $68m; Qatar (QPC and Shell) $71m; Abu Dhabi (ADPC and ADMA) $162m.

The compensation issue had been a difficult one, especially for the companies. To agree to compensation on the basis of "net book value"—the amount of money actually invested over the years by the companies minus the amount of depreciation taken for tax purposes—would be a bad precedent anywhere; in the Middle East, it was a derisory sum compared with the commercial value of the concession, that is, what the concession would have fetched in an arm's-length sale. The net book value (or net asset value, the same thing) of the companies' investments in the major Middle East concessions at the end of 1970 is shown in Appendix 7-1. In total, they amounted to some $1.3 billion for the five largest producing countries, Abu Dhabi, Iran, Iraq, Kuwait, Qatar and Saudi Arabia. This was about $0.23/B. of one year's production and less than half a cent per barrel of proved reserves. The companies were being offered little more than they were making in net profits in one year. The companies argued that this was confiscatory; the governments that profits were simply excessive, and asked why they should pay more for an equity share in their own oil resources than the companies had. The US State Department expressed its concern over the low level of compensation being offered and the Saudis at least indicated that the issue was negotiable. In the end, the companies settled for an "updated" net book value, that is, net book value corrected for inflation since the original investments were made. It was still far below the concessions' commercial value. There was therefore some poetic justice in the increase in the net earnings of the seven major oil companies during 1973—the first full year after the participation agreements were signed: they rose by 98 percent, over $4 billion, on the back of rapidly escalating market prices.

Thus ended an arduous negotiation different from any other negotiation between governments and companies that had preceded it. It was not primarily about money, but about control, about an orderly and gradual transfer of power from the companies to the government. It had a short life ahead ot it.

Things moved too fast and within a few months, even before the outbreak of the Arab-Israeli war of October 1973, the agreement was a shambles. Kuwait's Parliament refused to ratify it; each of the three remaining signatory countries, and their respective concession-holding companies were supposed to draw up detailed implementing agreements to the General Agreement. Before they managed to do so, they were overtaken by events.

Already, in October 1972, Libya had been able to pressure ENI into a 50 percent participation deal with compensation at net book value. In June 1973, Bunker Hunt, having refused the same terms, was nationalized but received some compensatory crude from the other companies under the Libyan Safety Net Agreement's provisions. In August 1973, Occidental accepted 51 percent participation with compensation at net book value. The Oasis partners (Continental, Marathon and Amerada-Hess, but not Shell) accepted the same terms. The following month, in September 1973, 51 percent of the remaining companies in Libya were nationalized.

By then, Nigeria had obtained participation at an initial rate of 35 percent (in June 1973).

By May 1973, Iran had renegotiated its agreement of the previous June, for a 20 year period, with the same financial effects as the General Agreement plus a commitment on the part of the Consortium to develop capacity up to 8 mbd by 1976 if technically and economically feasible. The Shah, of course, represented the agreement as 100 percent control, putting the participation agreements under further public-relations pressure.

Control Over Revenue

The first dollar "devaluation" was announced on 18 December 1971 and took the shape of a lowering of the price of gold against the dollar by 7.89 percent. Effective 20 January 1972, the Gulf Members of OPEC signed an agreement (which became known as "Geneva I") with the companies whereby posted crude oil prices were raised by 8.49 percent to compensate for the exchange losses resulting from the change in the dollar price of gold and the dollar's slide against other currencies. Government revenues of the Gulf Members rose by about nine cents per barrel.

It was a complex situation. Posted prices were quoted in dollars, but taxes were paid in sterling to all the Gulf countries except Saudi Arabia, where taxes were paid in dollars. Most prices for actual sales in international transactions of both crude and products were also quoted in dollars and payments made in dollars. However, sales to consumers in national markets were made in the currency of the country. Companies therefore received an array of different currencies, the relative proportions of which varied from company to company depending on their position in the markets. By the same token, different OPEC countries imported goods from different countries in different proportions. There was, therefore, no single measure specific to the companies or specific to the countries that would provide an adequate measure of the effect of the dollar devaluation on them, and any average would shift over time.

The result was the outcome of horse-trading. It was decided that future posted prices would be varied to compensate for changes in the value of the dollar in accordance with a basket of nine major currencies. Like most formulae of this kind, it didn't work, and when the next dollar devaluation came, on 12 February 1973 (the official dollar price of gold rose from $38 to $42.22 per ounce), the formula resulted in values that did not reflect the full extent of the loss in the value of the dollar. OPEC requested re-negotiation. After some of the usual to and fro, accompanied by suitable threats, a second agreement was reached ("Geneva II") on 2 June 1973, whereby posted prices were increased by 11.9 percent over the prices in effect on 1 January 1973 and 6.9 percent over the prices that would have come into effect on 1 April under the Geneva I formula. Government revenue was increased by about 9 cents per barrel, again depending on the type of crude. The formula applicable to posted prices to regulate further changes in dollar exchange rates was modified. The new formula was never applied because Geneva I and Geneva II would soon be swept aside.

Prices and the Markets

The bargaining position of OPEC and its member countries was immeasurably strengthened by the tight market situation that prevailed during most of the four-year period from 1970 through 1973, and most especially because there was no short-term alternative to the OPEC area itself as a source of incremental supply.

A few numbers for the four years: world energy demand was up 4.4 percent per year, but coal production was static. Supplies of natural gas and primary electricity (nuclear and hydro) barely kept pace with the average. Oil had to fill the gap and world production (excluding the CPEs) increased an average of 7.6 percent to do it. But US production, still without new supplies from Alaska, had begun to decline and neither the North Sea nor Mexico made any significant contribution to meet the increase.

The short supply situation was further aggravated by the switching of suppliers that necessarily accompanied participation. The emergence of governments over the long run as the principal source of crude oil supplies internationally, and, in the short run, as relatively minor suppliers, led to a scramble of buyers seeking to establish, through initial purchases of crude, the basis for a longer-term relationship that would protect the security of their supplies. Far from having any difficulty in disposing of their participation crude (the fear of which was the basis for the buy-back arrangements for "phase-in" crude in the participation agreements), governments were virtually besieged by buyers bidding up prices.

Prices took off, and scuppered everything.

The year 1973 had started most auspiciously. As noted above, a number of steps towards the settlement of outstanding issues had been taken. Qatar and Kuwait joined Saudi Arabia and Abu Dhabi in signing the General Agreement on Participation. Iraq and Syria signed an agreement on transit fees. Iraq and IPC finally reached a settlement of the issues outstanding between them. Abu Dhabi and BP settled a dispute over BP's sale of its 45 percent share in ADMA to a Japanese company. OPEC reached a new agreement (Geneva II) on exchange rates. Iran and the Consortium signed a 20-year agreement replacing the 1954 concession agreement. Nigeria signed a participation agreement with Shell/BP. True, there were still some icy patches on the road, notably Kuwait's refusal to ratify the General Agreement and Libya's thrust for 51 percent participation, Algerian-style; but on the whole, it looked once more like peace in our time. A stable relationship between companies and governments appeared to be a serious possibility.

The first signs of trouble came from product markets where prices began to rise, under the pressure of higher demand, higher freight rates, and higher producer country taxes. Crude oil prices were not far behind. Company profits started to shoot up, and the profit margins on crude sales out of the Middle East more than doubled. In February 1973, Abu Dhabi sold some 730 million barrels of "participation" crude at $0.13/B. more than the agreed price for bridging crude under the participation agreements, which was supposed to approximate a commercial price. In May, Saudi Arabia sold 69 million barrels of participation crude at $0.50/B. over the bridging crude price.

Sales of participation crude by Saudi Arabia and Iran were made at close to the posted price during the first half of 1973. Qatar's sales were concluded at $0.15/B. over postings. Actual sales prices had just about doubled since the low levels of 1969-70.

Company profits were soaring, and they were earning margins that were three to four times as great as the norm of $0.20 to $0.30/B. which obtained during the 1960s. These margins could not co-exist with a structure of agreements predicated on a significantly different level of prices. It was becoming clear that neither the Tehran-Tripoli agreements nor the Participation Agreements could survive. And they didn't. The seven majors ended up walking away with a 70 percent increase in net earnings in 1973 over 1972 (which had itself been a good year) but by the end of the year, the whole painfully negotiated system lay in ruins, and "participation" was increased to 100 percent—in other words, nationalization after all.

Politics Intrude

All the events related in these pages occurred in the context of a political atmosphere of seething discontent in the Arab world and domestic crisis in the United States. There was no way that oil could remain apolitical. This is not the place to enter into details; suffice it to recall that during the Six-Day War in 1967, Israel had taken Arab Jerusalem, Jordan's West Bank, occupied Syria's Golan Heights, moved into the Sinai Peninsula and up to the banks of the Suez Canal. And there they remained. It was an intolerable humiliation of the Arab nation, all the worse because it involved Islam's second most holy place, the Al Aqsa Mosque (the Dome of the Rock) in Jerusalem. Nor could US support for Israel be forgiven. With Israel's neighbors apparently crushed, no one could precisely foresee another conflict; but no one doubted that one was coming.

What the Arabs needed, and needed desperately, was some leverage that would neutralize, or at least moderate, US support for Israel, and, in the circumstances leading up to October 1973, oil was the obvious, indeed the only, candidate. US imports of oil were climbing fast and there was absolutely no way the country could do without Arab oil. The calls for the use of the "oil weapon" started to come from all sides, and even the super-cautious King Faisal of Saudi Arabia, when he saw how desperately the Americans needed Saudi oil, began in 1972 to threaten holding up the development of new capacity. (In 1971, plans had been initially drawn up for the expansion of Saudi producing capacity to 20 mbd.)

The four US major oil companies that were the shareholders of Aramco (Exxon, Socal, Texaco and Mobil) were urged to use their influence (largely imaginary) to sway the Nixon administration by pointing out the dangers to US investments in the Middle East of continued unlimited US support for Israel. They did what they could, and Mobil even took out a full-page ad in the *New York Times* calling for a more "even-handed" US policy towards Israel and the Arabs; Socal prepared a special letter along the same lines to its share-holders.

For their part, the Saudis issued numerous warnings and statements, from King Faisal himself and several of his key Cabinet Ministers, including Yamani. An intensive (by the standards of the usually reticent Saudis) press campaign was launched, with one of the last big salvos prior to the outbreak of hostilities in October 1973 being an interview King Faisal gave to correspondents of the *Washington Post* and the *Christian Science Monitor* in July 1973. His words were most diplomatic, without abuse or bluster, but he was saying in effect that Saudi Arabia was under great pressure from other Arab countries and that the expansion of producing capacity would have to be frozen or slowed down if the United States did not change its policy of virtually unqualified support of Israel. Similar but somewhat more detailed statements had been previously made or were subsequently made by Yamani, by Planning Minister Hisham Nazer and by Foreign Minister Omar Saqqaf.

They seem to have had no effect at all on US policy, and in fact Saudi Arabia never took any politically inspired steps to slow down the expansion of producing capacity. But they did have an effect on the oil companies, who believed that in the end, King Faisal might be driven to adopting measures against *them,* as surrogates for the United States, in the same way that Libya had retaliated against US policy by nationalizing Bunker Hunt.

By mid-1973, there was a mounting sense of panic. There was growing talk of an energy crisis; while the Arab countries in OPEC were pressing for a change in US policy towards Israel, others, notably Venezuela, were concerned with the transfer of technology and economic development. But throughout the debate and discussions, one thing was becoming crystal clear: security of supply mattered to the consumer; price didn't, or didn't matter very much. The consumer therefore got higher prices, accompanied by heavy-handed reminders of what could happen to the security of his supply in their absence. Speaking at the Royal Institute of International Affairs in London in June 1973, consultant and author Jack Hartshorn observed: "Since spring 1970, market prices for crude oil in the Eastern Hemisphere have more than doubled ..." Then, later in the same talk: "Japan and some governments in Europe, much as they regret the 1960s when they could have both security of supply and energy at knockdown prices, want to make clear that they now give the continuity of sufficient supplies a very definite priority over price." He was, of course, right. For the policies and politics of the oil-exporting countries, what could have been clearer?

The End of the Road

In September 1973, OPEC called for the renegotiation of the Teheran and Tripoli agreements, with talks to start on 8 October. On 6 October, war broke out between Israel and an alliance of Egypt and Syria. The talks with the companies commenced on schedule on 8 October, but were broken off after two days. On 16 October, an OPEC ministerial committee for Gulf member countries unilaterally raised posted prices (the tax base) by 70 percent. In the political circumstances, the companies acquiesced in the decision and the subsequent decisions of other OPEC member countries to do the same. For the companies, it was the end of the road in the struggle for control; all key decisions over taxes and maximum production levels now lay in the hands of the governments concerned.

NET BOOK VALUE OF PRINCIPAL OIL COMPANIES IN THE MIDDLE EAST
As of 31 December 1970 - Million Dollars

	Net Fixed Assets	Total Net Book Value
Abu Dhabi		
Abu Dhabi Marine Areas	90.2	116.9
Abu Dhabi Petroleum Co.	69.8	77.3
Total	160.1	194.2
Iran		
Iranian Oil Refining Co.	68.9	112.6
Iranian Oil Exploration & Producing Co.	266.9	248.2
Total Consortium	335.8	360.7
Iraq		
Iraq Petroleum Co. (IPC)		
Kirkuk Oilfields	14.4	na
Pipeline system (inc. Syria/Lebanon)	41.8	na
Tripoli Refinery (Lebanon)	10.6	na
Total IPC	66.8	244.6 (a)
Mosul Petroleum Co.	13.0	30.7 (a)
Basrah Petroleum Co.	32.2	51.4 (a)
Total IPC Group	111.9	326.6
Kuwait		
BP (Kuwait) Ltd.	96.7	566.6 (a)
Gulf Kuwait Ltd.	107.0	na
Total KOC	203.7	na
Qatar		
Qatar Petroleum Co.	7.0	32.4
Shell Company of Qatar	49.2	12.0
Total Qatar	56.2	44.4
Saudi Arabia		
Arabian American Oil Co. (Aramco)	563.4	469.9
Total Above	**1,431.0**	**1,395.8**
(cf.: Venezuela -All Cos.)	1,676.6	1,636.0

(a) Includes significant sums of 'Advances' or 'Loans' from parent cos.

Note: With the exception of Gulf Kuwait and Aramco, all the companies kept their accounts in pounds sterling. 'The above figures are based on the IMF par exchange rate for the year year 1970 of $2.40/pound.

Source: Company accounts, filed with Company House in the UK and with the SEC in the US.
Table published in 'Petroleum Industry Trends', 15 May 1972

Chapter 8
IMPORTERS TAKE HEED, 1971-1973

Passive Policies

The major importing industrialized countries ("consumer countries" in this chapter) had, until the 1970s, deliberately passive policies towards the international oil industry in general and the producing countries—the major exporting developing countries—in particular. Notable exceptions included US brokering of the 50/50 agreement in Saudi Arabia in 1950, Britain's last-gasp flirtation with gunboat diplomacy over the Iranian nationalization of 1951, US assistance in facilitating the Iranian Consortium Agreement in 1954, and French policy in Algeria. But the days of US Interior Secretary Harold Ickes' interventionism in the Middle East and the abortive Anglo-American oil agreements of 1944-45 had gone for good. There seemed to be no apparent need for interventionist policies.

When the time came, therefore, for a more activist policy, the major consumer countries were not well-prepared psychologically, and it would be a wrenching move away from passivism.

Consumer Reaction

How then did consumer countries—above all, the major industrialized importing countries, essentially the OECD area—react to the struggle for power that was taking place during the three years following the Tehran and Tripoli agreements that had been signed in early 1971? The events leading up to them had been viewed with some, but not much, apprehension. The agreements themselves were initially greeted with some relief, as ushering in a new period of stability in the triangular relationship between consumer countries, oil companies and producing countries; after all, the price increase was not much in the context of the preceding twenty years of declining prices (in real terms), and you had to be a pretty hardened neo-colonialist or an independent from the Texas outback not to notice that the old concessions suffered from a tinge of anachronism.

Nevertheless, prices were being driven rapidly upwards on the back of increases in government "take"—the sum of all taxes, royalties, etc. Government take on Arabian Light crude, for example, rose from about $0.80/B. in early 1970, before all the trouble began, to $1.61 in April 1973.

Another $0.10/B. had to be added to this for the extra cost of "participation" crude, which began to kick in at around this time. Prices increased by even more as demand surged (rather erratically) forward, especially after mid-1972, and supplies from several OPEC countries were restricted—not at this point as part of a concerted policy, but individually for policy rather than economic reasons.

To many, this began to seem like a case of prices being driven up by undisciplined consumer competition for supplies—competition among companies, and competition among countries. The situation was exacerbated because oil companies would seek to establish solid links with the producing governments' national oil companies that began marketing some of their own "participation" crude in the second half of 1972. Suggestions were soon being made, therefore, that the consumers should band together in some ill-defined buyers' cartel to suppress the competition for supplies. Nothing came of them.

The answer to the question of how consumer countries reacted is that they reacted rather slowly, considering that it was becoming clear that OPEC was moving toward the creation of an enormously powerful cartel. Then why was the reaction on the part of the consuming nations not faster and stronger?

Largely because the prime energy concern of the major consumer and importing countries since 1970 was not price at all but future availabilities and security of supply. As we have seen, people had started whispering "energy crisis" in 1969-70, but by mid 1972, it had become an obsession. A supply crisis was clearly approaching, it was thought, and a serious energy shortage would undoubtedly ensue unless crash programs to develop additional producing capacity were rapidly implemented. Saudi Arabia would go to 20 mbd, even 25 mbd, Iran to 8 mbd, Kuwait to 5 mbd, Iraq to 8 mbd, all within a decade, tripling output from 1970 levels. It would not have made any sense at all for the consumer countries to suddenly develop a hostile, aggressive anti-cartel policy towards a group of countries on whom they absolutely depended (or so they believed) for by far the greatest part of the increased oil supplies that they would need over the next decade or more. In addition, some account had to be taken of the overheated political situation: the air was thick with talk of the "Arab oil weapon"—withholding supplies from selected countries. No one in the consumer countries wanted a confrontation for which they were clearly unprepared.

For Japan and the Europeans, prices were secondary—but no one seriously imagined that they would be pushed up to the heights they were later to attain. The United States (or, rather, certain parts of the administration) actively wanted higher prices, and if OPEC member country taxes pushed them up, so much the better. Moreover, a distinction was made between the commercial interests of the major oil companies and the strategic interests of the importing countries—hence the emphasis on security of supply rather than price. Indeed, there was little sympathy for the major companies. The

US majors had been telling their government for many years that a "hands-off" policy would be the best one; and the majors were certainly not a political asset at home, where the public generally viewed them with hostility. Shell and BP, more savvy than their US counterparts, woke up early on and tried, in September 1970, to form a common company front against the producing governments as well as to enlist British and US government help, but to no avail.

In fact, little attention seems to have been paid anywhere to contingency policy planning relating to possible OPEC and producer country actions until sometime in 1972. But the way the companies had been jerked around by OPEC, between the Gulf and the Mediterranean, obviously could not be ignored, and once it became clear (which did not take long) that the Tehran-Tripoli agreements were not after all going to bring peace, policy-makers started thinking more seriously about alternatives to the previous reliance on the major companies.

I think it is probably fair to say that, before 1973, there was no policy at all envisaging a serious confrontation with OPEC in the event that its member countries took actions deemed to be excessive. To be sure, the United States and Britain on several occasions voiced their strong opposition to "illegal" nationalizations—nationalizations that were politically inspired, that were discriminatory, that had no public purpose and for which "adequate, prompt and effective" compensation was not paid. They were realistic enough to understand that the "adequate, prompt and effective" formula would not in practice be fully observed, and that tribunals would not submit the "public purpose" condition to close scrutiny. But there had to be reasonable compensation and the other conditions (non-discrimination, non-political) had to be met. Apart from that, contingency policy for confrontation was virtually non-existent.

Where might it have been formed apart from the foreign and energy policy departments of the individual governments of producing countries?

One possibility was, or should have been, within the OECD. The Organisation had an Oil Committee, but it, like all other international agencies to which the United States and Britain belonged, had been told, after the publication by the ECE of its study of *The Price of Oil in Western Europe* in 1955 (see Chapter 3) not to meddle in matters concerning the Middle East, and especially not to meddle in price. Consequently, the Oil Committee pottered around with studies of refinery expansion in Western Europe and other matters irrelevant to confrontation with OPEC, or any kind of counter-weight, until it was too late. It took some US prodding to get the organisation moving.

Nixon's Energy Message to Congress

In fact, the first steps came elsewhere, in the United States. In April 1973,

President Richard Nixon addressed an Energy Message to Congress in which he announced the phasing out of oil import quotas and asked for legislation on a number of other energy matters designed primarily to increase indigenous energy supplies, notably   to facilitate the construction of a trans-Alaska pipeline to bring North Slope crude oil to the market, the elimination of price controls on newly discovered gas, and the granting of tax credits on exploratory drilling. He also proposed tripling offshore exploration licensing and envisaged a series of other developments involving shale oil, coal, geothermal energy and nuclear power—but the United States was still some way from pressing the panic button on the development of alternative sources of energy.

Nixon's main concern was the rising US dependence on oil imports. At the time, oil imports were running at around 6 mbd, almost one-third of total consumption. The forecasts showed that by the year 1985, the United States would be importing over 15 mbd—more than half its total consumption, and that three-quarters of these imports would have to come from the Middle East. To make matters worse, the increase in imports was taking place as crude prices were rising, so that there was a doubly adverse effect on the balance of payments. But perhaps the main cause for concern was security of supply, in the broadest sense of the term, including anything from physical supply interruptions such as might occur in the event of war in the Middle East, to embargoes, to the attachment of political conditions to the sale of oil, a threat that had already been widely mooted in 1972, notably by Saudi Arabia, which had made it plain that it might not permit the expansion of producing capacity beyond a certain level unless US policy on the Arab-Israeli question was modified.   Until then, US oil and energy policy had always been a primarily domestic matter, impinging on the international arena mainly through its program of oil import restrictions. From 1971 on, it was to be closely involved in Middle Eastern politics.

Nixon's energy message had been some time in the making. In fact, during 1972, there had been a series of contacts with other importing countries, notably through the OECD and the EEC. There must have been some discussion about the adoption of a common policy vis-à-vis the exporting countries on price questions, but none of this was spelled out publicly.

Indeed, there was little mention in the message of the foreign aspects of the new energy policy apart from a general reference to coordination with the energy policies of other oil-consumer nations:

> Today, the United States is involved in a number of cooperative,
> international efforts. We have joined with the [OECD] to produce
> a comprehensive report on long-term problems and to develop an
> agreement for sharing oil in times of acute shortages. The European
> Economic Community has already discussed the need for cooperative

efforts and is preparing recommendations for a Community energy policy. We have expressed a desire to work with them in this effort.

The only indication at this point of anything concrete was, then, to take the allocation of supplies during a crisis out of the hands of the companies and have it administered by an intergovernmental body. There was no mention of strategic stockpiling at this point.

The EEC and Energy

Neither the European Coal and Steel Community (ECSC, established in 1951) nor its sister organisation, the European Economic Community (EEC, established in 1957), forerunners of the European Union, had ever developed (or had a mandate to develop) an energy policy, except in cooperative research ventures in Euratom; each country simply went its own way, several of them intent on finding socially peaceful ways of reducing if not eliminating high-cost coal production. There had been several oil supply interruptions, notably the closure of the Suez Canal in 1956-57, which might have sparked the creation of some kind of permanent inter-governmental body to deal with emergencies, but in fact only temporary oil-supply committees were set up. The energy situation in the various member countries was so different—some still with substantial coal-producing interests (Germany and France); Italy, with only natural gas; the Netherlands, with an important stake in a major oil company, Royal Dutch; France, with an interest in Algerian oil; and its *dirigisme* clashing with the *laissez-faire* policies of Germany.

A study of the long-term energy outlook[1] for the communities published in 1964 drew attention to the issue of security of oil supplies, observing that the means to ensure it were essentially confined to stockpiling of oil, for the short term, encouraging diversification of supplies, and encouraging domestic production of energy, especially nuclear power. That was as far as it went on the issue; the report carried no policy recommendations on security of supply, or any other matter, except by obvious implication. No measures were proposed. A common energy policy was still taboo[2] at the time, and the furthest the report would go was to qualify itself as "an essential reference point for the development of a European energy policy"—the earnest wish of a certain section of the aspiring European bureaucracy.

Nevertheless, it was clearly paradoxical for the group of nations to formulate a common economic policy, internally within the community and externally vis-à-vis the outside world, without including such an important part of the economy as the energy sector. In fact, though, the debate stretched out after 1964, focusing mainly on the protectionist policies for coal that existed in the coal-producing countries of the community. In 1966, the EEC Commission submitted a "first memorandum" (which became known as the "Marjolin Memorandum", after one of the commissioners at the time) to the ministers of its member countries, envisaging compulsory oil stocks equal to 65 days of the previous year's demand, and fiscal incentives for oil and gas exploration by "Community companies" in the Community. In June 1967, more than a year later, an *ad hoc* committee of senior civil servants from member countries endorsed most of the Commission's findings, and these were then formally adopted in July 1967 by the Council of Ministers, the Community's policy-making body, and recommended for adoption by member governments. The thorny question of oil import policy was not, however, resolved—thorny because of France's policy of preferences for "Franc Zone" oil, notably Algeria's.

Some progress was made during the following three years on a common energy policy, mostly on internal matters. However, on the key question of security of supply, stock requirements were raised from 60 days to 90 days of the previous year's consumption; on import policy, France abandoned its discriminatory policy on Franc Zone oil (not surprisingly, in view of the pressures, and eventual nationalization, in Algeria). At the beginning of 1972, however, there was still no Community policy towards, nor even a common view on the developments that were rapidly taking place in OPEC and the Middle East. Nevertheless, the events leading up to the Tehran-Tripoli agreements and the immediate aftermath, despite their relatively minor price consequences, had enough of an impact to make people think, especially in the light of the current oil demand forecasts that seemed to suggest that supply shortages might not be long in developing.

Rather tardily, in October 1972, the Paris summit conference of the European Community, now enlarged by the accession of Denmark, Ireland and the UK, and itself now the result of the merging of the three previous Communities (EEC, ECSC and Euratom), finally instructed the responsible Community organs "to formulate as soon as possible an energy policy guaranteeing certain and lasting supplies under satisfactory economic conditions"—in other words, secure supplies at reasonable prices.

As far as the international aspects of policy were concerned, the Commission duly came up, in April 1973, with recommendations for greatly increased cooperation with other consumer countries, notably Japan and the United States, largely with a view to avoiding competitive buying of oil, which would push prices up further. (By this time, crude and product prices had been rising rapidly in response to increased OPEC government taxes and sporadic supply interruptions.) Uniform policies on stockpiling were recommended, agreement should be reached on rationing and the allocation of oil supplies in the event of emergencies, and research on new sources of energy should be pursued. The Commission also threw a sop to the producing countries, stating that the recommended policies were in no way directed against the exporters and that the Community was, on the contrary, anxious to help exporting countries build up their national economies by industrializing.

The following month, in May 1973, the Council of Ministers noted the Commission's recommendations as an "appropriate basis" for further work. In effect, the core of a consensus had been formed, although, apart from mandatory stock levels (60 days at the time, to increase to 90 days) and no restriction on oil imports, there was nothing very specific about it. In any event, that is where matters stood when the struggle for control was resolved in Tehran in October 1973 with a clear victory for OPEC and its member countries.

The Council of Ministers meeting in May 1973 was followed by a visit to Washington of the EEC's energy commissioner, M. Simonet, where discussions had recently been held with a Japanese mission and Canadian officials. But these were merely tentative and preliminary discussions.

US Policy: Mid-1973

In July 1973, US foreign policy on oil was laid out by then Under Secretary of State for Economic Affairs William J. Casey, testifying before the Near East subcommittee of the House of Representatives. An even more detailed account of this policy had in effect been supplied by James Akins, head of the Office of Fuels, and in an article entitled The Oil Crisis: This Time the Wolf Is Here, which appeared in the April 1973 issue of *Foreign Affairs*. Akins in fact dismissed the idea of a world shortage (which was beginning to gain currency in some quarters) because of a physical shortage of reserves, and focused instead on the clear dangers of their concentration in the hands of a small group of countries in the Middle East, and in particular on the repeated threats that had been coming from Arab countries of a cut-off of oil supplies in one form or another. His major concern, reiterated by Casey, was the need to prepare a coordinated response to OPEC member countries' already coordinated actions, and he alluded to US efforts to awaken its colleagues in OECD to the approaching danger, efforts that started toward the end of 1969, and continued sporadically until October 1972. There was a positive response at last, and the EC committed itself in principle to some kind of cooperative approach. By then, it was clear to the European consumer countries that the Tehran-Tripoli agreements were not to be the source of stability that they had expected.

Akins also repeated in his article that oil prices might climb to $5, and possibly $7 per barrel by 1980, a possibility he had flagged at the Arab Petroleum Congress held in Algiers in April 1972. The price at the time of his article was around $2.60/B. (Arabian Light f.o.b Ras Tanura). In the event, of course, his suggestion, which appeared alarmist at the time, was woefully short of the mark.

The following excerpts are taken from Casey's testimony, pretty much summarizing foreign oil policy as it stood (apart of course from policy on imports, still regarded as primarily a domestic matter):

The second major feature of the international oil picture is the increasing concentration of the key supplies under the effective control of a small number of governments [which] have moreover shown a considerable degree of solidarity in pursuing their joint goals of achieving ever-increasing revenues from their oil production as well as control over the production of oil itself . . . Faced with an increasing possibility that oil will continue to be in short supply in the future, individual companies as well as governments have understandably acted to protect their own interests by seeking special access to sources of supply . . . it seems desirable to us that consumer governments consult to develop new sources of energy . . . the United States proposed, and the OECD oil committee accepted, a suggestion that an informal working group be established to develop and evaluate various issues and options of an OECD-wide agreement to share oil in times of emergency . . . It is clear that we must design measures of international cooperation to include producing as well as consuming nations which will bring about and sustain the willingness of the oil producing countries to produce the oil the consumers will require over the next several decades . . . It is the Administration's view . . . that the industrialized nations stand ready to assist the producing nations in their desire to marry their vital oil with the equally valuable technology, engineering, management and markets of consuming countries in order to reap lasting benefits for their peoples during the one brief generation when they will be in a highly favored market position . . . We must help here, not only in providing the plants, but also in marketing the product of those plants.

There are two strands here: fear of a physical shortage, that is, of supplies constrained by not enough oil in the ground; and, second, supplies constrained by the policy-determined actions of producer countries, or by political conditions of some sort. True, the development of alternative sources of supply would have made sense under either assumption. But if the first (physical shortage) had been true, where the producing countries would have had only "one short generation" to enjoy it, what would have been the point in helping them industrialize? Surely, only to encourage them to allow themselves to be sucked dry quickly. The fear of physical shortage on a worldwide scale was not intended, and this passage was addressed to those countries (notably Kuwait) that feared their own premature depletion.

The second strand was more real—fear of the actions that a small group of countries in control of most of the world's reserves might take: attaching political conditions to continuing increases in supply, and raising prices. Both were foreseen and both were to occur more quickly than anticipated. The creation of a countervailing bloc of consumer countries was therefore planned (with suitable public disavowals of confrontational intentions), plus the development of other sources of supply. A sop was thrown to the producers with an offer to help them industrialize, but it could not have been seriously thought that a useful or realistic policy goal could have been served by actually assisting in the industrialization of desert countries such as Saudi Arabia, Kuwait, Qatar, Abu Dhabi, Libya, etc. countries without water, agriculture, population, labor skills, or any need (or even real desire) to industrialize.

Neither Akins nor Casey gave much prominence to the question of price. Akins certainly seemed to regard a price of $5 to $7/B. by the year 1980 with equanimity and possibly welcomed the prospect, though in his position he obviously could not say so. But both expressed concern at the speed with which prices were being bid up, presumably because they feared that price would get out of hand—indeed, Akins specifically says so in his article:

> With OPEC production limitations in the future, or even with normal slow growth, with only Saudi Arabia and perhaps Iraq capable of substantial expansion, bidding for supplies could soon get out of hand, and the projected price of $5.00 per barrel in 1980, or even a price of $7.00, could seem conservative.

In summary, perhaps the most striking aspect of consumer-country policies vis-à-vis the producing and exporting countries during this brief period, from 1971 to 1973, was their relative lack of the sense of urgency that Akins tried to convey in his article. Certainly, the dangers were fairly clearly perceived: the shortages that could arise if capacity in the Middle East was not expeditiously expanded, the possible use of oil as a political weapon, and prices by 1980 possibly exceeding the currently anticipated (and implicitly acceptable) levels. Nothing was done in the way of measures to combat a cartel except a general consensus to encourage alternative sources of oil and energy (but then a cartel automatically does that); and apart from stockpiling in Western Europe and Japan, little was done to combat an eventual embargo beyond preliminary plans for some undefined concerted action by the consumer countries. It all happened too quickly.

Chapter 9
THE CRISIS OF '73

Matters of prices and supply may eventually be determined in the Arab world and the unpleasant day may come when Arab states can double oil prices and get away with it.
– Richard Funkhouser, internal State Department memorandum, July 3, 1953. Quoted *in extenso* in MNC Hearings, part 7, p. 135 *et seq.*, (1974).

A Political Maelstrom

During the second half of 1973, the political situation in the Middle East exploded and the already precarious status of the oil industry in the area disintegrated further. Oil was dragged into politics in a way it had never been entangled before.

The continued Israeli occupation of large tracts of Arab territory taken in the Six-Day War of June 1967, including the West Bank, Jerusalem, the Golan Heights and the Sinai Peninsula down to the Suez Canal, was a running sore. How to endure the intolerable was a problem that confronted most Arab governments: they recognized their military impotence and blamed the United States for its steadfast support of Israel, backed up with money and arms. A tightening market and growing US imports seemed to reveal a chink in US armor, and the Arabs came to view oil as perhaps a powerful political weapon. Algeria and Libya had demonstrated that the United States, Britain and France could not or would not defend their own companies, and first the Tehran-Tripoli agreements, then the participation agreements demonstrated that control over Arab oil resources could be wrested from the companies' hands.

The political tensions were worsening. There was little or no possibility of a settlement in the Middle East without a credible threat to Israel from the defeated Arabs. So Egypt's President Anwar Sadat decided some time in early 1972 to break the stalemate by attacking Israeli occupation forces across the Suez Canal, in an offensive to be coordinated with a Syrian attack on the occupied Golan Heights.

Sadat laid his plans carefully. In June 1972, he expelled the Soviet military "advisers" from the country, knowing that, for obvious political reasons, he could not possibly attack Israeli occupation forces while they were there. Then he set about forging a coalition in which *all* were expected to play their parts, including Saudi Arabia, whose role was to use "the oil weapon", that is, to apply pressure to the United States by withholding supplies.

In April 1973, Yamani and Prince Saud al-Faisal (deputy oil minister) visited the United States to deliver a new message, which was given wide publicity: Saudi Arabia would not expand capacity to the planned 20 mbd by 1980 if the United States did not modify its policy towards Israel.

Plenty of other things were happening in the Middle East, on and off the oil scene. In mid-1972, after a visit to Iran and discussions with the Shah, President Nixon authorized the purchase of sophisticated combat aircraft by Iran, which, along with the Shah's other purchases of US arms, amounted to allowing him to buy whatever he wanted in the way of arms from the United States. He also authorized covert aid to the Kurds for their struggle against the central government in Iraq—a diversionary tactic to keep Iraq busy and to leave Iran alone.

Action was not confined to the diplomatic front. In August 1973, there were aerial clashes over the Suez Canal between Israeli and Egyptian planes; naval units exchanged fire in the Gulf of Suez; Arab terrorists killed four people and injured many more in an attack in Athens airport; and, in September, Arab terrorists seized the Saudi Arabian Embassy in Paris, and flew with five hostages to Kuwait. Saudi Arabia was under severe pressure to abandon its conservative line.

The Runaway Market

The oil markets tightened during the fourth quarter of 1972 and prices took off, thereby kicking the stocks out from under the Tehran-Tripoli agreements as well as the participation agreements: they had both rested on the premise of a certain relationship between market prices and posted prices that vanished almost overnight.

The tight supply situation, which led to sharply rising market prices, was the result of a number of converging and largely coincidental factors: the imposition of production limitations in Kuwait and Libya; the continued delay in bringing Alaskan North Slope crude into production; the peaking out of oil and gas production in the United States and oil production in Venezuela; and delays in the construction of nuclear power plants in the United States and Western Europe. All these factors combined to place an unexpectedly heavy strain, to the tune of several extra million barrels per day, on those sources that could be quickly expanded, notably Saudi Arabia and, to a lesser extent, Abu Dhabi and Iran. At the same time, high levels of economic activity in industrialized countries had greatly stimulated demand, and by October 1973 oil consumption in the main OECD countries was running almost 9 percent above the previous year's levels; 1972 itself had been a banner year for world (excl. CPEs) oil demand, increasing 7 percent (2.9 mbd) over 1971.

But perhaps the most important single factor was the startling increase in US imports, which rose by 1.3 mbd in 1972 over 1971 (37 percent), and by 1.5 mbd in 1973 (31 percent). Nearly all of this was long-haul crude from the Persian Gulf, and spot freight rates rose correspondingly.

Company profits also reflected the higher prices, mostly more than doubling in 1973. The high freight rates were an immediate source of profit because the companies owned about one-quarter of the world tanker fleet, and had much of the rest under long-term charter at rates far below the spot rates. Consequently, the freight component of their total costs from crude source to the product markets was relatively small, whereas product prices had to be high enough to cover the high spot freight rate ruling at the margin. In addition, company profit margins on crude oil (as distinct from tanker transportation) rose sharply.

The Tehran-Tripoli agreements and the participation agreements were simply not working as intended. Calls for renegotiation, accompanied by the now standard dire threats, were viewed in consuming countries as tantamount to breaking the agreements (which had, of course, been reached by a similar process that had also been viewed as tantamount to breaking *previous* agreements). It was the penalty for making agreements that did not say what they meant.

What the governments wanted and what the companies would have agreed to (and probably thought they were agreeing to) was a tax or royalty that had a floor, but which could move up with market prices, preserving a company margin of around $0.40/B. in Gulf countries. But the agreements were geared to a tax based on an agreed schedule of posted prices, which were not prices at all, but simply a number masquerading as taxable income, and arrived at by grossing up from a target government per barrel revenue. When real market prices moved up above posted prices, the governments got nothing because their taxes were based on the previously agreed posted prices, and the companies took all of the market increase.

Saudi Arabia (but not the other OPEC countries) moved quickly to redress the balance as far as its Participation Agreement with Aramco was concerned, and after (again) the ritual pressure—this time threatening to reduce exports—an agreement was reached providing for the price of both the "bridging" and "phase-in" crude that Aramco bought from the government to be at the full market price. This would be determined by Petromin's price to third parties, fixed in Petromin's contracts at 93 percent of the posted price. More trouble was coming on this score.

Posted Prices: OPEC Takes Over

It was in this highly charged atmosphere that OPEC's Thirty-fifth Conference convened in Vienna in the middle of September 1973. It called for the renegotiation of the Tehran, Tripoli and Lagos agreements because the posted prices specified in those agreements were no longer "compatible with prevailing conditions and trends" (Resolution XXXV.160) and because actual inflation rates were about four times greater (1972 over 1971) than the 2.5 percent per year escalation provided for in the agreements, and were headed even higher in 1973. The Conference established a ministerial committee of the Gulf member countries to renegotiate the terms of the Tehran Agreement starting on 8 October.

On 6 October 1973, Egypt and Syria launched an attack on the Israeli forces in the occupied territories. On 8 October, the Gulf Ministerial Committee met with the oil company representatives in Vienna.

The companies were in a hopeless position, and they knew it. It was an incontrovertible fact that the intentions of the Tehran-Tripoli Agreements and the Participation Agreements were being frustrated by the market, and this was the result of the wretched mess of tax/price formulae established by the agreements. The formulae resulted in an increase of 30 percent in the posted price (and, therefore, in taxes) during 1972-73, but company profit margins on crude (determined by real market prices) actually rose by 100 percent. Having thought they'd plucked the goose, the governments now saw they had made a deal that left it fatter than ever. The fatal flaw in the Agreements was that no one had envisaged a situation where the market price would increase more rapidly than the posted price. The implicit assumption had been that crude prices were largely determined by tax-paid costs plus a small-to-moderate company profit margin. And, apart from momentary breaks, that had indeed been the case for the past twenty years, with the profit margins usually under pressure and eroding slowly.

It was with this background that the company and OPEC representatives met, the company team headed up by George Piercy (Exxon), and the OPEC Ministerial Committee comprising Saudi Oil Minister Yamani, Finance Minister Atiqi of Kuwait and Iranian Finance Minister Jamshid Amuzegar. The companies proposed an increase of 8 percent in the posted price, later raised to 15 percent. The OPEC Committee proposed an increase of 100 percent. The meeting was adjourned for two days, till 12 October, to allow the companies to consult among themselves and with the governments of major importing industrialized countries, namely Belgium, Britain, France, Germany, Italy, Japan, the Netherlands, Spain and the United States, as well as the EEC and the OECD. The companies asked these governments whether they should increase their offer to a point where it had a serious chance of acceptance, and the almost unanimous answer was no. (See MNC Report, p. 149.)

When they reconvened on 12 October, the companies requested a further adjournment of two weeks for more consultation. This was refused and negotiations were broken off. The ministerial committee then met in Kuwait on 16 October with the oil ministers of the other Gulf states—Iraq, Qatar and

Abu Dhabi—and issued a communiqué announcing a unilateral increase of 70 percent in the posted price, from $3.011/B. (Arabian Light f.o.b. Ras Tanura) to $5.119/B. effective that day. Other posted prices were set to be consistent with the Arabian Light posting, corrected for quality and geographical location. The new posted price was based on OPEC's assessment of the actual market price, $3.65/B., grossed up so that the posting would be 40 percent higher—the same relationship between posted price and actual market price that existed prior to the Tehran Agreement of 1971. And this relationship was to govern all future posted price movements.

The companies never again had any voice in the setting of posted prices.

Total government take rose from $1.77/B. to $3.048/B. (72 percent); the companies, assuming $3.65/B. was an accurate market price, were left with a margin of $0.50/B. (on Arabian Light).

The governments' communiqué left the status of the Tehran Agreement (assuming it still had any) unclear, but, although the agreed tax rate of 55 percent remained in force for the time being, the agreement was implicitly though never formally annulled. The communiqué did however say "The Geneva Agreement shall continue to be in force".

Uproar, Confusion and Farce

The communiqué from the OPEC Gulf members also reassured consumers that if the oil companies refused to comply and lift their entitlements (a laughably remote eventuality), the governments would make the oil available at the commercial price. Several days later they were imposing embargoes on shipments to certain destinations and planning production cuts.

Never had there been such uproar and confusion in the industry. The companies protested that the system was unworkable, because if they tried to pass on the increase in tax-paid costs to the consumer, the market price would go up, triggering a further increase in posted prices, and so on *ad infinitum*.

At around the same time, Exxon and Mobil were issuing public warnings that anyone attempting to buy Libyan oil from their properties, nationalized the previous month (1 September), would be sued. This was now descending into farce: by then, consumers were ready to buy anything that would burn, bootleg or not.

More farce, not inconsequential, followed: Iraq nationalized Exxon's and Mobil's remaining interests in the country (in the southern fields of BPC) while quietly assuring them that they could buy the same volume of crude at the going market prices.

Saudi Arabia's position with respect to the price of its participation crude sales back to Aramco was perhaps the most bizarre and farcical element of all in these events. Petromin's customers for Saudi Arabia's participation crude had agreed to a price of 93 percent of the posted price (the going market price at the time). In September, Aramco had also agreed to a revised price of 93 percent of the posted price for their purchases of participation crude. However, the posted price was now to be fixed at 40 percent (not 7 percent) above the market price, which was $3.65/B. at the time. But 93 percent of the new posting of $5.11 was $4.76, not $3.65. Which was the "real" market price? Herzollah, a senior official in the Saudi Ministry of Oil received an anguished call from Aramco asking whether they would in fact have to pay the higher price. He replied: "Look at your contract".

Three days after the Gulf countries' decision to raise the posted price by 70 percent effective 16 October, Libya jumped in and passed a new decree-law raising its basic posted price for 40°API crude from $4.604 to $8.925/B., effective 19 October, an increase of 94 percent—comprising a 70 percent increase on its basic posting plus increases in the sulfur premium, the shipping premium and the Suez Canal premium (a premium to account for the effect of the closure of the Suez Canal, which enhanced the value of the short-haul crudes available in the Mediterranean). For once, the market made the Libyan hike look almost moderate, as prices for Libyan crude rose to $8.50 - $9.00/B.

All this was to be swept away in the second, greater tidal wave of confusion and uproar that was about to hit the shore as the Arab oil embargo and production cuts went into effect. In the meantime, the US State Department, not surprisingly, remained uninvolved. For the time being, it was an almost trivial side-show compared with the war that was going on and the embargo and reduced production that accompanied it.

War and Peace and the Arab Oil Embargo

During the first few days of the war which had started on 6 October, Israeli forces bombed the export terminal of Banias in Syria through which 700 kbd of Iraqi oil moved, and the Syrian terminal of Tartus, from which about 100 kbd was shipped. Saudi Arabia cut back its movements of crude through Tapline by 50 percent (250 kbd) as a safety measure. All in all, that was a loss of 1 mbd of short-haul crude from the Eastern Mediterranean. The immediate effect of this was to push tanker freight rates (already extremely high) up even further, since the short-haul crude would have to be replaced by long-haul crude from the Persian Gulf. At their peak, the freight cost of moving a barrel of oil from the Persian Gulf to the US East and Gulf Coasts was about $4.50/B., compared with about $1.10/B. a year before. With the embargo and consequent lower volumes, freight rates dropped back precipitately the next month, November 1973, by about two-thirds.

On 17 October 1973, Arab oil ministers from ten countries met in Kuwait and decided to reduce production by 5 percent each month (from the previous month) until the total evacuation of all Israeli forces from the territories occupied during the Six-Day War of 1967 was complete.

On 18 October, Saudi Arabia announced its decision to reduce production by 10 percent until the end of November and to make further reductions at rates to be determined at the time.

On 19 October, the United States announced a massive new program of military aid for Israel.

On 20 October, Saudi Arabia announced a total ban on shipments of oil to the United States Over the next couple of days, all the other Arab countries embargoed shipments of oil to the United States, and several of them also embargoed shipments to the Netherlands, in retaliation for these countries' support of Israel.

On 22 October, the UN Security Council called for a cease-fire. This was promptly accepted by Israel, Egypt and Jordan (subject to certain conditions) and later by Syria and other countries.

But this did not mean the end of the embargo; on the contrary, pressure for a satisfactory settlement was stepped up, and on 4 November, Arab oil ministers met in Kuwait and decided to take production down to 25 percent below the September level. Actual production during November was 4.5 mbd below September levels. December 1973 and January 1974 production was 4.0 mbd and 2.6 mbd below September, respectively.

In early November 1973, the EEC met and issued a communiqué that was generally supportive of the Arab position on the occupied territories and the demand for Israeli withdrawal. This was followed in mid-November by a Japanese government statement reiterating support for UN resolution 242 and calling for an equitable solution to the Palestinian problem. King Faisal and various Saudi cabinet ministers reiterated the country's position that there would be no relaxation of the embargo or production cuts until Israel withdrew from the occupied territories. At a meeting of nine Arab oil ministers, the EEC (except for Holland) was excluded from the monthly 5 percent cut applicable to December, but cuts would be restored to EEC destinations in January. The Middle East Economic Survey (MEES) reported that Saudi Arabia had ordered Aramco to suspend work on all projects connected with the expansion of producing capacity in the country.

Things were getting hot. On 21 November, Secretary of State Henry Kissinger held a press conference at which he said that "If pressures continue unreasonably and indefinitely, then the United States will have to consider what countermeasures it will have to take". This was immediately interpreted as a threat to use military force, and Yamani made a statement the following day to the effect that if force was used, the oilfields would be blown up and destroyed.

A few days later, the Sixth Arab Summit Conference, meeting in Algiers, reaffirmed that the embargo and production cuts would continue until Israel withdrew from the occupied territories.

Peace negotiations got under way in Geneva between Egypt, Jordan and Israel on 21 December, and restrictions were gradually lifted as the talks made progress. Little by little, the situation returned to normal; but it was not until 18 March 1974 that a decision was taken by the Arab countries to lift the embargo on shipments to the United States (with Libya and Syria, however, dissenting).

The selective embargo had come to nothing, and hopes of a total Israeli withdrawal from the occupied territories (including Jerusalem) proved quite unrealistic. Egypt and Israel signed an agreement on disengagement on 17 January, and Israel completed its withdrawal from Egyptian territory on 21 February 1974. Nothing was to be gained from maintaining the embargo on shipments to the United States much longer.

The Oil Price Shock of December '73

In the meantime, confusion reigned in the oil markets. One day after the six Gulf members of OPEC had announced the new posted prices on 16 October, they met with other Arab countries in Kuwait and announced the embargo and production cutbacks.

The price effects were convulsive. The price of short-haul crude, being the scarcest, went up fastest. At the end of October 1973, Libyan crude was reported selling at $9/B. (from about $2.80 in October of the previous year). Venezuelan and Indonesian crude prices (and taxes) followed suit.

In early November, Iran increased its "direct deal" crude prices to Japanese customers from $2.88/B. to $3.70/B. for Iranian Light, for the period 16-31 October, and again raised the price to $3.85/B. for November. But Saudi Arabia, at the same time, raised the price of its "participation" crude to $4.76 (93 percent of the new posting) f.o.b. Ras Tanura for Arabian Light, a crude similar to Iranian Light. Iraq and Libya made large increases in their posted prices, to around $9/B. On 16 November, everyone was stunned by reports of a spot purchase of Tunisia's Zarzaitine crude (42°API) at a price of $12.64/B. f.o.b., the buyer being Coastal States. The market, it seemed, was going mad.

On 17 November 1973, the six Gulf states met once more with the oil companies in Vienna to discuss a pricing system that would bring order to the market. But the formulae or bases proposed by the companies were rejected as being too rigid. When the OPEC Conference met a few days later, it formally rejected the companies' proposals, saying that the organization believed "that the pricing of petroleum, like the pricing of other internationally-traded goods, commodities and raw materials, should be market-oriented". Some observers must have considered this a bit rich, coming from an organization whose governments had seen their oil revenues protected from market fluctuations for the past thirteen years (and not fully exposed even before), but the lapse on OPEC's part was only temporary. It was to be more than a decade before OPEC would again look to the market to set prices, and then in a totally different context.

Indeed, OPEC was now facing a problem it had never faced before. It was slipping, almost unintentionally, into the role of a cartel—though for the moment supply restrictions were purely politically oriented—and it would have to take a decision about what price it should charge for its oil. Not a fictitious posted price set for tax purposes, but a real sales price, with real market consequences. Its first attempt would come pretty much in the shape of a *diktat* from the Shah.

Before that happened, however, prices were still shooting up. In mid-December 1973, NIOC held an auction and sold 470 kbd, for the first six months of 1974, of direct deal and joint venture crude with prices up to $17.04/B. for Iranian Light crude. This was crude without embargoed destinations, and the US companies were correspondingly strong bidders; sales were being made to Sun, Murphy, Shell (US), Tenneco, Union Oil and Cities Service. (The Japanese bidders dropped out of the auction at around $10/B., and, in the event, some of the companies that bid successfully in the auction were already declining, in late February 1974, to lift the amounts to which they had committed themselves.) A week later, prices of over $16/B. were reported on sales of Algerian and Nigerian crudes, and a second round of sales by NIOC confirmed the $17+/B. price level. The stage was set for a huge OPEC price increase, and in Iran the idea was beginning to take hold that the price of oil should rise to the level of the cost of developing alternative sources of energy supplies.

Talk of "market-oriented" prices vanished. No one knew what "the market" was, or where it was going, or how it could serve as a guide for a cartel's price. In fact, the market was still thin. It was not institutionalized. There was simply no solid reference point, just a bunch of disparate deals erratically reported in the trade press. People's knowledge of the market was confined to the deals they did themselves, what they read in the trade press (not necessarily accurate and almost always with insufficient detail), and what they could glean from their business and personal contacts (information to be treated with great caution).

Nevertheless, after the sales of Iranian crude at $17, it was clear that posted prices were in for a big jump when the six Gulf states convened in Tehran on 22 December. This was the meeting they had scheduled five weeks earlier to fix Gulf postings for January 1974. It was not, strictly speaking, an OPEC Conference, but was nevertheless attended by other OPEC delegations from Algeria, Indonesia, Libya and Nigeria, with Venezuela along as an observer.

The Shah had been sitting on the sidelines for the previous two months, only intervening (probably with no more serious purpose than to appear statesmanlike to the United States, and perhaps to needle the Arabs) to urge the Arab countries to end their boycott. He now moved to seize the limelight and impose a price of his own choosing. On the morning of 23 December, before the final session of the OPEC ministers had been completed, he announced an increase of 130 percent in the posted price, to $11.651, effective 1 January 1974, which would take government revenue to $7/B. (from $3/B.)

Government take of $7/B. implied a market price of under $9/B. (adding in producing costs and company profit margins)—scarcely an outlandish price compared with recent sales. The justification for the increase was nice, too: producing countries had to offset the rapid inflation in the manufactured goods they imported from the industrial countries; they themselves (the producing countries) had a limited amount of time to generate the revenues they needed in order to industrialize before their oil, a depleting asset, ran out; and $7/B. was at the low end of the scale of costs that the industrial countries would have to pay to develop alternative sources of energy.

All these arguments were made in some detail by the Shah in his press conference on 23 December. To be sure, he admitted, the higher prices would impose hardship on other, non-oil developing countries, but these, he suggested generously, could be helped by the OPEC countries, such as Saudi Arabia and Kuwait, who would have large financial surpluses.

The Shah must have taken the measure of the industrialized countries and concluded that they would not try to retaliate. The Europeans had not responded favorably to Kissinger's 12 December speech with its call for an "Energy Action Group", and they were clearly too divided to take a united political stand. And had not Kissinger himself, in that speech, said "We must bear in mind the deeper causes of the energy crisis; it is not simply a product of the Arab-Israeli war; it is the inevitable consequence of the explosive growth of worldwide demand outrunning the incentives for supply. The Middle East war made a chronic crisis acute, but a crisis was coming in any event. . . . The only long-term solution is a massive effort to provide producers an incentive to increase their supply, to encourage consumers to use existing supplies more rationally and to develop alternative energy sources." In other words, the shortage was here to stay, and consumers would have to pay whatever alternative energy sources cost: that was the message Kissinger chose to send when he knew the OPEC Gulf members would be meeting a few days later to set a new price. The Shah was obviously listening. And if "a crisis was coming in any event", why not now?

The Blunt Instrument

The Arab oil embargo was a blunt and dangerous instrument. It was blunt because it was impossible to apply selectively; it was dangerous—not to its target, but to the major producers wielding it.

Since crude oil is by and large a fungible good, a selective embargo causes some inconvenience, but is easily circumvented by reshuffling suppliers: the countries selectively embargoed shift suppliers to non-Arab countries, and more Arab oil went to the countries previously supplied by the non-Arab producers. The selectivity of the embargo consequently had little effect, beyond being a nuisance and an additional cost. The overall reduction is what, eventually, hurts the target, but it hurts *all* consumers equally if they are in some sort of oil-sharing program and, therefore, none of them very much. And an embargo cannot be applied with immediate effect: a tanker takes about one month to move oil via the Cape from the Persian Gulf to the United States and to northwestern Europe (NWE), the major markets, and about three weeks to Japan. There was a normal amount of oil on the water when the production restrictions were announced on 18 October 1973, so it was only after mid-November that there would be any reduction in arrivals in the United States and NWE, and early November before Japan felt the pinch. The only pain on account of volume that was felt was in the loss of short-haul crude from the Eastern Mediterranean, noted above, and while this was important, it was still a relatively minor portion of total supplies and lasted little more than a month. In any event, by mid-December, the fighting had been over for almost two months and there was no question that the production restrictions could be maintained at damaging levels much longer.

But the embargo was a dangerous weapon for the Arab countries to use. The Gulf producers who controlled most of the oil and whose cutbacks were therefore sharpest, were all military midgets, and at some point withholding supplies from the United States and other industrial countries would have become a fighting matter. Threats, veiled and not so veiled, were in fact made, notably in speeches in 1974 by Kissinger and President Gerald Ford, who had by then succeeded Nixon.

The OPEC producers naturally objected to the implied military threats in the speeches and staunchly defended the current price levels. Western European governments and Japan reacted with alarm, condemned the idea of confrontation, urged cooperation instead, and characterized any attempt to roll back prices as unrealistic.

Subsequent statements by US officials were more conciliatory, and there were no more threats of an oil embargo from Saudi Arabia. The penny had dropped. Nor were there any more calls from Ford or Kissinger for a reduction in the price of oil.

The Scramble for Supplies

In fact, the embargo was for all practical purposes over quickly. Supplies were not significantly reduced and most countries emerged with oil inventories higher at the end of the embargo than at the beginning. But there had been a considerable scare, and the governments of many consuming countries had tried to assure themselves of sufficient supplies by paying some limited lip-service to the Arab cause in its struggle with Israel. More importantly, there was a scramble to line up supplies and supply-contracts on "direct deals" (in the Japanese jargon), government to government. The logic was clear: the oil producing countries wanted assistance in industrializing, their share of oil from the participation deals was growing and oil would be in short supply over the long term. Hence, a consuming government should bestir itself to assure supplies through bilateral agreements. France was particularly active, signing up long-term deals with Saudi Arabia in January 1974 for 820 kbd of oil over a 20-year period; Japan concluded a 10-year deal with Iraq for 330 kbd, also in January; the UK and Iran signed a deal for 100 kbd in 1974; Iran and Italy signed an agreement involving industrial investments of up to $3 billion, while Iran and France signed an agreement for about $5 billion of investments, mainly in petrochemicals. There were others during the first quarter of 1974, until market prices started to weaken, and then they trailed off, partly at least because the prices being asked by the producing countries were too high.

Consumer Reaction

The United States: Project Independence

The initial reaction of the United States to the embargo was muted, the only reason possibly being that too many other things of greater urgency were happening. Instead, President Nixon chose, rather sensibly, to concentrate first on measures to increase domestic energy supplies and put conservation measures into place. On 7 November 1973, he made an Energy Statement on radio and TV in the United States. He made no direct reference to the Arab oil embargo and indeed seemed to go out of his way to downplay it, saying, "Even before war broke out in the Middle East these prospective shortages were the subject of intensive discussions among members of my administration . . . From these discussions has emerged a broad agreement that we as a nation must set upon a new course."

He proposed allocating 10 percent less fuel for aircraft and 15 percent less for space heating, instituting a nationwide speed limit of 50 mph, preventing coal-fired utilities switching to oil, and speeding up licensing and construction of nuclear power plants. He called for legislation to enable the construction of the Alaska pipeline from the North Slope to Valdez, to speed up the development of the country's energy resources and fund a $10 billion dollar research and development program. Finally, he announced Project Independence, a multi-faceted program that would enable the country to become self-sufficient in energy by 1980. The idea was wildly unrealistic, and everybody in energy circles knew it; but Nixon needed the gesture.

Western Europe and Japan: Consumption Curtailed

The immediate reaction in most other consuming countries to the Arab oil embargo was highly defensive. In general, Western European governments, Japan and others sought to restrict consumption by a mixture of mild regulation and strong exhortation, and a series of measures was brought into effect in early to mid-November 1973, usually with a maximum duration of one year.

Typically, the measures (often voluntary) included no Sunday driving by private motorists (the Netherlands, West Germany, Italy, Belgium, Denmark, UK, Greece and Japan); speed limits reduced to 60 mph or thereabouts (same countries, plus Austria); temperatures to be reduced in homes and offices (mostly the same countries); limited lighting in shops for display purposes (Netherlands, Italy, Denmark, Switzerland and Japan); no sale of petrol in cans (France, Austria and Switzerland); service stations closed on weekends (Norway, Portugal and Japan); a cut of 10 to 25 percent in oil deliveries (UK, Denmark, Ireland, Austria, Finland, Norway, Portugal, Switzerland and Japan); exports and re-exports banned except by EEC countries to other EEC countries (Netherlands, Italy and Finland). Consumption did not in fact drop much: in November 1973, it was about 2 percent higher than November of the previous year; in December, about 3.5 percent lower.

The Netherlands presented a special case. It had been singled out by the Arab countries participating in the embargo for a total cut-off in all oil shipments because of its apparent support of Israel. Some EEC governments, notably France, fearful of offending their Arab suppliers by helping the Netherlands circumvent the embargo, indicated that they might not permit the free transit of oil to Dutch destinations. But the Netherlands was in a strong position, and only had to remind its EEC partners that if they were to violate the Treaty of Rome's free-transit provisions, the Dutch might find it necessary to suspend their natural gas deliveries to their neighbors.

In the UK, booklets of coupons for gasoline rationing were issued in November 1973, but never came into use.

The Companies Cope

For all their loss of position, the major oil companies were still by far the world's largest distributors of crude in international trade and the only means at hand for implementing some kind of equitable distribution. They were given no instructions by their home governments on how to allocate supplies (as had been the case in previous supply emergencies such as the Suez crisis of 1956-57), and, mercifully, there was no attempt by the Arab countries to exert pressure on the majors with respect to the disposition of their crude from other sources. Each of them (including non-majors engaged in the international crude trade, such as Amerada Hess, Continental, Getty, Marathon, Occidental, Phillips and Amoco) decided individually to spread the pain as evenly as possible, while still complying strictly with Arab embargo instructions. The companies sought an overall distribution of oil that was as even as possible, using non-embargoed crude to fill the gaps in embargoed countries,

For those consuming countries not home to important international producers and suspicious of how the majors would behave in a crisis (would they favor their home countries and leave the others high and dry?), the moment of truth had arrived. The companies passed the test with flying colors. But there were two special cases: the French companies (CFP and ELF), which didn't have to avoid bending anything because they were already supplying most of their production to France; and BP, in which the British government still had a majority shareholding and had, after all, been originally set up for national security reasons. In fact, however, the government did not force anything on the company, and if BP did bend the rules, it was a very English bend—discreet and imperceptible to all but the beneficiary, a cargo here and a cargo there, nothing obvious, you understand.

The re-allocations made by the US companies was not monitored, but the Federal Energy Administration (FEA) did make a study of them, from which the MNC Report summarized the following main conclusions:

> The US and other international oil companies helped to blunt the edge of the Arab oil weapon by redistributing global supplies so that the constriction of supplies was fairly evenly allocated, rather than targeted specifically against the United States and the Netherlands. Some pressure was exerted on oil companies by consuming nation governments, but it was rarely excessive. In most cases, governments were satisfied by industry assurances that supplies were being equitably distributed . . . The US companies did not on the basis of their nationality, treat the United States as a specially favored nation during the embargo.
> – MNC Report, pp. 147-8.

High praise, considering the source.

A New Reality

OPEC was now in control of supply and price. The industry would have to adjust to the new reality. But the aftermath would be a long one, and then a new catastrophe would strike. At the beginning of 1974, there was a host of problems (apart from winding up the embargo) to be confronted. Taxation at the producing end was far from settled; indeed, the Shah had specifically said that $7 was only a first step. Participation was up in the air again, putting into question the future role of the companies as investors. Pricing policy was undetermined. The effect of price on demand was unknown, and most especially its effect on the demand for OPEC oil. No one had a good handle on conservation, on alternative sources of energy, nor on new sources of non-OPEC oil. Inflation was roaring ahead. Policy alternatives for the importing industrialized countries were not sorted out. The oil-importing developing countries (OIDCs) had no means of paying for the higher level of imports they would require for development. It would take several years to clear up the mess.

Chapter 10
THE AFTERMATH OF '73

The United States and the rest of the non-Communist world face the most serious economic crisis since the depression of the Nineteen Thirties. If strong policies are not immediately adopted, this crisis can undermine the economic foundation of the non-Communist world and jeopardize our democratic form of government.
– Report of the U.S. Senate subcommittee on Multinational Corporations, 2 January 1975, p. 1

Perceptions

The opening paragraph of the Senate subcommittee's report, quoted above, was a gross exaggeration, hugely wide of the mark. In the 1930s, US GNP dropped 30 percent from its high of $204 bn. in 1928 to $142 bn. in 1933. In the 1970s, GNP stagnated but did not drop; and no one even suggested, let alone threatened, replacing democracy in the United States (or in any other country where it was established) by any other form of government.

The statement was an extreme example of a sentiment or perception that was rapidly becoming commonplace. There were plenty of others, some almost as alarmist, emanating from otherwise responsible sources. For example, here is the chairman of Exxon, Clifton C. Garvin in late November 1973, before the December OPEC price hikes:

> The world-wide energy supply problem was beginning to take shape long before the recent events in the Middle East occurred, and will remain long after the current production restrictions and embargoes are removed. . . . We are heading for continuing energy shortages during the next 10 to 15 years . . . which could be severe enough to have a dramatic impact on economic growth and living standards in many countries.
> – PIW, 3 December 1973.

I quote others elsewhere in this book. The slightly less alarmist message endlessly repeated was that the era of "cheap energy" had gone forever. (As I was writing these words, twenty-five years later, in mid-1999, gasoline was selling in the United States for under one dollar per gallon, cheaper in real terms than it had ever been at any time.)

Nor did perceptions wear off easily. Here is ex-US Secretary of State Henry Kissinger, writing nearly ten years after the event:

> It is now obvious that [OPEC's decision to increase the posted price from $5.12 to $11.65, Tehran, December 1973] was one of the pivotal events in the history of this century.
> – Kissinger, *Years of Upheaval,* (1982), p. 885.

It presumably ranks, in Kissinger's estimation, alongside the overthrow of the Czarist regime in Russia and the installation of Communism there, the First World War, the Great Depression, the Second World War, the decolonization of Asia and Africa, technological inventions galore from the flying machine to the personal computer, and the tripling of the world's population.

Diplomacy, Dialogue and Delusion

Even before the dust had settled on the Arab-Israeli armed conflict and the embargo, there began a period of unreal diplomacy and dialogue between producers and consumers, fed by their delusions.

There *was* a real issue: the diplomatic isolation of OPEC from other developing countries; there were also unreal issues: first, the extent to which OPEC could use its new-found power to impose structural changes in international trade on the developed countries (answer: none); and, second, the extent to which industrial countries could extract solid commitments from OPEC of assured supplies of oil at reasonable prices (answer: none). All were scrambled into a diplomatic mess and a froth of dialogue.

But first, the two sides had to get their ducks lined up.

The Washington Energy Conference, February 1974

In early January 1974, President Nixon addressed a proposal to the major consuming countries for a ministerial conference in Washington to formulate a "consumer action program" and "to develop a concerted consumer position ... for producer-consumer relations". A parallel message was sent to OPEC heads of state, expressing the hope that "an early joint conference of consumer and producer nations" could be held.

In February 1974, at Nixon's behest, an energy conference duly convened in Washington, with major European countries, Canada, Japan and representatives of the EEC and the OECD attending.

The main fruit of the conference was the establishment later that year (in November 1974) of the International Energy Agency (IEA), under the auspices of the OECD, with most members of the OECD except France and Norway joining. It had a broad remit of policy coordination, but its main task was to develop a working plan for the allocation of oil supplies internationally in the event of emergency. An Agreement on an International Energy Program was signed on 21 September 1974 in Brussels by the EEC countries, the United States, Canada and Japan, providing for stockpiling of oil and an emergency oil allocation and sharing program to be implemented through the IEA.

OPEC and the Oil-Importing Developing Countries

However, it was clear to OPEC at an early date that, under the supply and demand scenarios then current, it would be able to face the hostility of the industrial world that was so dependent on them for oil, but would not be able to live in a world where the developing countries were also united against them.

A first step in combating this danger was to set up a fund for economic aid to the importers, and this was duly done at the OPEC Conference in early April 1974, which provided for the establishment of the OPEC Development Fund, though it was to be more than a year and a half before it finally came into operation, as the OPEC Special Fund, with initial resources set at $800 million (later increased by an additional $800 million).

The New International Economic Order

A broader diplomatic effort was already underway. In response to a formal request by Algeria's President Houari Boumedienne, the UN General Assembly met in New York in April and early May 1974, and after much debate adopted a "Declaration and Programme of Action" for the establishment of a "New International Economic Order" based on twenty points enunciated in the declaration, all aimed at promoting the economic development of developing countries. It was wildly and hopelessly unrealistic, but gave OPEC the chance to pose as a sort of vanguard for the Third World in a struggle to redress what many developing countries regarded as an economic system rigged against them by the industrialized world. Predictably, it never came to anything.

European Initiatives

Nevertheless, there was initially some positive response: in September 1974, the EEC's Council of Ministers agreed to draw up a long-term energy strategy involving cooperation among consuming countries and between consuming countries and producing countries, and went so far (against US wishes) as to open a Euro-Arab dialogue, as well as promoting the development of alternative supplies of energy.

The following month, President Giscard d'Estaing of France proposed holding a tripartite conference on energy and related problems, among industrialized countries, oil producers and developing countries.

The Dakar Conference

The next grand move was the Conference on Third-World Strategy on Raw Materials and Economic Development which was held in Dakar, Senegal, in February 1975 and attended by 110 developing countries. A resolution was adopted expressing solidarity between oil-importing developing countries and OPEC, and demanding that the international conference proposed by France deal with problems related to all raw materials, not just oil.

The OPEC Algiers Summit

A month later, in March 1975, OPEC held a summit conference in Algiers of heads of state of member countries and issued a "Solemn Declaration" of fourteen points, setting forth general positions and concerns about the international economy and relations with developed countries.

It was a long and pretentious document, dripping with crocodile tears for the oil-importing developing countries, argumentative, tendentious, pompous at times, and generally hostile to the developed countries on major issues of international trade: a thoroughly Algerian document, drafted almost entirely by the Algerians, but aided and abetted by Venezuelans. As a wish-list, its substance was not in fact reprehensible, but it was a thoroughly unrealistic document, couched in obnoxious terms and offering in return only a readiness "to negotiate the conditions for the stabilization of oil prices".

On the key issue of the price of oil, the declaration laid out some criteria that were to be later embodied in the recommendations of OPEC's Long-Term Strategy Committee in 1980, namely indexation against inflation, and the value of alternative sources of energy.

The Conference on International Economic Cooperation (CIEC)

After further diplomatic to-ing and fro-ing, the first plenary meeting of the Conference on International Economic Co-operation (CIEC) was held in Paris, in December 1975, co-chaired by Venezuela and Canada. Eight industrialized countries participated (with the president of the EEC Council of Ministers representing all EEC members), with nineteen developing countries, including seven OPEC member countries. Four expert commissions were set up to study the various issues—on energy, raw materials, development and financial questions.

The conference dragged on for another eighteen months, with the expert commissions lagging behind schedule. Finally, in early June 1977, the second (and final) plenary session of CIEC was held in Paris. No substantive agreement emerged.

So much for dialogue. It was an embarrassing spectacle in which both sides displayed an extraordinary lack of realism. OPEC and the developing countries could not possibly have obtained the concessions that they sought, many of which were in any event under discussion in other fora, notably GATT and UNCTAD. The industrial countries on the other hand could never have obtained a commitment from OPEC on oil prices.

Three and a half years of diplomacy and dialogue had come to nothing. In the meantime, markets had weakened, the opportunity to bring prices down had been subverted, the companies in the OPEC area were being nationalized or taken over in other ways and OPEC itself transformed into an *ad hoc* cartel.

Unfinished Business: Participation

The tightness in the market that prevailed during the first three quarters of 1973, before the outbreak of the Arab-Israeli war, and the market panic of late 1973 and early 1974, sent a grievously false message to OPEC member countries. It suggested that there would be no problem in marketing participation crude and this, combined with the longer-term outlook for continuing shortages, convinced OPEC governments to accelerate the whole process of participation and bring forward the date of complete control and ownership. Still, no one except Yamani understood the dangers of "complete control and ownership", or, if they did, they weren't saying so.

Kuwait soon called for the renegotiation of the General Agreement on Participation (which it had not ratified) that provided for 25 percent participation immediately with a phased-in increase of the government share over a period of years. This was now out of the window. By the end of January 1974, Kuwait had signed a new participation agreement with Gulf and BP, whereby the government acquired 60 percent participation effective 1 January 1974. The agreement was to run for six years (to 1979), by which time the government would have acquired 100 percent of the facilities of the BP/Gulf operating subsidiary, the Kuwait Oil Company (KOC). Compensation was to be paid on net book value, amounting to $112 million for 60 percent. The agreement was ratified on 14 May 1974 by the Kuwait National Assembly.

Time and again, in looking back at this period, one is struck at how the *zeitgeist* played cruel tricks on the companies. They, and everyone else, were anticipating crude shortages in the long term and access to supply would, it was thought, be critical, even if it had to be shared with the host governments. They were in a hurry to settle. If Gulf and BP had kept their cool and played for time, they would, within a brief six months, have seen their position greatly strengthened by the growing surplus of oil and the inability of governments to put large quantities of participation oil onto the markets without a price collapse, or at least a serious drop. To preserve their position or some part of it, the companies desperately needed a determined common front; but by now, they were demoralized and believed that the impending "shortages" would give them no alternative and that opposition was futile.

The Kuwait agreement was another turning point. It meant, of course, that the countries that had signed the General Agreement—the UAE, Qatar and Saudi Arabia would inevitably move at least to Kuwait's 60 percent, and that Iran would demand "financial equivalence". And so it was, except for one thing. Yamani came to the conclusion that if 25 percent participation wouldn't hold, nor would 60 percent; he called for a 100 percent takeover which, in substance, would not be full nationalization, as he envisaged it, because he wanted to preserve some reasonably important part of the alliance with the companies. He therefore sought an arrangement that would leave the companies with a significant "economic interest", some equivalent, at least in financial terms, of an equity interest. At first, the companies would have none of it. On 10 June 1974, Saudi Arabia reached an interim agreement with Aramco for 60-40 participation, effective 1 January 1974, and both sides hunkered down for a struggle. But at least his call for a 100 percent takeover meant that Saudi Arabia could not now be portrayed as dragging its feet and catering to US interests.

There was good reason for the companies to try hanging on to what they could: the profit margin on their equity crude (at first, the 75 percent and then the 40 percent they retained under the participation agreements) was huge because taxes (royalty and income tax) were still based on an agreed posted price that was, unusually, below the market price. Thus the companies retained the whole of the difference between the two prices—tax-free. If the companies were doomed to sink, at least it would be in an ocean of profit. It was an absurd situation that OPEC had created.

Other Arrangements

Not all OPEC member countries chose what was at first called, with apparently little sense of the absurd, 100 percent participation. Some nationalized.

In March 1974, Libya nationalized Shell's remaining assets in the country. In June, the two parties reached a settlement whereby Shell was compensated at the net book value of its assets and in turn agreed to drop arbitration proceedings against Libya, which it had initiated when the first part of its assets were nationalized. In December 1975, Iraq completed nationalizing the industry by taking over the remaining holdings of BP, Shell and CFP in the Basrah Petroleum Company, which was part of the IPC group and operated in the south of the country. In August 1975, Venezuela nationalized the entire industry, effective 1 January 1976. This was to some extent only a matter of timing, as the concessions were due to expire in 1983-84 and the problems of transition, involving maintenance and ongoing investments, were getting too difficult to handle.

Some countries, notably Iran and Kuwait, chose to follow the Saudi example, though in Iran the form was different. Other countries, notably the UAE, Libya and Nigeria, chose to leave some of the concessionaire companies holding some equity. For a while, the OPEC area was had a mixed bag of different arrangements, but in most of them, the major oil companies retained a role as operators or providers of technical assistance, paid for on a fee basis, with or without privileged access to crude oil supplies from the government.

OPEC Surprised: The Birth of a Cartel

Absurd, implausible, improbable it may sound, but the historical truth is that OPEC's member countries were genuinely surprised to find that they had, seemingly overnight, metamorphosed into a cartel. Absurd, etc., because this was an organization that had been founded with the specific intention on the part of its two prime movers (Pérez Alfonzo of Venezuela and Abdullah Tariki of Saudi Arabia) of limiting overall production with a view to raising prices and allocating market shares among its members. What else does a cartel do? Indeed, OPEC's early years were partly spent in studying various bases (population, area, reserves, etc.) for pro-rationing production among the members—highly theoretical studies, one might add, because by 1963, no one in the organization was seriously contemplating production controls. (Some of them never had.)

Nevertheless, surprise it was, so much so that it took OPEC a long time to fully accept its consequential imperatives: production restrictions and quotas. The struggle by OPEC members for control had centered on nationalization in some countries but participation in most, and the question of how total output was to be determined was never addressed; indeed, it never seems to have occurred to anyone to raise the question. The implicit assumption was that the countries where nationalization had occurred would market their crude as best they could, and that in the participation countries, everything would go on in the same old way. The participation countries were at first nervous and doubtful about their ability to sell their share of the crude; hence the buy-back arrangements whereby the companies would have to buy back at a guaranteed price (which was now under the control of the governments themselves) any of the governments' share of crude that they could not sell. There didn't appear to be any need for cartelistic arrangements.

Moreover, by the time participation had been moved up from its original 25 percent to 60 percent in early 1974, the talk was all of long-term shortages, supply crises, pressure on reserves, etc., and there was still no thought of production restrictions as a price-support measure. Those that were thinking of restrictions at all (such as Saudi Arabia and Kuwait) and put them into effect were afraid of premature depletion, not market surpluses. Even when surpluses began to appear, by mid-1974, and proposals for production cutbacks were put forward by the OPEC Economic Commission in June of that year, at OPEC's Quito Conference, they were decisively rejected, mainly because Saudi Arabia, which had the largest amount of spare capacity, did not want to foreclose its option of bringing pressure to bear to keep prices down if the rest of OPEC decided on a price increase without them. Saudi Arabia was also pursuing its own particular struggle with Aramco at the time and knew that it might need to use its spare producing capacity to make the company's situation untenable.

Besides, it was generally thought in OPEC that the situation was a short-term, transitory matter, a brief period of temporary surplus before supply and demand balance would prevail, followed by increasing shortages. Nevertheless, at the Quito Conference, there was an informal, gentlemen's agreement among members other than Saudi Arabia, to hold production down to the then current levels until the next scheduled conference in September.

These were the birth-pangs of a cartel. But there was as yet no formal agreement on the cartel's basic functions, the restriction of supply or the distribution of market shares, and there was no awareness that here was a brand-new cartel emerging, a bigger and, to some, more menacing, cartel than the world had ever seen.

OPEC Prices: Saudi Arabia versus the Rest

OPEC Prices, January - June 1974

In the first of a long series of clashes between Saudi Arabia and most of the other member countries of OPEC that was to last for several years, with varying degrees of intensity, Saudi Arabia adamantly opposed a price increase at the OPEC Conference that met in mid-March 1974. As a result, posted prices for the second quarter of 1974 remained frozen at $11.651/B. (and the market price on direct deals at $10.84/B.). Saudi Arabia argued that prices were already too high and that they should be reduced, and while the country's main concern was over market reaction and the effect of the price increase on the economies of the industrialized countries (in which the Saudis had an important financial stake), there is little doubt that it was also responding to what it regarded as the US position.

OPEC Prices, July - September 1974

There was a repeat performance at the next conference, held in Quito in June 1974. The arguments were stormy, especially as Iran threw its weight behind the proposals for an increase, and Saudi Arabia had to threaten to walk out of the conference and open up spare capacity if necessary. In the end, a compromise was again reached and posted prices remained frozen. There was much debate within OPEC over what the market would bear, with most countries believing that, despite the current market weakness which they all recognized but considered temporary, a further increase was warranted.

The way to really test the market would be, it seemed to Yamani, to hold an auction of a substantial amount of crude. The lower prices that would undoubtedly be obtained would do their work as other member countries lost volume to Saudi Arabia. Plans were soon to be laid for a large-scale auction.

Once the worst of the Arab oil embargo was over, the market had weakened quickly. After years of vigorous growth, world demand (excluding CPEs) was to drop by almost 1 million bd in 1974, and by more than that in 1975. In mid-March 1974, it was reported that a scheduled Kuwaiti auction of 250 kbd had only attracted bids which were, for the first time in several months, below the posted price. The crude offering was withdrawn. By May, companies that had agreed to prices in the $17 range with Iran in December 1973 were dragging their feet on liftings and some were reneging. At the beginning of July, an auction of 1.25 mbd of Kuwaiti crude for the second half of 1974 was canceled (though this had been more of a ploy in negotiations with BP and Gulf over the price of "buy-back" crude than a serious attempt to go to the open market). In Iran, at the same time, no substantial sales were reported on an offering of 215 kbd, also for the second half, and the offering was withdrawn.

It is no exaggeration to say that the events that followed the Quito Conference—the announcement and then hasty cancellation of the Saudi auction—were of absolutely critical importance for the path prices took thereafter. These events have to be examined in the light of US policy towards OPEC under Kissinger.

US Policy and OPEC: Kissinger's Own

Kissinger was ill-equipped intellectually to confront the newly formed OPEC cartel. His mind-set was obsessively geopolitical, and while it is true that the OPEC cartel was born in a highly political context, it was nevertheless an essentially economic threat, the threat of excessive—extortionate, in the view of many—prices, jerked up suddenly, and ratcheted further up to ever higher levels. To make matters worse, Kissinger's fixation on geopolitical objectives, notably with Iran, conflicted with the administration's official policy of seeking to bring prices down.

Kissinger's first official involvement with energy policy came with his appointment to a Special Committee on Energy by White House Executive Order of 18 April 1973, along with Chief of Staff John D. Ehrlichman and George P. Schultz. The National Energy Office, established by the same executive order, was to be under the Special Committee's policy supervision. However, the committee was not notably active before it was replaced in June by the appointment of Governor of Colorado John D. Love to a new Energy Policy Office, reporting directly to the president.   Kissinger's other involvement in oil matters had been, and continued to be, through the Washington Special Actions Group (WSAG), which had a much wider brief than energy and was an interdepartmental group for coordinating policy during crises. The WSAG had considered oil issues in the context of Libyan demands on the oil companies following Colonel Qaddhafi's successful coup in 1969, but had concluded that there was little to be done because the United States had no leverage over the country, and that, at the time some action against Libya was being considered, the market was so tight that "Libyan oil was literally the only oil in the world that was irreplaceable . . ." Kissinger acquiesced in this judgment, but it was just another example of mistaking the very short term for the slightly longer term.

On 22 September 1973, two weeks before the outbreak of fighting between Egypt and Israel and three weeks before the OPEC decision to raise posted prices unilaterally, Kissinger was appointed secretary of state. With the Presidency embroiled in Watergate and Vietnam, the Middle East conflict and a few other matters on his mind, one can scarcely fault Kissinger for not concentrating at that point on the price of oil. When he did come to deal with the issue, his understanding of international oil prices was grievously distorted by his geopolitical mind-set: here, in his own words, is what he believed the situation to be, at least up to 1972:

> Oil imports were regulated through a system established by President Eisenhower in 1959, setting quotas for imports . . . In this way, the United States had a decisive influence over the world price of oil. If the price of foreign oil went up beyond what we thought desirable, we could increase our production, restrict our imports, and force our foreign suppliers onto world markets. Or, if we really wanted to make a point, produce more oil and sell it abroad. The Mideast producers therefore had an incentive to keep prices low.
> – *Years of Upheaval*, (1982) p. 855.

This was not a momentary aberration, committed to paper in haste. He repeated it several years later:

> Until 1972 the United States had been in a position to control the world price of oil because it was producing well below full capacity. Thus America was, in effect, able to set the price by increasing or withholding production.
> – *Years of Renewal*, (1990) p. 665.

Kissinger simply couldn't see the economics of oil prices. Indeed, he was the only person of stature, and influence over energy policy, ever to have put forward such a bizarre view of oil prices—and where he got it from is a mystery. It was absurd to suppose that a nation with a small amount of high-cost shut-in producing capacity (quite insufficient to cover domestic demand anyway), and importing ever higher quantities of oil, could possibly exert any influence at all over the international price of oil. As for the idea that the United States could at any time have unleashed its spare capacity onto world markets to drive international prices down, it was simply nonsense. He might as well have said that because Britain had a few coal mines with six-inch thick seams a mile underground, shut in, it could control the world price of coal. How could a secretary of state fail to understand that the point of oil import restrictions was to protect high-cost domestic oil against imports of low-cost foreign oil, and that the existence of some shut-in capacity in the United States was merely a reflection of a political balance between the high-cost US producers who wanted to produce at full capacity before *any* imports were permitted, and the many Americans, and American companies, who wanted to import low cost oil, produced mostly by US companies abroad? Economic analysis was decidedly not Kissinger's forte.

In October 1973 and the following months, it was of course right to accord a higher priority to the settlement of the Middle East conflict, and perhaps other matters, than to getting prices down, even after the much greater increase that OPEC imposed on the rest of the world in December 1973. But, again, listen to Kissinger:

> Both the Nixon and Ford Administrations had no higher priority than to bring about a reduction of oil prices by breaking the power of OPEC.
> – *Years of Renewal*, (1990), p. 668.

However, according to Dr. John C. Sawhill, administrator of the Federal Energy Office, testifying before the Senate Permanent Committee on investigations in early 1974, there *was* no policy on reducing oil prices:

> The United States does not have a policy or set of policies directed at halting and reversing the rise in world prices in the short run.
> – MNC Report, p. 155.

No doubt Nixon and Ford would have been startled to discover that "a reduction of oil prices" was their first priority. Nor was it ever communicated by Kissinger to either Iran or Saudi Arabia, the two countries in a position to do something about it, except, in the case of Saudi Arabia, in an act of bad faith, in early 1974. By late 1974, both Jamshid Amuzegar, minister of Finance of Iran at the time, in charge of oil, and Yamani, Saudi Arabia's oil minister, were left convinced, after several meetings with Kissinger, that the United States was quite happy with the high level of prices. Indeed, except for the initial reaction to the December 1973 price hike, Kissinger (as distinct from other members of the administration) never seems to have suggested to any OPEC member country, except Saudi Arabia in early 1974, that prices should actually be decreased, but only that OPEC should not increase them, or should at least exercise moderation. For example, here is an excerpt from President Ford's message (dated 9 November 1976) to President Carlos Andrés Pérez of Venezuela on the eve of the Forty-seventh OPEC Conference in Caracas in mid-December 1976:

> I wish to bring to your attention my deep concern about reports that Venezuela may seek an increase in the price of oil at the December OPEC meeting, and to urge you to bring your country's considerable influence to bear instead to oppose an increase . . . A further oil price increase would generate inflationary pressures which are not in any nation's interest . . . I am also concerned that an increase in the price of oil could undermine the fragile economic recovery and the already weak balance of payments situation in both developing and industrialized countries . . . Finally, I am concerned that a new increase in oil prices could prejudice the creative and constructive process of dialogue among developed and developing countries . . . I hope, therefore, that . . . the significant influence of Venezuela, and your personal stature and international leadership, will contribute to a decision by the oil-importing countries as responsible as that of May and that there will be no new price increase.[1]

Ford (read Kissinger) nowhere asks for a reduction in prices. All he asks is that they not be increased. Is this how, president-to-president, the United States expresses its top priority as the *reduction* of prices?

So, while paying lip-service to the price-reduction goal, Kissinger studiously ignored, even undermined, all short-term measures that might achieve it. Treasury Secretary William E. Simon, on the other hand, had no doubt that the United States should push for lower prices, and he was convinced that lower prices could be secured by the end of 1974. In the wake of the frantic world wide scramble for supplies over the winter of 1973-74 and the lifting of the Arab oil embargo, inventories everywhere were high. Uncertainty over prices and the direction they were taking led the Kuwaitis to put up several million barrels of oil for auction in March 1974, as noted above; they failed to get their reserve price and the sales were not consummated. The iron was clearly hot, and it was time to strike.

In July 1974, following a visit the previous month to the Middle East by Nixon and Kissinger, Simon visited the area on a basically economic cooperation mission rather than a purely political one. On his return to Washington, he testified (on 12 August 1974) at the MNC Hearings. The thrust of his testimony, as far as oil prices were concerned, was that: (a) the oil market was weakening because of worldwide oversupply; (b) the Saudis were favorably inclined to a drop in oil prices; (c) they would in the near future hold an auction of a significant amount of oil to test the market and they, as well as Simon, expected that the prices would reflect the market weakness; and (d) they would accept the prices bid. Here are some key excerpts from Simon's testimony:

> Our judgment [is] that there is today a surplus of worldwide production relative to current demand and that therefore, there would be strong, downward pressure on oil prices . . . Today we can see a surplus of oil, our estimates, slightly in excess of 2 million barrels a day, which is quite significant. The storage tanks are full all over the world at present and if production remained at this level it would create downward pressure on prices, and that is the most important thing I said. (p. 241)

> In our judgment, such high prices [present high price levels] are not in the interest of either the oil producers or the consumers. (p.235)

> In the interim we will work as we discussed with the Saudi Arabian Government on the oil auction that has been tentatively set for the month of August . . . Minister Yamani announced that the auction would be held in August while I was over there. (p. 244)

> The Saudi Arabian Oil Minister Yamani has told us that he will sell oil at what I anticipate to be lower bids than the 93 percent of posted price because of the surplus available and the lack of storage capacity in the world.

> Senator Symington: "Then . . . you expect the auction to result in lower prices?"
> Secretary Simon: "Yes, sir." (p. 261)

In the event, the auction was canceled. What happened?

Although Simon never said so, and perhaps was not fully aware of it at the time, a deal had been made with Nixon and Kissinger on their visit. Saudi Arabia would help in bringing prices down, but the Saudis made it clear that they were not prepared to try doing it alone: the United States would have to bring strong pressure to bear on Iran, and Iran would have to at least share in leading the way down. But, in fact, neither Kissinger nor his deputy at the State Department, Joe Sisco, made any effort to lean on Iran during their visit there, following their talks in Saudi Arabia. In the meantime, Algeria was appealing frantically to Saudi Arabia not to go ahead with the auction. Algeria was, of course, a price hawk: it had much smaller reserves than Saudi Arabia, and much greater need for revenue; it did not take a long view. In addition, there was the special bond between King Faisal and President Boumedienne: Faisal saw Boumedienne as a strong Arab leader, determined but measured, a dedicated nationalist but able to speak convincingly to the West, educated at Egypt's famous Al-Azhar University, with its traditional Islamic teaching.

What was Faisal to conclude? He must have concluded, when there was no move from Iran, that Kissinger was lying about his intention of putting pressure on Iran to reduce prices. So why should he, Faisal, get out in front without Iranian support and against the urging of others in OPEC, notably Algeria? The King dispatched Yamani to Tehran to talk with the Shah about reducing the price of oil. To Yamani's surprise, the Shah told him that Saudi Arabia would not be pleasing the United States by getting prices down; on the contrary, the United States wanted higher prices provided there were no sharp, abrupt movements.

Where was Kissinger in all this? By this time, he was practically in sole command of foreign policy. Nixon was beyond caring; mired in Watergate, he would resign in early August 1974. But Kissinger, instead of jumping in with vigorous support for Simon by strongly urging the Saudis to hold the auction, expressed his skepticism about its coming off. Indeed, he predicted to Simon that the Saudis would not go through with it, thereby putting his personal prestige on the line. Sisco, his deputy, told Akins, who was then ambassador to Saudi Arabia and who was reporting back to the State Department that the Saudis needed assurances that the United States would exert pressure on Iran, and that he, Akins, was "annoying the Secretary". Indeed, perhaps one of the oddest things in Kissinger's memoirs, as far as energy is concerned, is the way in which he recounts the auction incident—as though he were some disinterested observer watching the action from afar, instead of a key player with possibly decisive influence in the whole matter. Kissinger was in fact all the time in close touch with the influential Prince Fahd who was soon to become Crown Prince and later King. Fahd in turn lent his voice to urge cancellation of the auction.

The auction was canceled, and a golden opportunity was lost. From then on, the Saudis took little notice of US statements deploring high oil prices: they were so much window-dressing. For the next four years, prices were pushed up by the new cartel which, though wobbly and fractious at times, held together despite the surplus producing capacity that weighed on the market. It was not until after the next price explosion that came with the Iranian Revolution in 1979-80, that the cartel would finally succumb to market pressures and the price would fall precipitously. The apparently deliberate failure to push hard for the auction and lower prices in August 1974 cost US consumers billions of dollars.

Kissinger excused his inaction by saying, in effect, that nothing could be done. In an interview with *Business Week* (*BW*, 13 January 1975), he declared:

The only chance to bring oil prices down immediately would be massive political warfare against countries like Saudi Arabia and Iran to make them risk their political stability and maybe their security if they did not cooperate. That is too high a price to pay even for an immediate reduction in oil prices.
— *Years of Renewal* (1990), p. 674.

"The only chance . . . massive political warfare"? He didn't even *ask* them to reduce prices.[2] And, in fact, there were of course numerous points where carefully calibrated pressure could have been applied on both countries: both were dependent on the United States for the supply of arms and technical aid on how to use the high-tech weapons; dependent on US financial institutions to handle their growing funds; and deeply involved with the United States in economic development programs (for example, a Joint Saudi-US Economic Commission had been established in June 1974 for that purpose). They were dependent in the final analysis on the United States for defense against the Soviet Union or other predatory neighbors (as the Gulf War of 1990 was to show). And some undefined "massive political warfare" was the only way the secretary of state could think of to exert pressure on these two countries?

Instead of pushing for a price reduction, Kissinger concentrated (such was his mind-set) on the political isolation of OPEC by trying to cut OPEC off from the rest of the developing countries, and organizing OECD countries into an emergency supply-sharing scheme. He failed abysmally in the first, and at the end of the CIEC Conference in Paris in 1976, the non-oil developing countries stood solidly behind OPEC. The second became, as the International Energy Agency (IEA), a standby fire brigade for a possible repeat of what had already occurred. It never addressed itself to the problem of reducing oil prices.

But Kissinger succeeded in the geopolitical aim of bolstering Iran with as much money as it could spend on arms to ward off the Soviet threat and any other threat in the area. This was the central reason for Kissinger's aversion to exerting any pressure on Iran (or other OPEC countries) to reduce prices. Money for defense and arms was channeled into Iran via high oil prices, and there was no need to go to Congress for it. In his memoirs, Kissinger dismisses this allegation against him as "sophomoric"; but abuse is no substitute for evidence, and the evidence is overwhelming.

In a CBS television network program of 4 May 1980, the well-known CBS news correspondent Dan Rather interviewed ex-Treasury Secretary William Simon and a group of others, including Akins, and ex-Under Secretary of State George Ball. Rather asks Simon:

"Could we have kept the price of oil down if Dr Kissinger or anyone had fought the Shah on it?"

Simon replies: "Yes, we could have. And there was great belief, and there is belief still in some circles today, that the State Department – not necessarily Henry Kissinger – but the State Department – was in favor of high oil prices."

The program goes on:

Rather: "What do you personally think of the theory that Dr. Kissinger knew full well what he was doing, that he wanted the Iranians and the Shah to have the weapons; in order to get the weapons they had to have money, and the way they got the money was to raise the oil prices?"

Simon: "Well, there could very well be some truth in that . . . we had to make sure our allies were in strong positions . . ."

Rather: "But if that's true, we paid one hell of a price for arming the Shah."

Simon: "Yeah, and I suggested it was an unnecessary price to pay, if that were true."

. . . .

Rather: "Privately, you and any number of other people have said, 'Look, Henry did great work on a number of things, but here's one he blew.' "

Simon: "Well, obviously I believed at the time terribly strongly, and I think history has proven my position correct, and in that respect perhaps Henry did blow it."

In May 1972, Kissinger had accompanied Nixon on a visit to Tehran where, in Kissinger's words a year later, "we adopted a policy which provides, in effect, that we will accede to any of the Shah's requests for arms purchases from us (other than some sophisticated advanced technology armaments and with the very important exception, of course, of any nuclear weapons capability . . .)". In return, the Shah was to take on the role of protecting Western interests in the Persian Gulf region. As Gary Sick puts it in his book on US-Iran relations, *All Fall Down* (p.14):

> With the United States bogged down in Vietnam, with US domestic opinion firmly opposed to any new military ventures abroad, with the withdrawal of the British from their strategic role east of Suez, and with the oil of the Persian Gulf beginning to be recognized as a key factor in Western security, there was an inescapable logic in asking a strong regional power to accept a security role that the United States was simply incapable of undertaking at the time.

It was in this context that Kissinger was warned months before the January 1974 oil price increases that a big increase was on the way and would be pushed by the Shah, with Ambassador Akins transmitting Yamani's warnings to the State Department.

The policy of arming Iran and allowing the Shah to purchase practically whatever arms he wanted remained in effect[3] after the January 1974 OPEC price increases. When James Schlesinger, secretary of defense, uneasy about the virtually unlimited sales to Iran, asked his staff in 1974 for an evaluation of the security relationship with Iran, he was told that the White House directive of July 1972 (issued by Kissinger, confirming the May 1972 decision in Tehran in May) "was universally interpreted as a presidential order to the Defense Department to sell Iran whatever military equipment it required, short of nuclear weapons".[3] Within four years of the May 1972 decision, Iran had ordered nine billion dollars worth of military equipment, equal to about half of the country's entire revenue from oil during the fiscal year 1975/76, and twice as much as its entire revenue from oil during the year 1973 before the big leap in oil prices.

In the end, the surfeit of success of Kissinger's policy was thoroughly counterproductive: it contributed to the Shah's undoing as excessive spending on arms and the flood of foreign technicians into the country helped bring him down.

Kissinger recounts his and the State Department's involvement in energy during his period in office. But his last mention of OPEC and, by implication, of energy and the oil price issue is his reference to his December 1975 opening speech at the Conference on International Cooperation (CIEC) in Paris in December 1975. For the year 1976, during the whole of which Kissinger was in office, there is no mention at all in his memoirs of energy or oil prices—supposedly the highest priority. When he left the State Department in early 1977, oil prices were nearly 20 percent higher than in January 1974, immediately after the OPEC hikes of December 1973, and OPEC was anything but isolated. Kissinger was the best friend that the OPEC hawks ever had and his decision not to press seriously for lower prices was a monumental error. The token calls for lower prices made by President Ford and Kissinger towards the end of 1974 were in fact a reaction to threats from Saudi Arabia of a renewed embargo, and were never intended to spark a price decrease; once the threats of renewed embargo were dropped, there was no further call for decreased prices.

I have devoted a good deal of space to Kissinger's performance during this period because Kissinger flatly denies this version of events (which has, in less detail, been put forward by others before me), or anything resembling it, and because it was so important. In 1974, determined pressure from the United States on Saudi Arabia and Iran, and other OPEC members, would have brought a reduction in oil prices that could easily have turned into a competitive slide of the sort that did not come until 1985-86, under entirely different circumstances. There is, of course, no telling what would then have happened, but it could scarcely have been worse than what did in fact happen. But, to return to OPEC pricing.

Supply and Demand and Prices at the End of 1974

In mid-October 1974, the US Federal Energy Administration estimated that there were about 6 mbd of producing capacity shut in in the OPEC area, of which a substantial amount lay outside Saudi Arabia. Both Kuwait and Saudi Arabia had imposed production ceilings earlier in the year for conservation purposes, but were in fact producing below those ceilings. Abu Dhabi cut its production by 300 kbd in September 1974. Venezuela announced that it would cut its production for the year 1975 by more than 400 kbd. Libya was producing erratically but mostly well below capacity. All in all, by September 1974, OPEC's production, at 29.8 mbd was running almost 3 mbd below its previous peak of September 1973.

It was indeed a strange situation. Here was a cartel without a coordinated production policy. True, it had a price policy of sorts, but one that was full of inconsistencies and exceptions. The situation was possible for a while because the Organization's members were flush with cash and intent on maintaining the price control they had wrested from the companies. They preferred, individually and independently of any agreement on market shares, to close in production rather than sell below their official price. And, from the momentum it had, the system (if it can be called that) survived for several years.

OPEC Prices, October 1974

By the time OPEC's Conference met in mid-September 1974, market demand had remained weak for some months. OPEC faced three problems: first, how to resolve the dual price level, consisting of the companies' equity crude on which tax-paid cost was around $7.10/B., plus their purchases of government participation crude at 93 percent of postings or $10.83 (depending on the grade of crude) for a total cost (40 percent of the former and 60 percent of the latter) of $9.34/B.; but the price to everyone else was at least 93 percent of postings, which was what the governments could obtain from the companies from "buy-back" crude; second, whether to restrict production to support prices; and third, what to do about differentials—the appropriate and "fair" differences between the marker crude price and the prices of individual grades of crude oil in its member countries that reflected differences in geographical location and quality. This problem was not one that could possibly be solved in the sense that the differentials would ever reflect over a sustained period of time what was happening in the market, because product prices shifted too frequently and too suddenly.

The first was urgent: it was a situation that could not be allowed to continue much longer. The companies were getting huge margins which they were not passing on to the consumer, and OPEC saw in them a way to bring prices to the consumer down, and improving its image while maintaining or even raising its own income. Iran, sensibly enough, called for the abolition of the posted price system altogether, and the establishment of a single price for all. But this did not at that moment suit Saudi Arabia at all, because its negotiations with Aramco were still in progress.

The September 1974 conference was therefore unable to resolve the problem and it finally decided on a partial and quite unsatisfactory solution: to leave posted prices unchanged for the fourth quarter, at $11.651 (the price for Arabian Light marker crude of 34° API), but to raise royalty rates from 14.5 percent to 16.7 percent, and income taxes from 55 percent to 65.75 percent. This again left official sales prices on "direct deals" at $10.84, where they had been all year. The net increase in government take was 33 cents per barrel on the marker crude, raising the companies' total acquisition cost of crude from $9.41 to $9.74/B., and this meant only a partial correction of the large discrepancy between it and the sales price to other companies. Iran and Saudi Arabia were firmly opposed to a formal program of production restrictions, and indeed, at this point, nearly all OPEC countries were agreed that the market weakness was temporary and would soon give way to increasing strength. The conference ducked the issue by calling for further study of the Economic Commission's proposal that temporary, across-the-board production cuts be made. Nothing at all was done about the problem of differentials, which was not yet acute.

In mid-September, Iraq joined Iran in calling for the complete elimination of the two-tier price system; but it also called for the adoption of a comprehensive production program. Not surprising: Iraq had nationalized entirely and no longer had any safety net in the form of participation crude that it could force the major companies to take if it could not dispose of it itself. The cartel's constraints were beginning to make themselves felt.

OPEC Prices, November - December 1974

The next step was the Abu Dhabi meeting of the OPEC Gulf States in November. The posted price was reduced to $11.251, royalty was raised to 20 percent and the income tax rate to 85 percent. These changes responded largely to Saudi Arabia's needs in its negotiations with Aramco over a 100 percent takeover, but they did in fact also go a long way to resolving the dual pricing problem by drastically reducing the companies' margin on equity crude. A month later, on 10 December, the Aramco companies (Exxon, Mobil, Chevron and Texaco) agreed in London talks with Yamani to 100 percent government ownership and compensation at net book value. The volumes of oil to be made available to the companies and the fees for continued operation and expansion remained to be negotiated. That was the virtual end of participation, and the new basis, or its financial equivalent, was soon to be adopted by those countries that did not simply nationalize the companies outright.

OPEC Prices, January - September 1975

When OPEC reconvened for its December 1974 conference, to set prices and take up the other problems on the agenda, Saudi Arabia's struggle with Aramco had been concluded, though many important details remained to be ironed out.

OPEC's Forty-second Conference met in Vienna on 12 and 13 December, almost a year to the day since the OPEC meeting in Tehran on 23 December 1973 when the posted price had been increased to ensure a government take of $7/B. In the meantime, demand had slumped and some 20 percent of OPEC's producing capacity was shut in. But people's minds had not slumped—they were still in a state of high tension, over Israel and the possibility of a renewed embargo, over the imagined need to negotiate a basis for long-term security of oil supplies at reasonable prices, and over the energy shortages that seemed to loom on the horizon. All the talk was of conferences to fix the world economy with a "new international economic order" and to solve the "energy problem" (see above).

So, if you took the long view, as it was then perceived, there was little reason for OPEC not to increase taxes and prices further, or to panic into awkward and burdensome production restrictions. And consequently, when OPEC's conference met in Vienna it simply decided that the average government take from the companies should be fixed at $10.12/B. on the marker crude for the period 1 January to 30 September 1975, an increase of $0.90/B. from the previous level. The figure chosen derived from the average government take under the November Abu Dhabi arrangements, based on 40 percent equity crude at a tax-paid cost of $9.92 and 60 percent buy-back at $10.46 (93 percent of the new posted price of $11.251 set in Abu Dhabi), minus $0.12 production cost. Questions concerning buy-back prices and actual market prices were left unresolved pending the final 100 percent takeover of Aramco, but the general majority view was that the market price should remain at $10.46, in effect locking in a fixed company margin of $0.22/B. ($10.46 minus $10.12 government take, and minus $0.12 operating cost). It was also agreed that the posted price for the marker crude should remain frozen at $11.25/B. for the period 1 January to 30 September 1975.

Despite the crude oil producing surpluses, member countries rejected proposals for production limitations, believing that the market would firm up during the winter months and that the position could be reviewed at the next OPEC conference.

Again, nothing was done about the differentials problem.

By early 1975, the demand for heavy fuel oil (and, therefore, for heavy crudes) was sagging, and price decreases for heavy crudes in the Gulf, ranging between $0.10 and $0.17 per barrel, were introduced

In the meantime, as noted above, individual OPEC member countries were closing in production rather than lower prices. Saudi Arabia in particular had a large volume, around 3 mbd, of capacity shut in, and it raised serious questions over the country's publicly stated objective of lowering prices. Over the three or four years from 1974, Saudi Arabia was to be repeatedly accused of insincerity and duplicity in preaching lower prices while in fact happily letting prices be dragged up by the so-called OPEC hawks, when all along it had in hand more than enough spare capacity to bring prices down easily on its own if it decided to use it.

As will become apparent in this and subsequent chapters, it was never that simple. Saudi Arabia was, and still is, an essentially weak country and the survival of its regime depends on the skill with which it can navigate the many cross-currents that push it this way and that. Its policies are consequently almost always a compromise between conflicting pressures, more than an aggressive assertion of its own interests, and while it saw its own interests, economically and politically, in lower (or at least stable) prices rather than higher ones, it never for a moment contemplated taking on its relatively powerful neighbors in OPEC and other OPEC hawks alone. It had not heeded Kissinger's request for lower prices unless Kissinger could get Iran into a joint effort, which he did not even try to do; and after the aborted auction, when it had become clear that the United States did not want lower prices, Saudi efforts were mainly directed at holding back or restraining increases. That was as far as it was prepared to go on its own.

OPEC Prices to the End of 1978

During the period from the end of 1974 to the end of 1978, OPEC met eight times in full Conference. Some of the meetings concerned relations with the developing countries and the industrial countries, but most of them had to face questions of price. The questions were always the same: whether to increase prices again, and if so, by how much? It became a constant tug of war, the details of which need not be set out here except to mention that for a period during 1977, the differences between Saudi Arabia and Abu Dhabi on the one hand and the rest, on the other, became so acute that there was a two-tier price system in effect. Prices were reunified in July 1977 and frozen until the end of 1978.

But five years had passed since OPEC had effectively taken over the administration of prices. The new cartel had not yet squarely faced the problem of agreed production quotas and market shares; a coherent pricing policy had not emerged; and the problem of differentials was unsolved.

The Emergence of Spot Crude Oil Prices

The advent of government participation crude in 1974 led to a flourishing spot market for crude oils, with a substantial number of transactions being concluded through brokers. By 1976, they formed an important part of several sales made by the national oil companies, notably those of Iran, Iraq, Abu Dhabi, Libya and Algeria; and because they were not companies with extensive international marketing networks, many of these spot sales were made to traders or through brokers or other intermediaries. One consequence of this was that the spot market not only grew much larger but became significantly more transparent.

While it is impossible to know how much crude oil was moving into world markets on a spot basis, the volumes appeared to vary widely over time, even rather brief periods of time. It was thought that an average level of activity might be ten to twenty cargoes per month for Middle East and African crudes, equivalent to between 250 kbd and 500 kbd. But there were flurries of activity, particularly when an OPEC price rise seemed to be imminent.

The price data was perhaps better than the volume data, but still far from excellent. Prices reported in the trade press did not always specify whether they were bids, offers or actual sales; nor was the month of lifting always specified; and some of the reports were merely assessments of the spot market by brokers and traders, who were of course themselves interested parties.

However, it soon came to be accepted that despite the poor quality of the data on spot crude sales, spot prices were generally a good indication of the way the wind was blowing in the market. They were destined soon to become a much more potent force.

The Companies

After 1973, the major companies in the OPEC area were left clinging to the wreckage. By 1976, there was precious little of that left. Could they have come up with some imaginative "New Deal" that would have put their relations with the major producing countries of the OPEC area on a healthier basis? Perhaps, but it would not have averted the crisis of 1973 or the crisis of 1979. Neither of these had anything to do with the structure of the concession agreements, drastically modified as they already were by the Tehran-Tripoli price agreements and the participation agreements. There is nothing to suggest that even as early as 1969, they could have through their own initiative forged a new and lasting relationship that would have survived the political storms of 1973-74 and 1979-80.

Should they then, in the runup to 1973, have taken a tough stand and refused to budge an inch in the face of growing OPEC country pressure? They could not have done that in the prevailing climate without the strong support of their home governments, which was not forthcoming. On the contrary, the companies were being urged to work things out as best they could, and the companies themselves were divided in their approach: following Nixon's Energy Message to Congress, which called for some form of cooperation among consuming countries, both Sir Frank MacFadzean, chairman of Shell, and Sir Eric Drake, chairman of BP, came out publicly in favor. They were joined by the Common Market (EEC). In Zurich, a group of non-major oil companies held a meeting to discuss such a possibility.

Saudi Arabia's Yamani warned that such an approach would be confrontational and he was joined by Exxon chairman J. K. Jamieson. The whiff of grapeshot was enough and the nascent opposition came to nothing; but even if it had, it would not have withstood the storms to come. They were of a political dimension that clearly transcended government-company relations and the boundaries set by the concession agreements.

Exxon put the company attitude succinctly in its 1975 Annual Report (p.2):

> Since most industrialized nations will be dependent on the members of the Organization of Petroleum Exporting Countries (OPEC) for much of their oil in the years ahead, it is essential that Exxon find ways of working constructively with both producing and consuming countries even as we attempt to find new sources of oil and develop other forms of energy which will eventually lessen that dependence.

In other words, the battle is lost, forget confrontation and get on with the job as best you can.

Nevertheless, for the majors, the prospects for oil seemed bleak in the wake of the loss of their OPEC concessions. Despite the North Sea opening up and, for some, Alaska, there was nothing in prospect that could come close to replacing the Middle East; and even in non-OPEC countries that held good geological promise and (unlike Mexico) were open to foreign capital, the majors were pessimistically confident that if good discoveries were made and developed, they would soon be taken away from them by the governments seeking to emulate the OPEC example.

At this point (1974 and 1975), the companies were loaded with cash from the OPEC price increases. Most of them had seen their annual profits double from one year to the next and stay at high levels, due largely to the incredibly clumsy way in which OPEC had implemented participation. Giving the money to the shareholders was unappealing to management, who did not wish to see their companies permanently downsized.

Two routes, not mutually exclusive, were open: diversification; and retrenchment upstream to the United States, where there were still plenty of geological opportunities, especially at the new, higher prices, and where the dangers of nationalization were absent. The majors did indeed increase and to some extent concentrated their upstream oil activities in the United States, where, incidentally, they discovered another enemy—not government, but the environmentalist movement intent on preventing exploration and development wherever there was risk of a pollution and or other damage to the environment.

But diversification, in principle at any rate, seemed to hold some promise.

The majors had already diversified into chemicals, where they held an advantage in their access to the feedstocks (mainly naphtha and natural gas) and where some of the technology held similarities with the processing of oil. Further diversification had started on a relatively small scale before OPEC came along, but now it became something of a headlong rush. The most obvious (of many unattractive) candidates was coal, an industry which the companies had spent the previous twenty years running into the ground, so to speak. But at the new price level, coal could be attractive once more, and most of the majors went in for it heavily, acquiring mines and properties in the United States itself and in Australia and a few other locations around the globe (notably Exxon's Guajira Colombian mines).

After coal, in energy-related businesses, came the mining and processing of oil shales (mainly in Colorado), Canadian heavy oils and tar sands, and uranium mining and nuclear fuel fabrication, in which some of the major companies took a stake. Alternative sources of energy, especially solar energy, also attracted the attention and a little of the capital of the majors, but never came to much, though some companies (notably BP) have persisted and believe it holds great promise. Then (since they were now in the mining business) came non-energy minerals, mostly non-ferrous metals such as copper, zinc and silver mining.

At this point, the movement to diversify moved into other areas, and took other turns, sometimes bizarre, comic even, for these industrial oil giants.

Reviewing the major oil companies' annual reports, the monthly *Oil & Energy Trends* (20 May 1977) remarked "What with an energy crisis down the road and the drying up of oil resources, diversification remains the key to immortality [for the majors] . . . Powerful intimations of mortality are pushing the oil companies into other fields. But it isn't so easy for giants to turn into a bunch of conglomerate midgets with the same cash flow."

Indeed, the zany end of diversification illustrated the extremes to which the companies were being driven. Chevron reported:

> Garden and home product sales achieved record levels. Acceptance by the public of the Ortho garden book series was gratifying . . . The new Hilltop shopping center at Richmond California opened in September.
> – *Annual Report 1976.*

Mobil acquired Montgomery Ward (founder of the US mail order merchandise business), and the Container Corporation of America (part of the paperboard industry). Mobil reported that in 1977, Montgomery Ward distributed "more than 100 mn. copies of 16 seasonal and promotional catalogues . . . " *(Annual Report 1977).*

Shell went into scrap metal recycling, BP into computers, international travel and freight forwarding, and Exxon into office equipment with Startreksounding names like Qwip (fax machines), QYX (electronic typewriters) and ZILOG (microcomputer components).

The March madness did not last long and by 1979 the companies were backpedaling fast. Mobil said that it was "not actively seeking other major diversifications. We see ourselves essentially as a diversified energy company." Exxon said, "Energy resource development still represents the major portion of our business, and we expect this emphasis to continue". And Chevron: "The petroleum business remains our primary interest." *(1978 Annual Reports)*

It would not take many years before most of the ventures into diversification were dumped as quickly and quietly as possible (including many of the coal ventures), and the companies returned to their "core business" (in the buzz-word of the day).

Oil and gas were still big business, without the OPEC area concessions. Non-OPEC production kept rising in a large array of countries in addition to the North Sea. OPEC-style nationalizations did not sweep the industry, and then in the early 1990s, the collapse of the Soviet Union opened up a new world of upstream (and downstream) investment opportunities in the newly independent republics of the Former Soviet Union and Eastern Europe.

OPEC's New Role: 1974-1978

For a long time, OPEC really didn't get it. It understood, of course, that it was now setting world oil prices. However, surprised at the notion, it simply could not, or would not, quite accept its unexpected new role as a cartel. A cartel sets prices by restricting supply from its members and, necessarily, divvying up the market among them through a system of production quotas. This entails shutting in some existing producing capacity.

But this was not at all the way OPEC saw things. The world according to OPEC (and most other people), was entering a period of "continuing energy shortages", in the phrase of Clifton Garvin, chairman of Exxon. OPEC would simply set prices at a fair and reasonable level (e.g., the cost of alternative sources of supply), take it or leave it, period. Member countries would produce at capacity, or whatever lower level they preferred, and the world would have to do with whatever other energy supplies it could develop. Short-term surpluses were a temporary problem and no one within OPEC wanted to embark on production-quota commitments in order to solve it. Saudi Arabia subscribed to this view, but had an additional, more immediate reason for rejecting production quotas: it held most of the surplus producing capacity—a Damocles sword over the heads of other member countries, just in case the hawks got too far out of hand. Production quotas would have removed this weapon.

But what had in fact happened during the period to the end of 1978 and the Iranian Revolution? Without a plan or a purpose, its members divided among themselves on price objectives (some of them changing their minds from time to time), engaged in a fruitless dialogue with the industrialized consuming countries and a struggle for the hearts and minds of developing countries. OPEC simply stumbled from one *ad hoc* decision to another, with prices inching up, regardless of the market.

Everything was soon to change again with the Iranian Revolution in 1979.

Postscript

Two extraordinarily dramatic events occurred during the period we have been reviewing. They did not much affect oil policies, and are not really germane to the oil story, but they should be mentioned because they were emblematic of the troubled political times. The first was the tragic assassination in early 1975 of King Faisal, one of the most outstanding Arab leaders of modern times, by a disgruntled prince. The second was the kidnaping of the OPEC Ministers, meeting in Vienna in September 1975, by the Venezuelan terrorist Carlos and his gang. After flights to Algeria, Libya and back to Algeria, they were released unharmed.

Chapter 11
THE CRISIS OF '79

There is a high probability that an increasing tightness of international energy supply, especially of oil, will emerge during the late 1980s. If industrial societies do not develop and implement both domestic and international policies which succeed in reducing their collective dependence upon imported oil generally and Middle East oil in particular, the world community could be confronted by an unprecedented situation. Available oil supplies will be insufficient to sustain economic growth and achieve political and social objectives or even, perhaps, to maintain existing standards of living.

– Rockefeller Foundation. *Working Paper on International Energy Supply: A Perspective from the Industrial World.* New York: The Rockefeller Foundation, May 1978.

Prologue

The second oil price shock took the price of oil within a few brief months to undreamt-of heights. Nothing could have been more different from the 1973 crisis with which the second is sometimes twinned. Their genesis, convulsive lives and outcome were quite unlike each other: in 1979-81, OPEC, far from fighting for control over prices, was struggling to stop it from slipping away. Internally divided, driven by ill-conceived policies that destroyed the closest thing to allies that it had ever had—the major oil companies in the upstream—it failed totally in the face of a devastating market storm driven up at first by panic then down by competition. OPEC had been in the driver's seat for a scant five years; once prices started to tumble, it was at best the hand on the brake.

The Iranian Revolution of 1978-79 utterly changed the political landscape of the Middle East. It also ushered in the most turbulent period in the history of crude oil prices and markets. Afterwards, and after the senseless war with Iraq that followed hard on the revolution's heels, the international oil industry found itself once again transformed. The vestiges of the major companies' vertical integration had all but disappeared; OPEC's ambitions of price-administration lay in tatters; and for a while, prices and price-expectations distorted the whole world of energy as never before. And, astonishingly, everything happened without at any time there being the slightest shortage of

215

supply.

What occurred during these few fateful years cannot be understood without a firm grasp on a major OPEC aspiration and a major OPEC fear, because between them they dominated member countries' behavior throughout the period, and their behavior in turn dominated the course of events in the industry.

The aspiration was to administer oil prices. It was perhaps something more than an aspiration: OPEC member countries believed it was their function and prerogative to administer prices. In their experience, oil prices had always been administered, and in 1973 OPEC had deliberately wrested control over them from the major oil companies—and had in fact gone on to administer them with some success over the next several years. After 1973, it never occurred to them to do otherwise, that is, to leave the settlement of oil prices to the market. There was not even a whisper of discussion of such a possibility from any quarter of the industry. But even if it had occurred to them, it is not at all clear how they would have gone about it. There was no independent free market in crude, such as later developed for North Sea oil, that could provide market-oriented benchmark crude prices or a reference point on which to base term contract prices. Indeed, quite the opposite tendency took hold in OPEC: member countries soon realized, after endless squabbles over the setting of a base price for a marker crude and the consequent quality differentials, that they needed to formulate a coherent price strategy to achieve a clearly defined objective within a framework of rules or guidelines for how to get there.

This was the main purpose of the Ministerial Committee on Long-Term Strategy set up by OPEC in June 1978, and while member countries were generally conscious (sometimes painfully so) of the state of the market in general terms—whether in oversupply or not—they regarded it as only one factor among others to be taken into account in setting prices, and not as the price-determinant in itself. Its influence was mainly with respect to timing: after all, everyone believed that the world was heading for shortage in the longer term.

The Long-Term Strategy Committee was composed of the oil ministers of Algeria, Iran, Iraq, Kuwait, Saudi Arabia and Venezuela. In turn , it appointed a committee of experts to meet under the chairmanship of Saudi Arabia's Oil Minister Ahmed Zaki Yamani, draw up a study and recommendations, and report back to the Ministerial Committee in due course. It was to take more than two years to complete its work, during which there were long discussions at numerous meetings, studies prepared by outside consultants, and meetings held with representatives of governments in various countries, oil industry executives and other experts. But the main reason for the long drawn-out process was the turbulent price and market conditions that took hold soon after the committee started its work, as well as the important task of achieving a consensus at the political level (a job for the chairman) along the way. Its conclusions and recommendations were submitted to the Tri-Ministerial OPEC Conference which was held in Vienna in September 1980 (of which more later).

In the end, price administration, in the sense conceived by OPEC, turned out to be a vain ambition, as the Organization came to realize in the 1980s; but at the time, it was a strongly-held conviction, axiomatic and unquestioned.

OPEC's major fear was a deep-seated one of premature depletion, something that has been endemic to the oil industry since its early days (an odd phenomenon for an industry normally subject to large surpluses in producing capacity). In the Middle East especially, however, this fear had been powerfully aroused by the industry's extravagant development plans of the early 1970s. To be fully appreciated, it must be seen against the background of an almost universal belief in industry and consuming government circles that energy would soon be in permanently short supply. Producing countries would be pressured, perhaps compelled—there had been veiled threats by the United States to use force if necessary—to produce far in excess of their revenue requirements; their natural resources would be raped as the "West" gained time to develop alternative energy sources; then, after a period of disorderly development, they would be left depleted and cast aside, some of them to return to barren desert dotted with ghost towns on a grand scale. It was even reported that a group of Arab officials from Kuwait undertook a special visit to ghost mining towns of the US West to see their future for themselves. They returned, not surprisingly, shaken. Hence the crop of production ceilings that were decreed in many of the OPEC countries, in Kuwait, Iran, Venezuela, Abu Dhabi and above all and most fatefully in Saudi Arabia. The last-named set a ceiling in the early 1970s of 8.5 mbd and in fact never again budged from that position for many years, except in extreme circumstances, during parts of the period 1979-81. At that stage, however, in the early 1970s, the ceiling was still open to discussion and a number of different alternatives on the increase of producing capacity were discussed with Aramco, with a figure of 12 mbd being the one on which virtual agreement was reached. In the event, it was unnecessary.

Sight lost of these two factors (OPEC price-control aspirations and its fear of premature depletion) and it becomes impossible to understand what happened in the international oil industry immediately before, during, and immediately after the 1979-80 "crisis". To be sure, there were other factors, political ones, including events in the ongoing Arab-Israel conflict, US pressure for price-moderation, fear of the new regime in Iran, etc., but they were always within the context of, and subsidiary to, the deeply embedded beliefs of the times. The impending energy shortage meant that a rational pricing strategy had to be worked out to manage the transition from surplus to shortage, and production ceilings had to be enforced to prevent premature depletion.

These two factors are major ingredients of the crisis of '79. They explain why OPEC member countries behaved as they did, following policies that at times appeared to be perverse, predatory or, at best, simply contradictory. But they do not explain the tripling of prices that took place within a period of months in the absence of any shortage of crude oil, before or during the period, much less after. The economic disaster that started in late 1978 was a triumph of mind over matter, faith over fact and belief over the drumbeat of contrary evidence. Panic in a chaotic market swept everything before it, consumers, producers, companies, governments; but there was never a shortage of crude. For the explanation, we must look to the *zeitgeist* in the context of which the two factors operated.

The Mind-set of 1978

Dozens of studies and forecasts of 1977-78 vintage can be cited to show how widespread was the belief in impending shortage. The monthly *Oil & Energy Trends* (February 1979) remarked,

> Everybody's doing it. There are now so many energy forecasts around that people have started compiling opinion polls based on them . . . Among the most recent comparisons is the IEA's monograph entitled *A Comparison of Energy Projections to 1985*. Now the distinctive thing about opinion polls is that they tell you quite a lot about people's opinions and blessed little about the subject of their opining.

And so it was with the International Energy Agency's monograph, which cited several forecasts, all published within an eighteen month period from January 1977 to June 1978. The list included the IEA itself, a joint Pirinc/EPRI forecast, the US Department of Energy, Exxon, a joint Petro-Canada/PDVSA study, the US Congressional Research Service, the CIA, and WAES, among others. The focus of attention for the 1985 end-point of the forecasts was the amount of production "required" from OPEC by that year, generally arrived at by comparing estimated world energy demand with estimated world energy supplies other than OPEC. The shortfall was the amount of production "required" from OPEC, and the forecasts ranged from a low of 32 mbd to a high of 49 mbd, with an average of 41 mbd. (OPEC production in 1985 was actually only 17 mbd, but more of how it got down there, later.)

The mind-set of 1978 was unshakeable: the community of energy analysts was obsessed with the notion that an oil crisis was around the corner, and that it would take the shape of (most likely) physically or (perhaps) politically constrained supplies of oil. Demand would continue to rise until the reserve base could no longer support it, or producing countries would refuse to permit depletion rates sufficient to meet it. With rare exceptions, company presidents, prominent politicians in the major industrial countries, government officials, independent experts—all agreed that it was only a matter of time, to be measured in terms of a few years rather than a few decades, before production began to decline irreversibly, as reserves ran out. So when disaster did strike, in 1979, albeit from a totally unexpected quarter, and in a totally unexpected form, consumers were in principle already psychologically conditioned for it.

OPEC's Price Schedule for 1979

Despite the earlier market weakness in 1978, demand was beginning to strengthen by September 1978, and it looked as though 1979 would see a considerable increase over 1978. Most OPEC members, with the notable exception of Saudi Arabia, were gearing up anyway for a price increase in 1979, when the October 1978 oilfield workers strike in Iran occurred. Even though Iranian production had returned, briefly, almost to normal by mid-December 1978 when the OPEC Conference met to decide prices, an increase was by then a foregone conclusion.

Saudi Arabia's decision to go along with the rest of OPEC despite its desire to restrain price increases had little to do with the course of the Egyptian-Israeli peace talks which were then in progress and which were to end in the Camp David accords (and were not to the liking of the Saudis). Saudi Arabia had had its taste of oil as a political weapon, during the oil embargo of 1973, and wanted no more of it. In late 1979, it simply did not have enough muscle in the shape of spare capacity to prevent the increase.

The OPEC Conference duly met in Abu Dhabi in December 1978 and raised the price of the crude (Arabian Light) that it had designated as its "marker" or benchmark crude, by an average amount of 10 percent over the whole year 1979, with the price at the end of the year to be 14.5 percent higher than the end of the previous year. Price increases were to be introduced gradually, in small increments, each quarter. Significantly, the price increase itself was justified by OPEC not at all by reference to market forces of supply and demand, but by member countries' need to compensate for the decline of the dollar against other currencies and the high rate of international inflation prevailing at the time. In its press release No. 6-78 dated 17 December 1978, OPEC reported that the Conference had "noted with great anxiety the high rate of inflation and dollar depreciation sustained over the last two years, and hence the substantial erosion in the oil revenues of the member countries" but that "in order to assist the world economy to grow further, and also in order to support the current efforts towards strengthening the US dollar and arresting inflationary trends, the Conference has decided to correct only partially the price of oil by an amount of 10 percent on average over the year 1979."

In other words, OPEC would administer the price of crude oil in accordance with its revenue needs. Market considerations were to be of secondary importance.

At this juncture, it was a bad mistake. During the previous year, "administering" prices had meant trimming a few cents here and there to placate restive customers. But in December 1978, the political situation in Iran was still simmering and no one knew where it would go. No one knew what would happen in the product markets or in the spot crude market, the latter a sometimes false but always powerful signal, usually tending to exaggerate everything. Everyone knew, on the other hand, what was likely to happen if there were another supply crisis. To commit to a schedule of prices for the whole of the next year was a blindness born of the multiple misconceptions of the previous few years, and, like announcing a monetary devaluation in advance, the worst of tactics: the buyer now had an assurance that he would not lose money by filling his storage facilities.

Iran Again!

Three years that shook the world of oil had begun in October 1978 with the Iranian oil-workers strike that halted much of the country's production. In January 1979, the Shah left the country, a defeated (and terminally ill) man who had no stomach for the massive and no doubt bloody repression that would have been needed to put down a revolution that had spread throughout the country. Two weeks later, the long-exiled Ayatollah Khomeini was back in the country, passionately greeted with a religious fervor to make a Pope turn green with envy. Oil exports had been halted entirely, and would only resume at the beginning of March 1979, after a break of more than two months. That barometer of fear in the oil world, the spot crude oil price, rose from $12.80 in September 1978 to $21.80 in February 1979, paused for breath with the resumption of Iranian exports, then took off again in May 1979 after Iran announced a production ceiling, and kept going till it hit a high of almost $40 in November 1979. After that, a slow decline followed for several months; then in October 1980, war broke out between Iran and Iraq, exports were again halted, this time from both countries, and the spot price exceeded $40 in November 1980. Again, when supplies resumed and started to grow, the spot price declined and by mid-1981 was down to $31.

The panic was over but the consequences were not. As usual, the crisis ended in glut, but this time the price did not quickly revert to its previous levels. And OPEC had been transformed from a loose confederation of price administrators into a confused and divided cartel of production restrictions.

How did these unforeseen and largely unintended events unfold? The major and immediate cause of the price increases was the panic that gripped the market during most of 1979: the disappearance of supplies from Iran needlessly ignited a conflagration for which the mind-set of 1978 provided a vast psychological reservoir of fuel. But critical factors—OPEC's assumption that its natural role was now to administer crude prices, as well as the fear on the part of its member countries of premature depletion—had many consequences. Three of them, which were linked in the most unfortunate way, were the production ceilings imposed by Saudi Arabia and other OPEC member countries; the destruction of the majors' integrated supply channels; and the deliberate starving of the spot crude market. They figure prominently in the answer to the question posed. We should briefly examine the panic itself, and then the three factors—production ceilings, supply channels and spot crude prices.

Panic: the Markets Run Amok

OPEC may have thought that it was still in charge of prices when it took a decision in December 1978 to usher in a schedule of staggered price increases during 1979, but the North Sea producers in Norway and Britain weren't waiting. With spot prices already taking off, they immediately raised crude prices for the first quarter by almost 11 percent instead of the increase of 5 percent that OPEC had agreed on at its December 1978 Conference (along with a schedule of further increases). It was the first time that the North Sea had led prices up and it was a bad mistake: why should OPEC producers exercise price restraint when producers in industrial countries didn't? Within a matter of weeks, four OPEC countries raised their prices higher than the levels agreed in December (Abu Dhabi, Kuwait and Qatar, on 15 February 1979; Libya, a week later). The rest of the OPEC price schedule for 1979 was now uncertain—indeed, there was now more price uncertainty than if a schedule had not been agreed in the first place; for a while, holders of inventory were delighted.

When an oil company, or anyone else in the supply chain, believes that a severe shortage of supply is imminent, it does what any sensible individual consumer does: it stocks up as much as possible, because today's supply will not, it is thought, be available tomorrow. Crude oil goes into storage as much as possible; and so do refined products. Integrated companies keep as much for their own marketing chains as possible, eschewing sales to the spot product market. The buyers of products start scrambling for supplies, to keep their marketing (or onward processing, in the case of petrochemical companies etc.) operations going, and to build up stocks. This surge in product demand and some hoarding by the product-suppliers drives product prices up sharply, especially spot prices.

When the Iranian crisis struck in full force, in early January 1979, there was plenty of crude oil in the system and plenty on its way to the markets from the Persian Gulf (about one month's steaming time around the Cape to northwestern Europe; about the same to the US Gulf). But the surge in product demand was well underway: the refiner's margin (the difference between his crude oil cost and gross income from the sale of products), normally around \$1/B., already stood at nearly \$7/B., rose to a high of \$17/B. in February, fell back slightly, but remained extremely high until the last quarter of 1979. By then, storage facilities everywhere were bursting at the seams, and some of the largest tankers, in the category of "Very Large Crude Carriers (VLCCs)", were being used as floating medium-term storage in the Caribbean and off Japan. The refiners had had a good run for their money: anyone who could buy spot crude during the first half of 1979 was minting money; anyone who could buy at the official government selling prices (GSP) or GSP plus premiums was doing it on a grand scale. The market was not being driven by OPEC-induced crude price hikes, but by panic—fear of shortage rather than actual shortage, and fear of what OPEC might soon do to restrict supply (and eventually did do) rather than by what it had already done.

The huge margins soon showed up in company profits. The five US major oil companies saw their profits rise by almost 70 percent in 1979 over 1978. BP and Shell's rose by even more (largely because of different accounting practices for the valuation of inventory).

OPEC was dismayed, and said so. In its press release (no. 5-79) of June 1979, OPEC took the opportunity to "warn the oil companies of the irresponsible practice of taking advantage of the present situation to reap unwarranted profits." It was not an empty threat, as some of the later price increases were made retroactive in an attempt to claw back some of the companies' "excessive" profits—a large part of which were traceable to OPEC's price administration. Indeed, OPEC price administration had unintentionally resulted in the biggest give-away in history and these huge profits, as much as spot crude prices, stimulated further increases in government sales price.

It was not until OPEC's member countries saw what the spot crude and products markets were willing to pay that they decided where the money rightfully belonged—that is, with the producer; and it was only then that they began to understand what an enormously powerful cartel they had become and what sort of price levels they might be able to enforce. And if, as everybody confidently expected, consumer and producer alike, price would go to \$60 to \$70 in a few years, why not get there a bit sooner? It was an unfortunate but almost universal delusion.

Prices continued to escalate throughout 1979. Their development falls into two distinct phases, both of them played out against an acrimonious background where Saudi Arabia, for its own particular purposes, tried to practice, and enforce, some kind of restraint on the rest of OPEC.

The first phase lasted until the autumn of 1979. During it, the market was largely driven by panic buying of crude and products into storage. Product prices reached levels far in excess of crude costs even at spot prices, and stayed there until there was no more slack in the system, and storage could not accommodate any more. At that point (from October 1979), a second phase started with the decline both of spot product prices and spot crude prices until around mid-1980, when they converged closely with GSPs (at the official Saudi level or the other countries' levels minus premiums). The outbreak of the Iran-Iraq War towards the end of September 1980 caused little more than a short-lived blip in prices, largely because demand by then was dropping like a stone and inventory was full. Saudi Arabia had reinstated its 9.5 mbd ceiling from July 1979, and, with the drop in demand and full storage facilities, production in the rest of OPEC was in any event falling: indeed, OPEC production had dropped by more than 4 mbd by August 1980 from its monthly peak in 1979. The other member countries had little difficulty in making up production lost by Iran and Iraq due to the war. Prices soon resumed their downward trend. The crisis was over.

However, amazingly enough, falling spot prices, inventories bursting at the seams, burgeoning supplies of non-OPEC oil from the North Sea and Alaska, and plummeting world demand for oil did nothing to shake the mind-set of 1978 and the near-universal belief in an impending energy crisis. Consider the following passages, taken from the Staff Report to the US Senate's Committee on Energy and Natural Resources. It is entitled *The Geopolitics of Energy* and was published in December 1980, three months after the start of the Iran-Iraq War. Its opening sentence reads:

> The world will witness a growing struggle for secure access to oil through the end of this century and into the next. This gathering energy crisis deserves the highest priority in the councils of government. Few other problems are more complicated; few other problems will be more difficult to solve.[1]

By this time, the world was choking on a glut of oil. It didn't make any difference. Here are two more excerpts from the Committee's hearings which attract attention because of their authoritative sources:

> The next four to five years will be a period of crisis. All the preconditions for that already exist.
> – Henry M. Kissinger, Former Secretary of State, 31 July 1980.[2]

> Whoever controls the oil tap in the Middle East will possess sufficient leverage to dominate the world. The day is far gone. Let us take the necessary actions before the night is at hand.
> – James R. Schlesinger, former Secretary of Defense, former Secretary of Energy.[3]

In the face of the approaching apocalypse, the IEA did nothing. Indeed, one of the few moderately humorous episodes throughout the whole period was the IEA's inability to declare a crisis and thereby put its emergency supply plans into action. The problem was that the supply situation did not, by the IEA's definition, ever constitute a crisis—which was defined as the loss of a certain percentage of supply by any member country over a certain period of time (which had not happened), and the drafters of the agency's charter, with impeccable economic logic, had been unable to conceive of prices doubling and tripling without *something* fairly drastic happening to supply. They had not envisaged a simple nervous breakdown in the marketplace, and perhaps there is nothing they could have done about it if they had. Thus the agency specifically put in place after the 1973 crisis to deal with future price-explosions failed its first test. Another Maginot line.

The changes had nevertheless been truly shocking. Spot crude prices had risen to over $40/B. at times, from levels of well under $15/B. prior to October 1978. GSPs, mostly with various premiums, rose erratically, going from around $12 at the beginning of 1979 to around $28 by the end of the year, added a few more dollars in 1980, then ended up at a basic marker price of $34 in the Autumn of 1981. But in the meantime, there had been periods of chaos during which there was little relationship between the price of one crude and another, with quality and price differentials meaning virtually nothing. It was a cartel that did not know its mind.

But, to repeat, how and why did all this happen when there was never any physical shortage of oil? I mentioned three factors above; let us look at them.

Production Ceilings: Saudi Arabia et al.

The first of the three concerns was production ceilings, most especially Saudi Arabia's. If Saudi Arabia refused to expand its production, that by itself would be a powerful factor in creating a shortage. And, in fact, the Saudi government imposed a production ceiling of 8.5 mbd on Aramco in early 1978, well before the Iranian revolution and subsequent crisis.

It seems odd at first sight that Saudi Arabia, a country still nowhere near fully explored and with by far the largest proved reserves in the world, should want to limit its production. In fact, however, Saudi Arabia's fear of premature depletion went back quite a way, to the early 1970s, and built up gradually until it culminated in the government-imposed production ceiling. Unlike the case of other countries that shared Saudi apprehensions, a fairly detailed picture of the background to Saudi fears is given in a report for the US Senate Committee on Foreign Relations entitled *The Future of Saudi Arabian Oil Production*.[4]

It shows that the government and Aramco were in constant discussions over a considerable period of time (since the early 1970s) to determine an appropriate basis for the long-term expansion of capacity. The first target was to be 20 mbd by the early 1980s, later lowered to 16 mbd as demand slowed down. More importantly, the Saudis became concerned, rightly or wrongly, about the shortness of the period over which peak production could be maintained at the rates envisaged before irreversible decline set in. "In mid-1973," the report says, "the Saudi Arabian Government expressed concern to Aramco that oil production not decline for a long period of time." Based on proved, probable and possible reserves in already discovered reservoirs, a rate of 16 mbd could not be maintained for more than 15 years—from 1985 to 2000, at which point quite steep decline rates would set in. This was clearly too short a time, and a new target of 12 mbd was proposed, showing that peak rates could then be maintained until 2015.

To add to Saudi concerns, new discoveries during the period from 1970 to 1977 had not equaled total withdrawals from reserves. This should not normally bother a producer with a reserves-to-production ratio in excess of 100:1, but Saudi concern fits in with the always overly cautious outlook of the Saudi government.

Whether the assumptions on which the technical and financial studies were carried out were good or bad is neither here nor there. The fact is that a great deal of time and study were devoted to the question, and the apparent results pointed to brief peak production rates followed by decline rates that were not acceptable to the Saudis; it should not therefore be surprising that in the end the Saudis decided to postpone decline and (almost incidentally) reduce investment costs by making the same facilities enjoy a longer useful life. What emerges clearly from all this is that the final Saudi decision in early 1978 to impose a ceiling of 8.5 mbd on Aramco production was not capriciously taken, on short notice, in order to shore up prices which were then beginning to weaken. It was taken as a long-term strategic matter.

The Heavy/Light Ratio, February 1978.

One of the first measures to have a serious market impact was the decision, in February 1978, to limit the production of light crudes to 65 percent of total crude production, to accord more closely with the ratio of proved reserves of different quality crudes. Heavy and medium crude producing-capacity was a bit less than 3 mbd, so this meant total production would be limited to 8.5 mbd, on an annual basis.

Since Arabian Light was such an important crude in sheer terms of volume in the market, this limitation put a premium on all other light crudes and, pending the readjustment of refining patterns (which would require time and the construction of new conversion capacity), on light product prices relative to heavy ones.

Up, Down, Up and Down Again.

However, for the time being, the more important matter was the overall limitation. Demand was not bumping up against the Saudi production restrictions during the first nine months of 1978, and there was enough quota (set on an annual basis) at 8.5 mbd to allow production well above that level during the last quarter of the year and still meet the annual average.

On 16 January 1979, the Shah left Iran, after oil production had been largely shut down since late December. Exports would not be resumed until 5 March. Crude supplies were tight and deliveries uncertain in the short term. On 20 January, Saudi Arabia's Yamani announced that Aramco would be allowed to produce 9.5 mbd (instead of the previously decreed 8.5 mbd) for the first quarter of the year, but that the situation would be monitored and production would have to conform to quota on a month-by-month basis. But Aramco had been producing at over 10 mbd during the last quarter of 1978, using up under-utilized quota from the first three quarters. So the Saudi "increase" in allowable production actually meant a decrease for the first quarter of 1979.

The decision was greeted with some outrage and the net result of the Saudi decision was a further increase in the barometer spot crude price, which averaged $22/B.. in February compared with the official price of $13.40. But that was nothing: product prices in the markets were rising even faster, and averaged $27/B.. during February in Rotterdam on typical crude yields. The oil companies and traders and brokers were minting money. A crude price increase in mid-February by the four OPEC Gulf countries still left them far below spot crude and even further below product prices. So much for "administering" crude prices: the "administration" was quickly becoming the biggest giveaway in economic history, bigger even than the giveaway of 1973.

On 5 March 1979, Iran resumed crude exports, and the general expectation was that they would build up rapidly to their "normal" level. Accordingly, Saudi Arabia felt it was safe to reimpose its production ceiling of 8.5 mbd for the second quarter. At first, it seemed a correct decision: the spot crude market did not react immediately, but taken together with the moves in Iran limiting its crude production, the Saudi decision contributed to the biggest jump of all in spot crude and product prices, which leapt up by $9/B. and $6/B., respectively, as the four Aramco partners (Exxon, Mobil, Texaco and Chevron) entered the spot market to replace their lost crude.

The Saudi decision drew much criticism, and was interpreted as giving the lie to Saudi professions of an interest in "price-moderation". But the fact is that if Iran was re-entering the markets again and there was clearly no physical shortage of crude (the fact that the IEA had not declared crisis conditions was not lost on the Saudis), there appeared to be no reason why the normal 8.5 mbd ceiling should not be reimposed. The crisis got worse as spot prices rose followed by further increases in OPEC countries' GSPs. By the end of June 1979, spot crude oil prices had risen to $35, and OPEC GSPs to $19.50 for Kuwait (75 percent and 39 percent above March 1979 prices respectively). Pressure from the United States and the major companies continued and Saudi Arabia finally agreed to raise its production ceiling back to 9.5 mbd for the third quarter of 1979. In the meantime, OPEC prices were split into two tiers: Saudi Arabia had refused to go along with some of the increases in GSPs introduced by other member countries, and crude oil was being sold at two or more different basic GSP levels.

The 9.5 mbd production ceiling became a powerful instrument in eventually forcing prices down, as supply continued to exceed demand. It was not rescinded until November 1981, after OPEC crude prices had been re-unified around a $34 marker crude price the previous month.

Supply Channels Disrupted: the Majors Ousted

The second major factor was the disruption – virtual destruction – of traditional supply channels. By mid-February 1979, the markets were in chaos. At the end of the month, the new regime in Iran repudiated the 1973 agreements under which the major oil companies had been marketing much of Iran's production; they were told that they had no further role in Iran as anything other than buyers, on the same footing as any other buyer. Iran then announced that it was in any case limiting its maximum crude production to 4 mbd and shifting its marketing effort directly to other buyers (non-major oil companies).

The Saudi decision to restrict production to 8.5 mbd during the second quarter of 1979 lost the majors up to another 1 mbd. Most of this would have to come from supplies to their own integrated refineries or from their sales to third-party refiners in industrialized countries, since the Saudi government instructed the Aramco participants (Chevron, Exxon, Mobil and Texaco) to continue supplying the less developed countries (LDCs) with the full contractual quantity of crude to which they were committed prior to the ceiling reduction. The Aramco four wrote to Yamani in May 1979[5] urging the government to increase production. They said that production was well below their expectations under their "New Arrangements"[6] with the Saudi government, and that they were now not able to meet the needs of their own refineries and were being forced onto the spot crude market. But decisions are taken slowly in Saudi Arabia and they got no satisfaction until the end of the second quarter when the Saudis raised the ceiling to 9.5 mbd, partly to correct what had been an obvious error and partly in response to pressure from the United States and the IEA.

Third-party refiners previously supplied by the majors now had to scramble to the OPEC National Oil Companies and the spot market to fill their requirements as one major after another announced that it could no longer supply them, invoking *force majeure* clauses in their sales contracts. Spot prices jumped sharply in May 1979—almost $10/B.—sending another false signal to OPEC.

Other blows were to fall on the majors' supply sources. Nigeria nationalized BP's interests in the country at the beginning of August 1979, in retaliation for the company's alleged sales of crude oil to South Africa, an embargoed country; then, in early October 1979, Libya told its principal term-contract customers, including the majors, that it would reduce their liftings in 1980, and switch the oil to new customers, primarily governments and state oil corporations. In November, following the seizure of hostages in the US embassy in Tehran, the US majors and all other US purchasers lost their remaining supplies out of Iran as a result of the mutual boycott that was declared on crude oil trade between Iran and the United States In Iraq, in the renegotiation of contracts for 1980, the US majors had their volumes reduced by around one-half. In mid-November 1979, Abu Dhabi decided to lower its production ceiling and this brought pro-rata automatic cuts in quantities available to the majors operating there. In addition, the Abu Dhabi National Oil Company decided to reduce the volumes sold to the majors in order to diversify its sales. The loss of supply to the majors in Abu Dhabi was in excess of 100 kbd. Finally, Venezuela renegotiated its sales with its traditional customers (mainly the majors), reducing the volume available to them in 1980 by approximately 370 kbd. All in all, the total loss to the majors was put at 3 mbd by the end of 1979, with more to come in 1980. A report of the US General Accounting Office (GAO) said: "The major oil companies . . . lost access to an estimated 3 mbd of contract crude. Their combined role in international crude oil trade declined from about 55 percent in 1978 to between 50 and 45 percent by the end of 1979."[7]

It was the end of the road for the majors as integrated producers in the OPEC area. Operating under provisional agreements (known as the "New Arrangements" and a Crude Oil Sales Agreement, or COSA) that were never in fact signed, they retained preferential access rights in Saudi Arabia, and small equity interests in some other OPEC countries; but by and large they simply became purchasers of crude like any other company, though larger, with no remaining financial incentive to stick with one country rather than another. The "technical assistance" agreements which in some countries had been part and parcel of the deals under which the majors got preferential access to crude were soon phased out.

It had for some time been the stated and open objective of several important exporting countries to lessen their dependence on the international majors as outlets for their crude oil, and diversify their sales among other countries. In particular, some of the exporters (notably Iraq) showed a marked predilection for dealing with the state oil companies of importing developing countries. The exporters felt that the majors were too dangerous as large purchasers of crude oil, particularly during surplus conditions when they were in a powerful position to exert a downward pressure on prices. It was a mistaken tactic, an object lesson in how to turn powerful allies into important antagonists. The majors' very size should have made them desirable partners in times of surplus, even if that involved paying a price. It was a mistake the cautious Saudis were able to temper.

Of all the changes wrought by the 1979 crisis, this was certainly one of the most significant: OPEC countries were now on their own in the markets, and freer to compete with each other. When the debacle came, the majors—by then simple arm's-length purchasers—had no remaining equity share to make them prefer OPEC countries over other supply sources. Yamani's oft-expressed fears were soon to be realized. But in the short term, and of great consequence to the unfolding crisis, the main impact of the majors' ouster was to drive them temporarily into the spot market. Prices in the tiny market took another great leap up.

The Market: Out, Damned Spot!

A third factor impelling prices upward despite plentiful physical supply was the policy of OPEC member countries not to sell on the spot market—while at the same time perversely reducing supply to the majors and driving them, at least for a brief time, onto the spot market. Inevitably, spot prices went through the ceiling—demand had been increased and supply decreased—and, the higher prices were then used by OPEC to justify further increases in their official selling prices! All this wasn't even done deliberately, but out of a wildly misguided attempt to administer prices as, it was thought, they always had been.

Never have sales of such volumetric and monetary insignificance caused such monumental trouble in the international petroleum industry as did transactions on the spot crude market during 1979 and 1980. At all times, information on spot crude sales and prices was sparse, uncertain and sensational, this last quality causing untold damage.

No one knows what volume of crude oil was traded on the spot market during the critical years from 1979 to 1982. The only news service reporting systematically and promptly on the spot crude market at the time was *Petroleum Argus*. Their daily telexes to clients recorded amounts rising from 460 kbd in 1979 to 703 kbd in 1981, with a sharper rise to 1,411 kbd in 1982, and their comments are replete with remarks on the thinness of the spot market. These did not of course represent 100 percent coverage, and *Argus's* data bank was later updated to include more sales that had subsequently come to light, though it is not clear how many of these were resales of the same cargo *en route*. This source, along with estimates from other sources, concur in showing sharp fluctuations in the volumes from month to month, but clearly, with a *total* crude oil market volume of about 30 mbd, the spot volumes were insignificant.

A second source, the GAO, reported, on the basis of information submitted by importers, that "From April 1979 to February 1980 spot crude purchases averaged 9.4 percent of the foreign crude [the 31 largest US refiners] imported into the United States, ranging monthly from 2.6 percent to 14 percent."[8] There is no way of knowing whether this was typical of the spot market in general.

A third source, Exxon,[9] put the spot market at 1.8 mbd during the fourth quarter of 1979, with traders accounting for about one-third of all sales, and the governments of producing countries (mainly Iran, Dubai, Kuwait and Indonesia) accounting for the rest. Among the buyers, about 30 percent were Japanese refiners, another 30 percent US independents, and a further 30 percent accounted for by Shell and BP; the rest were a mixed bag. By March 1980, Exxon was reporting the spot crude market as "extremely thin with no discernible pattern. There have been buyers in and out of the market and no more than 1 - 2 cargoes per week have actually changed hands".[10]

In any event, it was clear that OPEC was openly and explicitly hostile to the spot market. Having established a system for setting and maintaining crude oil prices (a function in which it saw itself as successor to the major oil companies), OPEC was intent on enforcing it and imposing it on the market. Any other prices would be intrusive and a potential threat to the system and the OPEC order. This was something OPEC had incorporated into its way of thinking from the outset, from 1973, when it took control over price—and it seemed a natural thing to do, since the OPEC governments were in fact simply transferring to themselves the companies' previous price-setting prerogatives. OPEC even resolved that prices should be set by reference to the cost of alternative sources of energy supplies, and commissioned studies to determine what these were.

Already in February 1979, at a Ministerial Consultative Meeting, OPEC had expressed its concern about spot prices: "spot market prices of crude oil and petroleum products are such that speculative traders are taking advantage of the situation, thus creating further hardship for consuming nations, especially those of the Third World."[11]

At its Fifty-fourth Conference, OPEC reported that "It was also agreed that Member Countries would take steps to limit transactions in the spot market in a collective effort to stop the present price spiral."[12]

Compliance on the part of member countries was varied. Some abstained from spot crude sales entirely (Algeria, Saudi Arabia, Venezuela). Others found it more difficult to resist the temptation of making occasional spot sales, and even auctions (Abu Dhabi, Kuwait). By and large, however, the spot crude oil market was far from benefitting from a flow of supply that would have been considered normal and free of policy constraints in a market where there was no built-in bias against it. Indeed, had such a flow been available to the spot market, the differential between spot and term sales prices could not have existed in anywhere near the magnitude experienced: it would have reflected a normal premium or discount between spot and term.

For OPEC, the spot market was the result of speculation carried out mainly by a group of unscrupulous traders, performing no useful function as middle-men, and causing trouble, minor at first, then more disruptive, for OPEC's mission of price administration. Nevertheless, it was not long before several OPEC member countries could not resist sipping these forbidden waters where the difference between the spot price and GSP could easily reach $20 million on a single cargo. Iraq, Libya and Nigeria used the spot market more systematically, but far from exclusively. Iran tried for a brief period to use it exclusively, without success, and soon abandoned the spot market except for special purposes. But the real mistake was to suppose that the spot market could be killed by refusal to participate in it. Several OPEC countries, notably Algeria, Saudi Arabia and Venezuela, flatly refused to have any dealings on the spot market and forbade their customers to resell to it; others were hesitant; none was prepared to sell on the spot market without restraint, except for Iran, for a brief period. Thus starved, the market rose to unprecedented heights, goading OPEC into successive increases in official prices that received a sort of moral and intellectual sanction from the mind-set of 1978 and the inflation which was rapidly taking hold in the industrial world. Of course, if OPEC wanted the spot market dead as an "evil" price influence, the way to do it in would have been to sell spot as much as possible to all and sundry; prices would have come tumbling down. But in fact, OPEC was actively pushing the majors onto the spot market while starving it of supplies. What could they expect? Spot prices went through the ceiling.

The psychological impact of spot prices was enormous. Sensational increases made the headlines in the trade press week after week, and the spectacle of some refiners paying $30 to $40 for a barrel of oil that would not have fetched $13 a year or two before, made OPEC's increases in its official sales prices look tame by comparison. The spot market was frequently referred to as the "free" or "open" market and its prices presumed to be the "real" or "true" value of oil by pseudo-economists who had heard that market clearing prices were set at the margin but seemed to be quite unaware that the market in this context meant a competitive market, and the price in this context meant the price for *all* transactions. They thus lent a wholly spurious credibility to some of OPEC's claims that when it raised prices, it was only following the market.

In the end, despite all the brouhaha, the spot market had practically no direct impact on the overall flows of money. It was very small in terms of volume and money, and was only important because of the false signals that it sent out; people in OPEC circles began to believe (without quite having the courage of their convictions) that spot prices represented "open" market values for crude which could be obtained for much larger volumes. They were of course wrong and such volumetric data as exists on monthly spot crude sales (mainly from Petroleum Argus) shows price responding to variations in available supply over the period 1979 to 1982, and there are clearly identifiable and specific causes for the surges that occurred.

The amount of oil moving at spot prices was in fact so small as to be virtually invisible in the overall flows. Average import values for crude oil entering the United States, Western Europe and Japan track GSPs from 1979 to 1981 so closely as to be virtually indistinguishable from them. The direct

impact of spot prices on the import bill of industrial countries was almost
zero, though the air was filled, then and later, with invective about unbridled
"greed" (the OPEC countries), immoral speculation (the traders) and
"obscene profits" (the oil companies). In fact, of course, the spot market was
a marginal fun-fair where a good time was had by all except the consumers.

OECD countries were also hostile to spot market transactions about
which they were painfully conscious of knowing very little. The EEC, the
Group of Seven leading industrial countries (the G-7) at its summit meeting
in Tokyo in June 1979, and the US Department of Energy all urged the oil
companies to refrain from "abnormal" purchases on the spot market. The G-
7 resolved in Tokyo to establish an "international register of oil transactions"
to help inform them and monitor prices on the spot markets. This was duly
set up by the IEA but the information it yielded does not appear to have led
to any concrete actions. The EEC commissioned a report[13] on spot prices for
the period June 1979 to May 1980 known as the COMMA exercise
(Commission Market Analysis), but it dealt almost exclusively with product
prices. In the United States, all major US refiners were required to report
price and volume details of all their worldwide crude oil transactions (known
as Form ER-51) though a clear distinction was not made between spot
transactions and others. These did not give rise to any specific regulatory
action.

The World Reacts

The huge price increases that occurred in 1979 and 1980 stunned and
dumbfounded the consuming nations, industrialized and developing alike.
Their reaction was more rhetoric than action; there was abuse, cajoling,
pleading, threats, including the threat of military force,[14] and good resolutions,
but with the mind-set of 1978 still in sway, precious little was done because
practically nobody believed anything *could* be done.

Perhaps they were right; perhaps nothing could have been done without
an ugly confrontation that might have made matters worse. So the
governments of the major industrial nations confined their efforts to reducing
oil imports, promoting conservation and stimulating the development of
alternative sources of energy. In March 1979, IEA members set a target of a
5 percent reduction in demand for oil, amounting to about 2 mbd, each
member to meet the target in its own way. The target was reaffirmed by the
EEC Council of Ministers, meeting a few weeks later. In the event,
consumption during 1979 remained approximately at its 1978 level in the
OECD area, but net imports rose 3 percent as inventories were built up.
Apart from some counterproductive price controls, there were no widespread
compulsory measures to ensure attainment of the IEA target, though some
governments prepared plans for gasoline rationing and actually issued standby
ration books.

In June 1979, a summit meeting in Tokyo of the G-7 issued a lengthy communiqué, reaffirming and spelling out in more detail the targets for oil demand, committing to increasing domestic oil prices to world market levels, encouraging the use of coal and other alternative sources of energy, urging the oil companies to stay away from the spot markets, and others.

Despite the pro-forma obeisance to the power of price, the main thrust of the decisions taken was a vote of no confidence in the market response, the effect of price on supply and demand. No one seemed ready to believe that price alone, or even preponderantly, would solve the energy problem. The Tokyo G-7 communiqué declared that "New technologies in the field of energy are the key to the world's longer-term freedom from fuel crisis. Large public and private resources will be required for the development and commercial application of those technologies. We will ensure that these resources are made available."[15]

The EEC Energy Commissioner spoke in terms of investments in developing energy sources in the order of $50 billion required each year in the Community. An International Energy Technology Group was to be created to monitor developments and make recommendations on "the need and potential for international collaboration, including financing". President Jimmy Carter, with his remarkable gift for the infelicitous phrase, called the energy crisis the "moral equivalent of war". His Administration would create an Energy Mobilization Board, and $140 billion dollars would be spent over the next decade to solve the energy crisis. There were two abortive French proposals to set a maximum price for crude imports and to seek a pricing agreement with OPEC. Neither got a serious hearing.

There was also a fairly nauseating amount of cant about the developing countries. The G-7 Tokyo communiqué said:

> We are deeply concerned about the millions of people still living in conditions of absolute poverty. We will take particular account of the poorest countries in our aid program. . . . We will also place special emphasis on helping developing countries to exploit their energy potential. We strongly support the World Bank's program for hydrocarbon exploitation and urge its expansion.

In the event, the "deep concern" did not run to any net increase in the G-7's aid programs, and the World Bank's program did not add a single drop of oil to developing countries' production. The communiqué's words were nothing but a crude effort to drive a wedge between OPEC and the rest of the developing world, which didn't work because OPEC actually took the trouble to pay a small but not totally insignificant amount of conscience money to the importing developing countries through the institutions that it and its member countries had set up in the mid-1970s, notably as the OPEC Fund for International Development. Support, or at least acquiescence, by the developing countries was more important to OPEC than to the OECD, and OPEC cant (equally nauseating) had to be accompanied by some hard cash.

A year later, in June 1980, the G-7 Summit reconvened, this time in Venice. Commitments to the development and use of non-oil energy sources were re-affirmed; the link between economic growth and oil consumption was to be broken; OPEC was excoriated and lip service simultaneously paid to the desirability of a dialogue with producers. The final communiqué covered thirty-four points, nearly all to do directly or indirectly with oil supply and prices, composed mainly of worthy sentiments and little content.

As it turned out, the market was to wreak a devastating revenge on OPEC and accomplish most of the G-7's goals for them, developments which we will examine in the next chapter. But at that point, the politicians in charge of the G-7 governments might just as well have sat back and said nothing (though admittedly at the risk of being lynched by an outraged public). Most of the relatively straightforward conservation and regulatory steps had already been taken in the post-1973 crisis period, and in practice, few further steps were taken by government as a result of the 1979 surge in prices.

The Saudi Enigma

A large and quite disproportionate amount of analytic effort, scholarly and not so, was expended on trying to figure out the Saudis, and, in particular, during this and the immediately preceding period, why the Saudis opted for "price-moderation". Why did they insist on selling their crude at prices below levels at which other OPEC countries were selling? There was little doubt that they could have sold at the higher OPEC level, so why antagonize the rest of OPEC and why (apparently) decline to maximize? And if they were so keen on price moderation, why did they nevertheless raise their prices from $13 to $34 over the brief period of two years?

Opinions differ greatly over these questions and there were at least nine studies[16] by serious scholars and organizations as well as a host of shorter articles on the subject. Broadly speaking, the answers fall into two camps. The first ascribes primarily political motives to the Saudis; the second primarily economic ones. The political motives are identified mainly as reactions to US policy in the Middle East, especially with respect to Israel; and the need to retain US support and access to supplies of modern arms. The economic motives are identified mainly as a fear of pricing oil out of the market; fear of damaging the world economy, on whose health the Saudis were dependent for safeguarding their investments abroad and their oil markets; and the desire to maximize by ensuring that at a slightly lower price than the rest of OPEC they would always get full outlet for their crude, up to their chosen production ceiling.

I believe that the answer is a good deal simpler; it is to be found in the Saudis' deep (and justifiable) sense of insecurity. What would you do if the only significant power you had in the world was to set the world price of oil (and, indirectly, all energy), but at the same time you were militarily feeble, faced several hostile neighbors, were trying to maintain a regime and a way of life for it that you knew was universally rejected outside the country, and fear for your internal security because of (among other things) divisions between your eastern and the western provinces, tensions between your newly rich merchant class and the royal family, tensions between immigrant (especially Shia) and native populations?

You would keep your head down.

But if you are the natural price leader by virtue of producing 40 percent of all OPEC oil, the only way you *can* keep your head down is to make sure that whoever is seen to be leading the price extravagantly up, it isn't you.

There have been suggestions that much of the so-called Saudi moderation was duplicitous and that Yamani was merely leading from behind. This is quite untrue; the Saudis were being dragged along by the rest of OPEC though, as I remarked at the time, " ... if the Saudis are being taken for a ride, they certainly seem to be enjoying it ... "[17] Whether Saudi price-moderation had much effect in practice, apart from the apparent holding back of increases noted above, is a different question. There were, after all, other constraints, including (as also noted above) the threat of armed force if supplies were made available to the United States and other industrial countries only on economic strangulation terms. So the "hawks" in OPEC would probably have proceeded anyway with thin slice-by-slice tactics, and in this limited sense, the world *was* duped by Saudi "price-moderation": its practical effect was minimal. Official prices by the end of 1979 had about doubled during the year, and by the end of 1980 tripled. By the end of 1981, Saudi Arabia was swearing it would defend a $34 marker against all comers.

By the time that OPEC prices were reunified around a marker price of $34, the world was duly grateful to the Saudis for having exercised a moderating influence on other member countries, in particular for having brought the peak down from $36. Indeed, the new price level was so acceptable, especially in the light of rampant inflation that equalized $34 in 1982 to $24 in 1978, that the Saudis, together with the Kuwaitis, felt comfortable enough to pledge its defense. And again, why should anyone object? Forecasts had been pouring out of the United States and other industrial countries, from sources with apparently impeccable qualifications— such as Exxon and the US Department of Energy—to the effect that price would have to rise to somewhere between $50 and $100 (in real terms, from whichever year the forecast was made in) by the 1990s. And OPEC was more or less agreed (*vide* its Long-Term Strategy Committee) that price should proceed upward *pari passu* with a number of factors until it reached the cost of alternative fuels. In the meantime, the Saudis (and Kuwaitis) could allow themselves the luxury of trying to put the monkey on the West's back by preaching to it, at the height of the "crisis", about the need to conserve energy.

(In the end, they got rather more conservation than they bargained for.)

Viewed in this light, Saudi "price moderation" was more of a clever defensive move than a positive policy, serving, as it turned out, both political and economic ends more successfully than they could have hoped. For the fact is—though it is going too far to ascribe design to them (they weren't *that* clever)—by 1981, the Saudis had increased their revenues above 1978 levels by a higher proportion than any other major OPEC country except Nigeria, whose pricing "policy" during this period can best be characterized as systematized blundering. And the fact also is, I believe, that neither political nor economic motives were uppermost in the minds of the Saudis; they just wanted to stay out of trouble—more of a political than an economic objective if you like, but hardly the stuff that duplicitous Machiavellian policies are made of.

The Aramco Advantage

One of the curious sidelights of the multi-tier pricing that prevailed during the period from early 1979 until late 1981, with Saudi GSPs persistently lower than others in the Gulf, was the so-called "Aramco Advantage". The four US majors (Chevron, Exxon, Mobil and Texaco) who were participants in Aramco acquired their share in Saudi crude at the official government selling price, some two or three dollars per barrel (depending on the point of comparison) below the official prices of crudes in other OPEC member countries, giving them a substantial advantage over their competitors in their crude acquisition costs. However, in a letter dated 23 January 1979 addressed to the four, Yamani instructed them "to pledge that they will not sell to a third party at prices in excess of what we have specified herein". This became known among the participants as "the Yamani Edict", and it was backed up by requirements for the four companies to submit auditor's certificates on their resales to third parties, to ensure that the instructions were being followed. In addition, the four were required to continue supplying their buyers in developing countries their full contract requirements as they existed prior to January 1979, at the official prices. (Complaints received from the Philippines and Korea were in fact followed up by the ministry.)

Apart from the requirement to continue selling to the LDCs, the Aramco participants soon began to phase out other third-party buyers, since they were being left with less access in OPEC member countries to crude than was necessary for their own integrated operations. Thus, to the extent that they could sell products in the markets that reflected the acquisition costs of higher-priced crudes from other OPEC countries, they would be able to make a large additional profit. Yamani recognized this, that he could not control the companies' product prices, saying simply that it was a problem for the governments of consuming countries, and indeed several of them hedged product prices around with restrictions to prevent, in effect, the difference between the lower Saudi crude prices and the higher prices in other OPEC countries being pocketed by the companies.

This so-called Aramco advantage later became a contentious matter between the US Internal Revenue Service and the companies, with the IRS contending that the "Yamani Edict" did not have force of law and that the companies had in any event circumvented it to a large extent by exchanging Saudi crude for other crudes, then reselling the other crudes at higher prices. The IRS lost the case, and it is impossible to know by quite how much the Aramco advantage ended up benefiting the four companies. In any event, the four companies' worldwide profits in 1979 rose by no greater a proportion over 1978 than did the profits of the three majors (BP, Gulf and Shell) who were not Aramco participants. In 1980, however, they rose substantially faster than those of the other three.

The Aramco advantage soon turned into the Aramco disadvantage. After OPEC price reunification in October 1981 and in the face of falling demand, other OPEC countries started to discount their official prices, while Saudi Arabia maintained its own. The Aramco four were initially unwilling to cut back on their commitments, and continued taking their full entitlements until the pain became unbearable, at which point they started to reduce their liftings. On balance, over the whole period of the advantage/disadvantage, it is not clear whether the advantage was positive and substantial or not.

The End of Strategic Planning

In the meantime, the Long-Term Strategy Committee's group of experts had been busy elaborating its report, which was discussed at the OPEC Conference meeting in Taif, Saudi Arabia, on 7 and 8 May 1980, which "accepted it with some reservations on the pricing issue made by three Member Countries". (OPEC Press Release No. 3-80). The next conference, held one month later in Algiers, decided on the preparation of a plan of action for the implementation of the policy principles incorporated in the committee's report, for submission to the Joint Meeting of the Ministers of Foreign Affairs, Finance and Oil, scheduled for September. The Draft Plan of Action was duly submitted to the Tri-Ministerial Conference in Vienna in September 1980 and its main elements implicitly agreed though never formally approved. Its major principles were then incorporated in a Draft Declaration of Long-Term Policies of OPEC, which was to be adopted, if approved, by the Second Summit Conference to be convened in Bagdad in November, marking the twentieth anniversary of the creation of OPEC. No one can say the report didn't go through the hoops.

It dealt with prices and production policies; OPEC relations with other developing countries; and OPEC relations with industrialized countries. The latter two were mainly centered on the so-called New International Economic Order, and envisaged a number of modifications in the three groups' relationships, including the creation of a joint fund of OPEC and the industrialized countries to assist developing countries in realizing faster economic progress.

The Draft Declaration of Long-Term Policies was now ready for submission to the Summit Conference in Bagdad.

On 22 September 1980, five days after the end of OPEC's Tri-Ministerial Conference in Vienna, Iraqi President Saddam Hussein's army attacked Iran, and that was the end of that. There was no more long-term planning in OPEC; despite the Iran-Iraq War, the market for OPEC oil was about to collapse; there was no longer any need for production ceilings; and "price-administration" was soon to take an unexpected turn toward linkage with spot markets, to the exclusion of everything else.

The End of the Crisis

Spot crude prices during the whole of this later period were on the whole a good market indicator, despite the false signals they had sent out on previous occasions. They rose sharply throughout 1979, reaching a peak of almost $40/B. in the Gulf towards the end of the year, then, with demand sharply down and inventories full, slipping gradually to about $32 by the fourth quarter of 1980. OPEC production was down to 27 mbd (compared with a monthly peak of 32 mbd in 1979), and member countries were pledging to cut production by 10 percent in 1981.

The outbreak of the Iran-Iraq War in late September 1980 brought on a renewed bout of fever and prices hit $41, but it was short-lived as the rest of OPEC made up the short-fall in supply; by then world demand had anyway dropped by over 4 mbd from 1979 levels. Spot prices drifted down during 1981, and after a brief flare-up over the winter of 1981-82 kept floating down over the next few years. By mid-1981, the "crisis" was well and truly over: the market had recovered from its nervous breakdown. But OPEC would go down fighting, at great cost to itself and the rest of the world.

Epilogue

Although alarm and panic were concentrated in 1979 and, to a lesser extent in the final months of 1980, after the outbreak of the Iran-Iraq War, the greatest financial impact of the crisis occurred in 1980. The cost of net oil imports into the OECD area rose from $124 billion in 1978 to $180 billion in 1979, then peaked at $254 billion in 1981. OPEC, however, kept the bit between its teeth, and import costs, despite greatly reduced volumes, still totaled $200 billion in 1982—higher than in 1979, despite a decrease of 35 percent in the volume of imports over the period. OPEC revenues also peaked in 1980, at $287 billion, having risen from $136 billion in 1978. By 1982, they had dropped back to $207 billion and the volume of exports had dropped by 47 percent.

In 1973, OPEC imposed a price increase on the market; in 1979, market panic imposed a price increase on OPEC. In 1973, the producers led, and the Arab-Israeli conflict that provoked an embargo provided the opportunity to force through price hikes that were desired and sought after. In 1979, the market led, driven by a panic to which the incredulous but mainly delighted producers responded with confused and conflicting policies, finally settling for the worst of all—the maintenance of prices at a hopelessly unrealistic level.

The economic catastrophe of 1979-80 was mainly the result of the grand delusions that gripped the world of energy, both consumers and producers. For years, everyone had "known" that another crisis was coming: the IEA's compendium of apocalyptic energy forecasts published in January 1979[18] included 26 projections of world demand for OPEC oil in 1985, starting in 1974 (with four projections) and ending in 1978 (with five). Of this group of projections (there were others), the mean forecast demand for OPEC oil in 1985 was 40 mbd, which was regarded as imminent and unavoidable disaster: political dependence on OPEC would be unbearable and/or demand would outstrip supply and the world would be left permanently short of energy; this would be the much-feared, impending "energy crunch". In 1979, it was plain to see, the crunch was upon us. Add to this the belief in OPEC that its mission in life was to administer prices in a long-term transition from current levels to the cost of alternative supplies, and its parallel aversion to rapid depletion of its reserves, and you have the three main ingredients of the grand delusions.

Unlike the crisis of 1973, and partly because everything happened so quickly, there was little intellectual outpouring, few in-depth studies of the outlook for energy and the prospects for alternative sources, and of course no serious proposals for a grandiose dialogue between producer and consumer countries designed to lead to a New International Economic Order. How could there be? With two of its leading members at war, OPEC was incapable of dialogue with anyone about anything. Moreover, the new government in Iran was a reactionary, theocratic regime and, like its precursor in Libya, quite incomprehensible to the "West".

At least during the period of the previous crisis, from 1971 to 1973, there was a clear if helter-skelter process of adjustment as the old-style concessions were demolished and effective control transferred from companies to governments. In 1979, there was no serious plan, no grand design, no real strategy on anyone's part. The cartel was drunk with power, the consumers paralyzed by fear.

Chapter 12
BACKLASH: PRICES AND POLICIES

What we now need to discover in the social realm is the moral equivalent of war:
something heroic that will speak to men as universally as war does, and yet will
be as compatible with their spiritual selves as war has proved itself to be
incompatible. I have often thought that in the old monkish poverty-worship . . .
there might be something like that moral equivalent of war we are seeking. May
not voluntarily accepted poverty be the 'strenuous life', without the need of crushing
weaker peoples?
– William James, *The Varieties of Religious Experience.*

The energy crisis has not yet overwhelmed us, but it will if we do not act quickly
. . . Our decision about energy will test the character of the American people and
the ability of the President and the Congress to govern. This difficult effort will
be the 'moral equivalent of war' —except that we will be uniting our efforts to
build and not to destroy . . .The oil and natural gas we rely on for 75 percent of
our energy are running out.
– President Jimmy Carter in a broadcast address to the nation,
18 April 1977.

Introduction

The energy crisis of 1973-74 was a real political one that was, unhappily, grafted onto a grossly mistaken perception of a world running out of oil and gas. The melody lingered on for several years. A second energy crisis, also political (though in a quite different way), struck in 1979-80, and for a while reinforced the perception of a resource shortage.

Market reaction to higher prices (more supply, less demand) was in part conditioned by the perception of long-term shortages, especially as far as fuel-switching was concerned, because many people thought, much of the time, that high prices were here to stay.

Policy reaction was confused. Most governments recognized that allowing higher international prices to pass through to the national economy would have the desired effects of stimulating supply and depressing demand, but some tried to cushion the inflationary impact by controlling the price of domestically produced energy. They also tried subsidizing the development

240

of new (domestic) energy supplies; protecting domestic supplies by minimum prices (just in case the international price dropped); and mandating conservation measures. Conflicts arose between the need for more energy and the desire to protect the environment. A desire for economic equity and justice led, in the United States, to the taxation of excessive ("windfall") profits and the allocation of differentially priced oil (controlled, less controlled, decontrolled and uncontrolled) among importers and refiners.

But in the end, the market took its toll, helped along by some countries' policy measures, and in spite of policy measures taken by others. The growth in demand for oil slowed down and then collapsed, bringing prices down with it.

Price and Demand

In January 1974, OPEC raised the posted price for Arabian Light crude from $5.04 to $11.65/B. This had the effect of tripling market prices, from about $3.50 to $10.83/B. The increase had an immediate effect: as the brakes went on, demand fell for a couple of years during which GDP growth in the industrialized countries dropped to zero (not of course entirely due to higher oil prices). Growth in oil demand then resumed at (by oil industry standards) a crawl. World (excluding CPEs) oil consumption fell in 1974 (1.6 percent) and again in 1975 (2.8 percent), before starting to grow again in 1976. However, by 1979, it had regained some of its momentum and reached an all-time high of 52 mbd, almost 10 percent higher than 1973 (prior to the first big price increases).

Over the six-year period between 1973 and 1979 (the year of the next big price increase), demand rose on the average by only 1.5 percent per year compared with more than 6 percent per year during the previous six years, from 1967 to 1973. The return to growth that started in 1976 is attributable in part to the fact that oil prices did not keep pace with the general worldwide inflation during the 1970s, so in fact real prices dropped quite significantly between 1974 and 1979.

The year 1979 also saw OPEC reach peak production to date, even though 2 mbd of Iranian production had been lost in the runup to the Iranian revolution, and despite the fact that production from the Norwegian and British sectors of the North Sea, as well as increased Mexican production, were already making inroads. The high production rates of 1979 had been inflated by large liftings for inventory-building as the consumers once again panicked over the partial cutoff of supplies from the Persian Gulf. This was to have dire consequences for prices and production in the two following years.

The Iranian revolution took place in early 1979: the Shah left the country in January and Ayatollah Khomeini returned in triumph shortly thereafter. By the end of the following year, Iran and Iraq were at war. About 4 mbd were withdrawn from the market for a few months in early 1979, and prices again shot up, this time to $35/B., where they settled for a period of time at first widely regarded as a pause on their way up to $50 to $60/B.

When the price of oil almost tripled again during the 1979-81 period, from $13/B. to $35/B., the International Energy Agency (IEA) was unable, by the terms of its charter, to declare an emergency because none of its members was suffering a shortfall in supply of more than 15 percent. But the market had no such inhibitions, and, in time, reacted with a ferocity that perhaps should have been, but wasn't, anticipated.

Supplies and production of coal, natural gas, nuclear energy and non-OPEC oil all increased sharply; overall world demand for energy dropped, and OPEC not only lost market share to the increased supply of non-OPEC energy, but also had to absorb the decrease in the overall size of the market. Its production was cut almost in half, from its peak of 32 mbd in 1979 to 17 mbd in 1985. And for a while, until prices dropped back, there was a profusion of projects for the development of the Canadian tar sands with its huge reserves of (very high cost) oil, Colorado and other shale oils (even higher cost), fuels and electricity from the liquefaction/gasification of coal, from solar energy, geothermal springs, wind power, tidal power, gasoline from a species of euphorbia, methanol from corn, peat, biomass, city garbage, dried animal dung ("There's no fuel like an old fuel", and "Dung Ho!", quipped the wags), and several people invented internal combustion engines that ran on water but somehow never made it down to the patent office. Billions of dollars were to be committed on this basis to the development of high-cost sources of energy. Mercifully, the supply crisis was over before much of the funds "committed" to these high-cost projects was spent, and the projects themselves were either scrapped or postponed into oblivion.

But the writing was on the wall, in the shape of spot crude oil prices. While official prices were being held up by Saudi Arabia, Kuwait and Abu Dhabi, which were absorbing the lion's share of the cutbacks, most other countries of the cartel were cheating and selling some of their crude at well below official levels on the spot market. Spot prices for Iranian Light crude, for example, fell from $38/B. in January 1981 to $25/B. in June 1985, a loss of over one-third. It was the same story for other crudes.

The price increases of 1973 were finally coming home to roost as new supplies of non-OPEC oil flooded into the market and demand for heavy fuel oil vanished. This time, there was no getting away from it, inflation or no inflation: world demand for oil dropped and did not regain its 1979 levels for ten years, until 1989. OPEC production dropped 4 mbd in 1980, 4 mbd more in 1981, a further 3.5 mbd in 1982, and 2 mbd in 1983. Rarely has the market-place witnessed carnage on such a scale. By 1985, OPEC production had registered a cumulative loss of 15 mbd, nearly 50 percent, from its 1979 level. OPEC was stunned. Only one or two people could truthfully say, "I told you so!" and even they were startled at the strength of the backlash. There was never a forecast from any source whatsoever predicting such a fall in the demand for OPEC oil. How did all this happen?

The Demise of the Fuel Oil Market

The largest market losses were, of course, concentrated on fuel oil since this was the product most vulnerable to competition from other fuels, notably coal and gas for the generation of electricity. In the OECD area, the demand for fuel oil was cut in half during the period from 1978 (when demand totaled about 9.6 mbd) to 1985 (by which time it was down to 4.7 mbd). It was a tremendous boost to the coal industry (especially in the United States) which the oil industry had spent the previous twenty years driving out of the market. After years of stagnation, coal production in the United States increased from 350 million tons of oil equivalent (mtoe) in 1978 to 445 mtoe in 1985. But the oil price increases did little for high-cost (and heavily subsidized) coal in Western Europe, and production continued dropping in most of the important producing countries there. Fuel oil was being displaced by natural gas and nuclear power rather than coal.

Elsewhere, new investment was pouring into coal-mining, especially from the oil companies. Most of the majors bought up coal properties, both in the United States and other countries, notably Australia, with Exxon and Shell in the forefront.

The losses in the fuel oil market worldwide of course translated practically barrel for barrel into reduced demand for crude, all of it ultimately OPEC crude.

Refinery Yields

The loss of the fuel oil market had other, momentous consequences for the industry. Unlike motor gasoline and other products, for which there is no substitute anywhere near their cost of production, the market for fuel oil was limited in most uses by the price of other fuels, notably coal and gas. So the refiner would have to sell fuel oil at a price lower than the price of the crude oil from which it was manufactured—as he had been doing for many years, recovering the "loss" on the sale of other products. Only now, the amount to recover from other products was so great (because the difference between the price of fuel oil's competitors and the price of crude oil had increased greatly) that it justified the construction of conversion facilities in refineries to upgrade fuel oil into lighter products—that is, to get more gasoline and diesel fuel out of the barrel of crude. And that, over the years, was what happened, at very high investment costs, especially in Western Europe and the Caribbean (the latter having been the main supplier of fuel oil to the large US East Coast market).

US refineries had always had relatively low fuel oil yields, partly because their crude oils were lighter than the run-of-the-mill Middle Eastern crudes and partly because the United States relied on imports from the Caribbean of fuel oil made from heavy Venezuelan crudes. In the transition, therefore, less investment was called for in the upgrading of US refineries. In the United States and Canada, crude oil distillation capacity (the primary refining process) declined from 1980 to 1985 (see below, Scrapping the Surplus), but conversion (upgrading) capacity increased by 5 percent. In Western Europe, distillation capacity declined by 25 percent while conversion capacity increased by 47 percent.

Other Products

The demand for other products was not affected to anywhere near the same extent as heavy fuel oil. Unlike fuel oil, some of them had virtually no competitors at all in the short run, and little likelihood of any in the longer-term, even at the high prices that followed the crude oil price increases of 1979-80. There were no substitutes for jet fuel, motor gasoline or road diesel apart from some fringe fuels that either could not be produced in significant volumes or at competitive cost. The only escape route was to make engines that used the same petroleum fuels more efficiently.

Other petroleum products (apart from heavy fuel oil) for stationary uses, especially heating oil, were somewhat more vulnerable to competition from natural gas and coal, but not on the same scale. And the "minor" products—LPGs, naphtha (mainly for petrochemical feedstock), asphalts, lubricating oils, greases and a whole slew of specialty products—between them accounted for 23 percent of world (excluding CPEs) petroleum demand in 1980, and were also largely shielded from the competition of other products for the simple reason that there weren't any others to speak of. Again, the only thing you could do if you didn't like the price, was to use them more efficiently or go without.

In aggregate, then, the demand for all of these products kept on growing, though at much reduced rates, as economic growth itself slowed down and conservation efforts began to bite.

Before and After: The Pattern of Demand

The market transformation was profound. Oil became even more of a transportation fuel, an area where it could not be matched by its stationary-use competitors (natural gas, coal and nuclear energy). In the United States, heavy fuel oil's share of the market fell from 15 percent to 8 percent between 1975 and 1985, and the share of other products rose correspondingly. It was something of the same story in all of the other industrial countries, but in the developing countries, where there were fewer options, the demand for fuel oil did not fall in absolute terms. They had no electricity generating plants that could be easily converted to burn coal, and most of them would in any event have had to import the coal and invest in the infrastructure to handle it.

Scrapping the Surplus

As the demand for oil now fell, in the early 1980s, and the pattern of demand changed, the industry was faced with the painful task of adjusting to a new world of energy. One of the first things that had to be done was to scrap or "mothball" surplus refining capacity, in terms of total throughput, and upgrade the remaining facilities to produce proportionately more of the light products and less of the heavy ones. Secondly, the tanker fleet was now far too large, and many ships would have to be scrapped or "de-jumboized", meaning cutting a section out of the middle and joining the remaining two ends together to make a smaller tanker out of a larger one.

The decrease in refinery crude oil processing capacity was stunning. In the United States and Canada, 111 plants with a crude distillation capacity of 4.2 mbd were closed down or mothballed between 1980 and 1985; in Western Europe, which was hit much harder by the decline in fuel oil demand, distillation capacity was reduced by 5.8 mbd and 37 plants closed; and in Japan, busily shifting to nuclear power and coal, 1.0 mbd of distillation capacity was lost. All in all, more than 20 percent of refining (crude distillation) capacity was closed down in the OECD area during the five-year period.

The situation was even worse for tankers. Almost-one quarter of the world's tanker fleet was scrapped between 1980 and 1985. The surplus, caused essentially by the decrease in demand for crude oil, was exacerbated by the fact that most of the new supplies (of non-OPEC) crude was short-haul— in the North Sea for Europe, Alaska and Mexico for the United States— and this short-haul crude replaced the long-haul crude from the Persian Gulf. In some countries, notably Pakistan and the Philippines, the scrapping of vessels became a major industry.

Managing Demand and Supply

No doubt the near tripling of crude oil prices in the early 1970s, and again in 1979-81, was chiefly responsible for the massacre in the fuel oil markets and provided most of the market-driven impetus for the development of non-OPEC sources of energy. But in consuming countries, government measures, mostly taken or initiated before the second big price increases (in 1979-81), also played a part. Indeed, the reaction in consuming countries was on the whole stronger following the 1973-74 price increases (which were much smaller in absolute terms than the 1979-81 increases—$9 compared with $20) than after the second round. In part, this was only logical: most of the obvious and not too painful measures that could be taken by governments to assist the market in reducing consumption and increasing production of energy had already been taken by 1979, were in the process of being implemented, or had at least been agreed as policy objectives.

But there was also a political element to the reaction. In the period immediately following the 1973-74 price increases, their political content loomed large. It is true that at the time many people (Nixon, Schlesinger, Kissinger, Garvin) said publicly that an energy crisis had been on the way, regardless of the Arab-Israeli conflict that flared up in October 1973; but it must still be remembered that when prices tripled, it was against the political background of the conflict and the Arab oil embargo. The decision to triple prices at the beginning of 1974 was a deliberate political decision taken by OPEC on the embargo's coat-tails, and later maintained by production restrictions. Indeed, the view of the energy crisis as the inevitable result of a slowly developing shortage of energy increasingly gave way to a shorter-term political view of oil supplies. How else does one explain the attempts at "dialogue" with the producers to reach some sort of agreement on prices? Shortage is shortage, and you can't "agree" it away. And if OPEC could not be induced to reduce prices itself (Kissinger made sure of that, for short-term geopolitical purposes), then its oligopoly position had to be weakened over the longer term by the introduction of non-market measures to make the world less dependent on OPEC supplies.

The governments of the important consuming and importing countries reacted in three major ways to the price increases. First, through a variety of price, tax and regulatory measures, they tried to stimulate a higher degree of conservation (efficiency of use) into the markets than would have occurred naturally through market prices. Second, through tax incentives, subsidies and de-regulation, they tried to increase the domestic supply of energy. And, third, some tried to reserve domestic supplies of fuel for the domestic market, on national security grounds. The precise mix of policies adopted in each country depended on its own natural resource base and its domestic politics; the results were not always internally consistent and sometimes counter-productive, but on the whole, they had a significant impact on the consumption of energy and the reduction of dependence on oil imports over the long run, particularly with respect to the generation of electricity, speed limits on the roads, mandated fuel efficiency standards for new automobiles, housing (insulation) and domestic appliances.

From the outset, however, it was painfully obvious that some of the measures proposed would conflict with other important policies. Price de-control, where controls existed—which was nearly everywhere—would only fuel inflation, already high. The use of more coal for electricity generation would conflict with environmental policies for cleaner air. And subsidies for the creation of some high-cost alternative sources of energy would require the indefinite maintenance of high energy price—or the indefinite maintenance of the subsidies.

In the end, these problems were solved more or less satisfactorily—inflation being mitigated if not entirely cured by high-interest rates, and clean air standards achieved through technological advances in the control of stack emissions, among other things. Most of the projects for high-cost alternative sources of energy were to collapse of their own weight in the face of falling oil prices, soon to come.

IEA Principles for Energy Policy

The International Energy Agency (IEA), created in 1974, proved a convenient talk-shop and venue for the coordination of energy policies by the main industrial nations. By the end of 1977, its Governing Board of Ministers had adopted twelve "Principles for Energy Policy" (October 1977) and in December 1980 "Lines of Action for Energy Conservation and Fuel Switching", which were to "form a basis for priority action to bridge the oil supply-demand gap currently foreseen for the mid to late 1980s."[1]

A large number of measures were to be taken involving tax and financial incentives (or disincentives), straightforward regulation and pricing. They were however primarily focused on:

– De-control of crude oil and product prices, which "should reflect international oil prices". Energy prices generally should be allowed "to reach a level which encourages energy conservation, movement away from oil, and the development of new sources of energy".

– Establishment of fuel economy standards for automobiles and other vehicles.

– Regulation of heating and cooling insulation standards for homes and commercial buildings.

– Expansion of nuclear and coal-fired electricity generation and reduction of oil-fired capacity.

The Spectacular Results

Though masked by innumerable dead-ends and failures, particularly with respect to alternative sources of energy supply (alternatives to fossil fuels, that is), the combination of high market prices, especially after decontrol, together with fiscal and regulatory measures in OECD countries, produced results that were nothing short of spectacular in achieving the overriding objective—reducing dependence on oil imports from OPEC. It is true that some of the success must be attributed to slow and at times negative economic growth, scarcely the ideal way to get to the desired result. It is also true that many of the decisions taken had to be viewed in the context of a belief, still general, that the world was heading for "continuing energy shortages", but that, in a sense, made the objective more, and not less, political. An energy shortage could only mean increased dependence on OPEC countries, and if that happened, there would, sooner or later, be both an extortionate dollar price and some form of political price to pay, or at least demanded. That much was obvious from the proposals for a restructuring of the international economy and the so-called "New International Economic Order" put forward during the dialogue period of the mid-1970s (which had collapsed as soon as it seemed to become obvious, by 1976-77, that oil prices were settling down and being seriously eroded anyway by inflation). What was meant by reducing dependence on oil imports was simply reducing dependence on OPEC—a purely political objective and nothing else.

Nevertheless, success in achieving the objective can be mainly ascribed, though with no great precision, to conservation, to fuel switching, and to the development of non-OPEC sources of oil supplies, all of them driven by price and regulatory activity on the part of governments, in proportions that I shall not attempt to measure here—indeed, they overlap in the sense that it took government action to de-control prices and allow price to play its part.

Conservation

As a rough, back-of-the-envelope measure of conservation, one can look at total primary energy requirements (TPER) per constant thousand dollars of gross domestic product (GDP). This shows how much energy is required to produce $1,000 worth of goods and services. It dropped sharply over the period from 1973 to 1985 encompassing the two major oil price hikes.

Overall, in the IEA group of countries (basically the OECD area minus France) the TPER/GDP ratio fell from 0.57 tons of oil equivalent (toe) in 1973, to 0.46 toe in 1985, a decrease of almost 20 percent. Star performers were Japan (down 31 percent), the United States (down 23 percent) and the United Kingdom (down 20 percent), though to some extent this may merely reflect a high level of waste at and prior to the beginning of the period.[2]

Admittedly, the TPER/GDP ratio is an imperfect measure of conservation (efficiency of use) because it takes no account of structural change in the economy, such as a shift to inherently less energy-intensive forms of economic activity (heavy industry to services, for example). But speed limits, where enforced, and fuel economy standards played an important role: gasoline consumption per car dropped by 22 percent in the IEA area (by 18 percent in the United States) from 1973 to 1984, a substantial saving per car (though overall gasoline consumption increased in most countries because the number of cars on the road increased faster).

Energy intensities in the industrial and residential/commercial sectors in industrial; countries also dropped during the period, by 30 percent in the former and 6 percent in the latter.

Data for the less-developed countries is not available in such detail, but there seems to have been less scope for this kind of conservation.

Fuel Switching

By far the largest part of fuel switching from oil to other sources occurred in the generation of electricity, and the effect on fuel oil consumption was devastating, as noted above. In the IEA area, oil as a percentage of inputs in electricity generation fell from 23 percent in 1973 to 11 percent in 1984. The United States, with its vast reserves of low-cost coal, recorded a drop of almost three-quarters, from 18 percent in1973 to 5 percent in 1984. Japan, moving fast to nuclear power, dropped from 64 percent in 1973 to 34 percent in 1984.

Non-OPEC Oil

The price increases that started in 1971 and continued almost unabated for the next ten years were, quite naturally, an enormous stimulus to non-OPEC supplies of crude. In some respects, the circumstances were peculiar: the three areas from which massive amounts of new non-OPEC oil would come were all discovered before the major price increases started. The North Slope Alaska discovery well came in when the outlook for prices was still gloomy, in 1968; the North Sea Ekofisk discovery in 1971; and the string of discoveries and new producing provinces in Mexico in 1972-73.

These areas would have been developed slowly in the absence of the OPEC price increases—indeed, it is possible that Alaska's North Slope would not have been developed at all in view of the environmental opposition. But the Tehran Agreement of November 1971 assured their future by reversing the long-term trend towards lower oil prices and raising their general world-wide level. The price increases that followed, particularly in 1973-74, made sure that development would be rapid.

The contribution of other non-OPEC to the increase in crude supplies was not insignificant though more dispersed over a number of different producers. Some old ones were able to respond to the price hikes by increasing their production, and some new, smaller producers that might not have come onstream quite as quickly without the price increases now went ahead rapidly.

All in all, new non-OPEC crude supplies increased by 11 mbd (59 percent) from 1973 to 1985 (the year when OPEC prices collapsed). Mexico, Norway and the UK accounted for over half of it, and a scatter of other countries for the rest (including a substantial increase in Soviet bloc exports). Once the geologic potential of the new areas had been grasped and the potential for expansion in some of the older areas understood, the speed of development was inhibited only by government policies and the sheer physical constraints on mobilizing capital, equipment and people to do the job. We look more closely at this diverse and phenomenal surge in production in Chapter 13.

Failures: Alternative Sources of Energy

If the increases in non-OPEC oil production and coal production, as well as conservation, were a stunning success, there were also a number of failures during the period from 1973 to 1985, notably in the development of alternative sources of energy. The basic reasons were either concern over the environment, or the very high cost of the alternatives which became impossible to justify when prices began to falter.

Nuclear Energy

Nuclear energy was a runaway success at first, especially during the period when it counted most, from 1973 to 1985, with efforts by the industrialized countries to reduce dependence on OPEC at their height. Led by the United States, France (nuclear power's most ardent devotee) and Japan, consumption of nuclear-generated electricity in the OECD area rose by 17 percent per year. Measured in terms of oil equivalent, or the amount of oil it would have taken to generate (in a typical modern oil-fired plant) the amount of electricity consumed, this was an increase from 44.4 mtoe to 284.3 mtoe, or 240 mtoe (4.8 mbd). Not all of this came out of OPEC's hide—some of the new nuclear power plants coming onstream would have been coal-fired or gas-fired; but a substantial amount must have been translated into a barrel-for-barrel reduction in OPEC crude production.

Later, the large amounts of electricity generated by new plants coming onstream masked the incipient decline of the industry. The huge capital cost of nuclear power plants compared with fossil fuel ones; the longer lead times (especially in the United States) from the planning stage to the commissioning of plants; and environmental opposition soon reduced new orders to zero in many countries of the OECD area. The heyday of this new technology had no sooner begun than it was over.

After 1979, it was all downhill. A relatively minor accident at the Three-Mile Island nuclear power plant near Harrisburg, Pennsylvania, in March 1979, spelt the end of new orders for nuclear power plants in the United States. In April 1986, a major accident at the Chernobyl plant, 100 kms. north of Kiev, in the Ukraine (then part of the Soviet Union), was the kiss of death for new orders in Western Europe. After Chernobyl, construction was started on only three new reactors in Western Europe. Afterwards, construction would be limited to Japan and a few other countries (notably India and China).

Nevertheless, as new plants on which construction had started many years before came onstream, nuclear power's contribution kept growing at a healthy pace. It is not clear to what extent higher costs played a part in the industry's decline, compared with environmental and safety fears. It was an expensive disappointment. Nevertheless, it made a substantial contribution to lessening dependence on OPEC during the critical years from 1973 to 1975.

Other Sources of Energy

Apart from hydroelectric power, all the other sources of energy touted in the early 1970s were unmitigated failures, mainly on purely economic grounds, as significant contributors to world supplies of energy. People were quick to see it, too. The IEA, in its annual report *Energy Policies and Programmes of IEA Countries—1982 Review,* lists a *selection* of energy projects cancelled or postponed [p. 57]. They include the Alsands and Cold Lake oil sands projects in Canada; the gas pipeline from Alaska through Canada; five coal gasification projects in the United States, Germany and the Netherlands; five coal liquefaction projects in the UK, the United States, Germany and Australia; the Colony (United States) and Rundle (Australia) oil shale projects; and 26 nuclear power plants in the United States. None of these had been crackpot schemes dreamt up by ignorant speculators (of which there were plenty elsewhere). They were all initially backed by serious energy companies.

There were minor contributions. In the United States and Brazil, alcohol fuel from agricultural products had to be subsidized. It still maintains a level of production that is not negligible on the national scale. Similarly, production of oil from the Athabasca tar sands (not subsidized) started up, but never expanded. Shale oil never got off the ground at all; fuel cells, biomass, solar energy and wind power remain insignificant, whatever their potential for the future, even though some (like biomass) can be significant in a small number of countries.

Developments in the United States

The goals generally agreed by the major consuming countries, as embodied in their stated objectives in the IEA, have been noted. These must suffice in the context of this book: a more detailed examination would require too much space and be of limited interest for international oil policies. There is, however, one exception: a more detailed, yet brief, look at developments in the United States is worthwhile because the United States was by far the largest consumer of energy in the world, and its actions and inaction had a far greater impact than those of other countries.

Policy Prior to the 1973-74 Price Increases

As noted in an earlier chapter, US concern with energy policy, as far as international aspects of oil were involved, had been largely limited to imports. The question quite suddenly became more serious than simply a matter of balancing domestic producers' interests against the benefits of freer trade, when it became apparent in 1970-71 that rapidly growing demand and declining domestic producing capacity would soon be translated into massive increases in oil imports which would be available only from the Middle East.

This naturally raised the question of national security in the shape of dependence for a vital commodity on a politically unstable and, on the whole, hostile region.

President Nixon's first Special Message to the Congress on Energy Resources of June 1971, highlighted the need for an expanded nuclear power program, conversion of coal to clean gaseous fuels, Outer Continental Shelf (OCS) oil-leasing, and an oil shale program. The message was virtually ignored by Congress.

A second message followed in April 1973, which was largely a tarted-up repeat of the 1971 message, with an urgent plea for the removal of obstacles to the construction of the Trans-Alaska Pipeline (destined to bring North Slope crude to the ice-free port of Valdez in southern Alaska).

Nixon and Project Independence

The outbreak of the Arab-Israeli War in October 1973 and the subsequent imposition of an embargo on oil shipments to the United States galvanized the government. On 7 November 1973, Nixon addressed the nation on policies to deal with energy shortages and called for a new national endeavor, Project Independence:

> Let us set as our national goal, in the spirit of Apollo, with the determination of the Manhattan project, that by the end of this decade we will have developed the potential to meet our own energy needs without depending on any foreign energy sources.

The aim to make the United States self-sufficient in energy by 1980 was absurdly unrealistic, and everyone in the administration knew it, as did anyone at all familiar with the oil industry.

On 16 November 1973, Nixon signed legislation (the Federal Lands Right-of-Way Bill and the Trans-Alaska Pipeline Authorization Bill) enabling the secretary of the Interior to issue the necessary permits for the construction of the Trans-Alaska Pipeline. (First supplies of equipment and pipe were transported to the north coast of Alaska in the summer of 1974; construction started at the beginning of 1975 and the line was completed in mid-1977. The first oil arrived at Valdez on 29 July 1977, nine years after the discovery well at Prudhoe Bay was completed.)

The Emergency Petroleum Allocation Act (EPAA) was now rushed through Congress and signed by Nixon on 27 November 1973. It authorized the imposition of price, production, allocation and marketing controls and required the administration to prepare allocation plans within 30 days.

Ford: the Energy Policy and Conservation Act (EPCA)

Apart from international energy relations (especially the Washington Conference and follow-up), the rest of 1974 was given up to wrangling over policy matters that were more concerned with conflicts between different groups of interests than with doing anything to increase supply or decrease demand for energy.

In January 1975, President Gerald Ford sent proposals to Congress for an Energy Independence Act the broad objectives of which were to reduce import dependence, establish a free market in petroleum and provide revenue for energy research and development.

It took almost a year to get the bill passed, and by the time the final version was signed into law as the Energy Policy and Conservation Act in December 1975, it had been considerably modified. It emerged from its lengthy gestation as less of an energy act than an oil act in which the main powers clustered around the price of oil and there were few teeth to bite into demand or stimulate the use and production of alternatives. The short-term effect was to roll back prices to $7.66 from the previous composite ("old" and "new" oil) price of $8.75. Thereafter, prices would be increased by stages to $11.21 in April 1979.

It was widely perceived as a monument to political expediency, not an adequate response to the energy problems facing the country. In fact, however, the act did include some important positive measures: it authorized the creation of a strategic petroleum reserve (SPR); mandated an automobile fuel efficiency program; called for the doubling, over a ten-year period, of the average miles-per-gallon capability of car production, from 13 miles to 27.5 miles per gallon; and granted the authorities requested on coal conversion and product labeling.

Carter: The National Energy Act

Energy had not been an issue in the elections of 1976, and when President Carter took office in early 1977, nothing on the national or international scene appeared to require urgent action.

What gripped Carter's imagination, however, was the dreaded pincer movement of rising US demand for oil and declining domestic production. The inevitable result would be rapidly increasing imports, made all the more dangerous because it spelled growing dependence on the Middle East. Moreover, this scenario was set in the context of a world supposedly running out of oil, even, eventually, in the Middle East. The economic and strategic implications of this apocalyptic view were enormous. Unfortunately, Carter chose as his chief energy adviser and secretary of Energy—James Schlesinger—a man who was equally if not more obsessed with this doom-laden vision of the country's energy future.

Carter's anguished appeal to the country (from which the second quote at the beginning of this chapter is taken) on the eve of sending his energy policy proposals to Congress came almost three and a half years after the 1973-74 price hikes. His call for the American people to wage the "moral equivalent of war" was not of course a proposal that they accept monkish poverty voluntarily, which is what William James, philosopher, psychologist and coiner of the unfortunate phrase, had in mind as equivalence (see the first quote at the beginning of the chapter). The president was, rather, doing his utmost to imbue Americans with a sense of urgency and the need for action in the face of an impending catastrophe. His speech (of 18 April 1977) was full of nightmare:

> We could use up all the proven reserves of oil in the entire world by the end of the next decade . . . if we wait, we will live in fear of embargoes . . . our factories will not be able to keep our people on the job with reduced supplies of fuel . . . Inflation will soar, production will go down, people will lose their jobs . . . If we fail to act soon, we will face an economic, social and political crisis that will threaten our free institutions.

The public at large did not believe much in an approaching "energy crunch", or if they did, only as modern Christians believe in Hell in the hereafter—a prospect not to detract seriously from the pleasures of life on earth in a four-wheel-drive, gas-guzzling SUV.

Carter's legislative proposals, summarized in a "fact sheet" which he submitted to Congress on 20 April 1977, stressed conservation and accelerated price de-control of domestic crude, and was on the whole far more interventionist than Ford's program. Carter's short-term objective was to "reduce dependence on foreign oil"; medium term, to "weather the eventual decline in the availability of world oil supplies", and long-term, "to develop renewable and essentially inexhaustible sources of energy for sustained growth". Carter was clearly obsessed with the notion of a world running out of oil, and Schlesinger, who was similarly preoccupied but should have known better, must both bear much of the responsibility for the misdirection that US energy policy took as a result.

On 9 November 1978, eighteen months after he had submitted his energy plan to Congress, President Carter signed the National Energy Act into law. His plan had undergone much modification. Carter's proposed gasoline standby tax and a crude oil equalization tax were both rejected by Congress. The other proposals were considerably mutilated, and the five main parts that emerged into the light of day (and law) were:

– *Natural Gas.* Price controls on newly-discovered gas to be removed entirely by January 1985.

– *Utility Rates.* Utilities required to justify any decision not to move to types of rate structures encouraging conservation, such as reduced rates for off-peak use.

– *Coal Conversion.* New power plants required to burn coal; existing plants to stop using gas by 1990; plants with the existing capability of using coal, to do so if required by the department of Energy.

– *Conservation.* New efficiency standards for major appliances (air conditioners, refrigerators, furnaces, etc.); increased penalties on car manufacturers not meeting fuel efficiency standards.

– *Energy Taxes.* A new excise tax for car manufacturers not meeting fuel efficiency standards (starting with 1980 models).

By November 1978, when Carter signed the act, the Shah's regime in Iran was on the brink of collapse. Oil workers in Iran had gone briefly on strike in October; in January 1979 there would be renewed strikes; by the end of the month, the Shah had left the country. In April 1979, the new regime announced a new production ceiling. Spot prices rose to $23. Other OPEC countries, now under pressure to produce even more, also announced they would cut output. By the end of the year, spot crude prices in the Gulf had reached $39.

The market reaction (described in the first part of this chapter) was particularly savage because it was the cumulative effect of the 1973-74 price increases, all the conservation and fuel-switching measures put in place between then and 1979, and the 1979-81 price increases themselves.

The impact of the second price shock was relatively short-lived because of the very violence of the market backlash that soon cut OPEC production (and prices) in half, but in the United States it spawned the Energy Security Act and the passage of the long-awaited Windfall Profits Tax (enacted in April 1979).

The Synthetic Fuels Corporation was created by the 1980 Energy Security Act, and provided for the expenditure of $20 billion in a first phase, to be followed by a further $68 billion in a second phase. The corporation was to provide a final, sad comment on the Carter-Schlesinger view of world oil resources: in late 1985, before it was finally shut down by Congress and President Reagan, it was still guaranteeing companies working on oil shale projects in Colorado an oil price of $67 per barrel. By then the market price had fallen from a high of $39 to $27, and was still dropping. Union Oil Company, one of the beneficiaries of large loans to develop oil from shale had built a plant designed to produce 10,000 bd—mere peanuts—which had been completed more than a year behind schedule and had never been able to run continuously for more than thirty hours at a time.[3]

The second price shock was, perhaps surprisingly, accepted with far greater equanimity among the industrial importing nations than the first, despite the price increase being much greater in absolute terms.

There are several reasons for this: the second price shock, of 1979-81, was seen as more of a simple market reaction to the loss of several million barrels per day of Iranian crude (though it was in fact backed up by production restrictions in other countries); there was no embargo or threats of embargo. The Iran-Iraq War, after an initial scare, was not perceived as posing much of a threat to supply; surplus capacity soon reappeared, bringing weakening prices (albeit from a higher level); demand for OPEC oil decreased dramatically and supply of non-OPEC energy increased. Finally, there was a certain sense of *déja vu* about it: the public was simply not as inclined to believe that oil shortages were here to stay.

In the end, after prices had dropped to a less damaging level, and inflation had eroded them further, most governments opted for inaction, or at least for no further action, leaving the market to take its course. This fitted in well with the more general move away from government control and intervention in the economy, toward free, competitive markets. Better news for the consumer was soon to come, as OPEC member countries fell to competing with each other.

Chapter 13
THE DEVELOPMENT OF NON-OPEC OIL
SINCE 1970

The enormous quantities of oil needed to satisfy demand in the seventies and eighties will have to be sought for and developed in more and more difficult places ... the investment for this will have to come largely out of retained earnings ... Oil, which is still a relatively cheap fuel ... will have to become more expensive— exclusive of taxes—if adequate supplies for the future are to be forthcoming.
– Petroleum Press Service, August 1971, p. 282.

Overview

One of the heaviest blows to OPEC, once it had seized power over prices in 1973, was the rapid development of large quantities of crude oil from other areas, mitigated only by the decline of production in the Lower 48 States of the United States. The new supplies came too late to avert the crises of 1973 and 1979, but quickly enough to make a major contribution to the collapse of the market in the early 1980s.

It would be well, before going into any detail, to take an overall look at the course that OPEC and non-OPEC production were to take during the relevant period, from 1970 to 1990. As shown in the chart below (which excludes production in the Centrally Planned Economies, but includes their net exports to countries outside the Soviet bloc), OPEC production grew very rapidly from 1970 to 1973, in response to burgeoning world demand and limited supplies from non-OPEC sources. At the end of 1973, OPEC tripled crude prices. Demand fell for a couple of years and then started to grow again, but more slowly than before. OPEC production remained at extremely high levels—over 30 mbd—for another few years, and then plunged as non-OPEC sources flooded into the market, coal pushed heavy fuel oil out, and demand dropped once more. It was not until 1986, after prices had collapsed (though they were soon to regain part of their loss), and non-OPEC production leveled off, that OPEC production began to climb again.

The number of non-OPEC crude oil producers has grown from well under twenty of any significance (say, over 10 kbd) in 1950 to over fifty in 2003. Excluding the United States and the Soviet Union (or FSU), production has risen from 0.8 mbd to 25 mbd. Less than half of the non-OPEC producers are net exporters—fewer than twenty in recent years. Of these, only eight are volumetrically important in international markets. They are Mexico, Norway, Russia (and other FSU), Oman, Malaysia, Angola and Yemen. The United Kingdom occupies a special position because it is an important exporter (but not on a *net* basis), its crudes are widely traded and their prices widely quoted, including the most important 'marker' crude price, for Brent blend. Canada is a large exporter, but to only one destination, the United States.

From 1973 on, non-OPEC producers have been able to produce at full capacity as OPEC took up the role of swing supplier by holding up prices. The only exception was the brief period of 1985-86 when prices collapsed, and a substantial segment of high-cost crude from US "stripper" wells (producing only a few barrels per day) was closed down for good.

Mbd   **WORLD CRUDE OIL PRODUCTION**

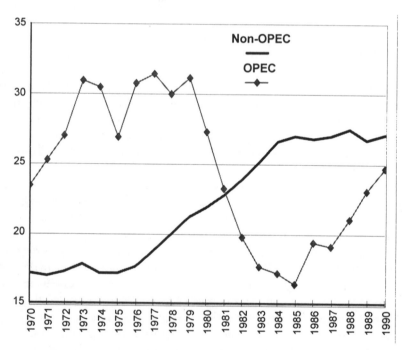

Volumetrically, *all* non-OPEC production is important because every additional barrel is one less for OPEC. However, it is the net exporting countries, competing directly with OPEC in the international markets, that have a much sharper and more direct impact on price—especially when they have the potential for expansion. We look, in particular, at these, below.

Non-OPEC Net Exports

The net exports of non-OPEC producing countries have been through five phases during the period from 1973 to 2000, doing varying degrees of damage to OPEC.

From 1973 to 1979

The price increases imposed by OPEC in late 1973 and the much smaller ones agreed in Tehran in late 1971 had little immediate effect in increasing competitive supplies into the export market, largely because of the long time-lags involved in the development of new production. In the export market whose total size was then around 30 mbd, non-OPEC exporters managed to increase their share by only 1.4 mbd over the six-year period to 1979. About half of the increase came from the Soviet Union which, with its command economy, was able to cash in rapidly on the bonanza price increase. Indeed, it was important to the Soviets whose main source of hard foreign exchange was from oil and gas exports. An additional one-third of the increase came from Mexico, and the rest in bits and pieces scattered around, including incipient net exports from Norway (it was still early days for the North Sea). Alaskan production had also become available in quantity, and took some of the pressure off import demand in the United States.

In any event, OPEC did not much care. All member countries were producing as close to capacity as they wanted, and indeed some of their spokesmen were lecturing the industrial countries on the crying need to adopt more and sterner conservation measures. In 1979, when the Iranian revolution took hold and supplies from Iran were cut in half, the rest of OPEC was producing at close to capacity and the only immediate constraints on price were political.

From 1979 to 1985

The following six years were an entirely different story. Things could not have gone worse for OPEC. Non-OPEC oil invaded the export markets in huge quantities, more than doubling and shooting up by 4.2 mbd. Fully one-quarter of this increase came from Mexico, almost one-quarter from the United Kingdom, 15 percent from the Soviet Union, and the rest mostly from Norway, Canada and Egypt. All of this was oil that would otherwise have been supplied by OPEC.

But, bad as it was, it was only part of the bad news for the organization. Overall world demand for oil dropped, and in many net importing countries domestic production increased, thus reducing their import demand still further. As a result, OPEC production was cut in half, from nearly 30 mbd to almost 16 mbd, and prices collapsed in 1986.

From 1985 to 1990

This next period, from 1985 to 1990, was curious (and worth examining in a little more detail) because, while there was a surge in net exports from quite a number of countries, notably Norway, Oman, Malaysia, Colombia, Angola and Yemen (about 2 mbd in aggregate), there were very substantial decreases in the United Kingdom (down 777 kbd), as well as Mexico and the Soviet bloc. These offset much of the increase and consequently net exports from the non-OPEC countries as a whole were up a mere 780 kbd over the five-year period. It was another of those odd coincidences. The sharp fall in exports from the countries concerned was not due, or not due primarily, to the price decreases of 1985-86, but rather to a combination of local political circumstances and simple bad luck. After all, if Norway *et al.* could profitably increase their exports so substantially during this period when prices collapsed for a short while, the sharp decline in British, Soviet and Mexican exports must have had causes other than price.

In any event, the drop almost certainly saved OPEC from disintegration. The Organization might not have held together at all if it had been faced with another loss of, say, 3 mbd in its market to non-OPEC sources. As it was, OPEC now took the lion's share of the increase in world export markets for the next five years, and production rose rapidly from 16.8 mbd in 1985 to 25.0 mbd in 1990, thus regaining much of the lost ground.

– The United Kingdom. In the United Kingdom, development was no doubt affected to some extent by the declining price of oil but an ill-timed increase in taxes was also partly to blame. The number of wells drilled dropped sharply in 1985 and 1986, in response to shrinking company cash flows; taxes had been increased in 1981 with the introduction of the Supplementary Petroleum Duty (replaced in 1983 by the Advance Petroleum Revenue Tax). But, more than anything else, simple bad luck seems to have been the major cause of the decrease in UK production. Licensing had proceeded steadily, with new rounds in 1980-81, 1982-83 and 1984-85, albeit subject to more stringent conditions than before, especially with respect to participation and a carried interest for the state-owned British National Oil Corporation (BNOC). However, while there were a good number of new discoveries during the period 1980-85 which should have been coming onstream during the period 1985-90, they were, as luck would have it, generally small. Worse still, the major finds (notably Brent, Forties, Ninian and Piper) of previous years had already peaked and were in decline. All in all, of 13 major fields, 11 had peaked prior to 1987, and by 1998 their aggregate production was down 35 percent from their highs.

As if all this were not enough, there was a series of accidents in 1988 and 1989 that took out a major amount of production. In July 1988, the Piper platform was destroyed by an explosion; the floating storage at the Fulmar field was lost in winter storms; equipment failure at Brent Delta and a gas explosion at the Cormorant Alpha platform shut down the whole of the Brent pipeline system; and finally, the St Fergus gas treatment plant had to be closed down. By May 1989, production was running at only 1.5 mbd (down from 2.5 mbd in May 1988) and for the time being the United Kingdom was out of the export market altogether.

– *Mexico.* The slump in Mexico's exports that occurred during the period 1985 to 1990 was, it is true, indirectly related to the slump in oil prices, but much more directly to gross political mismanagement.

Mexico had become one of the world's largest net exporters of oil following the discovery and rapid development of two major new producing areas in the early 1970s. They were the Reforma (Chiapas-Tabasco) fields onshore, in the south of the country, on the Gulf of Mexico; and the Gulf of Campeche fields, offshore Tabasco, in the southern part of the Gulf of Mexico. They were developed rapidly, and during the period of fastest expansion, from 1973 to 1982, Mexico's production grew at the phenomenal rate of over 50 percent per year, going from 525 kbd in 1973 to 3.0 mbd in 1982.

In the general euphoria, the country borrowed heavily on the basis of its new-found assets, and by the time oil prices tumbled, it was saddled with an external debt of almost $80 billion. When the bottom dropped out, the government did the easiest and worst thing possible: to meet foreign debt servicing requirements and its other obligations, it starved Pemex, the national oil company, of investment funds. Drilling dropped abruptly and development of new producing capacity virtually stopped. Even the maintenance of existing capacity tailed off. As a direct consequence, net exports, which had peaked in 1984 at 1.7 mbd, slid down to 1.3 mbd in 1989, a decrease of 400 kbd.

– *Soviet Union.* The Soviet Union's contribution to OPEC's survival came a little later, in 1989 and 1990. True, net exports to non-Comecon countries dropped about 300 kbd in 1985 (18 percent), but this was for market reasons, and before the price drops of 1986. Indeed, the following year, they recovered somewhat, and climbed again in 1987 to reach an all-time high in 1988 of 1.9 mbd (so much for the Soviet promises to reduce exports in support of OPEC).

It was not until the Soviet economy began to implode in 1989 that exports dropped. Everything seemed to grind to a halt all at once. The oil industry was severely hampered by shortfalls in the supply of oilfield equipment from its plants located in Azerbaijan, largely due to ethnic unrest; there were industrial stoppages elsewhere and workers in the large Tyumen producing province cut production deliberately in an attempt to pressure the government into improving work conditions.

Net oil exports fell by 260 kbd in 1989, 285 kbd in 1990, and a disastrous 525 kbd in 1991—a total of 1 mbd in three years, which all in effect accrued to OPEC.

By 1991, OPEC production was back up to 25 mbd, from 17 mbd in 1985: the organization had escaped by the skin of the teeth. The price debacle of 1986 had had little to do with it. Of the 8 mbd gained by OPEC during the five-year period, not much more than 1 mbd can be ascribed directly to price, and that was almost all concentrated in the United States, the aggregate production of thousands of stripper wells that were permanently shut in. Most of the rest was the providential effect of the political situation in Mexico and the Soviet Union, and the fiscal situation in the United Kingdom, combined with some extraordinary bad luck there in the small size of recent discoveries and a truly disastrous run of serious accidents in its North Sea producing facilities.

From 1990 to 1995

The next five years saw a huge resurgence in net exports from non-OPEC countries, which rose by 4.4 mbd, chewing up most of the increase in world demand. But (providentially, again, for OPEC) demand was strong and enough growth was left over for OPEC's own exports to grow, though much more slowly than during the previous five years.

Norway, the United Kingdom, the FSU, Canada and Mexico between them accounted for 76 percent of the total increase in net exports from non-OPEC countries during the period. Fifteen other countries accounted for the rest, notably Angola, Colombia, Malaysia, Oman, Syria and Yemen.

As a result of a remarkable surge in development, Norway's net exports shot up by 1.3 mbd during the period 1990 to 1995. Several new fields were brought onstream, three of them very large (Brage, Draugen and Snorre).

The UK experienced a wonderful reversal in its fortunes. About forty new fields came on stream from 1990 to 1995, all medium to small. Their development was substantially helped by three factors: first, advances in technology were bringing costs down; second, declining production in some of the older and larger fields meant that there was spare capacity in some of the infrastructure that could be put to use by the new fields; and, third, the fiscal situation was improved by the reduction of the Petroleum Revenue Tax (PRT) from 75 to 50 percent in mid-1993, and abolished altogether for fields approved for development after March 1993. As a result, production increased rapidly once more and net exports were up by 870 kbd in 1995 over 1990.

The other three major contributors to the increase in non-OPEC production and exports during this period were the FSU, Canada and Mexico, between them accounting for 1.2 mbd of the total increase of 4.4 mbd.

From 1995 to 2000

After 1995, there was a marked slowdown, once again, in the expansion of non-OPEC production and net exports. Exports climbed by about 1.5 mbd between 1995 and 2000, presenting a relatively minor irritation to OPEC and only a small threat to price stability. The FSU's net exports kept expanding, though not reaching their former levels; but increases in Mexico, Norway and the UK were relatively small (340 kbd in aggregate), and there were serious declines (relative to their size) in the net exports of Egypt and Syria. But new discoveries offshore West Africa and the development of new areas and the FSU promised a fresh onslaught.

OPEC and the Non-OPEC Producers and Net Exporters

How did the OPEC cartel try to deal with the outsiders, the non-OPEC producers and exporters that were eating into its markets? At first, it tried inviting them in, then it tried crushing them, then it tried inviting them in again. Neither way worked well.

Given high prices supported by a cartel, outsiders produce and develop as much as they can as fast as they can. They become a serious threat to the cartel's market position and are then accused by the cartel of free-loading, and threatened with dire consequences. With professions of penitence and acts of duplicity, they cry all the way to the bank, and continue as before.

Perhaps a bit unfair as a description of the non-OPEC exporters that pledged cooperation with OPEC from time to time, but not, with the important exception of Mexico and, to a lesser extent Norway, too wide of the mark.

OPEC preoccupation with loss of market share to non-OPEC exporters first surfaces in statements made by Dr Mana Said al Otaiba, UAE Oil Minister, after an OPEC Consultative Meeting in Qatar in March 1982, following sharp price cuts by Britain's British National Oil Corporation (BNOC), Norway, Egypt and the Soviet Union. He qualified the price cuts as "hostile" to OPEC and urged the non-OPEC producers to support OPEC's attempts to maintain the price structure. By March of the following year (1983), OPEC officials were reported contacting non-OPEC producers, notably Norway and Britain, trying to persuade them, without success, to restrain production increases. Indeed, in Britain, an Energy Department spokesman went out of his way to emphasize that there was no question of cutting back on North Sea production, especially since the government had recently assured the companies that there would be no production cuts until at least the end of 1984.[1]

But Mexico, at least, was well-disposed, and adopted a ceiling of 1.5 mbd on its exports for the year 1983. The country's position was confirmed in a joint statement issued on 25 May 1983 by Mexico's energy minister Francisco Labastida and Pemex Director General Mario Ramón Beteta which said, in part:

> Mexico has committed itself to an export ceiling of 1.5 mbd of crude oil during 1983 . . . In spite of its evident need for foreign exchange, and the current excess demand for Mexican crude, we will continue to hold to this export target . . . Mexico is committed to furthering an open dialogue with other oil exporting countries, both members and non-members of OPEC. We have established contacts both at government and corporate levels, ane seek to intensify them.[2]

There were unkind suggestions from some quarters that Mexico could not at this juncture produce enough to export more than its ceiling, and there were indeed, for a while, some limitations on export terminal capacity; but in fact, customers were turned away and the limitation was real, if small.

Later it was a different story. In 1987, Mexico adopted a ceiling of 1.35 mbd on crude exports, starting in the third quarter, and stuck to this limit during 1988, but there was serious doubt, given Pemex's lack of funds whether it could have exceeded it anyway.

In January 1987, Norway announced that it would place restrictions on production in order to support price and OPEC's efforts. Production became subject to a sort of "floating roof" whereby it was to be limited to 92.5 percent of total deemed producing capacity. The deemed capacity figure was to be established periodically by the Petroleum Directorate on a realistic and, it was claimed, conservative basis. However, obviously, as capacity continued to expand, the production ceiling would also rise.

Initially, the restrictions would take a mere 80 kbd off the market. Thereafter, "only" 85 kbd of each 100 kbd of additional new capacity would be put on the market. It was a Norwegian compromise between the well-established policy of keeping the development (and expansion) of the country's offshore resources progressing at a measured pace, and being seen to be doing something to support the market and back OPEC's own measures. Norway also made it clear that the restrictions could be rescinded on short notice if it transpired that OPEC member countries were themselves not maintaining adequate discipline in observing their own production quotas.

The Norwegian "restrictions" may have initially provided some sort of psychological fillip for OPEC, but as a market-support measure, it was nugatory. Norwegian production increased 17 percent in 1987 over 1986, 13 percent in 1988 and 27 percent in 1989. By 1992, it was more than double its 1987 level. OPEC must have wondered, *With friends like these* . . . Between 1985 and 1995, the increase in Norway's net exports accounted for 40 percent

of the total increase in all non-OPEC net exports. Norway wasn't helping to
solve the problem; Norway *was* the problem.

OPEC's ongoing concern about the rising level of non-OPEC exports
was given official expression in the opening speech of the OPEC President,
Libya's Oil Minister, Kamel Hassan Maghur, to the July 1984 Conference:

> It has all along been OPEC's policy to create a conducive atmosphere
> for co-operation and dialogue with the non-OPEC producers, who
> must seriously consider the long-term advantages of co-operation
> with OPEC, because without such co-operation the market cannot
> hold.

For the next ten years, there were statements at practically every OPEC
conference urging the non-OPEC exporters to cooperate with OPEC (i.e., to
restrain production) in order to support prices: "It is very much in the interest
of the non-OPEC producers to join with us." (Seventy-second Conference,
December 1984); "OPEC and non-OPEC producers should make every
possible effort to avoid a price war detrimental to all . . . OPEC would not be
able to avoid such a situation if non-OPEC producers do not recognize the
harmful effects of a chaotic market and do not act responsibly." (Statement
of the OPEC President, February 1986);   "Some non-OPEC countries,
including some of those which had publicly supported OPEC's stand, in fact
increased production . . . They should also appreciate that OPEC cannot
continue to bear the heavy burden of price stability alone." (OPEC President's
address to the Eighty-first Conference, June 1987);   "I am referring to our
repeated calls to non-OPEC producers to assist us in establishing a framework
for durable stability in the international oil industry—exhortations which have
brought only a limited response and, in totality, an inadequate one." (OPEC
president's address to the Eighty-fourth Conference, November 1988). And
so on.

There were numerous contacts and meetings between OPEC and non-
OPEC officials, non-OPEC countries including Angola, Brunei, China,
Colombia, Egypt, Malaysia, Mexico, Norway, Oman, the Soviet Union and
even the states of Alaska and Texas, and the province of Alberta. The regulars
started calling themselves the Independent Petroleum Exporting Countries
(IPEC), though they never acquired a formal structure. Some of them
attended OPEC conferences as observers from time to time.

OPEC slogged on for several years. Among the middle-rank non-OPEC
players (after Mexico and Norway) , Oman—largely through its membership
in the Gulf Cooperation Council (GCC)—was the only country willing to take
up the cudgels and have a go. In January 1994, it announced that it would cut
its own production during the first quarter by 5 percent (but production for
the year would be up 4.4 percent over 1993—an increase quite in line with the
previous trend). Oman had already undertaken to try coordinating production

cuts among other non-OPEC producers, and at the GCC meeting in December 1993, received support from a now skeptical Saudi Arabia and Kuwait for its continued efforts. But the support was at this point a political cynicism: Saudi Arabia, fed up with OPEC and non-OPEC production increases in violation of previous pledges, had not wanted to discuss oil market stabilization matters at all at the GCC meeting, but when persuaded to do so, made future OPEC cuts conditional on matching cuts by non-OPEC producers. The GCC communiqué (22 December 1993) read, in part, as follows:

> The [GCC] Supreme Council affirmed the need to work for the stability of the oil market, and to this end the GCC countries are ready to participate in reducing present production levels if all producing countries, both within and outside OPEC, agree upon and commit themselves to a comprehensive plan to cut production in a balanced fashion.[3]

That is, when pigs fly.

Nevertheless, Omani Oil Minister Said al-Shanfari duly made the rounds of non-OPEC exporting countries, and reported back. Britain, Norway and Mexico pointblank refused; the Russians said they would maintain their exports at their then current level; and others made polite noises but no commitment.

As far as this kind of coordinated attempt to round up non-OPEC support, it was pretty much the end of the line. There was some residual grumbling (articles in the OPEC Bulletin, asides in OPEC ministers' speeches, etc.), but the grand design was dead. It had become obvious that the only non-OPEC players worth talking to about "market-stabilization" were Mexico, Norway and Russia.

The rapid growth of the second-rank non-OPEC exporters (Angola, Colombia, Egypt, Malaysia, and Oman) was alarming: even when the increases in their production were relatively small, they tended to chew up a disproportionately large part of the total increase in world demand. But it should nevertheless have been clear that the whole exercise was a ludicrous waste of time. None of these countries ever had the slightest intention of cutting production one jot: they were all busy signing new exploration and production agreements in the hope of expanding production; areas recently granted for exploration were being drilled up and developed—there was no way the companies could be told not to produce what they had found. Moreover, in absolute terms, they were all small net exporters, mostly well under 500 kbd. In aggregate, even by 1991, these five countries, plus Brunei (which, though a mature and possibly declining province, was in on the earlier talks), had net exports of only 1.8 mbd. Even if they could all have been persuaded to reduce production by as much as 10 percent, the result—180 kbd—was well within the range that several OPEC member countries could, individually, cheat by on their quotas (and more than one did).

The sorry chapter came to a close; later, in the late 1990s, Mexico and Norway would play an important role in helping OPEC push prices back up after the collapse on 1998-99.

The Development of Non-OPEC Supplies: The North Sea and Alaska

Two areas, the North Sea and Alaska, merit special comment because they illustrate how oddly fortuitous it was that major, but high-cost, reserves should have been discovered before OPEC appeared to be a threat to the economies and national security of industrialized countries. The outlook for price was dismal in the late 1960s, so there was no sense of urgency in the search for oil in these areas. Indeed some of the companies involved were close to abandoning it when the lightning struck. OPEC's actions shortly thereafter did not ignite the fire of non-OPEC supplies, but they did fan them into a blaze.

The North Sea

Well before the first, relatively small price increases of 1970 and 1971, a substantial number of companies, usually operating in risk-spreading consortia, were actively exploring in the extremely tough (expensive) environments of Alaska's North Slope, the northern sector of the UK North Sea, and the Norwegian offshore. Extensive gas discoveries in the relatively benign southern parts of the North Sea had sparked hopes that similar or larger deposits would be found to the north. Few people expected significant oil (rather than gas) discoveries; indeed, one well-known, highly reputable (and presumably thirsty) geologist was reported to have promised to drink any oil discovered under its waters.

However, the northern areas in the UK and Norway did attract considerable interest, and the first rounds of leasing were awarded in 1964 and 1965. First results in both areas were, typically enough, disappointing. Finally, on Christmas Eve of 1969, a group headed by Phillips, the operator, with participation by Petrofina, Petronord and Agip) struck oil in the Norwegian sector. The weather was terrible, and proper testing was not possible; so the discovery was not confirmed until June 1970 with the completion of a second well that flowed at rates of almost 4,000 bd of 35°API low-sulfur oil. It was a major find, soon confirmed with stepout wells, and the field was christened Ekofisk.

It was a very large field with recoverable reserves originally put (conservatively) at over 1 billion barrels by the consulting firm, DeGolyer and MacNaughton, assuming a relatively low recovery rate of 25 percent of oil in place. Production from the field started in June 1971. By the fourth quarter, production was being obtained from three wells.

The UK sector's turn came soon after Ekofisk. While the first shows of oil in the northern North Sea had been made by Amoco in May 1969, they deemed uncommercial. The first big UK discovery came when BP, which had been lukewarm (before Ekofisk) about prospects for the northern sector and had not thought that even a medium-sized field would be economic at prices prevailing in the late 1960s, drilled the exploratory well that found the Forties field, in November 1970. The following year, in July 1971, Shell-Esso brought in the Brent discovery well.

Probably by the end of 1970, a year in which crude prices started to strengthen, but certainly by the end of 1971, when the Tehran Agreement was signed, providing for a scheduled increase in prices, companies had lost most of their reservations over price. The outlook was now bullish, and the gold rush was on.

It was the first of the coincidences—the price increases came at exactly the right time though there was nothing inevitable or even expected about them. To the extent that they reflected, in 1970, a certain tightness in the market, the circumstances were temporary; there were also temporary shortages caused by purely political circumstances in the Middle East. The price increases of 1970 were followed by more political pressure which resulted in the Tehran and Tripoli agreements of 1971 and 1972. But there was certainly no question of "shortages" developing, or any tightness in supply which would in the normal course of events have sparked price increases.

Nothing, of course, could have less resembled the gold rushes of California and the Yukon of the previous century when hordes of penniless fortune-seekers, armed only with pick, shovel and sifting pans, descended on the prospective areas. Here, billions of dollars were being bet by the world's leading oil companies, and it soon showed up in the figures. The number of exploratory wells drilled in the Norwegian and UK (north) sectors of the North Sea rose rapidly, from 16 and 15 in 1967 and 1968, respectively, to 42 in 1972 (plus several field extension wells). By this time, the constraint on the drilling of wells was more the availability of drilling platforms and other physical constraints than anything else. Field after new field was discovered and within a few years, production began to take off. The first big year was 1976, when production from Britain and Norway reached a combined total of over 500 kbd. It was just the beginning: by 1980, production from the two countries was up to 2.2 mbd, and 3.5 mbd by 1985, the year that OPEC prices started their tailspin into collapse.

Once the first discoveries of oil (notably Ekofisk) in the North Sea had been made, without the benefit of much strengthening in price, there is little doubt that other discoveries would follow in due time. The Tehran-Tripoli agreements providing for successive price increases, and, even more, the much greater price increases imposed by OPEC at the end of 1973, ensured development at breakneck speed. Even so, the "breakneck" speed was still six to seven years from the first discoveries in 1969 to the materialization of a goodly flow of oil in 1976.

Alaska

Almost two years before the discovery of the Ekofisk field at the end of 1969, another momentous discovery had been made. A partnership of Atlantic Richfield and Humble Oil (an Exxon subsidiary) completed the 1-Prudhoe Bay discovery well in February 1968, to be followed in short order by the 1-Sag River confirmation well. But it was BP that had led the way. Attracted by the enormous structures in the area, the company had taken acreage at a time when most attention in Alaska was focused on the Cook Inlet area in the south, and had drilled a number of unsuccessful wells. When the Prudhoe Bay area came up for leasing, it lost out in the bidding for the "high" of the structure (the area where oil was most likely to be found) to Exxon/Arco, but it got much of the adjacent acreage—and, in the event, about half of the reserves discovered.

The North Slope had long been known to have particularly attractive geological structures. Situated north of the 70th parallel on the north coast of Alaska, this was probably the most costly area in the world to carry out exploration and the development of any fields that might be found. It would surely not have been deemed economic if the price of oil in the United States had not been propped up by domestic production restrictions and import controls. Domestic crude prices in Texas at the time were well over $3 per barrel, approximately three times as high as export prices in the Persian Gulf. Moreover, the Prudhoe Bay discovery was extremely large. DeGolyer and MacNaughton said in late 1968 that it might have recoverable reserves of 5 to 10 billion barrels, making it one of the world's largest fields.

Exxon/Arco immediately planned a pipeline from Prudhoe Bay to Valdez on the southern coast of Alaska, "to start North Slope crude oil on its way to markets by 1972."[4] In September 1969, a lease auction of 179 tracts brought in bids of almost $1 billion in aggregate from scores of companies.

Nearly all of them were destined for disappointment, and the proposed pipeline from Prudhoe Bay (the Trans-Alaska Pipeline System, owned by the group of producers with interests in the North Slope, including BP) ran into regulatory problems, so that it was not until the Spring of 1974 that the shipment of materials could start, following the passage of legislation in November 1973. Actual construction of the line started in early 1975 and the line was completed in mid-1977. Alaska's effect on OPEC power was therefore not felt until nine years after the Prudhoe Bay discovery, and it was felt not directly in export markets, but indirectly by reducing US import requirements that were incrementally supplied by OPEC.

Policy Issues: the United Kingdom and Norway

Countries wishing to explore for and, if the exploration is successful, develop their oil resources are always faced with a number of policy choices in different areas. The main ones concern (a) leasing/concessions; (b) taxation; (c) control (depletion and participation); and (d) other matters such as labor, safety, environment, supply industries and infrastructure.

These policy issues acquired greater importance, and became more political, after the OPEC prices increases for the simple reason that so much more was at stake: the economic rents had become a glittering prize that (everyone agreed) rightfully belonged to the country that owned the resources. Private companies, especially foreign ones, should not be allowed to walk away with any of it.

Leasing/Concession Policy

The main question for countries with oil resources is usually whether leases should be granted by auction to the highest qualified bidder, or whether they should be granted on a discretionary basis.

The auction system has two considerable advantages. First, it tends to capture much of the economic rent (or so most economists believe): general conditions are drawn up that apply to all blocks to be leased and these are then awarded to the highest bidder. Second, it is simple to administer: there is only one criterion for the award, and it is unambiguous—the money bid.

On the other hand, a discretionary system permits the government to favor its own nationals, establish criteria for awards that are not strictly financial (such as work programs proposed) and, if necessary, make plain to companies already operating under prior leases in the country that a certain pliability in negotiations on unrelated issues might be appreciated. Indeed, in Britain, Amoco was excluded from the fifth licensing round in 1976 because it refused to enter into voluntary participation agreements on its existing leases, allowing the newly created British National Oil Corporation (BNOC) to acquire a share of them.

Among major industrialized countries, the United States (where state or federal lands are concerned) has traditionally chosen an auction system. This is not surprising. In the United States, the domestic oil industry is huge, and there is absolutely no danger that, under the auction system, foreign companies would get a politically unacceptable preponderance of the acreage under license. In Britain and Norway, no such guarantee exists. The auction system will not ensure that a diversity of companies—big, medium and small— will emerge, and that everything will not end up in the hands of a few of the giants. For this reason, a discretionary system has been favored in most of the industrialized countries, most significantly in Britain and Norway, though Britain did experimentally try (in 1971) an auction for 15 of the 436 blocks up for licensing in the fourth round.

In Norway especially, the discretionary licensing system was adopted with the primary objective of retaining a wide measure of control over the industry. From the beginning, there was considerable concern about the government's participation in the industry, and a state oil company, Statoil was established in 1972 as a vehicle for it, but the discretionary licensing policy was also used to reserve an important place in the industry for the private, or partly private, sector Norwegian companies, notably Norsk Hydro and Saga Petroleum. In the third round (1974), a 50 percent interest in all licenses was reserved for Statoil, which had an option of increasing this to 75 percent in the event of a commercial discovery. All subsequent licensing rounds made provision for Statoil participation, and some awards of important blocks were made to a consortium of exclusively Norwegian companies.

Taxation

With the new pricing levels, there were huge rents to be captured, that is, margins between the sales price and the "full-cycle" cost of the oil, including an attractive margin of profit for the companies. What system of taxation would do this best? Certainly, the traditional system of royalties plus income tax was not up to it. If prices had been stable, a system of auctioning licenses might have done the job well enough, but couldn't work when prices kept on rising beyond any expectation.

In the United States, the solution adopted was to impose a mixture of price controls and a windfall profits tax on producers. Other countries, notably Britain, chopped and changed as they grappled with the problem of reconciling the twin objectives of encouraging vigorous exploration and development on the one hand and appropriating all of the economic rent on the other, and the overall tax structures that resulted were unnecessarily complex.

The tax structure in Britain for the oil industry was originally the classic one: royalty plus income tax (i.e., a percentage of gross revenue plus a percentage of net profits). Before production from the North Sea had even begun, it was clear from the rising international prices following the Tehran-Tripoli agreements and the OPEC 1973 increases that this structure would be insufficient. However, instead of imposing a windfall tax of so-many cents per barrel on oil priced above a given level, the government opted in 1975 for a Petroleum Revenue Tax (PRT) assessed on each individual field's profits (and therefore "ring-fenced"), with complex rules to define field profits, different from rules applicable to the definition of corporate profits.

Production began in earnest in 1976. In 1978, crude prices began to rise sharply again as a result of Iran's revolution and the partial shutdown of its industry. In 1981, a Supplementary Petroleum Duty was introduced to increase taxes and accelerate their payment. It was short-lived and was replaced at the end of 1982 by the Advance Petroleum Revenue Tax, similar to the SPD but subject to a couple of important differences. The PRT was the cornerstone of the fiscal system applicable to oil production, and reached levels of 75 percent.

In Norway, the tax structure, as it evolved, was composed of a royalty payable in cash or kind, a "special tax" based on gross income from production from the Continental Shelf, a corporation tax on a company's overall profits, and a capital tax on the net book value of capital equipment The system, with its strong element of taxation of gross income, tended to penalize the smaller higher-cost fields, and subsequent revisions were made to correct this. However, one of the most important features of the Norwegian tax system was the adoption of a "norm" price to determine gross income for the purpose of the special tax and the corporation tax, rather than using the actual sales price, as in Britain. The "norm" price, set quarterly by the government, was its assessment of the value of the oil in a free market—in other words, the price that a company could have obtained for its crude in an arm's-length transaction.

Control

One of the thorniest problems confronting governments dealing with oil companies engaged in exploration and production has been the question of control. The interests of any commercial entity do not necessarily coincide with the government's interest, but control has always appeared to be an especially sensitive matter in the international oil industry because of the industry's domination by a small number of large multi-national companies and their high degree of vertical integration. The multi-national makes decisions based on its overall worldwide interests, and these are imposed on its various subsidiaries operating in different countries. This lays them open to *prima facie* suspicion. Any oil produced is then kept largely within its vertically integrated circuit, a matter that may not work well for the host country, and this is a second ground for suspicion. But, importantly, there is always a strong feeling on the part of governments new to the game that they are at a disadvantage in their dealings with the companies because of a lack of inside knowledge, and that they must therefore acquire some direct experience of the industry. The argument has been used time and time again to justify the establishment of national oil companies, which are then given participation rights in new licenses and concessions.

— *Depletion Policy.* Apart from the United States, it is unusual for a non-OPEC country to restrain production or slow down development. But in Norway especially, and to a much lesser extent, Britain, the question of calibrating development and controlling (i.e., restricting) production was important. Conscious decisions were taken in both countries to license acreage gradually, in order to phase in exploration and development over an extended period of time. But depletion was a relatively minor consideration at this stage. A program of phased licensing had other obvious and more immediate advantages: not flooding the market for acreage all at one time, and providing a longer life-expectancy for the support industries that would be built up around successful producing operations. These two reasons loomed larger in the minds of policy-makers than the question of depletion.

Depletion policy in the sense of restricting production from existing, developed fields in order to prolong their life has in fact never been a serious issue, for a simple reason: it would be absurd and counterproductive for future leasing, not to say politically irresponsible, to lease acreage, encourage investment in development, and then prevent the investor from reaping his proper reward.

In Britain, it is true, there was much discussion of the issue, engendered in part by the 1973 energy crisis, which rapidly became in the popular perception a resource-crisis rather than a purely political one that happened to affect the price and supply of oil; and in part by the then current fears about the long-term availability of resources generally, inspired by (among other things) MIT's report on The Limits to Growth (1971), prepared for the Club of Rome. The Club of Rome was an informal international group of eminent persons with a strong scientific and research orientation that had undertaken a Project on the Predicament of Mankind to examine major problems confronting the world over the long term. The MIT report was given much publicity and left the widespread impression that, as far as non-renewable resources (including, of course, petroleum) were concerned, the world was fast running out of everything.

The British government accordingly took powers, notably in the 1975 Petroleum and Submarine Pipelines Act and the 1976 Energy Act, to exercise depletion controls by imposing limits on production rates or, more suitably, by imposing extensive delays on the development of new fields. It was all deadly serious at the time, but in retrospect appears to be slightly farcical, and the 1975 act was preceded by assurances (non-binding, of course), embodied in the Energy secretary's guidelines (the so-called Varley Guidelines laid out in December 1974) that the government would not impose production cuts within a given time-frame. These assurances, given by a Labour government, were renewed by Energy Secretary Nigel Lawson in 1982, in a Conservative government. The government retained its powers, of course, "just in case".

– *Participation.* Broadly speaking, "participation" outside OPEC and the Middle East meant the acquisition by the government, on favorable terms, of an equity interest in existing concessions/licenses, or the reservation to it of such an interest in new ones. This interest was usually vested in a national oil company owned 100 percent by the state. The arguments usually advanced in support of participation were, first, that it would increase government control over a vital industry; second, that it would enhance national security; third, that it would improve the financial return to the state of a national resource; and, fourth, that it would enable the government, through its national oil company, to gain direct experience in the industry, thus providing a better basis for government decisions.

There were only four developed countries that were important producers in the 1970s: the United States, Canada, Britain and Norway. In the United States, the participation issue was never seriously raised; in Canada, the government created a wholly owned state oil company, Petro-Canada, but it did not go the participation route, operating instead through commercial acquisitions, like any other oil company, though government-financed. Its principal raison d'être was to put in the hands of a truly Canadian company some part of the nation's oil and gas resources, given that all the other important oil companies operating in Canada were wholly or majority-owned by US companies.

The Norwegian government set up a wholly owned state oil company, Den Norske Stats Oljeselskap AS (Statoil), in 1972 to acquire and hold participation rights and direct licenses in the industry. Neither "control" nor national security nor financial advantage were at stake. The Norwegians simply did not want to become the Abu Dhabi of the north (though at one point during tough negotiations, some oilman called them "blue-eyed Arabs"). Norway had a small but highly educated population, and as a matter of national pride rather than economics, it was not about to stand aside and let what was clearly to become its major industry be run entirely by foreign oil companies. Besides, there was no doubt some merit to the argument that it would be better to have state oil policy executed by a willing servant rather than a reluctant foreigner (though the premise of "willing servant" was not universally accepted as a description of national oil companies' managements). In any event, Statoil became a partner with the foreign oil companies and then an important operator and producer in its own right, and a large seller of crude oil on the international market.

When a Labour government under Harold Wilson came in shortly after the 1973 crisis, North Sea development was well under way (the first big oil field, Forties, was discovered in 1970) and the Labour program called for the establishment of a national oil company and 51 percent participation in North Sea ventures. Once in power, Labour set up the British National Oil Corporation (BNOC) and went ahead with plans for participation. BNOC took over the relatively small equity holdings of the state-owned Gas Council and the National Coal Board, acquired in the first rounds of licensing, but 51 percent participation proved totally unacceptable to the existing companies in the North Sea, and the government settled for a purchase and sell-back arrangement (but no equity holding) at market prices and access to all the operating data and information it required. BNOC went on to acquire considerable equity interests in several fields as a result of the provisions for equity participation stipulated in the fifth and sixth rounds of licensing, and was also granted several blocks directly, in 1978, outside the regular rounds.

The Labour government policy on participation was not simply inspired by Conservative Prime Minister Edward Heath's unfortunate experience with BP (he had been unable to persuade BP to allocate Britain a greater share of oil during the 1973 "crisis", at the expense of BP's foreign markets), but more generally on a desire for control over a major industry, reflecting its ideological background. The concept of control encompassed the protection of national security and entailed the acquisition of detailed information on companies' operations. In fact, however, participation could alter nothing with respect to the disposition of foreign oil owned by UK-based companies, and it was on the other hand quite unnecessary for control over oil and gas from the Continental Shelf: the government had all the powers it needed to protect those national interests that fell outside the purview of the companies, mainly of a national security nature. In the event, BNOC contributed nothing to the enhancement of national security or any necessary state control.

Instead, it made its mark as a large trading organization in the emerging open market that was fast replacing the closed, vertically integrated structures of the major oil companies that had until then dominated world oil. It became an important player in the international market and its term prices were closely watched by OPEC. There was a complex and at times disruptive interplay between them and, in particular, Nigerian prices. But BNOC's role as trader and seller was not of ideological significance to either of the major political parties in the country, and when a Conservative government returned to power in 1979, its days were numbered. In 1982, BNOC's exploration and production assets and operations were transferred to a new company, Britoil, whose shares were then sold off in stages. BNOC was left with only its trading arm, and it was finally closed down altogether in 1985 after incurring trading losses in the previous years. It had all been pretty much of a pointless exercise.

Chapter 14
OPEC AT BAY

Real energy costs are likely to rise throughout the period [1980 to 2000] as a result of a limited supply of conventional oil and the high cost of most alternate energy sources.
– Exxon Corporation, *World Energy Outlook,* December 1980, referring to supply.

Where have all the barrels gone?
– OPEC Spokesman in 1981, referring to demand.

Between a Rock and a Hard Place

By 1981, OPEC was trapped: non-OPEC sources of oil and new supplies of other energy, especially nuclear and coal, were coming in fast; at the same time, conservation measures and economic recession were reducing world demand for energy. Practically the whole of the increase in competing oil and energy supplies, as well as the reduction in overall demand, was coming out of OPEC's hide. OPEC was caught in a squeeze and the pressure on it was to prove unbearable. But the organization's members were slow to see the extent of the danger and at first the market downturn was viewed as a temporary phenomenon not requiring a long-term response. True, the Long-Term Strategy Committee was revived, held some inconclusive meetings, but came to nothing because it did not address the problems at hand.

The collapse of the market and the reluctant acceptance of the need to take some collective action restricting supply was considerably delayed by the reductions in production that were forced on Iraq and Iran by the appalling war that Iraq had so rashly started in September 1980. Iraq's production dropped from an average of 3.5 mbd during the year 1979 to 0.9 mbd in 1981; Iran's production dropped from 3.2 mbd in 1979 to 1.3 mbd in 1981. Between the two countries, the decrease totaled 4.5 mbd. Without it, price would undoubtedly have collapsed in 1981.

The market backlash, described in Chapter 12, began in the 1970s, but its full force was not felt until the early 1980s. The years 1981 and 1982 in particular were a catalog of price and demand disasters for OPEC. Refinery closures and partial closures came thick and fast: in October 1981, Shell announced that it would reduce the capacity of its giant Pernis refinery in the Netherlands, and that it would close its Ingolstadt plant in Germany. In November, BP announced a reduction in the capacity of its Rotterdam refinery and Exxon announced the closure of its Cologne refinery. In January 1982, BP said it would close its Dunkirk refinery and Gulf said it would cut its Western European refinery capacity by 43 percent. In May 1982, Texaco announced the closure of its Belgian refinery in Ghent, and Gulf was reported to be selling all of its downstream assets in Western Europe to Kuwait.

The first cracks in the structure of official crude oil prices came in early 1982. In January, Venezuela cut heavy crude prices by $0.58 per barrel and Mexico cut its prices by $2.00. These cuts were followed by reductions in Algeria and Malaysia. By the end of January 1982, oil markets had begun a seemingly inexorable slide under the impact of weak demand and a massive stock drawdown of about 4 mbd. A number of sellers, both OPEC and non-OPEC, were obliged to reduce their official prices sharply. The first major OPEC country to go was war-torn Iran whose customers had deserted it in droves owing to a combination of the political stigma still attached to trade with Iran in the wake of the US Embassy hostage crisis, and the previous ultra-hawkish stance on oil prices adopted by the Iranian authorities. In early 1982, Iran's oil exports had dropped to a mere 500 kbd as against about one mbd in the first quarter of 1981. Such a meager volume was not nearly enough to sustain any kind of reasonable level of economic activity in Iran, let alone to finance the conduct of the continuing war with neighboring Iraq. In a desperate and, in the short term, fruitless bid to rebuild its oil sales, Iran resorted to three separate cuts in its official prices, totaling $4 per barrel in the space of a few weeks in February 1982. The non-OPEC exporters were not far behind. Under heavy pressure from its customers, Britain's BNOC chopped $1.50 off its contract prices in February 1982 and a further $4.00 in March, thereby bringing the price of Forties crude down from $36.50 to $31.00/B. Mexico too announced fresh cuts of up to $2.50 in March. By the end of March 1982, the spot price for Arabian Light crude had fallen to $28/B., compared with its official price of $34.

The competitive process was warming up, and the heat now switched to the African exporters, with the focus on Nigeria. In early March 1982, buyers of Nigerian crude, both equity holders and third parties, warned that a huge fall in liftings would be inevitable unless Nigeria matched the price cuts in the North Sea. By mid-March Nigeria was on the brink of agreeing to a reduction of $5.00/B. in its official prices, from $36.50 to $31.50/B.

Cartelized at Last

It was time for OPEC to do something different. Crucial consultations took place in early March 1982 in Qatar among the oil ministers of the Arab members of OPEC. Yamani reiterated his government's commitment to the $34 marker price and let it be known that Saudi Arabia would support an OPEC-wide stabilization scheme based on temporary production controls provided that the OPEC members manifested the proper spirit of discipline. As an earnest of their good intentions, the Saudis promptly announced a cutback in their production of one mbd, to get back to their production ceiling of 7.5 mbd for the month of March.

At the Conference in Vienna that followed hard on the heels of the Qatar meeting, an agreement of sorts was finally reached. A total allowable or ceiling for OPEC production was set at 17.5 mbd and quotas assigned to member countries. With the byzantine logic of the sometimes paranoid Saudi mind, Saudi Arabia declined to participate formally in the plan that it had so assiduously promoted, on the grounds that production levels were a matter of sovereign prerogative. Yamani did, however, make it clear that Saudi Arabia would cooperate fully with the scheme, and after the end of the Conference, announced a further reduction in the country's output ceiling to 7 mbd for the month of April 1982. It should be added that Saudi Arabia was one of the few OPEC member countries, if not the only one, to fulfill its obligations, however couched, under the production program adopted.

The market strengthened for a short while after the announcement of the OPEC agreement, largely because of the Saudi pledges. But the new cartel's first attempt to operate jointly-agreed production restrictions and quotas got off to a bad start and soon fell apart in total disarray. The agreement suffered from certain fatal defects.

In the first place, it was relatively easy to allocate and implement the required quota ceilings in the crisis atmosphere that prevailed in March 1982. The 17.5 mbd ceiling was in fact somewhat above the level of actual production at the time, and in the case of several key countries that had lost substantial export volumes as a result of the market crisis (Nigeria, Iran, Libya and Algeria) the quotas allocated were in excess of current output. Only in the cases of Saudi Arabia, the UAE, Venezuela and Indonesia did the OPEC plan entail cutbacks in actual export volumes. But the quota plan did not include any agreed procedure for revising the quotas once the market improved, and so the seeds of future discord were to a large extent inherent in the plan itself.

Secondly, by no means all OPEC member countries were truly committed to the program. Iran, in fact, never formally agreed to abide by the 1.2 mbd quota allocated to it (although this was glossed over at the time) and Iranian officials were soon making no secret of the country's determination to pursue an export target of at least 2.5 mbd with or without OPEC's leave. Nor did Iran make any attempt to raise its selling prices in the light of OPEC's renewed determination to defend the $34 marker price, and these therefore remained $4 below the official OPEC level.

The general inclination in OPEC circles at the time was to tolerate Iran's maverick behavior: in effect a recognition of Iran's special circumstances in fighting a desperate war in which OPEC solidarity had to take a poor second place to the struggle for survival. It was hoped that the overall operation of the program would be sufficiently rigorous to neutralize the effects of Iranian non-compliance.

However, although the program could probably have tolerated such an individual stance if it had been confined to Iran alone, it could not withstand the pressure of fresh infractions when other producers, such as Libya, began to follow Iran's example of seeking volume increases through price discounting of one kind or another.

The first test of OPEC's program came in Nigeria, where many customers walked away when the government confirmed the new official price at $35.50/B. rather than the $31.50/B. that the companies had been led to expect. Nigerian production plummeted to 600 kbd at the end of March 1982 (as against 1.4 mbd prior to the OPEC Conference). Saudi Arabia and Kuwait threatened sanctions against the companies that had refused to buy, and talked of putting together a financial package to help Nigeria weather the difficulties. In the event, however, there was no need for confrontation, as demand for lighter crudes strengthened, and Nigerian production gradually picked up again.

All went more or less well for two months, and OPEC production was actually below the ceiling. Then, in June 1982, things started to fall apart: OPEC production took a substantial leap upwards, with some key producers, notably Iran, Libya and Venezuela, pushing volumes far above quota by substantial discounting of their official prices. The Gulf Arab producers, meanwhile, were losing markets by sticking to their official prices, so that, once again, a *de facto* two-tier price system developed: buyers took all the discounted crude they could get, from whatever source, and only turned to sources of crude at official prices for the balance of their requirements.

When OPEC met again, in July 1982, the production program had degenerated into farce. To add insult to injury, Iran and Libya now demanded much higher formal quotas than their previous allocation, with the increases to come out of the Saudi share! Saudi Arabia demanded a doubling of the light crude-marker differential to a more realistic $3.00/B. No agreement was possible, and the program collapsed, everyone going his own way. OPEC's first attempt at a working cartel based on agreed supply restrictions never got off the ground. It lasted barely two months, and even that achievement was due almost entirely to external circumstances rather than internal discipline. By the end of 1982, Iran, Libya and Venezuela were producing, in aggregate, more than twice their second-quarter quotas, an excess of 3.6 mbd, and selling at sharp discounts under their official prices. Some of the discounts were simply outright price reductions; others were thinly disguised, such as extended credit terms, processing deals yielding netbacks on crude lower than official prices, barter deals based on artificially high prices for the goods received in exchange for oil, package deals of crude, at the official price, and underpriced refined products (for which there were no official prices), freight absorption by the seller on c.i.f. sales, and, finally, favorable tax treatment of companies still holding equity interests in some countries.

No one was deceived. Buyers were only too keen to show Saudi Arabia and other countries still clinging to official prices, how much better were the deals they could get elsewhere. Something had to give, and Saudi Arabia determined to bring prices down to more realistic levels. It took some time to muster a minimum of political support, achieved mainly within the Gulf Cooperation Council (GCC), though with the momentary support of Nigeria and Indonesia. These two very soon abandoned the pro-reduction group which, thus weakened, could not find the willpower to go it alone. In the event, they didn't have to: in February 1983, the state-owned British National Oil Corporation dropped its price for North Sea oil by $3.00/B., down to $30.50/B. The move was immediately countered by Nigeria with a sharper drop of $5.50/B., down to $30.00/B., giving Nigerian crude a competitive edge over the North Sea.

The London Agreement, March 1983

The bleak market prospects following the North Sea and Nigerian price reductions brought home to even the most hawkish of the OPEC member countries the seriousness of the threat now facing them. The necessity of a substantial price cut was finally accepted by all as inevitable, as was the need for a production program to defend the new price. These elements were eventually put into place in an agreement reached in London on 14 March after three weeks of grueling consultations and negotiations between the OPEC oil ministers in Riyadh, London and Paris.

The key pricing and production provisions of the agreement were: (a) to reduce the official price of the marker crude, Arabian Light of 34 °API, by $5.00/B., to $29.00/B., and (b) to set an overall production ceiling of 17.5 mbd for OPEC for the rest of the year. Saudi Arabia, however, was not assigned a specific quota, it being understood that it would act as "swing producer", supplying the balancing volumes to meet market requirements within the overall ceiling.

"Market requirements" for OPEC crude were in fact running well below 17.5 mbd, and Saudi Arabia's production was under 4 mbd, though an improving position was expected during the rest of the year. However, it was felt at the time that much depended on the behavior of other, non-OPEC producers, especially Mexico, Britain and the Soviet Union. Mexico agreed to hold its exports down to 1.5 mbd; the Soviets declined to do anything, and the British, typically, sat on the fence waiting to see.

It was a seriously flawed agreement. The provisions concerning differentials remained unrealistic, making an important exception (for Nigeria). Other conditions weakened it further. Nevertheless, it survived and

functioned more or less well for more than two years, until mid-1985, largely
as a result of Saudi Arabia's willingness to act as swing supplier, absorbing a
greatly disproportionate share of OPEC's lost volume.

The London Agreement Crashes

But in the end, a still weakening market and OPEC indiscipline brought the
London Agreement down.

First, total demand for OPEC crude oil shrank, as non-OPEC supplies
expanded, especially from the North Sea. OPEC production averaged 18.5
mbd in 1982, but was down to 15 mbd by March 1983, when the London
agreement was signed. It recovered somewhat during the rest of the year and
during the year 1984, but then reached a low point, slightly below 14 mbd in
June of 1985. By then Saudi Arabia's production was down to 2.2 mbd and
its exports were getting close to zero. The situation had become untenable.

Second, it proved impossible to operate a realistic system of price
differentials. The value of crude oils relative to each other depends largely on
their product yields, lighter crudes yielding more of the higher value gasolines
and distillates than heavier ones. But the prices of the various refined
products vary over time, depending on seasonal and other factors, so crude
price differentials that may be realistic in one situation rapidly go askew in
another. OPEC could not possibly keep up with the shifting market, and even
if it could, frequent renegotiation of the differentials would have been
politically impossible. Compromises were therefore made that had nothing
to do with the market but were politically inspired. In particular, the North
Sea was a critically important competitive factor for Nigeria, and Nigeria had
a great deal of trouble trying to balance its obligations towards OPEC (on
differentials) with its market need to maintain parity with the very similar
North Sea crudes, that, like Nigerian, were light, low in sulfur and close to the
markets. An exception to OPEC rules for differentials had to be made for
Nigeria.

Third, cheating was endemic, with member countries exceeding quota
through a variety of different devices, of which unrealistically-set differentials
was only one. Others included straight discounts off official prices, barter
deals, freight absorption by the seller, and extended credit terms.

Nevertheless, through a series of meetings during which OPEC twisted
and turned, the London Agreement survived the rest of 1983, the seasonally
low demand of the second quarter of 1984 and into the fourth quarter of the
year when it might have been reasonably hoped that demand would pick up
substantially. Indeed, when OPEC ministers ended their July 1984
Conference in Vienna, they were confidently expecting to meet again in
October for the purpose of distributing additional quota, over and above the
17.5 mbd OPEC output ceiling, in view of the projected increase in demand
for OPEC crude oil to something like 19 mbd in the fourth quarter.

No such luck. In October 1984, everything went wrong at once for OPEC. Britain pushed 250 kbd more North Sea crude onto the markets than the previous month, mostly onto the highly visible and volatile spot market. Nigeria produced almost 300 kbd more in October and Norway chipped in with an additional 30 kbd. This was all short-haul or medium-haul crude that impacted quickly on the markets. At the same time, demand in the main industrial markets scarcely rose at all in October. Inevitably, spot prices weakened and Norway felt compelled to bring down its contract prices closer to spot levels. It had already done some price-cutting, through covert price discounts in August and September 1984 and gotten away with them undetected. It tried again in its contract prices for October and November. But you can't fool all of the people all of the time, the discounts were leaked to the press and the fat was in the fire.

Within a few days, without even gaining full knowledge of the Norwegian price situation, Britain's BNOC responded with an official price cut of $1.35/B., while Nigeria, true to its policy of hair-trigger reaction to North Sea price developments, leap-frogged with a $2.00/B. reduction on its light crudes. Market perceptions were now of plentiful supplies of short-haul crude with no need to step up long-haul crude liftings in preparation for peak winter demand.

As if stagnant demand, rising non-OPEC oil production and falling spot prices were not enough, OPEC had been further hit by the unannounced policy changes in Norway and Britain that led to these price reductions.

The situation was characterized by a number of curious features. For one thing, it was Norway that took the lead in cutting prices, rather than simply being content to follow Britain as it had done in the past. For another, there was a distinct change in the attitude of Britain. Since the historic 1983 OPEC price and production agreement, the UK had been adopting an increasingly interventionist line on oil prices, permitting a degree of tacit cooperation and consultation with OPEC on price matters—though not on production volumes—in order to safeguard a key mutual interest in the maintenance of the OPEC structure. In January and July-August 1984 Britain had held back from unilateral action on prices in order to allow OPEC sufficient breathing space for action to steady the market. This time, however, Britain acted without waiting to see what OPEC would do.

OPEC rushed into an emergency session at the end of October 1984 and pulled down its overall production ceiling from 17.5 mbd to 16.0 mbd, effective from 1 November. All might have been well if normally cold winter weather had followed; but it didn't. Unusually mild weather prevailed in Europe, Japan and along the US East Coast. The usual seasonal surge in winter demand failed to materialize and prices remained weak.

In the end, Saudi Arabia, as swing supplier, was driven to the wall. It was perhaps the only country continuing to sell at the full official price, which, by early 1985, had been reduced to $28 for the marker crude, and which was still

$1 to $2/B. above the market prices of other crudes. The prospect of zero exports loomed close, and production had dropped so low that at times not enough associated gas was produced to fuel the power stations. In a land of seemingly infinite oil and gas reserves, frequent brownouts were being experienced! By May-June of 1985, Saudi Arabia's production was only about half the volume required to cover the Kingdom's financial requirements, and the drawdown from financial reserves was running at $1.5 to $2.0 billion each month. This was obviously a severe drain on the country's financial reserves, the liquid portion of which was $70 to $80 billion.

To make matters worse, Iraq was seeking a substantial increase in its quota, of at least 500 kbd when its new pipeline link to Saudi Arabia's Red Sea coast came onstream in the fourth quarter of 1985, and it was simultaneously resisting any reduction in the 300 kbd war-relief crude being delivered to it by Kuwait and Saudi Arabia.

The first concrete sign of Saudi disquiet emerged in late May 1985 when Shaikh Yamani invited all OPEC oil ministers to hold informal consultations in the Saudi summer capital of Taif, high in the mountains above Mecca. Eight turned up, plus non-OPEC Mexico. King Fahd delivered a message to the meeting the gist of which was that every Member Country would be free to "act in a manner that will secure its own interests" if OPEC quotas continued to be violated. A few weeks later, the message was repeated at the full ministerial meetings in Vienna in early July and in Geneva in late July, and Yamani made it clear that Saudi Arabia was no longer prepared to act as swing supplier but would reassert its right to a fixed quota of 4.35 mbd allocated as a result of the November 1984 OPEC decision, under which the OPEC ceiling had been reduced from 17.5 mbd to 16 mbd .

Saudi Arabia quietly started signing a series of netback contracts designed to assure it a minimum volume outlet. These netback contracts provided for the price of crude to be determined *ex post facto* by deducting from the price of the products manufactured from it the cost of marketing, refining and transportation, plus a fixed profit margin. The buyer couldn't lose, and did not need to be concerned about sales: he sold his products at whatever it took. There was further icing on the cake: the contracts did not necessarily specify actual product yields obtained from the crude in question, but ones that were simply set by a process of horse-trading. They were of course more or less realistic, but the refiner did not have to account for what he *actually* got out of the crude, which could in fact be a more profitable slate of products. The deductible cost of refining and freight were similarly negotiable. A refiner's dream come true!

The London Agreement was stone cold dead in the market.

OPEC's first attempts at operating a cartel were based on fixing price and letting volume find its own level. The central cause of failure was the assignment of the key role of swing supplier to a single country, Saudi Arabia, which accepted it in the belief that it would thereby regain, in time, the market losses that it had already sustained. In the event, despite its best and bravest efforts, it was unable to support the role: a combination of growing non-OPEC oil supplies, cheating on quotas by other OPEC member countries, and a stagnant market defeated it. It would never again openly and explicitly agree to act as swing supplier for OPEC.

The Netback Wars: The Saudis Steal a March

Considering the frequent and explicit warnings issued by Saudi Arabia throughout the summer of 1985 to the effect that continued indiscipline among the OPEC countries would eventually oblige Saudi Arabia also to accord itself freedom of action as regards oil pricing and production, no one should really have been surprised at the way things turned out. However, the Saudi warnings were, generally speaking, either disbelieved or ignored.

But the Saudis meant precisely what they said. By August 1985, the Kingdom's production had sunk to around 2.2 mbd, yielding exports of only around 1.4 mbd, and the Saudis evidently felt that they could not afford to wait any longer before taking action to restore their sadly eroded market position. Negotiations were initiated with the four Aramco partners (Exxon, Mobil, Texaco and Chevron) to work out new sales arrangements based on market-related crude prices, netted back f.o.b. from spot product realizations in the major markets.

Agreements covering the supply of around 900 kbd of Saudi crude to the four Aramco majors were concluded in early September 1985, and from then on the Saudis went to work to convert all their export sales of crude oil to netback pricing. By early February 1986, Saudi Arabia had more or less reached its target for the conclusion of sales contracts covering some 3 mbd of netback-priced crude exports.

The Saudis had stolen a march, and, indeed, the success of their strategy depended, as was soon to become evident, on being there first with the most.

Impasse Over Quotas, October 1985

If Saudi Arabia's switch to market-related pricing sounded the death knell of the official OPEC price structure, OPEC's Extraordinary Conference held in Vienna on 3-4 October witnessed the formal collapse of the production regulation program.

The impasse at Vienna was clearly predictable. The Conference had been convened specifically to discuss demands for higher production quotas by Iraq, Ecuador and others, consideration of which had been postponed from the previous conference in Geneva at the end of July. The Iraqi demand constituted a particularly hot issue, on which no agreement could conceivably be reached within the OPEC framework.

In many ways the Iraqis had a good case. They pointed out that Iraq had only accepted the absurdly low quota of 1.2 mbd allocated to it at the London conference in March 1983 because that figure represented the limit of its physical export capacity at the time, which had been severely constrained as a result of war damage and the politically motivated closure by Syria of the Iraqi-Syrian pipeline. Iraq had made it clear, at the time of the March 1983 conference and on subsequent occasions, that its acceptance of a quota of 1.2 mbd was purely temporary and that it fully intended to produce more as and when its physical export capacity increased.

By October 1985, Iraq had indeed expanded its export capacity with the commissioning of a 500 kbd pipeline link to Saudi Arabia's Red Sea terminal at Yanbu, and a further 500 kbd increment was scheduled when the expansion of the Iraqi-Turkish pipeline was completed towards the end of 1986. The Iraqi oil minister, Mr. Qasim Ahmad Taqi, went on record as saying that Iraq considered its fair OPEC quota should be 2.35 mbd, and that his country was planning to produce an average of 2 mbd in 1986, regardless of whether this was endorsed by OPEC. The nature of the Iraqi demand, intractable on the Iraqi side and unassimilable within the OPEC framework, opened a Pandora's box of competing claims among the OPEC members. Iran, Iraq's adversary in the five-year-old Gulf war, riposted that it would produce two extra barrels for every one produced by Iraq. Ecuador, Qatar and Gabon formally requested higher quotas, while others, among them Nigeria and Libya, let it be known that they would want to raise output if others did.

The Vienna meeting broke up in utter disarray, agreeing only to postpone the redistribution of the ceiling production of 16 mbd to a later date. But, for the moment, this had little effect on the world oil market where prices were in the process of strengthening under the impact of low inventories, higher winter demand and a cutback in Soviet supplies. The short-lived bull market peaked at the end of November 1985 when the spot price for Brent reached nearly $30/B. Shortly afterwards things began to fall apart again as the tide of netback crude from the Gulf started to reach the US and European Markets.

OPEC Adopts a Market Share Strategy, December 1985

When the OPEC ministers met again, two months later, in Geneva in early December 1985, it became more than ever apparent (now that Saudi Arabia was insisting on taking its full quota of 4.35 mbd) that attempting to squeeze the OPEC countries back into their previous straightjacket of 16 mbd, let alone the15.5 mbd that might be required for 1986 or the 14.4 mbd for the second quarter of the year, was not in the cards. Non-negotiable demands for additional output by individual member countries had actually inflated OPEC's projected production to something like 17.5 mbd for 1986.

It was the sheer impossibility of solving the quota conundrum that drove the OPEC ministers to conclude that OPEC's share of the market had now been reduced to a point where it was no longer, by any stretch of the imagination, divisible among its members, and that therefore the only way out was to reclaim a portion of the market share appropriated by those non-OPEC exporters who had for so long been maximizing their production at OPEC's expense. Hence the OPEC decision, in the words of the official communiqué of the Geneva Conference, "to secure and defend for OPEC a fair share of the world oil market consistent with the necessary income for member countries' development." This was a momentous decision in that it set the seal on what was effectively a total reversal of OPEC's traditional policy. Defense of a minimum market share would now, for the time being at least, take precedence over price maintenance as the number one objective of the OPEC member countries .

There were now two netback wars going on simultaneously. The first one was the one initiated by Saudi Arabia, directed essentially against the rest of OPEC and designed to regain market share for the country. It was very rapidly successful, and Saudi production had already risen from a low of 2.2 mbd in August 1985 to 4.5 mbd by December. The second was initiated by OPEC as a whole and was directed at clawing market back from non-OPEC producers, especially the North Sea ones. In October, the president of OPEC, Indonesia's Dr. Subroto, had been told by Britain's energy secretary, Peter Walker, that Britain had no intention of imposing production cutbacks on the companies. At the same time, Norway pointedly announced that it was planning a 40 percent increase in production by 1990.

Given the rigors of the impending price war, with Britain and Norway publicly and repeatedly announcing that they had no intention of reducing North Sea production, it was hardly surprising to find that the price hard-liners within OPEC (Algeria, Iran and Libya) later dissociated themselves from the December "fair market share" decision on the grounds that volume gains by the OPEC countries would not be sufficient to compensate for the drop in prices resulting from a price war with the non-OPEC exporters.

In any event, prices crashed very soon after the December 1985 decision. Britain's North Sea Brent crude had emerged as a reference point. At the end of the year 1985, its spot price was almost $27/B. In the second half of January 1986, it took a plunge to $18.50 and by mid-March was down to $13.30, a loss of fifty percent in two-and-a-half months. All other crudes underwent similar drops. The world was stunned. Even the OPEC perpetrators of the action were taken aback; they had not expected the price to drop significantly below $20. Disbelief that such prices could last was followed by general rejoicing on the part of consumers and the gnashing of teeth by producers of energy everywhere, including especially the high-cost areas of the United States

The whole of 1986 was spent in a series of frenetic meetings of OPEC conferences, ministerial consultative meetings and contacts with non-OPEC producing countries. OPEC met in Geneva in March and April, in Taif (Saudi Arabia's summer capital) in May, Brioni (Yugoslavia) in June, Geneva in

August and again in October, Quito in November and Geneva once more in December where, at last, an agreement of sorts was reached.

In Taif in May, a target price of $17 to $19 was set, but no measures adopted to get to it. The Brioni Conference also ended in failure despite a heroic quota allocation exercise by the indefatigable Dr. Subroto, by then Secretary General. The market went into a tailspin, prices dropping below $10/B, with Dubai crude touching $7/B. at one point. And the gloom was further deepened later, in July, when Saudi Arabia finally abandoned its lingering commitment to its former 4.35 mbd "quota" and boosted production to over 5.5 mbd. Evidently, the Saudis had decided to turn the heat up, because it was clearly no use having a target price without production restrictions to support it, and, since Saudi Arabia now rejected the role of swing supplier, there was no use having production restrictions without quotas. Moreover, to boost its production, Saudi Arabia was now giving substantial discounts off its netback contracts, well in excess of $1.00/B.

In Geneva (August 1986), OPEC reached an interim agreement to reduce production from over 20 mbd to below 17 mbd. Prices began to strengthen, and the production ceiling was renewed at OPEC's October conference until the end of the year.

In Saudi Arabia, policy was being quietly taken out of Yamani's hands. A surprising development at both the August and October conferences was the formal espousal by Saudi Arabia of a speedy return by OPEC to a system of fixed prices based on a minimum yardstick of $18/B., although it was clear that such a restoration of a fixed price structure did not enjoy Yamani's whole-hearted support. At the same time, a Saudi government statement issued in Riyadh on 17 October, while the Geneva OPEC conference was still in progress, spoke both of the government's desire to obtain a higher production quota after the expiry of the interim agreement at the end of December, and its aim to raise prices to a fixed level of at least $18/B.—twin objectives that seemed to most observers to be incompatible. In fact, these straws in the wind were signals for a very sharp change of direction in Saudi oil policy.

Despite these portents of things to come, the promulgation on 29 October by King Fahd of a royal decree dismissing Shaikh Yamani as Oil Minister, and appointing Mr. Hisham Nazer, the Minister of Planning to replace him, sent shock waves through the oil world. Yamani had served as Saudi Oil Minister for 25 years under four kings and his name had become almost synonymous with Saudi oil policy. However, it soon became clear that Yamani's departure was the consequence of deep-seated differences between himself and King Fahd on various aspects of oil policy, including both price-production strategy in general and Yamani's opposition to various oil barter deals then in effect or under consideration. For one thing, Yamani felt that the simultaneous advocacy of higher prices and higher production manifested a basic inconsistency in Saudi policy. More specifically, he also had deep reservations in principle against the readoption of any system of fixed prices for the present time. Given the precarious state of OPEC discipline, he felt that successful maintenance of any such fixed price system would inevitably require Saudi Arabia, whether it liked it or not, to resume the role of swing producer and risk the erosion of its market share to an unacceptable level, as had happened in the fateful summer of 1985. However, in the aftermath of Yamani's departure it also emerged that the King's espousal of an $18/B. fixed price was the result of a complex politico-economic deal involving a number of disparate elements—including the United States, Iran and Libya—and represented a commitment that could not be retracted.

There was one more significant development before the December 1986 agreement: in Quito, in November, the Ministerial Committee on Pricing, in an effort to remove the exclusive burden of the marker crude, with its swing producer connotations, from Saudi Arabia, recommended that the calculation of the now official $18/B. reference price should be based on the values of a basket of seven representative crudes—six OPEC and one non-OPEC (Mexican). They were Arabian Light, Dubai, Minas, Bonny Light, Saharan Blend, Tia Juana Light, and Isthmus.

Accord, December 1986

OPEC's 80th Conference, held in Geneva from 11 to 20 December, 1986, was preceded by a flurry of ministerial committee meetings (committee on quotas, committee on pricing, market monitoring committee). With all the preparation, the actual technical work of formulating quotas and calculation price differentials went relatively smoothly. On the production side, the objective was to arrive at a set of graduated quotas for 1987 that would be sufficiently low in the first half to mop up some of the accumulated stock overhang resulting from previous overproduction, while allowing for some output growth in the second half; and on the price side to work out, by a combination of negotiation and computerized netbacking, a set of relative values aligned as closely as possible to market realities. But the really thorny problem—one that almost blocked the agreement and turned the conference into a cliffhanger right up to the last moment—centered around the conflict between Iran and Iraq.

Given their improved clout within OPEC, the Iranians clearly decided that the time had come to deprive Iraq of the legal basis to produce freely that it had enjoyed within OPEC since September and put it back in a recognized quota box. And this objective struck a sympathetic chord in quite a few other OPEC members. As elaborated and agreed upon by a ministerial working group composed of Nigeria's Lukman, Indonesia's Subroto, and Saudi Arabia's Nazer, with the collaboration of Iran's Aghazadeh and Algeria's Nabi, the quota schedule provided for a first-half allocation of 1.466 mbd for Iraq–somewhat better than the woefully inadequate 1.2 mbd fixed in the special circumstances of March 1983, but falling way short of Iraq's aspirations and capacity (around 2.0 mbd now, due to rise to 2.5 mbd by mid-year with the expansion of the Turkish pipeline). It came as no surprise that the offer of 1.466 mbd, even backed by an intense effort at persuasion by Saudi Arabia, should have been turned down flat by Iraq. Iraq had often made it plain that it would never under any circumstances accept a quota less than that of Iran. In the end, after much sabre-rattling and Iranian-inspired threats of public censure of Iraq by the rest of OPEC, and even eventual Iraqi expulsion from OPEC, it became clear that either the remaining 12 members would have to go ahead without Iraq, or the whole agreement would collapse in ruins. Sensibly the 12 finally decided to make the best of it, and the agreement was signed by all except Iraq. At the same time political initiatives from the Gulf were able to prevent a projected condemnation of Iraq from appearing in the official OPEC communique.

OPEC had at last achieved an accord of sorts to extricate itself from the damaging netback wars that had held sway until the interim agreements of August and October. True, Iraq would not sign up, but the rest would get along without it.

The organization now had a brand new, fixed-price system, based on a reference price of $18/B. for its basket of seven crudes complete with the appropriate differentials as computed on a netback method, and backed up by a set of production quotas. Arabian Light crude was posted at $17.52/B. f.o.b. Ras Tanura effective 1 February 1987 (a one-month grace period had been allowed to phase out the netback contracts); other crudes were priced consistently with it. The new system worked like a dream for a few months, but only because Saudi Arabia, despite heated denials, was forced to slip back into the role of swing supplier, as Yamani had predicted. In August and September 1987, the Aramco partners (Exxon, Mobil, Texaco and Chevron) put it on the line: either their contract prices would have to be reduced or liftings would drop drastically. The Saudis were left with no alternative but to cave in. The new arrangement simply collapsed; the new official prices became as meaningless as posted prices had been in the late 1960s. The fixed-price system metamorphosed into a "target" price system based on an OPEC-wide production-ceiling divided into quota shares among member countries. And there it remained until its further transformation into a price range, as we shall see in chapter 16. The truth was of course that a single-figure target price was never a realistic objective because the OPEC system was and remains a blunt instrument, incapable of operating on price with any precision.

US Intervention

OPEC's frenetic activity during 1986 (four conferences, two split into two parts, and innumerable consultative meetings and meetings of the various ministerial committees, not to mention meetings at the technical level, spread out around the world) did not of course take place in a political vacuum. Two major member countries, Iran and Iraq, were still engaged in a particularly bloody war, in which both sides, but particularly Iran, were dependent for financing on oil revenues. (Iraq was receiving large amounts of aid from other Arab countries, notably Kuwait and Saudi Arabia.) Relations with non-OPEC producers and exporters took time and effort; relations with buyers and the shift to netback contracts, then to discounts off netback prices were a central part of the process; but by far the most important political influence from outside of OPEC itself was the United States.

No producing area in the world was harder hit by low prices than many of the US high-cost fields where more than 450,000 "stripper" wells, each pumping only two or three barrels per day of oil, contributed in aggregate about 1.3 mbd or one-quarter of the country's total production.[1] More than half of this—about 700 kbd—was soon to be closed in as prices plunged from $26 at the beginning of 1986 to $12/B. by the end of March (spot West Texas Intermediate). The loss of production was permanent because these wells had to be plugged and abandoned after a period of time. They also happened to belong to a large number of politically influential independent producers.

Loss of domestic production inevitably meant increasing imports and increased dependence on the Middle East. With the memory of the Arab oil embargo still fresh in people's minds, the question of national security naturally emerged as an important issue. Once again, the United States found itself favoring higher rather than lower prices, and what the administration meant by "higher" was around $20/B., a level which, it had been estimated, would result in only a relatively small loss of production. An import fee of $4.00/B. was mooted but faced fierce opposition in Congress from oil-consuming states. There were also proposals to buy substantial quantities of oil for the Strategic Petroleum Reserve stocks, thereby sopping up some of the surplus on world markets. In the end, it was decided that some pressure should be put on Saudi Arabia to cease and desist from "irresponsible" competition.

Vice President George H. Bush, who had himself been an independent producer and could therefore empathize with the plight of Texan oil millionaires, was accordingly dispatched in April 1986 to Saudi Arabia to deliver an appropriate message. US Energy Secretary John Herrington had told the press that Saudi Arabia's policy of "forcing prices down by excess production" had "ramifications among its allies" and that the Saudi government should weigh the political considerations. Bush said that it was essential to "talk about stability". So much for competition and the free market. He added that a strong domestic oil industry was essential to the security of the United States, and that he would be "selling very hard" to convince the Saudis on this point.

But what could the Saudis do on their own? As swing producer, they had been driven to the wall in 1985; Yamani was even doubtful whether OPEC as a whole could bring stability to the market without the help of non-OPEC producers. Besides, the whole issue was bound up with the sale of arms to Saudi Arabia, which Bush characterized as "essential to the US national interest" but which was blocked, though only temporarily, by Congress in May 1986. In addition, there was the delivery, under a previous agreement, of several surveillance aircraft (AWACS), which began at the end of June 1986. The Saudis were also purchasing a number of Tornado and other aircraft from the British, under the so-called Al-Yamamah Agreement that had been concluded in February 1986. With rock-bottom oil prices, the Saudis would be hard pressed to pay for all these arms purchases and they were now running a huge budget deficit (almost $20 billion for fiscal 1985/86, equivalent to over 5 mbd at the then current prices).

In the event, the Saudi reaction following Vice President Bush's April 1986 visit was to actually increase rather than reduce production. The Saudis must have persuaded Bush to give them more time to "sweat" the rest of OPEC into an agreement. They were already giving substantial discounts on their netback contracts; now they abandoned their restraint and pushed their output above their OPEC quota of 4.6 mbd. By August 1986, Saudi production had risen to over 6 mbd, and spot prices in the Gulf had fallen to a little over $7/B. (Dubai spot, last three weeks in July and first week of August.) Saudi Arabia pushed volume to get higher revenue, to turn the heat up on the rest of OPEC and to push non-OPEC producers into bearing some part of the cutbacks necessary to get prices back up. In the end, it worked, more or less, though it took from August until December 1986 for a credible agreement to emerge.

Exit Ahmed Zaki Yamani

Shaikh Ahmed Zaki Yamani was appointed Minister of Petroleum and Mineral Resources in April 1962 and served without interruption in that capacity for the next 25 years. It was an achievement without parallel and his role in formulating and executing policy was critical during that extraordinary period when the Saudi Arabian government's position was transformed from one of a relatively passive collector of royalties and taxes to a commanding place in the international petroleum industry. A man of vision, he was the longest-lasting and most skillful of an especially talented crop of OPEC oil ministers of the 1960s and 1970s. They included Iran's Jamshid Amuzegar, Kuwait's Shaikh Ali Khalifa al-Sabah, Algeria's Belaid Abdessalam and Venezuela's Manuel Pérez Guerrero. These were not simply political appointees (though of course they were that as well); all of them brought experience and dedication to the job, a deep knowledge of the larger world outside of oil, and exceptional political and negotiating skills.

Yamani's achievements in the field of oil are too many and too varied to catalog here. He had to start from practically nothing—first of all cleaning up the considerable mess that Tariki left behind. This entailed negotiations with

Aramco that started in 1962 and in fact continued sporadically throughout Yamani's tenure. Yamani understood that Saudi Arabia could not get everything that was ultimately obtainable right away, and that he could not get too far out of step with the rest of OPEC.

Attacked by the companies (who at one point early in the game had threatened him to his face to "get him"), he was fortunate in enjoying the protection and patronage of King Faisal. He survived Faisal's death and remained for another decade the preeminent voice in Saudi oil policy. As minister, he had many qualities, but I think the one that served him best during his long career was patience. Yamani was a man who knew how to wait. He also, whether by nature or design, never seemed to offend anyone personally and consequently retained the respect of friend and foe alike.

Chapter 15
WAR IN THE GULF, 1990-1991

Dependence and Security of Supply

The history of international oil is intertwined with the security issue. From the consumer's point of view, oil was found in all the wrong places—difficult of access and almost always far away, usually in backward countries that became increasingly difficult to deal with as they developed economically and politically. The industrialized countries' dependence on imported oil grew rapidly in the second half of the last century: in 1948, the United States became a net importer and today imports almost 60 percent of its requirements of oil; Japan and South Korea are almost wholly dependent on imports, and so was Western Europe until the advent of North Sea oil; but even today, with the large production from the North Sea, Western Europe's net imports account for well over half of its total consumption.

Oil has for many years now been essential to modern economies, and imports have become a matter of economic life or death. Access to major supply sources on reasonable terms and the integrity of supply routes are a fighting matter.

The security threat has been centered on the curtailment of oil supplies from the Middle East, either because of local or regional events, such as the Iranian nationalization of 1951 and the periodic outbursts into war of the Arab-Israeli conflict; or for deliberate, political purposes, directed mainly against the United States and its allies, notably the Arab oil embargo of 1973; or because of the disruption of transportation routes, notably the Suez Canal crisis of 1956/57 and the numerous occasions when the pipelines from the producing countries of the Gulf to the Eastern Mediterranean export terminals were deliberately closed or sabotaged. The major importing countries were acutely aware of the danger from an early date. Their strategic response has been consistent over the years: to encourage the geographic diversification of supplies and to maintain emergency stocks. These have been supplemented at times by the establishment of bilateral relations between some major importers and major exporters, notably France and Algeria, but one could also include the more amorphous relationship between the United States and Saudi Arabia as well as bilateral deals involving government-to-government purchases of oil, sometimes tied to the sale of arms to the producing country concerned. On the whole, the experience of these bilateral relationships has not been a happy one, though the US and Saudi Arabian relationship occupies a special place.

No one, however, has attempted to achieve security of supply by deliberately encouraging competition among the suppliers, and the advocates of this course of action have been few. It is no doubt an ideal solution—to have numerous suppliers competing ferociously for markets, knowing that any attempt to exert political pressure by withholding supply would simply result in the loss of market to someone else. But the overarching risk of pursuing this course is that the Middle East would drive out too many other sources of higher-cost oil, and, in the end, dependence on that area might be even higher than before. It might be possible to protect other sources by preferential import tariffs and quotas, but this would require agreement among the major importers, energy-rich and energy-poor alike. It was never on the cards that countries such as Japan, Italy and Germany would agree to this. A few countries did attempt to encourage diversification by establishing or subsidizing national companies to explore for oil abroad. Such was the purpose of the Japan National Oil Corporation (JNOC), Spain's Hispánica de Petróleos (Hispanoil) and Germany's Deminex, all of them consortia of independents plus some State participation, direct or financial. Their resources and therefore efforts were quite inadequate and they contributed little to total supplies and nothing to national security.

In practice, diversification of supplies was left to the private sector (mainly the major oil companies) and their profit motive. It worked well enough, but was certainly not brought about as a result of the search for security; enhanced security was merely incidental. The maintenance of emergency stocks, on the other hand, was motivated and implemented solely for security purposes. In Western Europe, the level established was at first 60 days of anticipated demand, and later 90 days. The United States established a strategic petroleum reserve after the Arab oil embargo, but, as a security measure, emergency stocks are by their nature essentially short-term. No other measures were taken over the long term to cope with serious supply disruptions except the logistical arrangements set up, at first through various company coordinating groups and later through the International Energy Agency (IEA), to manage the fair distribution of available supplies in an emergency.

The fears of the major importing countries have been amply justified by events over the past fifty years, but, with the exception of Suez in 1956, the numerous crises were always resolved, prior to 1990, without the use of force by the West. Indeed, in the invasion of Egypt over the nationalization of the Suez Canal—the only occasion when force was used—it was to forestall a hypothetical *future* crisis; instead it became itself the proximate cause of the supply disruption so much feared, caused great disruption to all shipping, and incidentally spurred the development of the supertankers that were already on the way to making the Suez Canal of secondary importance for the oil trade.

Iraqi Oil Revenues, Kuwait and the Price of Oil

The war precipitated by Iraq's invasion of Kuwait in August 1990 was different. It was also the first oil war—a war fought primarily over the control of oil; other motives were at best secondary.

Iraq's war with Iran had ended in 1988 with Iraq winning by a technical knock-out. A major preoccupation for Saddam was now the country's financial situation and immediate prospects. Iraq was almost $100 billion in debt, a debt incurred largely during its war with Iran, and much of it owed to Kuwait, the Emirates and Saudi Arabia. By June 1990, the price of crude oil in the Mediterranean (Iraq's crude was mostly exported from Eastern Mediterranean and Red Sea ports), had dropped by nearly one-third since the beginning of the year, wiping out more than half a billion dollars of Iraq's oil revenues per month. (The spot price of Libya's widely-quoted Es Sider crude averaged $21 in January and only $14.50 in June.)

OPEC was overproducing. Its overall production ceiling of 22 mbd for the first half of 1990 would probably have maintained prices quite nicely at over $20, but excess production was running in the order of 2 mbd—and much of the blame could be laid at the door of Kuwait and Abu Dhabi, both of which were exceeding their quotas recklessly.

Iraqi efforts to get higher oil prices through OPEC had been going on since the end of 1989, and pressure had specifically been brought to bear on Kuwait. Instead, prices deteriorated, and by May 1990, matters within OPEC were reaching crisis proportions. An Arab Summit of Iraq, Saudi Arabia, the UAE and Qatar, held in Bagdad at the end of May, primarily to demonstrate Arab solidarity against Israel but also to discuss other matters, came to nothing. But in closed meetings[1],Saddam Hussein accused Kuwait and the UAE of waging economic warfare on Iraq by refusing to observe their OPEC production quotas and thus keeping oil prices depressed. Saudi Arabia's King Fahd tried to defuse the situation by suggesting a further meeting on the oil issue, and this was duly held in Jiddah on 11-12 July. It went well, by all published accounts; agreement was reached on acceptable quotas and both Kuwait and the UAE gave firm assurances that these would now be strictly observed, Kuwait's quota remaining at its previously set (though blatantly disregarded) level of 1.5 mbd.

But in the meantime, Saddam Hussein's anger had grown to encompass other matters, more serious than the mere non-observance of OPEC quotas (scarcely an unprecedented transgression in OPEC's ranks).

In a memorandum to the Secretary General of the Arab League dated 15 July 1990, and a speech by Saddam Hussein on 17 July 1990, Iraq accused Kuwait and the UAE of joining a US conspiracy to overproduce and drive the price of oil down in an act of economic warfare against Iraq; and accused Kuwait specifically of occupying Iraqi territory, erecting "military installations, border posts, oil installations and farms on Iraqi territory" and producing oil from the southern part of the Iraqi Rumailah field. He said, "The government of Kuwait is determined to cause the collapse of the Iraqi economy during this period when it is confronting the vicious imperialist Zionist threat, which is an aggression no less serious than military aggression." Saddam Hussein threatened "action", saying that if words could not prevail, "then action will have to be taken to restore matters to their normal course."[2]

These were new issues, and extremely serious ones. Saddam Hussein was deliberately widening the conflict. Perhaps he had already decided that war with Kuwait might be an attractive and viable option, for if the price of oil and the non-observance of OPEC quotas had been the only issue, he would surely have awaited the outcome of the end-July OPEC Conference and its probable ratification of the quotas agreed in Jiddah, as well as giving Kuwait and the UAE time to prove their good faith.

Kuwaiti denials and counter-accusations followed Iraq's new accusations, accompanied by a good deal of diplomatic activity; but there was no sign that Kuwait would yield on anything other than what it had already agreed at the Jiddah meeting of July 11-12.

The United States reacted by sending a cable on 19 July 1990 to its Middle Eastern embassies instructing them to stress that disputes should be settled by peaceful means and not threats of force; and that the United States was not taking any position on the substance of bilateral issues concerning Iraq and Kuwait. The UAE, alarmed by the Iraqi troop movements now being observed, wanted a joint military exercise staged with the United States as a warning to Saddam. The United States obliged on 23 July.

This must have upset Saddam Hussein, who promptly summoned US Ambassador April Glaspie on 25 July 1990. This was, as Saddam put it, to be a "message to President Bush" and covered the resumption of diplomatic relations between the two, US policy in the Gulf, and Iraq's dispute with Kuwait. On the last point, Glaspie told Saddam that the "U.S. had no opinion on the Arab-Arab conflict, like your border dispute with Kuwait." Taken out of context, this may have seemed like a green light to Saddam, and indeed Glaspie was later criticized on these grounds. The fact that she had already emphasized to Nizar Hamdun, Iraq's deputy foreign minister, that the United States could "never excuse settlement of disputes by other than peaceful means" must have carried little conviction coming from a country which had actively aided and abetted Iraq in its war with Iran. Besides, Glaspie's remarks on the other matters that Saddam had brought up were distinctly friendly and encouraging, given the relations between the two countries.[3] And Glaspie herself did not believe that Iraq would invade and take over the whole of Kuwait; neither did anybody else, not the State Department, not Israel, not the Kuwaitis, nor any Arab leader. After the meeting, she cabled the State Department, suggesting the Administration go light on criticism of the Iraqi regime at least until the outcome of the further Iraq-Kuwait negotiations, which had been fixed for 31 July in Jiddah, were known.

Saddam must have felt reassured. But, reassuring or not, nothing Glaspie could have said within the framework of her instructions would at this point have deterred him from his course: it was the 25th of July, Iraqi troops were already in place and one week later the attack would be launched. The decision had been taken; the timing awaited only the inevitable breakdown of renewed talks in Jiddah, a breakdown that could only at this point have been averted by the total capitulation of Kuwait on all the issues involved. The little tête-á-tête with Glaspie seems just to have been a last-minute double-check, to make sure that the United States would not intervene militarily to protect Kuwait or help it at a later date. In a subsequent message to Saddam, President Bush cabled that his administration "continues to desire better relations with Iraq."[4]

At the same time, OPEC was meeting in Geneva, and hastily agreed to the proposals had been put forward by the Arab group in Jiddah on 11 and 12 July. The trade journal *Oil and Energy Trends* (August 1990) remarked:

> With indecorous haste, OPEC reached an agreement at its 25-27 July Conference in Geneva on an overall allowable for the second half of 1990 and its apportionment by country quota. It must have been the first time in the world's economic history that a cartelistic arrangement to limit supplies of a commodity to international markets has been rammed through by one member's threats to use military force against others.

The Jiddah Meeting of 31 July 1990

The OPEC meeting did not of course address the wider political differences between Iraq and Kuwait which had been brought to the fore by Saddam Hussein. In the meantime, President Mubarak of Egypt and King Fahd of Saudi Arabia had been busy trying to seek some means to resolve the dispute. At their insistence, Saddam Hussein and Shaikh Jabir, Ruler of Kuwait, agreed to have high level delegations meet in Jiddah on 31 July to try to sort out their differences.

Shaikh Sa'ad, Kuwaiti prime minister, headed the Kuwait delegation; Izzat Ibrahim al-Duri, deputy president of the Revolutionary Command Council, headed Iraq's. Compromise was on neither's mind nor in their instructions. At the end of the first day, with no concessions from Kuwait on the main issues, the Iraqi delegation was ordered to return to Baghdad and left the next day. Sa'ad later claimed that he had been flexible, and had tentatively offered to cancel Iraq's debt (Kuwait was not likely to get paid anyway), and to grant Iraq military facilities on the islands of Warba and Bubiyan.

It was too late. Kuwait was fully aware of Iraqi troop movements and positions on its border, but, along with everyone else, did not take them as a serious threat of invasion.

Invasion

In the early hours of 2 August 1990, Iraqi troops crossed the border and invaded Kuwait, swiftly overrunning Kuwait city. Troop numbers were reported of about 100,000 with 350 tanks. By evening, they were in full control of the city. The Emir, Shaikh Jabbar al Ahmed al Sabah, escaped to Saudi Arabia overland.

Kuwait, which had spent billions of dollars on arms over the previous ten years, offered virtually no resistance to the only plausible military threat it had ever faced, in spite of the repeated, open and public warnings emanating from Baghdad during the previous weeks. Kuwait paid a fearful price for its misjudgment of Iraq's intentions and the foolhardy policy it had followed in trying to force the rest of OPEC to agree to a much higher quota for it by pushing its production to a point where the price of oil was collapsing. Kuwait was not Saudi Arabia, that could and did "sweat" the rest of OPEC in 1986, and it was certainly not crystal clear that the United States would come to its assistance as it would without any doubt have come to Saudi Arabia's.

Iraq was now about to pay an even more fearful price for misjudging how quickly the US administration under President George Bush would conclude that the occupation of Kuwait could not be tolerated. And after urgent consultations and meetings, Bush declared publicly, forcefully and repeatedly that "This will not stand, this aggression against Kuwait."

Of course it couldn't. In a lightning strike, Iraq had seized control of over 94 billion barrels of proved oil reserves—about 10 percent of the world's total—and was within a stone's throw of the major Saudi oilfields with over one-quarter of the world's reserves. If Iraq could not be dislodged from Kuwait, how long would it be before it attacked Saudi Arabia and the UAE? Alternatively, letting Iraq keep Kuwait but being prepared to defend Saudi Arabia militarily would have necessitated the permanent deployment of a massive US force to be stationed somewhere in the Gulf, not to mention many other unpleasant consequences.

Coalition and War

Bush's first job, as he saw it, was to put together a broad-based coalition of countries to force Iraq out of Kuwait, working as far as possible through the United Nations. Diplomatic pressure, economic sanctions, a blockade on exports and, ultimately, force would have to be used if necessary. But the United States was not psychologically prepared to go to war over Kuwait, and even if it had been, it would have taken (and eventually did take) a considerable period of time to get the military forces in place. In one sense, the time requirement was not unfortunate. Saddam Hussein's army was ensconced in Kuwait, but he couldn't go forward and wouldn't go back. President Bush's timetable had, up to a point, no urgency and putting the coalition together and proceeding with the military buildup, dubbed "Operation Desert Shield", could move forward with all deliberate speed.

Gathering allies was essential. Turkey, whose main trading partner was Iraq, had to be in—not an easy decision for the country. Saudi scruples about allowing foreign (non-Islamic) troops on its soil had to be overcome. Syria, of all countries, previously branded by the United States as a "terrorist" State had to be at least neutralized. More general Arab scruples about Western interference in what was for a time seen as an essentially Arab dispute also had to be overcome. And Israel had to be kept out, even if attacked by Iraqi missiles (as it later was). Above all, perhaps, Russian support had to be obtained; Russia had to suspend all military aid and sales of equipment to Iraq, and to make it clear that Iraq could not count on Russian support in any sense. President Mikhail Gorbachov and his foreign minister Eduard Scheverdnadze obliged: it was not the moment for confrontation with the United States UN endorsement and active support had to be obtained. Western European countries enlisted easily enough, some reluctantly but Britain, under its pugnacious prime minister, Margaret Thatcher, enthusiastically.

The pressures on Iraq escalated: economic blockade, cutting off of oil export routes, cutting air links, trade embargo, and warnings from all quarters to withdraw. Nothing worked. Weeks, then months, went by, until towards the end of the year it became clear that force would soon have to be used. In the meantime, the price of oil moved up and down, sometimes violently, and down, as the danger of war approached and receded with every belligerent statement or peace initiative.

At the end of November 1990, the UN Security Council adopted a resolution, by a majority of 12 to 2 with one abstention, authorizing the use of force if Iraq had not withdrawn from Kuwait by 15 January. On 12 January, the US Congress adopted a resolution supporting the use of force by the United States if Iraq did not meet the 15 January deadline. But it was not plain sailing: the resolution passed with only a small majority in the Senate (52 to 47) and a more comfortable one in the House (250 to 183). It was clear that the country was not at that point solidly behind President Bush, with many fearful of the severe casualties that might result.

On the night of 16/17 January, intensive bombing started of Iraqi troops and military installations in Kuwait and Iraq and the destruction of Iraq's industrial base and physical infrastructure continued without letup during the whole of the period up to and after the start of the ground war at dawn on Sunday 24 February.

Saddam's Rationale

In retrospect, Saddam Hussein's invasion of Kuwait and his subsequent actions seem suicidal. But they didn't at the time. Saddam, after all, saw in the

United States a country that had helped him in his war against Iran and had afterwards repeatedly sought better relations, despite bitter public criticism of him in the US media and the Congress. It had overlooked the atrocities he had committed against his own people in putting down a revolt; and Ambassador Glaspie's words in her interview with him on 25 July could be interpreted as a hands-off attitude by the United States in any purely Arab conflict. It was clear that the United States wanted a strong Iraq as a bulwark against enemy no. 1 in the region, Iran (and, of course, it did). For these reasons, Saddam Hussein must have been convinced that the United States would not go to war over Kuwait; and there were additional ones which did not directly concern the Middle East at all. The United States had been traumatized by its experience in Vietnam and, though by far the most powerful country in the world, would be extremely reluctant to undertake any major effort abroad involving the use of armed force, for fear of being sucked into a conflict from which there could be no clear victory and no easy withdrawal. Moreover, the lesson of the Soviet Union in Afghanistan was there for all to see.

His opinion was shared. Certainly, Secretary of State James Baker did not think the Administration had sufficient backing at that point to go to war over Kuwait:

> If the President had said prior to August 1990 that we were willing to go to war to protect Kuwait, many members of Congress would have been muttering impeachment. Even after Saddam had invaded Kuwait, there was little, if any, domestic support for using our military. We had to build that support painstakingly.[5]

It should be remembered that, at the time, there was considerable fear that war would mean unacceptably high casualties. The most popular "estimate" or, rather, guess around Washington before fighting started was 10,000 to 15,000. General Norman Scharzkopf, Chief of Central Command at the time, when pressed, thought about 5,000. Powell said 3,000. Although not related to any of the estimates, according to Powell, the Defense Department ordered 15,000 body bags—word got out.[6] Saddam Hussein's conclusion that the United States would not go to war over Kuwait coincided with the judgment of Colin Powell, who was after all the chairman of the Joint Chiefs of Staff and a man of some political experience (as, among other things, national security adviser to the president). Shortly after the invasion, Schwarzkopf briefed the National Security Council on the military situation in the Gulf. He recounts his conversation with Powell prior to the briefing. According to Schwarzkopf, Powell said, "I think we'd go to war over Saudi Arabia, but I doubt we'd go to war over Kuwait."[7] Some days later, according to Schwarzkopf, Powell repeated this view: "I don't see us going to war over Kuwait. Saudi Arabia, yes, if we had to; but not Kuwait."[8]

It is surprising in retrospect that anyone should have doubted that Iraq's occupation of Kuwait was a fighting matter. Kuwait could not remain an isolated issue. A Kuwait occupied by Iraq meant a Saudi Arabia (and the Emirates) perpetually under threat, the threat of eventual control of all oil exports from the Gulf in Iraqi hands, including Iran's, and a series of totally unacceptable consequences, from the price of oil to the fate of Israel.

Possibly, at the outset, only President Bush himself clearly understood that if all else failed, the United States would have to fight, and it is to his great credit that he was able to steer the country and the uneven coalition to that conclusion.

War and Expulsion: Desert Storm

After three weeks of merciless and sustained shelling, bombing and missile attacks which destroyed much of Iraq's military capability and the country's infrastructure, Saddam Hussein's resolve was weakening. On 10 February, Iraqi Foreign Minister Saadoun Hammadi said in a press conference in Jordan that his country was ready to negotiate a peaceful settlement of the conflict; but there was nothing to negotiate. After days of diplomatic activity leading nowhere, on 22 February, President Bush set a deadline of 8.00 pm Baghdad time of the following day for the beginning of a large-scale Iraqi military withdrawal from Kuwait, to be completed within one week. Eight hours after the expiry of the deadline, at 4.00 am Baghdad time, the UN coalition forces launched a massive ground attack on Iraqi forces in Kuwait. Encountering little resistance, they moved rapidly into Kuwait and southern Iraq, taking large numbers of Iraqi prisoners. After massive destruction of Iraqi armor, but little significant fighting, it was all over. There was virtually no resistance from Iraqi troops: the lucky ones surrendered and were taken prisoner; the unlucky ones (along with many civilians) were massacred from the air in what one pilot termed a "turkey-shoot", as they tried to flee along the road (Highway 80) from Kuwait to Basra in any vehicle (most of them laden with loot) that would move. They left behind them a murdered city, a blazing inferno of 600 or more wells on fire and a sea of ecologically deadly oil.

Relief and jubilation among the coalition forces at the tiny number of fatal casualties suffered by them—about 150, 10 percent inflicted by "friendly fire"—obscured the massive overkill of perhaps 100,000 and possibly many more Iraqis, take soldier and civilian. Estimates of total Iraqi casualties during the war range from 200,000 to 150,000 (Schwarzkopf), to 82,500 (Hiro).[9] Many of them—perhaps most of them—were killed from the air while in full retreat; they didn't even have the option of surrendering. In any event, coalition forces were in full control of Kuwait city on the 27th of February and hostilities were suspended on 28 February.

US Post-War Policy Objectives

What were US post-war political objectives? A difficult question to answer, because foreign policy is rarely monolithic in the United States, split as it is between the State Department, the National Security Council and the Department of Defense, with the President as ultimate arbiter, but one who has to keep his eye firmly fixed on Congress and sometimes defer to it. Secretary of State James Baker's statement on 6 February 1991 to the House Foreign Affairs Committee may have represented the Administration consensus views at the time, but if they did, they would reveal only a startling lack of realism.

Baker defined policy objectives for the United States after the war as: (a) help from the UN Coalition countries in the reconstruction of Kuwait and Iraq; (b) new regional security arrangements, to include Iran and Iraq itself; (c) the withdrawal of US ground troops from the area and their replacement by a new force, possibly under the control of the Gulf Cooperation Council; and (d) US commitment to resolving the Israel-Palestinian dispute.

None of these was met (as Baker later acknowledged, at least as far as the first three were concerned),[10] and it is easy to see why. The first three were little short of laughable, and the fourth was never particularly relevant to the war, which was over oil, not Israel. Israel was relevant only inasmuch as some attempt by the United States to help settle the Israeli-Palestinian conflict was promised as an inducement to bring other Arab countries along in the coalition against Iraq. Baker did pursue this objective with some vigor, but despite considerable apparent progress, the intractable remained just that.

In truth, the major war aims were simpler: first, the elimination of potential Iraqi control over Saudi Arabia's and the UAE's oil; and, second, retention of Iraq as a single political unit strong enough (eventually) to act as a counterweight to Iran. The war was a resounding military success in expelling Iraq from Kuwait, and Iraq was indeed left as a single political unit—because Saddam Hussein remained strong enough to put down, with atrocious ferocity, the Shi'a and Kurdish uprisings that followed the war. It was not an episode that did credit to the United States. The Shi'a and Kurds were encouraged by the United States to rebel, and they expected material help when they did. It was not forthcoming because, while Saddam's ouster would have been heartily welcomed, the United States wanted an Iraq with a strong central government, and civil war was not likely to lead to it.

Reparations, Sanctions and Controls

From the second of August 1990 (date of the Iraqi invasion of Kuwait) to the end of 1991, the UN Security Council passed some twenty-seven resolutions relating directly to Iraq, and more than another thirty subsequently. Taken with the measures "hung" on them later (sometimes via imaginative interpretations), they reduced Iraq to a status unlike anything ever seen before in international politics. The Iraqi "surrender" was not unconditional in any formal sense, as were the surrenders of Germany and Japan after World War II; but neither was it conditional in the sense of a formally negotiated settlement.

Instead, the UN devised and imposed a system of external sanctions and internal controls which were to last until Iraq had complied fully with all the relevant UN resolutions. In addition, reparations were to be paid to damaged parties, mainly Kuwait and Kuwaiti nationals.

Briefly, the system developed as follows:

The first UN Security Council resolution (660 of 2 Aug 1990) simply condemned the Iraqi invasion and called for an immediate and unconditional withdrawal.

Iraqi funds abroad were immediately frozen, in the United States and elsewhere, and the Security Council imposed a complete trade embargo (Resolution 661 of 6 Aug 1990), except for medicine and foodstuffs for humanitarian purposes. The resolution also set up the "661 Committee", composed of all members of the Security Council, to monitor Iraqi compliance with UN resolutions, and determine the circumstances under which food and medicine could be imported for humanitarian reasons. Resolution 665 (25 Aug 1990) called on member states to enforce the embargo with a naval blockade.

On 29 November 1990, the Security Council passed a key resolution, No. 678, which authorized member states "to use all necessary means" to compel Iraq to withdraw from Kuwait if it had not done so voluntarily by 15 January 1991. This was the authorization by which the United States sought to justify the use of force and the employment of the massive buildup of troops that it was undertaking. Final sanction for the use of force came on 12 January 1991 when Congress authorized the Administration to "use all necessary means" to eject Iraq from Kuwait.

After the fighting was over and Iraq had been duly routed and driven from Kuwait, the Security Council adopted Resolution 686 on 2 March 1991, setting out terms for a final cease-fire, but at the same time affirming the "independence, sovereignty and territorial integrity of Iraq".

This was followed by Resolution 687 (3 Apr 1991), which did two things: first, it provided for the destruction of all of Iraq's biological and chemical weapons, ballistic missiles and "nuclear-weapons-usable" materials, to be carried out by a UN Special Commission (UNSCOM), in cooperation with the International Atomic Energy Agency (IAEA); and, second, it decided to create a Commission to administer a fund to pay compensation for damages caused by Iraq, with Iraq to contribute a percentage of the value of its future oil exports (later fixed at 30 percent). The embargoes (trade, financial, etc.) on Iraq were to be continued and reviewed periodically to determine whether they should be lightened or lifted.

On 5 April 1991, Resolution 688 was adopted, condemning the repression of the Iraqi civilian population, meaning the Kurds in the north and the Shi'a in the south. This resolution was used by the United States and Britain to establish the no-fly zones north of parallel 36 and south of parallel 33.

Resolution 692 (20 May 1991) established the UN Compensation Commission to administer the Compensation fund..

There followed a key resolution for oil, Resolution 706 of 15 August 1991, providing for the sale of Iraqi oil to fund compensation claims, weapons inspection and humanitarian needs. Periodic sales were authorized on an *ad hoc* basis until 1995 when, under Resolution 986 (14 Apr 1995), sales of one billion dollars worth of oil every 90 days were authorized. All payments were to be made into an escrow account controlled by the UN.

A number of subsequent resolutions regulated the export of oil by Iraq and modified the amounts of oil that could be sold in specified periods.

Dilemma and Anomaly

The appalling political mess, full of anomalies, left behind after the Gulf War was the result of the unresolved dilemmas posed by the Coalition's war aims. The situation's great complexity arose because the Coalition members, united only by their desire to see Iraq ejected from Kuwait, had significantly different interests from each other in the final political outcome of the conflict. The accommodation of these interests in a workable compromise capable of producing a stable situation has proved impossible.

Iraq had to be left in one piece, nominally sovereign, with a (penniless) central government strong enough to keep it that way. It had to be stripped of its weapons of mass destruction. It had to pay reparations. And it had to be stopped from any more excessively brutal repressive measures to *keep* the country in one piece. Nor could the Coalition intervene with force to change the government which, obviously, remained hostile, breaking the trade embargo at every possible opportunity and obstructing, in every possible way, UNSCOM's work of stripping it of weapons.

Over the next twelve years since the sanctions were put in place, the trade embargo became increasingly leaky. Unauthorized imports and the hidden export of oil grew apace. UNSCOM was finally driven out by Iraqi non-cooperation, but was later replaced by the UN Monitoring, Verification and Inspection Commission (UNMOVIC), created by Resolution 1284 of 17 December 1999, with functions essentially similar to those of UNSCOM. Apart from the United States and Britain, most other members of the Coalition lost their stomach for sanctions that did not work and had little prospect of working in the future, but which had clearly visited great hardship on Iraq's civilian population. This was essentially where matters stood until President George W. Bush, son of President George H. Bush, anxious to finish the job his father left incomplete, turned his attention to Iraq after the

11 September 2001 terrorist attacks on the Trade Center in New York and the
subsequent routing of the Taliban regime in Afghanistan. (See Epilogue.)

The War, Its Aftermath and Oil

How were the supply of oil to the markets, prices and the oil industry itself
affected by the war and its aftermath? The war was, after all, about oil,
although sometimes its wider political implications, for the balance of power
in the Middle East, for relations between the Arab world and the "West", and
for relations among the Coalition's members, obscure that simple fact.
Unexpectedly, the effect of the war on oil supplies and the markets was quite
unremarkable compared with the previous crises of 1973 and 1979/80.

Supply and Price During the War

Prior to the invasion of Kuwait on 2 August 1990, OPEC was producing in
excess of 25 mbd of crude oil and natural gas liquids, of which Iraq and
Kuwait were, between them, contributing around 20 percent, and Saudi Arabia
about 25 percent. With the invasion, Iraqi and Kuwaiti oil exports came to an
immediate and abrupt end. Prices more than doubled, on fear more than
shortage, with the spot price of Brent, a major reference point, going from an
average of $17/B. in July 1990 to $36 in September.

Other members of OPEC, particularly Saudi Arabia, moved rapidly to
make up the shortfall in supply: Saudi production jumped from 5.7 mbd in
July 1990 to 8 mbd in September (and maintained production at levels in
excess of 8 mbd for the next year). Total OPEC production had dropped
from 25 mbd in July to 22 mbd in August, but by September was up at over
24 mbd and by November was well above its pre-invasion level. The August
shortfall was easily covered out of inventories, which were high and were soon
to be replenished. Prices started to weaken already in November 1990,
dropping further (except for a blip during the actual fighting in February 1991)
until they were almost back to their pre-invasion point by June 1991, a couple
of months after the cease-fire. Spot Brent averaged $18/B. during that
month. There were no Iraqi exports and the Kuwaiti oilfields which had been
set ablaze by Iraq's retreating forces, were still burning though being rapidly
doused by the redoubtable Red Adair and his team , of international fame in
the industry for their exploits in quelling oil-well fires.

OPEC Production Performance

Yet there was a glut of oil in the market.
How did all this happen?
The short and simple answer is that there was more than enough surplus
capacity in other OPEC countries to more than make up for the loss of Iraq

and Kuwait.

The keystone of the OPEC effort to make up for the Iraqi/Kuwaiti output shortfall was, of course, Saudi Arabia—and, in the event, the Kingdom's production performance was even better than the most optimistic prior estimates.

In August 1990, Saudi Arabia's sustainable production capacity was reckoned to be in the region of 7.5 mbd—roughly 2 mbd above actual output in July—and the received wisdom at that time was that it would take six to nine months to raise it by a further 1 mbd. As it turned out, as a result of a crash program of de-mothballing previously existing above-ground facilities, Saudi Aramco achieved a sustainable crude production capacity of 8.5 mbd by December 1990. In total, the 11 OPEC countries (i.e., excluding Iraq and Kuwait) succeeded in boosting output by as much as 4.9 mbd. Saudi Arabia alone accounted for over 3 mbd of the increase, but quite a number of other members came up with (in some cases surprisingly) substantial contributions, including Iran, the UAE, Venezuela, Libya, Nigeria and Indonesia. In other words, if Saudi Arabia was determined to prevent prices from rising too high, the price-hawks would have to make as much hay as possible while the sun shone: they increased production by as much as they physically could, thus contributing to, if not ensuring, an eventual collapse in price.

This buildup of OPEC production helped to progressively decrease the war-scare price-premium and finally, after fighting actually broke out in mid-January 1991, to almost extinguish it. OPEC production actually declined by 760 kbd in January 1991. This was partly due to the immediate effects of the war: lower production for local consumption in Iraq and Kuwait; shutdown of the Khafji field in the offshore Neutral Zone previously producing 260 kbd; and the reluctance of tankers to load at Iran's Kharg Island terminal. But a more compelling reason was that an already amply-supplied market did not want or need the extra output.

For the year 1990 as a whole, OPEC crude production registered a substantial 8.5 percent rise to 23 mbd, from 21mbd in 1989. As for the overall 1990 supply/demand balance, reported supply exceeded estimated demand by a wide margin—nearly 1 mbd.

OPEC: Normality Regained

After the Gulf War, which had affected supply so little and prices for so short a time, OPEC slid slowly back to normality, a state of alternating high- and low-tension bickering over production quotas and their enforcement. It took time because in some important respects, the game had changed. Eighteen essentially quota-free months, courtesy of Iraq and Kuwait, had done nothing to sharpen member countries' taste for discipline. Saudi Arabia had gained 3 mbd and was not about to go back on a stringent diet, especially after having had to foot the lion's share of the war's costs. Iraq was sidelined, though it would shortly be allowed to export limited amounts of oil. Kuwait was coming back slowly. But there was no question of going back to the July 1990 quotas, even if it included an open sharing out of Iraq's quota (that had already been done *de facto*, with Saudi Arabia bagging most of it). Besides, the market demand situation had changed, and there were, for a while, sharp differences of opinion in the Organization about future developments and, therefore, the total size of the pie to be divided.

Nevertheless, a sort of steady-state price-volatility emerged, which the industry got used to even if it didn't like it very much. Over the rest of the decade of the 1990s, crude prices fluctuated mostly within a band of $15 to $20/B.

Iraq on the Rack

Sorry political episodes seem to have a long life: ten years after the end of the Gulf War, Iraq continued to be punished and its government continued unrepentant.

Immediately after the war, Kurdish uprisings in the north and Shi'a in the south were brutally repressed (see above), and "order" re-established in what one author dubbed The Republic of Fear. The Coalition forces gave the Kurds some protection on the ground, the Shi'a less; no-fly zones were established in the north and south of the country. But the major problem on the road to some kind of normality in international relations with Iraq was Iraq's failure to comply fully with UN Resolutions, particularly those dealing with disarmament under UN supervision, and weapons of mass destruction. For this reason, trade and other sanctions were not lifted on the country.

Iraq was heavily dependent on imports, including food and the products necessary to sustain its own agricultural production, such as fertilizers and agricultural machinery. Two successive years of severe drought, in 1994 and 1995, added to the general hardship, and per capita food intake dropped by around 30 percent, to about 2,300 kcals per day, meaning levels close to starvation for the poorest sections of the population. Misery was compounded by the unavailability of medical supplies. Naturally, the spectacle of semi-starved children and rapidly rising infant mortality rates aroused much revulsion in the "West", and it became clear that the boycott/embargo would not be politically sustainable for much longer without some alleviation of the Iraqi population's hardships.

A catch-22 trap had, inadvertently, been well and truly set by the victorious allies for themselves. On the one hand, one of the purposes of the boycott/embargo had been to make life so difficult for Iraq that Saddam Hussein and his government would be overthrown by some internal coup. But the only people capable of mounting such a coup—army officers—were either well looked after and therefore not suffering, or in exile, or dead. The rest of the population, it was clear, would receive no military help from outside if they tried to overthrow the government by force, as had already been demonstrated by the refusal of the Allies to come, militarily, to the assistance of the Kurds and Shi'a when they had tried it. So the Allies were compelled to mitigate the boycott/embargo by sending food and medicine to the Iraqi people, thereby reducing the pressure (on the Saddam Hussein regime) which, according to the Allies' own reasoning, the embargo was supposed to create. In the meantime, the power-elite in Iraq was filling its pockets with lucrative, two-way smuggling—oil out, food and a wide range of other goods in, across borders that were leaky and through countries with complicitous governments, including Iran and Turkey.

The Allies had simply underestimated Saddam's staying power. Right after the war, in August 1991, the UN Security Council passed two resolutions (705 and 706) setting war-compensation to be paid by Iraq at a maximum of 30 percent of earnings from the export of oil, and allowing the emergency sale by Iraq of certain amounts of oil to fund compensation claims, weapons-inspection costs and humanitarian needs. But these and several subsequent resolutions dealing with oil exports remained a dead letter until 1995, by which time the situation in Iraq with respect to food and medicine had become desperate.

By 1995, Iraq was still (officially) exporting no oil and earning no foreign currency. It could therefore make no payments for reparations and damages resulting from the war. The creditors, not unreasonably, were restless. Together with the proponents, growing in number, of some relaxation of sanctions so that Iraq could import and pay for food and medicine, they became another source of pressure on the Allies to allow at least limited exports of oil. In April 1995, the Security Council adopted a resolution (No. 986) providing for the export by Iraq of one billion dollars' worth of oil (at "fair market prices") each 90 days, for an initial trial period of 180 days, subject to certain conditions. (At prices prevailing at the time the Resolution was passed—April 1995—this would have equated to about 600 kbd, enough to cause some market disruption, but not excessively so, particularly in view of the limited periods involved.)

The conditions to which the implementation of the resolution was subject included: (a) payment of all receipts from the sales into an escrow account from which the UN would make disbursements to cover the costs of food and medicine to be imported by Iraq, instalments on war reparations and the costs of administration; (b) approval of oil sales contracts by the UN; (c) payment of 30 percent of receipts from the sale of oil into the Compensation Fund (via the escrow account) set up by the UN for the payment of damages and war reparations; and (d) payment of part of the receipts from the sale of oil to the UN Inter-Agency Humanitarian Programme for direct distribution by it in the northern (mainly Kurdish) provinces of Iraq.

Serious discussions to this end started with Iraq shortly thereafter, but it was an agonizingly slow process. It was not until the end of May 1996, more than one year after the adoption of Resolution 986 by the Security Council, that a Memorandum of Understanding was signed by Hans Corell, UN Under-Secretary-General and Dr. Abdul Amir Al-Anbari, Iraq's Ambassador to the UN, who had, it must be said, exercised his considerable diplomatic skills with great dignity throughout the difficult period.

The Memorandum of Understanding dealt mainly with procedural matters for the procurement and distribution of the humanitarian supplies involved. It was followed in August 1996 by a letter from the Chairman of the so-called "661 Committee" to the President of the Security Council, mainly setting out detailed procedures for the oil-sales permitted under Resolution 986, which were to be handled by the Iraqi State Oil Marketing Organization (SOMO).

Several sales contracts were signed and approved by the UN, transportation facilities repaired and brought back into usable condition, and the pipeline from the Iraqi Kirkuk fields to the Turkish export terminal at Ceyhan began to function once more in mid-December 1996, six and a half years after the invasion of Kuwait. The line would initially carry about 450 kbd of Iraqi crude; Iraq would export the rest of its "allowable" via the Mina Al Bakr terminal in the south, on the Persian Gulf, plus about 90 kbd of "exempted" crude (exempted from the ceiling of $1 billion worth of oil) for export to Jordan in payment of debt due and food imports from Jordan.

In June 1997, the first period of 180 days for Iraqi exports was renewed, to 4 December, not without some wrangling over conditions, and continued thereafter via a process of periodic renewals, including the raising of the allowable value to $5.26 billion in early 1998. Iraq was initially unable to fill this quota at the then prevailing prices because its producing facilities had been degraded from lack of maintenance and repairs. It was allowed to import supplies to restore its oilfields to better condition and upgrade producing capacity, but essentially every time the matter of export authorizations came up for renewal, the two sides engaged in some minor brinkmanship over conditions, usually to be resolved at the last hour or with only a short suspension of shipments.

Unfinished Business

Iraq, at the turn of the century and for some time thereafter, was high on the list of unfinished business. The oil part of that business, less dramatic than the UN's attempts to complete and tighten the arms-control agenda, or the protection of the Kurdish and Shi'a minorities, was characterized by increasing UN requirements for Iraqi oil to pay for war damages and the humanitarian "oil for food" (and medicine) program, pitted against the government's determination to do everything possible to evade sanctions, mainly by smuggling.

By 2000, the sanctions were in any case under attack on a broad front and no one except the United States and Britain believed they were achieving anything, or were likely to achieve anything in the future. There was a half-hearted attempt on the part of the United States to sharpen the sanctions so that they would inflict more pain on the Iraqi government and less on the Iraqi people, and a resolution designed to do just that was accordingly drawn up for submission to the UN Security Council in May 2000. Iraq immediately suspended all export shipments and in the face of an almost certain veto by Russia, the proposed resolution was withdrawn in July 2000, although there was some talk of reintroducing it in the wake of the terrorist attacks of 11 September 2001 in the United States and the start of the war in Afghanistan.

The Iraqi government's tenacity at chipping away at sanctions was manifested in other ways. The restrictions on the volume of exports was lifted by the UN in December 1999 (under Resolution 1284) as well as the ban on export routes other than the previously approved ones, via Turkey's Ceyhan port and the Iraqi gulf port of Mina Al Bakr. In fact, Iraq and Syria had already signed an agreement in August 1998 for the reopening of the existing pipeline from Iraq's northern fields to the Syrian export terminal of Banias. (The pipeline had been closed since the early 1980s.) Maintenance and repair work on the pipeline and pumping stations took some time, but in November 2000, there were reports that pumping through the line had started. Iraqi crude was then delivered to Syrian refineries, freeing up Syrian crude for export.

The next step was for Iraq to set its export prices at lower than fair market value, but demand a payment of $0.50/B. from purchasers, to be paid directly into Iraqi accounts and not the UN-controlled escrow account into which all export payments were supposed to go. This was to start in December 2000. Iraq's proposed prices for crude were not approved by the UN Sanctions Committee, and Iraq suspended all exports. A revised pricing formula was then submitted by Iraq to the Sanctions Committee which approved it even though it still appeared to be below "fair market value". Some companies were known to be making the surcharge payment to Iraq but there is, naturally enough, no published data on these nor their extent.

Inching Back

There was a long way to go to "normal" control over the oil industry by the Iraqi government. The UN Resolutions setting conditions for the export of Iraqi oil were at pains to emphasize that these should not be interpreted as in any way infringing on Iraqi sovereignty, requiring great skill in interpretative jujitsu, but the fact was that control (presumably the essence of sovereignty) over the industry was split. Exports were controlled by the UN, but not production. The import of oilfield equipment was controlled by the UN, but not oilfield maintenance. Foreign investments were embargoed by the UN, but not contracts for future investment. Iraq pushed on all fronts.

Export controls were circumvented to some extent by smuggling, through

Iran, Turkey and Syria. Estimates of the value of smuggled exports ran between $500 million and 1 billion dollars for the year 2001, but in the nature of things, these estimates were highly speculative. Oilfield maintenance and the resulting production capacity were in the hands of the Iraqis, and no one knew what capacity was, except that it certainly must have been significantly higher than the amounts required to produce sufficient for the domestic markets plus allowable exports, because enough was also being produced to cover substantial smuggled exports, estimated at around 450 kbd in 2001.

Production in the year 2001 was running at rates of up to 2.87 mbd at peak (much lower at times of serious dispute with the UN). About 0.45 mbd was for the domestic market, 0.08 for Jordan, and 1.85 mbd for other legal exports, leaving 0.45 mbd being smuggled out. Legal export sales were being made to a wide variety of buyers, Russian, Italian, French and Chinese. Much of the oil purchased by the Russian companies was resold, mostly to US companies which in 2000 accounted for about 600 kbd of Iraq's total exports. Buyers included ExxonMobil, Chevron, Koch, Phillips, Tosco, Citgo, Clark, Marathon, Ashland and others. In the meantime, contracts had been signed or were being negotiated with various foreign firms (non-US) for the development of Iraqi oilfields, but little work had started pending the lifting of UN sanctions. In addition, a pipeline to Jordan was agreed.

Stopping: Too Much, Too Soon

The most persistent criticism of US conduct of the Gulf War was that Saddam Hussein and his regime were left in power, with all the appalling consequences for ethnic minorities in Iraq, for the pursuit of weaponry, conventional and unconventional, by Iraq, and for the stability of the Middle East generally. Sanctions were not working and support for them dropped away, leaving the United States and Britain virtually isolated on the issue. And Saddam Hussein was still there, presumably rebuilding his arsenal of weapons of mass destruction.

The United States, it was repeatedly said, should have gone in and finished the job. Why didn't it?

The United States, rather confidently, bet that the people of Iraq would quickly get rid of Saddam Hussein after the war, and that some kind of regime would emerge that was strong enough to hold the country together and, ultimately, remain as a counterweight to Iran, but abandon its arms program and its aggressive policies towards Kuwait and Saudi Arabia. Here is Colin Powell on the subject:

> The UN Resolution [Resolution 678 of 29 November 1990] made clear that the mission was only to free Kuwait. However much we despised Saddam and what he had done, the United States had little desire to shatter his country. For the previous ten years, Iran, not

Iraq, had been our Persian Gulf nemesis. We wanted Iraq to
continue as a threat and counterweight to Iran. Our Arab allies did
not intend to set foot beyond Kuwait. Saudi Arabia did not want a
Shiite regime breaking off from Iraq in the South. The Turks did not
want a Kurdish regime splitting off from Iraq in the north . . . In
none of the meetings I attended was dismembering Iraq, conquering
Baghdad, or changing the Iraqi form of government ever seriously
considered. We hoped that Saddam would not survive the coming
fury. But his elimination was not a stated objective. What we hoped
for, frankly, in a postwar Gulf region was an Iraq still standing, with
Saddam overthrown.[11]

In March [1991], the Iraqi Shiites in the south rose up in arms to
demand more recognition from Baghdad. Saddam responded by
sending in his troops to suppress the uprising. In the north, the
Kurds tried to shake off the Iraqi yoke. Neither revolt had a chance.
Nor, frankly, was their success a goal of our policy. President Bush's
rhetoric urging the Iraqis to overthrow Saddam, however, may have
given encouragement to the rebels. But our practical intention was
to leave Baghdad enough power to survive as a threat to an Iran that
remained bitterly hostile toward the United States.[12]

Would it have been possible to have occupied Baghdad, overthrown the
Saddam Hussein regime and replaced it with a less obnoxious one, then
quickly withdrawn? Disregarding legal niceties such as the terms of the UN
resolutions, the United States could certainly have done that, but at the cost
of losing Arab support everywhere and probably Turkish and Russian support
as well. It is difficult to think that the situation the United States would have
left behind would have been the one they wanted.

In the end, a small defensive force was set up under the name of
Peninsula Shield. It numbered around 5,000 to 10,000 personnel from the
armed forces of the six states comprising the Gulf Cooperation Council, but
in addition, about 25,000 US military personnel remained stationed in the Gulf
region, including the units enforcing the no-fly zone over southern Iraq. Over
7,000 US military personnel remained in Saudi Arabia. Together with US
contractors' personnel and other civilians, the total number of Americans
stationed and working in Saudi Arabia was about 30,000 at the end of the year
2000.[13] Their continued presence there was high on the list of Osama Bin
Laden's grievances against the United States.

Chapter 16
OIL'S NEW WORLD

The commonly held view in recent years has been that the existing oil surplus will gradually be replaced by a growing tightness of supply which will exert upward pressure on prices. This is based on the expectation that world demand for oil will continue to expand, that non-OPEC supplies will fail to keep pace, and that imports into the free world from the communist bloc will at best be maintained at the present level.
– Petroleum Economist, October 1987, p358.

An Industry Challenged

Until the Iranian Revolution of 1979-80, it was possible to believe that the international petroleum industry might continue in a form that was at least a recognizable offspring of its former self, still dominated by the seven majors, now partly in partnership with the producing governments of OPEC countries, and enjoying price conditions that seemed more or less stable and acceptable to the consumer. The Iranian Revolution brought in its wake a second huge price increase that looked permanent at the time, and the near-total expulsion of the majors from their concessions in the Middle East. It became clear that the world of oil would be radically different from the past. A psychologically shattered industry would have to redeploy its incomparable human resources and its great financial assets to restructure its physical ones and redirect its strategies.

It may seem strange but is nevertheless true that, as innovators of policy and political initiatives, the seven majors were scarcely visible during the years from 1950 to 1973. These were years of extraordinary growth in the industry, and there was no question about what had to be done; deep thought and new policy directions were not required. Such as they were, company policies were confined to developing, consolidating and then hanging on to what they had, yielding afterwards only inch by reluctant inch. They generally advocated free trade and the virtues of the private sector, still questioned at the time; fretted about "low" prices and high taxes; and rallied around at times of crisis. But these were more attitudes than policies leading to specific action. To be sure, each company had its corporate objectives, policies and strategies—for example, BP was always painfully aware of its narrow base, and sought to

313

diversify—but it is impossible to discern, outside the United States, an industry-wide response to industry-wide challenges and opportunities.

By the early 1980s, the international petroleum industry, which by now meant something very different from just the seven majors, was confronted by broad challenges that were truly staggering—and which spelled opportunity for some newcomers. The industry now included a substantial number of sizable independents, the huge, newly born or greatly enlarged national oil companies (NOCs) of the OPEC and other exporting countries, and much larger state oil companies in importing countries (many soon to be privatized).

The industry now had to adapt to new conditions governing the major sources of supply; to the increasing transparency of prices; to the emergence of different product demand patterns; and, above all else, to much slower growth in demand. The companies themselves also had to become accustomed to dealing with each other in a different mix from before, and with a different market structure that included a strong and quite new dose of traders and speculators.

These were the strictly oil issues, but the industry would also have to face increasing pressure to work without damaging the environment; to comply everywhere with the highest ethical standards and to take on board the requirements of a new but ill-defined "corporate social responsibility". In the meantime, the investors were developing an increasingly voracious appetite for short-term returns, and tending to dismiss talk of "responsible" long-term investing as so much pie in the sky.

The Face of the Future

The seven majors and CFP would have viewed the loss of their concessions in the Middle East and other OPEC countries as a disaster before it actually happened. The concessions were, they and everyone else thought, their commercial backbone and most of their muscle combined. The downstream was merely the alchemy that turned the oil into gold; but you had to have the oil first.

When the loss actually occurred, the companies did indeed panic for a moment, trying to flee into a diversification that never had a chance of working. It did not, however, take them long to realize that the OPEC concessions, far from being backbone and muscle, were merely the fat on large and powerful bodies that had few rivals. They had formidable assets: organized know-how; and a well-established, though not invulnerable, position in diversified markets around the world with a network of refineries. They became huge net purchasers of crude oil but they also retained substantial diversified reserves and production of oil and gas which gained immeasurably in value through the high, OPEC-supported prices; and, with all this, sufficient cash flow and financial resources to pursue a vigorous program of research and exploration around the world. Only one of them—Gulf Oil—did not survive the loss of its OPEC concessions for very long. Another two were later to disappear, but for other reasons.

At the outset, however, things were not at all clear. Here is how Exxon, the largest company of all, saw the future. Its 1979 Annual Report (issued in Spring 1980) had the following passage, expressing views that were broadly shared by the industry at large:

> It seems clear that we have entered a period of energy transition. . .
> Some of the elements of that transition which will shape the 1980s
> are already discernible.
> – The world's need for energy will continue to grow, despite a
> slowdown in the rate of general economic growth . . . Some of this
> slower economic growth will be attributable to rising energy costs.
> – There will be a reduction in the intensity of energy consumption in
> industrialized countries . . . Conservation will be an important factor
> in this reduction, but it will also result from other efficiencies in the
> use of energy.
> – The balance between world energy demand and available supplies
> will be precarious.
> – Virtually all new petroleum reserves will be expensive to find and
> develop.
> – Coal and nuclear power . . . will have to meet the bulk of the
> growth in the world's energy requirements during the 1980s.
> – A synthetic fuels industry may emerge toward the end of the
> decade, primarily in North America.

Exxon was wrong about the world supply and demand balance, and about the emergence of an important synthetics fuels industry (so was nearly everyone else), but right on other matters. However, it was far from the whole story. Serious damage was done by misdirected investment on the part of a broad range of companies, based on the view that energy supplies would somehow be constrained. Matters became no clearer in the early 1980s despite the slide in prices towards eventual, though temporary, collapse in 1986. The passage from the *Petroleum Economist* of October 1987, quoted at the head of this chapter, is based on the same general expectations as Exxon's eight years earlier. It is a view that persisted for several years, though weakening greatly during the 1990s, and soon to be generally discredited.

The Markets: An End to Rapid Growth

But, in the supply-demand equation, the key changes have not been so much on the supply side (despite the majors' loss of their concessions and the emergence of the NOCs), but in demand and market structures.

The demand for oil has its own momentum, regardless of price. When prices increase sharply, the consumer has no sure way of knowing whether the increase is long term or whether it will soon be reversed. The car manufacturer cannot switch to production of more fuel-efficient engines overnight, in response to consumer demand or government regulation. The car-owner does not immediately scrap his gas-guzzler and rush out to buy a smaller car. Some electric power plants could switch to cheaper coal or gas quite rapidly, but many could not; and new power plants to take advantage of nuclear power have long construction lead-times. The expansion of public transportation systems do too, perhaps even more so. Regulatory measures imposing fuel-efficiency standards on new appliances and conservation standards on domestic and commercial buildings have an impact relatively slowly.

In other words, inertia of all sorts is built into a modern industrial society's energy consumption, and this makes initially for a deceptive price-inelasticity: the system is simply incapable of responding quickly to price increases in a technical way. It can, and does, respond more quickly on the income side: economies slow down and consumers consume less oil with the same equipment (planes, cars, trucks, boilers, household appliances, whatever), and when the technical and fuel-switching response comes along in addition, the resulting drop in demand can be massive, and it certainly was that in the post-1980 period.

World oil consumption kept right on growing after the large price increases of 1973-74, and did not reach its peak until 1979. The growth was, it is true, considerably slower than before, but it was still of sufficient magnitude to inspire the kind of fears for the future epitomized in Exxon's forecast: oil surpluses were at an end and prices would remain high forever.

World oil demand, outside the Centrally Planned Economies (CPEs) which were largely isolated at the time from market prices, had risen from 39 mbd in 1970 to 52 mbd in 1979 (nearly 4 percent per year) before much happened. This was a good deal lower than previous growth rates but still substantial. Disaster struck in the early 1980s. Total demand for energy dropped, and all of the decrease was absorbed by oil, especially as the heavy fuel oil market was wiped out, with electric utilities switching to coal and gas. In addition, the first crop of nuclear power plants was coming onstream. Other users of fuel oil also switched to coal or gas where they could, and the result was a total loss of 5 mbd within a few years—10 percent of world oil demand; 50 percent of world fuel oil demand. And that meant a barrel for barrel reduction in world crude oil production.

Demand (still excluding the CPEs) dropped from 52 mbd in 1979 to 46 mbd in 1983 before some slow recovery got underway, but it took six years for demand to climb back to 52 mbd, in 1989, at what, by the oil industry's previous standards, seemed to be the glacial rate of 2 percent per year. Since then, demand has risen more or less steadily at about the same pace, and stood at 65 mbd in 2000.

In the meantime, the CPEs were transformed. Eastern Europe broke away from Soviet political domination and joined the world's market economies; the Soviet Union itself simply collapsed, economically and politically, and some thirteen countries were spun off to lead independent lives. Almost half (about 140 million) of the Soviet Union's population went with them; what was left became the Russian Federation, still a country of formidable geographic size (almost twice as big as the United States), but a population barely larger than those of the United Kingdom and Germany combined, and an economy not much bigger at the time than that of the Netherlands. With the collapse of the economy went a collapse in oil demand – indeed scarcely one of the former CPEs experienced any growth in demand from 1990 to 2000: the FSU declined catastrophically—by about 60 percent.

In one respect, however, Russia remains a world-class player: it is the world's largest net exporter of oil (4 mbd in 2000) except for Saudi Arabia, and the largest net exporter of natural gas, bar none. It is therefore a force that the market and the OPEC cartel must reckon with.

China, however, is the gigantic exception to the decline of the CPEs since 1990. There, demand has more than doubled, to nearly 5 mbd, making it the world's third largest consumer of oil, and a major net importer (about 1.5 mbd in 2000).

All in all, then, the disintegration of the Soviet Union and the beatific conversion of China to capitalistic free enterprise virtues has had, considering the magnitude of the events, relatively little effect so far on the international oil industry's markets and marketing. No new markets have opened up except for increased exports to China, and that's about it. Industry restructuring, as far as markets are concerned, remains for the moment confined to the areas that were of concern before.

But to return to the structure of demand: if, as remarked above, inertia of all sorts is built into a modern industrial society's energy consumption to slow down its short-term response to sharp increases in the price of oil, the same is true, perhaps *a fortiori*, when prices drop sharply and stay down, slowly eroding further with inflation. Fuel-efficiency and conservation regulations, drawn up and passed into legislation with some sense of urgency, are not rescinded; nuclear power plants that would never have been built at the now lower prices prevailing, are not shut down and scrapped; and car manufacturers do not (are not allowed to) revert to making gas-guzzling engines, despite some loop-holes such as the sports utility vehicles (SUV). Mostly, the changes are irreversible; and so, the lower prices do not bring a resurgence in demand sparked by a return to the regulatory and technical past. Consumption increases more normally, in line with the growth in the economy and its reaction to lower oil prices. However, it may be remarked that in some countries, notably much of Western Europe, the price reductions were not reaching the consumer at all. Instead, governments were offsetting the decreases by increasing indirect taxes. This was notably the case of excise taxes on motor gasoline which, in some countries, actually rose by more than the drop in crude prices.

By and large, then, the growth in oil demand has moderated from previous levels, and the past fifteen to twenty years have witnessed a pace of increase of only 1 to 2 percent per year (compared with 7 percent per year during the greatest years of growth, from 1950 to 1973).

The Market: the Emergence of Prices

The major oil companies agreed in 1972 to the principle of "Participation" by the governments of OPEC member countries in their concessions. It meant that the governments would acquire an equity share in the concessionaire companies that accounted for nearly all of the crude production in their countries, a share that would increase over a period of time until it reached 51 percent in 1985. For a brief time, it was not clear how the governments would dispose of their crude entitlements under these agreements; so the agreements had buy-back clauses which provided for the government to opt for a sale of their share of crude production back to the companies. These fears were soon dissipated in the market panic that followed the political upheavals of 1973 and 1979-1980; the ante was upped on the participation share, and it soon became 100 percent, and the companies were left with no equity crude at all. The governments on the other hand found no trouble at first in selling all they could produce, and a spot market quickly emerged. At first, spot represented a premium over the governments' official selling prices, then, quite quickly, a discount off them.

The pricing mechanism that the OPEC governments at first chose for their crude oil sales was a carbon copy of the old "posted price" system used by the majors since the early 1950s, and suffered from all the same defects—most particularly widespread discounting when the market weakened. The new system entailed the adoption by the governments of "official selling prices" or "government selling prices" (OSPs or GSPs) which were supposed to be coordinated within the OPEC circuit in such a way as to be consistent with differences in quality and transportation cost-differentials.

The system worked poorly, and after the price crash of 1985-86 (which came for reasons not related to the pricing mechanism itself), a system of production quotas was adopted, in early 1987. This soon led to the final and welcome demise of the GSP/OSP system and its replacement by evergreen or serial-spot supply contracts at formula-derived prices set monthly by the selling governments. (See below.)

In the meantime, spot markets for crude oil had been flourishing, and with them, of course, considerable price-transparency in the publicly reported prices at which the now numerous spot sales were concluded. The emergence of the spot markets owed much to the availability of substantial and growing volumes of oil from North Sea fields. North Sea oil was produced by a large number of companies, majors and independents, integrated and non-integrated, many of whom needed to sell because they were not themselves refiners and marketers. Importantly, the British National Oil Corporation (BNOC), which was not a refiner, had substantial quantities of oil to sell which it received from the participation agreements that had been imposed by the British government on the producing companies. But the other companies, integrated refiners, including the majors, also had a keen interest in the development of the spot market because the UK fiscal system required (or strongly encouraged) the use of arm's-length crude oil sales prices in the establishment of values for the taxation of ring-fenced sales by producing to refining affiliates within the same company.

By the mid-1980s, North Sea crudes, particularly Brent (or, more accurately, Brent blend, a mixture of crudes from different fields), were a major feature of an increasingly price-transparent market. It was a new kind of market for the oil industry in two senses.

First, it was no longer a spot market in the established sense of the term: trading was already far removed from the occasional one-off cargo which companies would sell and buy to balance out supply and demand at the margin. It had become, rather, over the years since 1979-80, a feature of the mainstream supply channel, constituted to a large extent of serial spot transactions, and functioning through standardized contract terms, notably "Dated Brent" transactions, each for the sale of a single cargo to be delivered within an agreed date range at a price specified in dollars per barrel.

Second, Brent became a "marker" crude: the contract prices of other crudes came to be fixed by reference to the price of Brent, subject to appropriate adjustments for quality and location. This was no longer a spot price that could be represented as an aberration, reflecting the special and transitory circumstances of an isolated buyer or seller, barely connected to the prices at which the vast majority of oil sales were made; on the contrary, it was this price, the price of Brent (or the similar prices that were emerging for West Texas in the United States and Dubai in the Persian Gulf) that became the basis for prices throughout international crude markets. Nothing like it had ever existed in the industry before.

Side by side with the emergence, for the first time, of a significant open market for crude oil (one where the prices of a large number of transactions between arm's-length buyers and sellers were promptly reported and became known), a forward market also emerged. The Dated Brent market dealt entirely in transactions for oil (wet barrels) physically delivered by the seller to the buyer. Another type of Brent transaction also developed—the 15-day Brent, a contract for the purchase and sale of oil at a date at least fifteen days after the date of the transaction, and typically anywhere up to three months after that date. This was forward trading that could result in physical delivery of the oil but did not necessarily do so. Forward trading was developed and with it came the financial trading instruments which were a feature of other commodity markets—futures, options and a panoply of derivatives—the paper markets dealing in "paper" barrels. The markets themselves became interrelated, Dated Brent influenced by 15-day Brent and the futures market.

Futures were developed over several years, the first ones for oil products being introduced by the New York Mercantile Exchange (NYMEX) for gasoil in 1978 and the International Petroleum Exchange (IPE) in 1981. Crude oil futures contracts were a later arrival, with a West Texas Intermediate (WTI) contract launched in 1983 by NYMEX and a Brent contract in 1988 by the IPE.

With the growing markets, a flourishing service of price-reporting sprang up of which the most prominent, reliable and hard-data oriented was *Petroleum Argus* and its affiliated publications. But there were others, notably the long-established Platt's *Oilgram* and *Price Service*, and these were joined over time by more, functioning first by telex and then increasingly available online.

Thus, the 1980s were pivotal years for the development of market prices that you could see, hear, touch and feel. For a number of reasons noted above, the action centered around the North Sea Brent crude, and, to a lesser extent, West Texas Intermediate (WTI) and Alaska North Slope (ANS) in the United States, and Dubai in the Gulf. The circumstances were indeed peculiar and unusual for the oil industry—the number of companies involved in the North Sea, the presence of BNOC, the fiscal regime in the UK, the volumes of crude involved, etc. It is already difficult to imagine the oil industry today without the price-transparent markets that have developed. And one of the most extraordinary features of this development was the absence of any contribution to it by OPEC or any other major crude supplier to the international markets, such as Mexico or the Soviet Union.

OPEC: The Change to Formula-Pricing, 1987-88

The emergence of real and reliable, visible and verifiable, independently market-determined crude oil prices, published daily, was a god-send to OPEC. They provided, just when it was most needed, an escape-hatch from the fixed price system that OPEC had previously clung to, with unworkable differentials and its heavy reliance on a swing country.

After the debacle and price crash of 1986, OPEC had painfully patched together a new agreement complete with production quotas and a fixed-price reference point of $18/B. for its "basket" of crude oils. Arabian Light crude was priced at $17.52 f.o.b. Ras Tanura, and other OPEC crudes were priced consistently with it.

Why Saudi Arabia or anyone else in OPEC imagined that a fixed-price system would work now when it had just led to disaster in the previous year is a bit of a mystery. It had, for several reasons, become impossible to maintain a system of fixed official selling prices, among them being the fact that oil markets were increasingly taking on the characteristics and functions of regular commodity markets, incompatible with the rigidities inherent in fixed pricing. But the most vulnerable aspect of the fixed price system was the fact that its maintenance was entirely dependent on one or more OPEC members acting as swing suppliers, that is to say, allowing their output to fall in order to support official prices at times of market weakness. And, despite its loud denials, Saudi Arabia did in fact almost immediately resume that role for a short period in the first quarter of 1987 (as Yamani, now out of office, had warned) in what was evidently a last-gasp attempt to shore up the newly reinstated fixed official-price system.

It did not carry the burden for long. By September 1987, under threat from its main customers in the Aramco group (Exxon, Mobil, Texaco and Chevron) that Saudi crude liftings could no longer be sustained at contract levels unless the fixed price was replaced by market-related pricing, an arrangement was reached, under cover of the strictest secrecy, providing for the adoption of prices related to spot prices for Alaska North Slope (ANS) crude for deliveries to the Western Hemisphere, Brent for deliveries to Europe and Oman/Dubai for deliveries to the Far East.

There was, of course, no possibility of keeping the secret for long, and the arrangement was openly confirmed in January 1988. Faced with the impossibility of selling any oil at all at official prices, the rest of OPEC soon shifted to market-related pricing, adopting formulas based, like Saudi prices, on benchmark spot price indicators in various markets. By the end of the first quarter of 1988, the fixed price system had sunk, leaving hardly a trace. The new system, with some refinements, notably the discarding of ANS as a reference price and its replacement by West Texas Intermediate (WTI), has lasted ever since.

Generally speaking, Saudi Arabia's crude prices were set monthly in advance in accordance with a formula in which the only indeterminate element was an adjustment factor based largely on quality and freight differentials as well as an assessment of the strength or weakness of the market at the time. For example, the price for Arabian Light for delivery to Europe during a given month was set at Dated Brent, whatever that turned out to be on the delivery date during the month, plus or minus an *ad hoc* adjustment factor of x cents per barrel. Other crudes followed the Saudi prices, with variations on the precise formula used.

An odd but surprisingly durable system had emerged. World crude oil prices were now being set by reference to the prices of the "marker" crudes—Brent, WTI, Dubai. Sellers, starting most importantly with Saudi Arabia, hung their prices on these pegs. But what determined the prices of the marker crudes? Supply and demand, to be sure. And supply was determined at the margin by whatever OPEC chose to produce (or, more accurately, not to produce). So OPEC ended up indirectly controlling the market prices of the marker crudes.

The control was, and remains, long-distance, erratic, imprecise and unpredictable—but, in the end, very real. OPEC cannot calibrate prices with any precision, nor within a set time-frame. It depends entirely on increasing or decreasing supply at the margin, and then waiting to see what happens. If the market's reaction does not produce the desired target price (or overshoots it), supply is decreased further (or increased). The system is slow, clumsy, partly dependent on necessarily inaccurate demand forecasts, and bedeviled by indiscipline within OPEC's ranks. But, by and large, it works.

Within this system, OPEC's initial target price in 1987 was $18/B., which it hoped to achieve by reducing overall production sufficiently to influence the price of the marker crudes, but apart from a few months during the Gulf War of 1990-91, it never managed to reach that goal more than sporadically until 1996. It only averaged $14 in 1988, strengthened somewhat thereafter as OPEC quota discipline improved, then, after the Gulf War in 1990-91, it hit the target (during 1992) but fell back to well under $18 for the next three years, through 1995. Prices then recovered in 1996 (the average basket equaled $20.29 during the year) and continued relatively strong in 1997, until the end of the year. OPEC overconfidence then led it to loosen quotas—just as the economies of Southeast Asia were rushing into recession. Prices collapsed, and averaged only $12.32 in 1998. OPEC, it seemed, had lost control once more.

But OPEC had been written off so many times since its establishment in 1960 that it should have come as no surprise when it suddenly swung into action once more in April 1999 and, with a bit of help from Mexico and other non-OPEC suppliers, cut production by a targeted 1.7 mbd and raised prices to their highest level since 1981, $31/B. Of course, not surprisingly, what had started out as an effort merely to restore prices to a range of $18 to $20/B. soon lost its appeal and in March 2000 the unofficial target range was raised to $22 - $28/B., with an "automatic" adjustment factor consisting of a 500 kbd increase if the OPEC basket price rose above $28 for a sustained period, and a similar decrease if it dropped below $22/B. These were the figures and objectives mooted in OPEC at the time, and in some circles they were taken as an OPEC commitment, but they were never that. It would indeed have been rash for OPEC (or Saudi Arabia, to be more precise) to make any such commitment which could entrain unforeseen consequences, and might have to be exercised (or reneged on) when unforeseen circumstances arose. Understandings on price would later be reached behind closed doors between the two most important players, the United States and Saudi Arabia.

The Industry: Life in the Slow Lane

The end of rapid growth in demand was perhaps the greatest challenge of all to the industry, greater, I think, than the loss of their upstream assets in the OPEC area. Companies generally look to growth for the increasing prosperity of their shareholders—and the oil industry was accustomed to a very large helping of it. Company managements rightly detest stagnation, because their shareholders want (for a variety of reasons, including tax ones) growth above all, more than current dividends, and when they don't get it, they start to look elsewhere. A no-growth company is a failure, doomed to a falling share price and thus vulnerable to takeover and perhaps dismemberment, or, even worse, to slow decline and extinction.

With demand stagnant or growing only slowly, a company's path to growth must therefore be by streamlining operations, a process that can take several years; or by the acquisition of other companies; or by competing with other companies and taking markets from them; or by going into new areas.

Streamlining

The buzz word, or phrase of the day in the mid-1970s became "core business", on which the companies resolved to concentrate. That meant oil, gas and chemicals. All of the major companies hived off operations that were peripheral to the company's overall business (not a "good fit"), did not contribute much to profits, had little potential for growth, and took too much management time.

First to go were the non-energy ventures into which companies had rashly plunged in an effort to diversify; next were the non-oil and gas energy operations; then the peripheral oil and gas operations. Actually, some of all three categories was being shed simultaneously, but it was a rough order of priorities, and today's major international oil companies now have no operations of much significance outside their oil, gas and chemical "core". In 2001, for example, ExxonMobil earned a mere three percent of its net profits from non-core business (coal and copper), and the company was in the process of selling its remaining coal interests.

The effects of "streamlining" were most striking on the companies' direct employment. The numbers were difficult to credit. In 1980, the five US majors employed a total of 556,000 people worldwide; in 1999, the five (by then merged into three, soon to be two) were down to 161,000. Net assets per employee had gone from $143,000 in 1980 to $580,000 in 1999—and there was more (or, rather, less) to come. True, it is impossible to tell what the overall impact on employment was, because some of the operations which had previously been undertaken directly by the companies themselves were now being out-sourced, and the numbers employed by the industry's contractors must have increased (though they themselves were doing some of their own out-sourcing, and so on, down the pyramid).

Nevertheless, the direct and indirect payroll savings must have been very considerable, or they would not have been pursued with such vigor, and the savings seem to have come largely from the jettisoning of peripheral operations (along with their employees), shedding fat in the core operations, making the remaining employees work harder and longer, and the computerization of operations and administration.

Acquisitions and Concentration

A second, sometimes overlapping, path to growth was through the acquisition of other companies. In the oil industry, there have been innumerable acquisitions and mergers over the past twenty years. In the early 1980s, the *Oil & Gas Journal* started listing annual data on the 400 top publicly traded oil companies in the United States (the *OGJ400*). The list shrank to the *OGJ300* in 1991, then to the *OGJ200* in 1996, and the listing for the year 2001 fell below 200 companies. Part of this may reflect the sharp decline in US production, with the remains of some of the smallest companies simply being swept up into larger entities; others were the victims of the price-crash of 1985-86 and disappeared altogether; most were, by oil industry standards, pathetically small, each with total assets (in 1986) under $500 million. (The total number of companies of this size made up over 300 of the *OGJ400* in 1986.)

But by far the most significant part of the shrinkage in numbers came at the top end of the list. Of the top ten US companies in 1986 (ranked by total assets), only four survived as independent entities into the year 2002. Mobil, Texaco, Amoco, Arco, Tenneco and Sohio had all been taken over by others.

Among the most voracious hunter-gatherers was BP, which started off in 1987 by completing its acquisition of Sohio, paying £4.7 billion ($7.5 billion) for the 45 percent of the company's shares that it did not already own. (Sohio—Standard Oil (Ohio) as it was officially called—owned important producing interests in Alaska, four refineries in the United States and a substantial marketing position in certain areas of the country.) BP then went on to acquire Britoil, in 1987 and 1988, for a total of £2.8 billion ($4.5 billion). Britoil was one of the offshoots of the privatized British National Oil Corporation (BNOC), and had producing interests and attractive undeveloped acreage in the North Sea. A few years of digestion and consolidation were followed in 1998 by a merger with Amoco to form a new company, BP Amoco, owned 60 percent by former BP shareholders and 40 percent by former Amoco stock holders. Amoco was a huge company in its own right, producing nearly 700 kbd of oil in the United States and abroad, refining about one million bd, and selling 1.6 mbd of products plus substantial quantities of natural gas. From a management point of view, however, the merger was a takeover; within a couple of years, "Amoco" had been dropped from the merged company's name, which reverted to being just "BP". In any event, it was now twice the size of its former self, with net assets at the end of 1998 of $43 billion.

In 1999, the new, bigger BP went on to acquire the Atlantic Richfield Company—ARCO—for $31 billion. ARCO was another very large company, producing (like Amoco) nearly 700 kbd of oil at the time, in Alaska, the Lower

48, and outside the United States; and had refineries and markets in the United States, mainly on the West Coast. Finally, Burmah Castrol was another large BP acquisition during the year.

By the end of 2001, BP's net assets stood at $66 billion, and it was producing nearly 2 mbd and refining 3 mbd worldwide. It had become the largest producer of hydrocarbon liquids and natural gas in the United States, and the second largest refiner.

Other mega-mergers are just as impressive: in 1999, Exxon and Mobil merged into a single company—ExxonMobil Corporation. Mobil's shareholders received 30 percent of the shares of the new company with Exxon shareholders in effect retaining the remaining 70 percent. Like the BP-Amoco deal, it was in substance a takeover, the formal merger aspect of it being merely the manner of payment. In fact, Exxon management took over and Mobil's simply disappeared except for a few survivors that remained as officers of the new, merged entity. Unlike the BP-Amoco deal, however, Exxon was taking over a company that operated in areas worldwide with which it was already familiar and had operations itself. In addition, it had had many joint operations with Mobil, either through partnerships, notably Stanvac (which had for many years operated in South and Southeast Asia in integrated operations) and in jointly-owned producing operations in the Middle East, notably in Iran, Iraq and Saudi Arabia. BP's takeover of Amoco was quite different in nature: Amoco's operations were to a much larger extent, both in the United States and elsewhere, in different areas: Amoco was a real add-on for BP, and not the absorption of a close relative.

In any event, ExxonMobil retained its position as the world's largest oil company. Its net assets jumped from $43 billion at the end of 1998 to $71 billion at the end of 2000. Crude production worldwide jumped from 1.6 mbd to 2.5 mbd, and refinery runs from 3.9 mbd to 5.6 mbd.

The third mega-merger—Chevron's takeover of Texaco—was again quite different from the first two. Both Amoco and Mobil (as well as ARCO) could probably have survived as prosperous, well-run companies on their own account, with coherent operations and strategies. Their takeover was not the result of terminal weakness, but much more a recognition of the likelihood that their shareholders could do even better from melding into larger entities. Texaco, on the other hand, had become a mangled mess of a giant, had been in and out of Chapter 11 bankruptcy proceedings, run up a colossal debt between the cost of acquisitions (Getty Oil), fending off a hostile takeover bid (Bass Brothers), paying damages to Pennzoil in a case brought by the latter for tortious interference in contract negotiations, and expensive restructuring and legal fees. It had had to sell off some of its best assets (Texaco Canada, Deutsche Texaco and a 50 percent share in much of its US downstream refining and marketing facilities) to pay off debt. By 1999, it had recovered somewhat, though a shadow of its former self; it still had some valuable assets, such as its highly profitable producing operations in Angola, but now had practically no wholly-owned operations and its prospects for growth were poor.

In 2001, Chevron took it over. Chevron had already taken in one international major, Gulf, in 1984, which at the time was staggering toward dismemberment at the hands of T. Boone Pickens, president of a small US domestic producer, Mesa Oil Company, bidding for Gulf's shares on the basis of a plan to strip and sell off the company's assets for a total value considerably in excess of value to shareholders at the time.

Now Chevron acquired the remains of Texaco, and its net assets rose by 70 percent, to $34 billion. It knew the company well. Chevron and Texaco had a long history of joint ventures through their jointly-owned subsidiary, Caltex, which had important producing, refining and marketing operations in South and South-East Asia, Australia and Europe (a sort of twin to Stanvac). In addition, Chevron had been a partner with Texaco and other majors in the principal concessions and producing operations in Saudi Arabia and Iran.

Other large acquisitions included Phillips Petroleum Company's acquisition of Conoco and USX/Marathon's acquisition of Ashland, an independent, non-integrated refiner.

In Europe, Total (successor to CFP Compagnie Française des Pétroles), the "eighth major", first took over the privatized state oil company Elf Aquitaine towards the end of 1999, then the Belgian refiner/marketer PetroFina in 2000, and renamed itself TotalFinaElf. With net assets of 32.4 billion euros at the end of 2000, net earnings of 6.9 billion euros in 2000 and worldwide refining capacity of 2.5 mbd, it had become the world's fifth largest oil company.

Whatever happened to Antitrust? Not so long ago, mergers on this scale, particularly in the oil industry, would have been inconceivable. The US Department of Justice would never, in, say, the 1960s, have given the green light for Exxon to take over Mobil, nor for Chevron to take over Texaco. But attitudes to bigness in business had changed radically. Size and market share were not necessarily seen as bad: fewer and larger players in a given industry were seen as sometimes creating more efficient markets and benefitting consumers by keeping prices low. Size *per se* was no longer seen as harmful unless prices were likely to go up as a result. Antitrust regulators in the second Bush administration, for example, were reported as being "particularly vocal in telling competitors of large players not to expect help just because a rival gets even bigger."[1] By the same token, there seemed to be some recognition (perhaps misplaced) of the need to create larger units capable of competing globally (as if that had not been the case before, in the oil industry).

Competition

Nevertheless, companies are sensitive to the charge of suppressing competition through their mega-mergers, and they were at pains to stress, in their justification of them, that they would be better able to compete in the global economy once merged; or, that they *needed* to merge, in order to survive in a "more competitive global economy".

Of course, the mergers do nothing to increase competition; that can scarcely be done by eliminating an actual or potential competitor. But the suppression of competitors was not the primary purpose of the mergers either. For BP, the acquisition of Sohio, Amoco and ARCO was the gateway to its long-desired expansion into the United States, and the diversification of the company operations. The acquired companies had not been significant competitors with BP. Chevron picked up two lame ducks when it acquired first Gulf, then Texaco, albeit ducks—or geese—with one or two golden eggs still inside them, and certainly not competitive threats. Exxon's acquisition of Mobil might have raised raise more eyebrows, but they tended to operate in different markets, and Mobil was scarcely much of a threat to Exxon.

However, none of the companies saw aggressive competition as the road to expansion in an essentially low-growth market, which is not surprising. The history of the international petroleum industry is of partnerships, joint ventures, risk-sharing, and, to some extent, government regulation in the market-place inimical to all-out competition. Joint operations in one form or another have been the rule rather than the exception in the upstream, from the Middle East, the rest of the OPEC area, developing countries generally and the North Sea. Nor is the situation much different in refining, outside the United States and Canada: jointly-owned refineries abounded in Europe, Japan and elsewhere. In some cases (notably Caltex), these partnerships extended downstream into marketing.

In these circumstances, competition among the large international companies may not be entirely absent, but it does not consist of cutting your upstream partner's throat when you get into refining and marketing downstream. And no one tried it.

New Areas

Going into new areas was a different way to restructure and expand. All large companies were now dependent on the purchase of some (usually a large part) of their crude requirements, essentially at OPEC prices, and mostly from OPEC countries. OPEC prices meant volatility, but at levels likely to be considerably higher than the cost of producing and delivering oil from almost anywhere else to the markets. The big money was still in the raw material—oil or marketable gas—and all of the companies wanted to replace as much as they could of the reserves that they had lost during the OPEC takeovers, as well as to replenish from other sources their waning reserves of crude oil in the United States.

This did not appear to them as a necessary restructuring: the majors and some other companies had been exploring in many areas throughout the world long before; it just became more attractive, first because any oil discovered would be equity oil; second, because it was not subject to OPEC's sporadic production restraints; and third, because OPEC would provide a price-umbrella under which it could be profitably developed. The search for, and development of, non-OPEC oil were at a premium, and in fact non-OPEC production in many different areas surged ahead.

In practice, truly "new areas" meant, first and foremost, the former Soviet Union (FSU) which was the main new area holding promise of big oil. Political risk was particularly high because it also attached to the problem of transportation from the producing fields to the port of export. All of the majors and a good handful of other companies accordingly took positions in Russia and various other FSU countries, notably the most promising of all, Kazakhstan. But there were other new areas. In some (such as Chad and Sudan) oil had been discovered but not developed for a number of reasons, mostly political; others were genuinely new (such as Equatorial Guinea); still others were "new" in the sense of new fields in older areas (deeper reservoirs in the Gulf of Mexico; smaller fields in the North Sea), and these benefitted from existing infrastructure.

However, all in all, there was no replacing the OPEC area, and an outstanding feature of the new, restructured industry was the high proportion of arm's-length crude oil purchases that refiners now had to make from OPEC national oil companies.

New areas can also mean new activities, and among the chief one taken up by many oil companies, including notably the multinationals, is trading. Trade or supply sales now figure prominently among many companies' operations, and product sales now far exceed the products available to a company from its own refineries. They are products which are bought and resold only partly because the company's direct marketing is larger than its refineries; many of them are bought for resale to other oil companies, or large oil marketers and large unbranded resellers. In 2001, for example, ExxonMobil's sales of this sort (identified as "Supply Sales" in its accounts) totaled 2.6 mbd; BP's amounted to 2.4 mbd. But there is so far no indication in the companies' published accounts of the contribution these activities make to net earnings.

The Limits to Growth

These strategies have worked for some companies, but, apart from the acquisition of reserves and production in essentially new areas, they have to be viewed as "shakeout" strategies: they cannot continue indefinitely for all. There is a limit to the cost-cutting and streamlining a company can do, though technology will no doubt continue to surprise for a time. There is a limit to takeovers for international companies of a significant size: there aren't many left. And there is a limit to new areas where international oil companies can expand, although it may still be some way off. But in the longer term, the road to growth has to be in the market-place, in growing demand—not something the industry can influence significantly so long as OPEC continues to favor a high-price objective that, in effect, sets or strongly influences the price of energy for the whole world.

For individual companies, the only alternative is competition—taking market share from someone else. But so far, in international oil's big league, no one has ever died of competition.

The Industry: Companies

The outcome of the many mergers and acquisitions noted above, of the majors' loss of their concessions in the OPEC area, of the collapse of the Soviet Union, the worldwide rush to privatization, and the commoditization of oil was, of course, a mix of companies vastly different from what had gone before.

The Multinationals

Multinationals are companies that have a significant proportion of their exploration, oil and gas producing, oil refining, chemical and marketing operations in several different countries. In the industry, they are now usually referred to as IOCs—international oil companies. Today, there are only five large ones left: BP, ChevronTexaco, ExxonMobil, Shell and TotalFinaElf. As a rough definition, these are companies that have significant production in fifteen countries or more, refine in fifteen countries or more, and market in forty countries or more. Between them, they account for roughly 13 percent of world production, 21 percent of world refining, and 35 percent of world product sales. They are of course nowhere near as well vertically integrated as before the OPEC takeover, but no other company comes anywhere near matching the (admittedly somewhat arbitrary) geographical spread of operations noted above. For example, Phillips, the third largest US oil company (not including BP or Shell), had nearly 90 percent of its crude oil production in just two countries, the United States and Norway, and amounts ranging from small to negligible in seven others. It had almost no refining or product marketing interests outside the United States, and its acquisition of Conoco did little to diversify its geographical spread.

Other large companies that operated and had significant production in more than one country included Amerada Hess, Anadarko, Conoco (soon to be taken over by Phillips), ENI/Agip, Kerr McGee, Occidental, Repsol, and Unocal. However, outside their home countries, their interests were mostly confined to one or two countries, notably in the North Sea, and Indonesia, and they had scant refining and marketing operations.

True, the Five are a shadow of their former (Seven) selves in some respects, notably crude oil production, but they still dominate the *international* aspects of the industry—indeed, they still *are* the international industry; others look quite parochial by comparison, even if the parishes are sometimes large.

National Oil Companies and Other Major Exporters

The large national oil companies (NOCs), mostly the companies that took over from the seven majors in the OPEC Countries, plus Pemex in Mexico, and Petronas in Malaysia, are very large in terms of production and some of them are substantial in refining, but they are, for the most part, just what they say they are—national—and, with the exception of Petroleos de Venezuela (PDVSA) and Saudi Aramco, they have virtually no refining or marketing operations outside their own countries. But between them, they account for about one-third of world crude production.

Apart from these, there are other large exporting companies, most of them now privatized former state-owned corporations (or offshoots of them). The principal ones are the Russian companies such as Lukoil, Yukos, Sibneft and others. Through privatization, the mix of their shareholders is complex, with substantial holdings by non-Russian companies and institutions. The nine largest produce over 6 mbd among them (8 percent of world production) and export over 2 mbd. They have scant holdings or operations outside the FSU. Other large export companies include notably the Norwegian companies, Statoil and Norsk Hydro.

Others

Companies not in the first two groups cover a vast array; what they have in common, however, is that they are all primarily oriented toward operations in a single importing country, which is their home country. Some of them are very large, such as the Chinese national companies, producing over 2 mbd and refining over 4 mbd, Petrobras in Brazil, producing over 400 kbd and refining about 1,500 kbd, and India's Oil & Natural Gas Corporation, producing about 500 kbd.

Apart from Petrobras, which has substantial direct investment interests in the oil industry outside of Brazil, most of them have little inclination to operate abroad on a large scale. True, it is always tempting to go upstream and try to secure your own crude oil sources abroad. But it is a long haul, requiring stamina and money—and many are called, but few are chosen. This does not mean that they do not have important international concerns: they buy substantial quantities of crude and products from abroad and therefore have a strong, almost vital, interest in international markets.

There are also innumerable small producers, and over 50 refiners in the United States, well over 100 refining companies outside the United States, and countless traders, distributors, jobbers, bulk storage owners and retailers.

The Industry: Peripherals

Corporate Social Responsibility (CSR)

Multinationals at the turn of the century were under public scrutiny as never before. Their role was no longer accepted, or regarded as acceptable, if exclusively concerned with profit, and large, vocal segments of the public in special-interest non-governmental organizations (NGOs), as well as some governments and international organizations now appear to believe that these companies must shoulder obligations beyond what is required of them by law, with respect to the environment, with respect to ethical behavior, and with respect to the fostering of "sustainable" economic development and the promotion of social justice, including of course human rights, all now deemed part and parcel of a newly devised "corporate social responsibility" (CSR). A few business leaders agree, more in Europe than the United States, with varying degrees of enthusiasm; many others simply accept the need to do, with good grace, what has to be done (but not much more) to qualify as good corporate citizens.

Large oil companies—the multinationals in particular—have long accepted that they should do enough in their communities to cultivate a generally good image and that their behavior everywhere should conform to high ethical and environmental standards. It matters little whether this is done primarily out of "enlightened self-interest", or because company managements are composed of ordinary human beings who care about these things as much as the next guy (and perhaps cared as little about them as the next guy did fifty or sixty years ago). But faced with these demands—some new, some merely intensified—managers have trodden warily, as well they might. No one wants to see his company's products boycotted or the company name vilified (with in addition some unpleasant innuendo about the personal morality of those in charge).

Nevertheless, the primary function of companies is to be economically productive—that is, to make money—by harnessing the capital of its shareholders and the knowhow of its employees in their chosen field. They may do it well or poorly; conscientiously or unscrupulously; wisely or rashly, but in the end there is only one bottom line: investors invest for the sole purpose of financial return. Their other objectives are best pursued by other means.

The function of government, on the other hand, is to provide an adequate regulatory infrastructure for companies to work as economically productive units, and to make sure they do not swindle the public, exploit their workers, pollute their surroundings, prosecute their business unethically, or do anything else that is morally or socially reprehensible, including allowing management to enrich itself illegitimately and defraud the shareholders. On the whole, governments in the "West" have learned to do this quite well, despite occasional spectaculars to the contrary.

Companies may wish to go beyond their legal obligations, and usually do, in pursuing their corporate social responsibilities, but there is a financial cost and there are financial limits which currently seem to be around one percent of net profits (not including necessary environmental costs which must be reckoned separately and depend to a large extent on the company's particular circumstances). But if voluntary gifts and grants for civic and community services, education, the arts and other items goes much higher, investors will no doubt seek to put the brakes on. As for the political role being urged on multinationals with respect to human rights and the promotion of sustainable development (the definition of which soon becomes political), it holds the potential for more harm than good.

Corporate Power

The oil industry got its bad name mainly because of unscrupulous business dealings based on monopolistic strength (John D. Rockefeller and his Standard Oil Trust being the chief perpetrators), price-gouging in the market, and the widespread impression that oil companies enjoyed too much power, were able to influence government excessively, and manipulated international markets in world-embracing deals splendidly concocted in Scottish castles, between bouts of grouse-shooting, by the chairmen of huge companies. The deals have disappeared, but the public, both in the United States and Western Europe, remains convinced that the large multinationals, especially in oil, retain undue power over governments, and that it is exercised (among other ways) to promote legislation favoring the industry and subverting the broader public interest. Indeed, there are few areas where the general public's perception of the corporate power of multinational oil companies is so at variance with the facts—laughably so, for anyone remotely familiar with the amount of management time devoted to complying with the (sometimes unduly burdensome) oceans of governmental regulations applying to their companies. Obviously, some lobbying is done—industry views have to be conveyed somehow to the powers that be—but in today's world, as practiced by the multinationals, it is for the most part no longer either sinister or corrupt. Tellingly, in the long list of large-company scandals, pillage and corruption during recent years, the private-sector multinational oil companies have been notably absent.

But the issue of corporate power has in recent times yielded pride of place as a matter of public concern to the environment.

The Environment

Oil pollutes. It pollutes when spilled accidentally, it pollutes when discharged deliberately at sea (as tankers flush their tanks of unwanted residues), and it pollutes when burnt as fuel.

Public concern over the environment has risen steadily during the past fifty years and some of it has, rightly, focused on oil spillages. Regulations have been introduced to prevent spillages as far as possible, often with stiff penalties attached. Companies, fearful of bad publicity and a bad reputation even more than the penalties, have reacted sharply, and most, especially the large internationals, no doubt do as best they can to prevent spillages. This doesn't need any special measure of "good citizenship" or the like: the costs incurred avoiding spillages are usually much less than the cost of the penalties involved and the bad publicity engendered.

The world consumed about 70 million barrels per day at the turn of the century, much of it produced offshore under hazardous conditions and all of it having to be transported from the point of production to the point of consumption–a journey, whether short or long, involving its transfer, several times, from one kind of physical facility to another. Spillages are and always were inevitable, originally because of a measure of indifference, latterly because of human carelessness, accidents (avoidable or otherwise), natural catastrophe and the work of saboteurs. Among the great headline accidents were the grounding of the Exxon Valdez tanker in Prince William Sound off the Alaskan coast in 1989 and the resulting spillage of about 250,000 barrels of crude oil; and the grounding of the Amoco Cadiz off the French coast of Brittany in 1978, with spillage of some 1.6 million barrels. But hundreds if not thousands of smaller spillages occur every year around the world, and they must be cleaned up and measures taken to prevent reoccurrences. In the United States, for example, the Oil Pollution Act of 1990 was aimed mainly at reducing the number of spills each year and the quantity of oil spilled, and the industry claims (as of the year 2001) to have spent some $17 billion complying with its requirements.

Forms of pollution other than spillages, notably automotive emissions, have been greatly reduced, standards set and the industry has, in its own interests, developed cleaner fuels and carried out research on fuel cells and hybrid cars – cars fueled by a combination of gasoline and electricity.

Nevertheless, the public generally sees the oil industry, and the big companies in particular, as the enemy when it comes to the environment. In the public view, it is only by public pressure that they (the industry and the big companies) have been dragged along into being much more careful about the environment and have only begun to take spontaneous measures, beyond the strict legal requirements, to protect the environment as a consequence of these pressures. Much of this may be true, but it is a disconcerting argument. After all, if there were no public concern over the environment, why should the companies, or anybody else, care? Nobody opens an umbrella before it starts raining.

Public antagonism seems to boil down to: (a) resentment at the slowness of industry responses to public concern, and (b) disagreement over the facts.

For example, Exxon has publicly dissented from the general public's judgment over what would, *in fact*, be the result of full implementation of the Kyoto protocols; and there is disagreement between the industry and the general public over what would, *in fact*, be the environmental effect of drilling in the Arctic National Wildlife Refuge (ANWR). The issues are highly contentious and arouse deep feelings of, at times, religious intensity; at present (2003), it seems likely that public sentiment will carry the day on most environmental issues where the facts are in dispute. Perhaps indeed it is better to err on the side of caution (if that is the side being erred on).

Chapter 17
THE POLITICS OF PRICE AND THE PRICE OF DIVERSITY

At the close of the twentieth century, the international petroleum industry, like nearly everything else, looked very different from its 1950 self. World population had more than doubled, in a geographically uneven way; world consumption of oil had risen almost sevenfold, from 11 mbd to 74 mbd. The industry had been transformed by technology, by politics, by public concern over the environment, and above all by the OPEC price revolution and the sometimes painful adjustment and restructuring that followed. This book, concerned primarily with the policies and politics swirling around and within the industry, touches only lightly on the environment and scarcely at all on the technology. A dominant theme has been price, because it affects everything else (including technology and the environment), and because price in the industry has always been a political price, in the broadest sense of the term.

The important players in the industry have policies on price, which means they can, or think they can, influence it (otherwise there wouldn't be any point in having a policy). The market is not characterized by the kind of intense competition where price for one and all is a "given", set by the forces of supply and demand, and everyone is a "price-taker" who must accept what he finds. That supply and demand do not by themselves determine prices does not of course mean that they are not powerful forces in the industry. On the contrary: the battle with them is what it's all about. One of the industry's central features, the huge disparity between costs and reserves in the Middle East on the one hand, and everywhere else on the other, remains what it was in the late 1940s when US Interior Secretary Harold Ickes was wondering how to fit low-cost Saudi Arabia into a structure dominated at the time by high-cost Texas.

The world has moved on since then, in the way the matter is perceived; but the essential dilemma, with the emphasis now on security rather than protectionism, remains: to reconcile diversity of supply with price. You can have high prices and ample diversity of supply, but they, both supply and price, must be managed; or you can have competition, low prices, but supply, dangerously, in the hands of the few—who would drive out high-cost diverse sources out and might then not continue competing among themselves.

However, it doesn't actually *feel* like a central problem, for several reasons

335

which do not quite add up to a conspiracy of silence, but which do explain people's reticence. First, the problem is an evolving state of affairs without any particular point of urgency. Second, the industry—the oil companies, major or not—can't do much about it any more though their lives depend on how it develops. Third, important consumer interests, represented particularly by the US government and the IEA, don't like to talk about it because they are ideologically committed to free markets and competition and won't speak plainly and in public about the need for compromise in the case of oil. Fourth, the non-OPEC producers are of course delighted with the OPEC price umbrella and keep as quiet as church mice about it (as well they should). And, finally, OPEC, fearful of being blamed for everything, pretends that its prices are really set in the market-place (by reference to Brent and WTI), and that member countries' constraints on development and production are merely helpful attempts to "stabilize" the market, in the general interest.

So, over the years, and particularly recently, an informal consensus has developed among the major players. Attempts to fix crude oil prices by restricting supply recur again and again in the history of the international petroleum industry, and I have briefly described them in various parts of this book. Some worked well for a while; others never got off the ground. In the early 1960s, OPEC started to play around with the possibility of prorationing, and even considered a commodity agreement as a way of boosting prices. Nothing serious was done, and neither the major international oil companies nor the governments of the principal consuming countries would hear of it.

Then, for the first time in the history of the industry, there actually was a formal agreement, reached between the companies and the OPEC producing governments in Tehran in late 1971, with the acquiescence if not connivance of the United States, on the setting of prices, or at least of the fixed tax base which was by far the largest component of price. The Tehran Agreement (and the related Tripoli and other agreements that followed it) was short-lived and fell apart when OPEC member countries unilaterally seized control over prices in late 1973. In a rather narrow but important sense, failure came because the accords were badly crafted and simply could not cope with the situation that developed shortly after their conclusion. In a broader sense, there was never much hope, in the evolving political circumstances, that OPEC governments would be happy to continue negotiating price with a group of now visibly weak (in the political sense) companies that, after all, had no clear mandate from anyone.

Since late 1973, price has been set unilaterally, directly or indirectly, by OPEC and its member countries, and has been maintained at levels hugely in excess of anything that would emerge in a truly competitive environment. This has been possible by constraining supply in one way or another—by quotas on current production and by limiting the development of new capacity. But the price "set" by OPEC, or the price-target adopted by it, has not often been reached and sustained for more than a few months at a time during the past thirty years, either because production quotas are set too high for the market, or, more frequently, because member countries exceed them with whatever spare capacity they have on hand. So prices have risen and fallen, often sharply, usually unpredictably, driven partly by the internal politics of the OPEC cartel and its member countries. Volatility became, and remains, an uncomfortable fact of life in the oil industry. It has several contributory causes, such as exchange rate fluctuations, the industry's "just-in-time" inventory practices, the seasonality of demand, but, most importantly, the control (or lack of it) exercised by OPEC over the supply of crude oil.

However, the roots of the difficulty lie elsewhere, in the wide disparity in producing costs in different areas. In a rare public pronouncement on costs, the Saudi oil minister, Ali al-Naimi, said (in October 1999) that Saudi Arabia's "all-inclusive cost of production is less than \$1.50/bbl".[1] Similar, though slightly higher costs, obtained in the rest of the Middle East. Indeed, the Middle East with its vast reserves (65 percent of the world total) and highly prolific oil wells could have, if it had been so minded, developed reserves to produce and sell enough oil to satisfy total world demand at under \$5 per barrel, and still enjoy substantial government revenues. That is what would happen in a highly competitive world.

Nobody in fact wanted, or wants, price at that level, and when competition did break out in 1985-86, as Saudi Arabia pushed to regain market share, no one in the "West" liked it.

When prices fell again in the late 1990s, and when everybody (exporters and other producers, including the United States) had had enough of prices of around \$10/B. (by early 1999), a few OPEC producers, mainly Saudi Arabia and Venezuela, got together with non-OPEC Mexico, Russia and Norway (a member of the International Energy Agency), and cobbled up an agreement to reduce output. The deal was later ratified by the full membership of OPEC. Further cuts in production proved necessary, and these plus the recovery of the Southeast Asian economies, took price to over \$30 per barrel.

The problem now was that prices were too high for comfort. OPEC went into reverse, cautiously increasing production each month from April 2000—without any visible effect on prices for eight months. The whole episode should have been an occasion to take greater cognizance of the abiding dilemma of low costs in the Middle East and the West's need for oil prices high enough to protect higher-cost oil elsewhere and the diversity of supply it provides.

The West has never wanted free, competitive markets in international oil. President Clinton said (in August 2000) that the price "needs to be, I think, in the low 20s somewhere",[2] and a spokesman for the European Union's Commission said, approvingly, that most observers considered a price of around \$25/B to be justified.[3] Then US Energy Secretary Richardson came out in favor of a price between \$20 and \$25 (a difference of only tactical competitive market would have been miles below this.

OPEC in the meantime got a lot of stick for not achieving the impossible when prices rose above $30 in early 2000. It would simply not have been possible to fine-tune a market which is truly global, where the main centers of consumption in North America and Western Europe are more than 30 days' steaming time from the new supplies that can only come from the Persian Gulf, and on which reliable data is non-existent or incomplete for several months after the event. However, in this instance, fine-tuning was not the problem: the problem was the absence of competition.

To elaborate: when OPEC (or certain of its members), in the light of sharply rising prices, proposed making increased supplies available, the buyer had to ask, "At what price?" The reply was, "At the going market price." And what was the going market price? The going market price was the price that prevailed *without* the increased supplies, take it or leave it. In other words, for increased supply (availability) to work on price, there must be competition— somebody must be actively pushing to displace another supplier, by cutting price, or to increase total demand by cutting price, or a bit of both. That this element was lacking went unremarked at the time, but it revealed a serious flaw in the emerging price-management system, and it was directly traceable to the supply/demand/market-rules fiction spilling over into real life. People's actions (in this case, Saudi Arabia's) were governed by the fiction: increase supply, price has to drop. But this is only true in a competitive environment, where supply means sales pushed onto the market, and not merely increased availability at the previous price.

Hence the puzzlement over why price was not responding to increased supply, with many vain conjectures about time-lags, stocks, market data, even a brief shortage of reformulated gasoline in the US Midwest. Secretary Richardson was among the puzzled: "In fact, OPEC's four production increases . . . have been positive steps, but they haven't reduced oil prices significantly. So what we need are other factors . . . ", he said, but did not elaborate.[4] But neither Saudi Arabia nor anyone else made any attempt to push additional supplies onto the market by aggressive price-cutting. True, Saudi crude price-formulae over the year showed a widening differential *vis-à-vis* the WTI and Brent reference crudes, but these merely reflected the growing differences in their respective gross product worth in the markets as well as increasing freight rates. When prices finally tumbled with a short, sharp shock in early December 2000, they were led down by falling crude oil demand: buyers were full up, short-term requirements dropped off, and producers fell over themselves scrambling for the cargoes that were left to be supplied.

***

In the early 1970s, OPEC (at first with the tacit blessing of the United States) grabbed the reins and has in effect been managing prices ever since, sometimes well, sometimes very badly indeed. But if OPEC cannot do a good job for itself and for the world at large, who will? Can they be fixed by a formal agreement between producer and consumer? Almost certainly not. On the producers' side, there is no group—certainly not OPEC—that would or could make a formal treaty agreement worth the paper it was written on. On the consumers' side, there is no stomach for attempts to institutionalize the setting of oil prices by treaty. The dismal failure of the Conference on International Economic Cooperation in the mid 1970s put paid to that, and after long and fruitless discussions, occasionally bordering on the surreal, no further efforts have been made in that direction. So the world, it seemed for a while, was stuck with OPEC stumbling along, as it had done since 1973.

But a lot has changed. Much of OPEC, with its development of new capacity lagging, has become irrelevant to the setting of price. Only a few members of OPEC, in a shifting coalition with a few non-OPEC exporters, have been active in manipulating supply, and the formal blessing of OPEC as a whole has simply been an expedient exercise in political correctness to cover Saudi et al's flanks. Realism has crept in, and the world of oil is the better for it: notably, there is no more talk of setting the price at some chimeric cost of alternative sources of energy, nor, in the Middle East, of embargoes and the use of the "oil weapon", and countries are once again opening up exploration and development to the international oil companies. OPEC has set an objective for oil prices, a band of $22 to $28, clearly acceptable to the major countries of the OECD, and a mechanism for achieving it. Above $28, production will be increased; below $22, production will be decreased. However, the mechanism does not kick in automatically.

Nevertheless, it is appropriate to ask, What progress was being made? Did we get a tacit agreement between producers and consumers on a long(ish) term price of crude oil? Could the producers really deliver? And the answer is a qualified "Yes".[5]

Qualified by the fragility of the structure, the survival of which depends in large measure on a dangerous reliance on essentially one country—Saudi Arabia, and its continued good will—as sole guardian of the world's spare producing capacity. If demand continues along its present path and if non-OPEC oil supplies keep on increasing more slowly than they have done in the past, the Middle East will have to supply an ever greater share of world demand. Ever greater dependence on two or three OPEC members for increases in supply inevitably puts at risk the agreeable consensus that now seems to have been reached.

On the other hand, the development of spare capacity in other OPEC and non-OPEC countries is devoutly to be wished by prudent consumers. There is a glaring ambivalence here because such spare capacity would, of course, be even more life-threatening for the "agreeable consensus" on prices, but (one can only assume) it takes precedence over consensus-preservation, in a kind of "we'll-cross-that-bridge-when-we-come-to-it" attitude. For the development of spare capacity, time and technology are everything. Today, the latter is an article of faith which most of us are confident will not be frustrated. The former is there, in some good degree, for the having. In particular, the United States could help everybody and most especially itself by reversing its long-standing policies prohibiting US petroleum investments in Iran and Libya. As a result of these policies, the development of new capacity has been seriously curtailed. But, alas, revanchiste policies die hard.

Everything is temporary, and much depends on developments in Iraq after the 2003 war and invasion. It seems unlikely that the basics will change much, for it will certainly be several years before Iraq's oil industry is on its feet again and ready to expand aggressively. Until then, it can hardly become a disruptive force for the "agreeable consensus", which may therefore work for an agreeably long period of time. It would be helpful if it received greater public recognition. Proforma babble about competition and "letting the markets decide" is an unnecessary distraction and an implicit denial of the consensus, which should be talked up, not down. When the President of the United States, and later, a spokesman for the European Union, brand prices of over $30 as excessive, and call for prices in the low to mid-20s as "reasonable", no one thinks to ask what is reasonable about them, and certainly no one volunteers an explanation. US Energy Secretary Richardson (in the Clinton Administration) stated repeatedly that the United States regarded a price range of $20 to $25 as desirable, though he felt it necessary to preface his remarks by saying that he stressed "three points for the future: First, rely on open competition, market forces, is the first principle"—rather like saying grace at a meal for hungry atheists. Perhaps it is simply too embarrassing to admit that OPEC or an OPEC-equivalent is needed to impose a sort of inverted protectionism on the rest of the world to facilitate the survival of high-cost oil outside the OPEC area and encourage its further development. After all, this was the idea of the "minimum price" adopted back in the 1970s (at then Secretary of State Kissinger's urging) and still technically on the books.

The meeting of the International Energy Forum in Riyadh in mid-November 2000 was a welcome development. The United States came out clearly and unequivocally in favor of a price range which overlaps, to a large extent, the range advocated and pursued by Saudi Arabia and OPEC. There was agreement on the price objective. There was agreement on how to get there (managing supply—forget the free market camouflage). There was agreement as to who should do it (Saudi Arabia). In fact, it looked almost like a commodity agreement, except of course there was no formal agreement *between* the parties—they merely, individually and separately, stated their views, in a conscious parallelism of action. Nor was there likely to be a formal agreement, with the commitments that it would entail. But this should not obscure the very considerable progress that had been made over the past few years in bringing producers and consumers to a consensus. And it was soon clear that this consensus, reached during the Clinton Administration in the

United States, would be preserved under President Bush's, with an energy policy wholly dependent on a managed price.

The practical side remains fraught with difficulties. Today's world market is not like Texas sixty years ago under the Texas Railroad Commission, and fine-tuning it is virtually impossible: turning the tap on to produce large additional amounts of sour crude in Saudi Arabia is certainly one way to influence the spot price of small amounts of sweet crudes, Brent and WTI, several weeks away by tanker, but it does not invite comparisons with high-tech surgical instruments. And as a way of changing the price of sour crude in Saudi Arabia,[6] which is what you're trying to do in the first place, it is positively bizarre.

The search for an objective, independent,[7] market-determined peg on which to hang the price of Arab Light (the world's marker crude) was understandable but was, in the end, a mere subterfuge to get the monkey off Saudi Arabia's back. Saudi Arabia did not want to set the price of its crude itself, directly, because that made it too obvious that it was the world's swing supplier, a role it has repeatedly and emphatically repudiated in recent years. There was indeed some justification for this when other OPEC Members had surplus producing capacity and were exceeding quota, notably Venezuela. At the time, Saudi Arabia was quite rightly insistent that others share the burden of cutting back production in order to strengthen prices; but spare capacity outside Saudi Arabia has all but disappeared and making the system work depends more than ever on the Saudis acting, like it or not, as swing supplier while the world waits for Iraq to fulfill its geologic promise.

EPILOGUE

The United States should invade Iraq, eliminate the present regime, and pave the way for a successor . . . Today the shock of the September 11 attacks is still fresh and the U.S. government and public are ready to make sacrifices—while the rest of the world recognizes American anger . . . The longer the wait before an invasion, the harder it will be to muster domestic and international support for it, even though the reason for invading would have little or nothing to do with Iraq's connection to terrorism.
– Kenneth M. Pollack, "Next Stop Baghdad?" in *Foreign Affairs*, March/April 2002. (Mr Pollack was Senior Fellow and Deputy Director for National Security Studies at the Council on Foreign Relations.)

President George W. Bush was inaugurated on 20 January 2001. Neither his inaugural speech nor his first State of the Union message, delivered on 27 February 2001, betrayed any anxiety about terrorism or threats to national security from abroad. The emphasis was all on tax cuts and reform of the school system.

At the time, Iraq was subject to UN and US sanctions of unparalleled severity, designed to pressure Saddam Hussein's government into full compliance with the UN resolutions passed during and after the Gulf War of 1990-91, particularly those dealing with disarmament. The principal sanctions were the control of oil exports, with the proceeds being paid directly into an escrow account administered by the UN; the control of imports to exclude items deemed of possible use for the manufacture of weapons; and the banning of flights by Iraqi aircraft over two "no-fly" zones, one in the north and another in the south, that between them covered more than half the country. They were monitored and patrolled by US and British aircraft.

The trade sanctions were slowly falling apart as Iraq found more and more ways to circumvent them, and more accomplices abroad to help them do so. The lack of any visible weakening of the Saddam regime and the well-publicized, and very real, hardships that the sanctions were inflicting on the ordinary Iraqi, especially on the children, were making it increasingly difficult to justify their continuation. But for the time being, in early 2001, US efforts were confined, first, to making clear to Iraq, by renewed air attacks on Iraqi military installations on the ground, that the new Administration would not

342

take a softer line than the previous one; and, second, to seeking a revamping of the sanctions to hurt the government more and the people less.

Iraq was not at this point an actual or prospective candidate for a pre-emptive strike by the United States on the grounds of national security, though some thought, on other grounds, that Saddam should be forcibly removed.

Everything changed after the appalling terrorist attacks of 11 September 2001on the World Trade Center's twin towers in New York and on the Pentagon in Washington. The reaction was swift. War was declared on international terrorism and, in effect, on any country sponsoring it. Top of the list was the Taliban regime in Afghanistan, harboring the ring-leaders of the terrorist organization, Al-Qaeeda, and its head, Osama Bin Laden, member of a wealthy Saudi business family, and fanatically religious. When the Taliban refused to hand Bin Laden over, the United States launched air strikes (the first on 7 October) on Afghanistan which continued for two months. Military intervention on the ground jointly with dissident Afghan factions quickly routed the Taliban government and Al-Qaeeda resistance. Though Bin Laden himself escaped, the fighting was virtually all over by early December, and an interim government, under tribal leader Hamid Karzai was installed in Kabul on 22 December. National elections were to follow by 2004.

A group of well-placed US neo-conservatives had for some time been advocating the violent overthrow of Saddam Hussein's government, but it was only at this point, in late 2001 and early 2002, that Iraq started to emerge into prominent public view as a possible second target, especially after Bush's "axis of evil" speech (State of the Union address, February 2002). With a nexus of troops already in place and various airbases potentially available (some in use for patrolling Iraqi airspace), and with the American public's anger still high, here was an opportunity not to be missed.

But if Iraq was not engaging in international terrorism and presented no immediate threat to US national security, or anyone else's, why go to war? The United States had three reasons, one to do with Israel, two to do with oil, and none with the bogus ones given out to muster public support.

The bogus reasons were that Iraq under Saddam Hussein had amassed weapons of mass destruction that it was preparing to unleash on the United States and its allies; and that it had close links with the Al-Qaeeda terrorist movement. Further justification was sought in the truly loathsome and brutal nature of the regime, but this was merely to further inflame anti-Saddam sentiment. On the positive side, it was given out that US troops would be going into Iraq as liberators, not conquerors, that the path would thus be opened for the installation of democracy in the country, that this would be a salutary example to other authoritarian regimes in the area, and that it would open up the way for a lasting settlement of the conflict between Palestinians and Israelis.

No one explained what possible interest Saddam Hussein could have had in attacking the United States with such weapons, assuming he had them or any way of delivering them. The absurd allegations of close links with Al-Qaeeda were made knowing that the general public, unfamiliar with even the basic elements of Middle Eastern politics, would accept them. And it did. None of the other justifications, by themselves, could serve as a casus belli, nor would they have been accepted as such.

Why then go to war?

First, US policy towards the Middle East is strongly influenced by a deep concern for Israel's security, to which the Saddam regime posed a serious long-term threat. "Regime change" (in the phrase of the day) consequently became a prime objective—but not only for this reason: the oil objectives could not be achieved without it.

The stalemate over sanctions had to be broken sooner or later—the second reason for going to war. They were clearly having no effect on Saddam's iron grip on the country. The alternative was to stand by and watch them slowly crumble away as "smuggling" of oil out and other goods in grew out of control, aided and abetted by any number of other countries, neighboring and otherwise. And as long as sanctions, however leaky, remained nominally in effect, Iraq's oil industry could scarcely be maintained adequately let alone expanded significantly, especially insofar as the exploration of new areas was concerned. So, with Iran embargoed, dependence on Saudi Arabia and the Emirates would inevitably continue to grow. Which brings us to the third reason the United States had for going to war.

US dependence on imported oil has been growing steadily over the years and by the year 2000 was up to 55 percent of total demand. The Department of Energy was forecasting an increase in net imports to nearly 70 percent of demand by 2025. On the supply side, two-thirds of the increase in world production needed by 2025 was forecast to come from the OPEC area, mostly from the Middle East—and most of that from Saudi Arabia. The figures spelled growing world dependence on OPEC oil and on Saudi Arabia in particular.

Different grades of crude oil are to a large extent interchangeable, and it does not much matter which countries are the actual, physical source of imports into the United States; *any* increase in demand will ultimately have to be reflected in an increase in OPEC production. For much of the world, without much of an international political agenda, that might be of some economic concern, but that is all. For the United States, on the other hand, the possibility that unacceptable political conditions might be attached to increases in producing capacity (as had been threatened by Saudi Arabia in the early 1970s), or the possible replacement of the current friendly Saudi monarchy by a hostile fundamentalist Islamic regime, loomed large on the horizon.

Iraq was and is an important part of the answer to this growing danger.

The country has a geologic potential for oil generally considered to be second only to Saudi Arabia's—even greater by some—and its development would represent a considerable dilution of Saudi Arabia's power over supply.

After the resounding US military success in Afghanistan, the opportunity to invade Iraq and thereby solve the relatively short-term problem of sanctions as well as the long-term one of dependence was not to be missed.

But there was a problem: timing. The United States needed to strike while the iron of American anger over the atrocities of September 11 was still hot.

The Taliban regime collapsed in December 2001, US troops were in Kabul within days, and the decision to invade Iraq was taken shortly thereafter, if not before. But it was clear that the invasion could not take place before the winter of 2002 at the earliest, and would have to take place before the spring of 2003 at the latest.

After Bush's State of the Union address in February, the rest of 2002 was spent in talking up the war with Iraq and preparing for it, including troop movements reportedly starting in February, and some not very fruitful attempts at coalition-building. From a purely military point of view, the United States needed little help from elsewhere (beyond the availability of bases) for the invasion and subjugation of Iraq, and the Administration proceeded accordingly, obtaining a blank check from Congress in October 2002, in the shape of a resolution authorizing the president to use force against Iraq if necessary.

Resort to the United Nations Security Council was had mainly to mollify public opinion, at home and abroad, and to indulge the British government under Tony Blair which was the only significant ally the United States had in the venture. The Security Council passed a resolution—No. 1441 of 8 November 2002—demanding the readmission of UN inspectors into Iraq and threatening Iraq with "serious consequences" if it continued violating its disarmament obligations toward the United Nations. The resolution was later deemed a more or less adequate fig-leaf for US and British unilateral action.

The UN arms inspectors, now under Hans Blix, a former head of the International Atomic Energy Agency, were readmitted into Iraq, but received scant cooperation from US intelligence services (which claimed to know the probable locations of Iraq's weapons of mass destruction), and insufficient cooperation from the Iraqis. In February 2003, the UN inspectors asked for several months more time, but that would have meant a delay of the invasion until late 2003 and US troops were by now already in place, mainly in Kuwait and Qatar. They could not be left doing nothing for several more months during the hot summer.

The rest of the world was greatly upset. Bush's clear determination to go ahead, with or without a further UN resolution specifically authorizing the use of force, created a rift between the United States on the one hand and France, Germany, and Russia on the other, but the question of timing was critical to the United States, which was backed vigorously by Britain and Australia, less vigorously by Spain and a group of Eastern European countries. And so, despite worldwide protests on an unprecedented scale, the United States went to war, riding rough-shod over world opinion, and in the event achieved its military objectives with ease and few of the dire consequences, such as popular uprisings throughout the Arab world, predicted by its critics. But the episode stoked growing world aversion to US unilateralism, and US contempt for the United Nations caused further alarm.

Hostilities started in earnest on 20 March with an air strike intended to decapitate the resistance by killing Saddam Hussein. The Iraqi army put up little resistance and by 7 April US forces were in Baghdad and the British in Basrah. It had been the "cakewalk" the US Administration had predicted. There were few US or British casualties (less than 200 fatalities), and the Iraqi casualties, military and civilian, numbering a few thousand, had to be weighed against the many deaths which would have been caused by a continuation of the UN sanctions. (For the period from 1991 to mid 2002, the probable number of deaths attributable for the most part to sanctions was estimated at 400,000 to 500,000 Iraqi children under five years, according to the Global Policy Forum report, *Iraq Sanctions: Humanitarian Implications and Options for the Future*, dated 6 August 2002.)

There were many issues, political, legal, administrative and humanitarian, to be resolved at the end of the war, all vastly complicated by an almost total collapse in the security and administrative apparatus of the state and by the widespread looting that took place in the wake of the Iraqi defeat.

As in the 1990-91 Gulf War, oil markets did not suffer sustained price dislocations, or even short ones that were in any way serious. Brent crude rose to a peak of $34.50/B. on 6 March, but fell back sharply to $24.20 on 7 April after it became clear that the war was virtually over and that little damage had been inflicted on the Iraqi oilfields, which were not set ablaze as had the Kuwaiti ones in 1991.

For oil, the path ahead was now relatively straightforward in the sense that the problems, though they would take time, money and diplomacy to resolve, were clear.

First, the industry required thorough rehabilitation. Years of minimal maintenance due to lack of equipment which could not be imported had to be made up, and substantial investments were required simply to bring producing capacity back to its level prior to 1990. The task was complicated by the looting and sabotage of oil installations at the end of the war.

Second, plans for the ongoing development of existing proven areas had to be drawn up and implemented.

Third, plans for the development of new areas had to be formulated, including areas for the development of which agreements had been signed but not put into operation, and the legal status of which was open to question.

Fourth, Iraq had to mend relations with its neighbors, through which its export pipelines run (one to Ceyhan in Turkey; another through Saudi Arabia to the Red Sea; and a third through Syria to Banias).

Fifth, Iraq needed to resume its place in OPEC with a realistic policy of expansion that did not unduly disrupt the Organization's efforts to maintain prices within the agreed range.

It will be some time, a matter of years rather than months, before it becomes clear if the US government's long-term objective of having Iraq serve as a counter-weight to Saudi Arabia is fulfilled. In the meantime, toward the end of 2003, American and British forces remained in Iraq keeping order and overseeing the efforts to get the country on its feet again—a daunting task, for while unlimited military power confers unlimited power to destroy, it contributes little to the capacity to build, particularly in the face of hostile elements.

It may be appropriate to end this Epilogue and the book with a few words on security of supply, which is what the two Gulf Wars were about—the first, obviously and directly, the second not so obviously and in any case rather indirectly.

For the "West", any discussion of security of oil supply starts from the tacit assumption that the major suppliers are members of a potentially dangerous cartel, and are politically hostile for a number of reasons of which US support for Israel is the main one.

As noted at several points throughout this book, the "West" needs relatively high prices to provide an umbrella under which higher-cost non-OPEC sources of oil can be developed. It needs an OPEC (or surrogate) to produce them. But it needs a relatively weak OPEC, and most certainly not one virtually or actually in the hands of a single hostile country in the Gulf—which could all too easily happen with a change in the current Saudi regime. So, at this—tactical—level, policy needs to be directed at keeping OPEC diverse enough, or sufficiently under control, to forestall the emergence of prices greatly in excess of the level required to protect non-OPEC development.

On a strategic level, what lies ahead is the much more difficult task of eliminating or at least blunting the major suppliers' hostility. This can only be done by settling the Arab-Israeli dispute. It is certainly not inconceivable, some might even say likely, that things can simply go on in much the same way as they have for the past twenty or thirty years, since OPEC countries took over. That need not be unmanageable, but it would be a dangerous choice to make deliberately, for even if Iraq does emerge as a counterweight to Saudi Arabia, that does not mean that a political element will necessarily be absent from supply considerations.

And in any event, in the end, perhaps technological advances will one day, one way or another, in the not too distant future, make oil strategically irrelevant.

Who knows?

NOTES

CHAPTER 1. CORNERSTONE CONCESSIONS

1. The seven major international companies were:
– British Petroleum Company (BP), since 1954. Formerly the Anglo-Iranian Oil Company (AIOC), formerly the Anglo Persian Oil Company (APOC).
– Chevron Corporation, since 1984. Formerly Standard Oil Company of California (SOCAL). Renamed ChevronTexaco in 2001.
– Exxon Corporation, since 1972. Formerly Standard Oil Company (New Jersey). Renamed ExxonMobil in 2000.
– Gulf Oil Corporation (acquired by Chevron in 1984).
– Mobil Oil Corporation since 1965. Formerly Socony-Mobil Oil Company, formerly Socony-Vacuum Oil Company. Acquired by Exxon in 2000.
– Royal Dutch Shell Group (usually referred to just as "Shell").
– Texaco Inc., since 1959. Formerly The Texas Company. Acquired by Chevron in 2001.

In addition, the French company Total (formerly the Compagnie Française des Pétroles - CFP) was a partner with the majors in the Iraq Petroleum Company group and the Iranian Consortium. Total acquired Fina and Elf in 2001 and was renamed TotalFinaElf.

I have referred to the companies throughout by the names that seem most appropriate to the context, not necessarily their actual names at the time of the events referred to.

2. The "Red Line" Agreement of 1928 was an agreement among the companies that jointly owned the Iraq Petroleum Company, namely BP, Shell, CFP, Exxon, Mobil and Partex (Gulbenkian). Under its terms, none of the signatory companies was permitted to acquire concession interests in any of the areas of the Middle East delineated on a map by a red line that included Turkey and only excluded Iran, Kuwait and the Saudi Arabian-Kuwaiti Neutral Zone.

3. *The International Petroleum Cartel* was the title of the Staff Report to the Federal Trade Commission submitted to the Subcommittee on Monopoly of the Select Committee on Small Business of the US Senate (dated 22 August 1952). It was a basic document in the Department of Justice's antitrust case against the major oil companies.

4. Richard Funkhouser in a speech on "The Problem of Near Eastern Oil" given on 4 December 1951 to the US National War College.

5. Irvine H. Anderson, "The American Oil Industry and the Fifty-Fifty Agreement of 1950," in *Mussadiq, Iranian Nationalism and Oil*, p. 148.

6. Ibid., p. 154. Anderson's quote is from a Memorandum of Conversation, McGhee, Harden et al., in Report and Hearings of the US Senate on *Multinational Corporations and United States Foreign Policy*, part 8, pp. 345-8, cited hereinafter as MNC Report and Hearings. Support from these quarters for such an unorthodox legal doctrine strains credulity, to say nothing of the contradiction inherent between such a position and the 50/50 agreement itself, signed on 30 December 1950 (less than two months after the meeting) in which Aramco "submitted" to the Saudi income tax decrees provided that taxes never exceeded 50 percent of profit and provided that "Aramco's exemptions and immunities set forth in Article 21 of the Concession

Agreement shall continue in full force and effect." (Article 1(b) of the Agreement Concerning Amendments to Aramco's Concession, 30 December 1950.)

7. Ibid., p. 155.

8. Kuwait's 50/50 was initially based on Gulf and BP's long-term contract prices with Exxon, Shell and Mobil. Saudi Arabia's 50/50 was based on Aramco's price to its parent companies, which was, in 1951, $1.43/B. or 18.3 percent off the then posted price of $1.75. It was not until 1955 that Aramco moved to a posted price basis, though there had been an interim upward adjustment. See MNC Report, pp. 86-7.

9. Farmanfarmaian, Manucher. *Blood and Oil*, pp. 249 & 250.

10. See Lauterpacht, *International Law Reports – Year 1952*, pp. 518 et seq.

CHAPTER 2. BIG BANG AND THE GROWTH OF THE MARKETS, 1950-1973

1. Socony-Vacuum (Mobil) *Annual Report, 1947*.

2. The texts of the first and second agreements were published in *Petroleum Press Service*, September 1944 and October 1945.

3. John M. Blair, *The Control of Oil*, p. 73, quoting testimony published in *MNC Report and Hearings*.

4. Professor M. A. Adelman, *My Education in Mineral (Especially Oil) Economics*, Center for Energy and Environmental Policy Research, MIT, Cambridge, Mass., 1997.

5. My translation from the original French in the 1964 edition of the Communities' *Etude sur les perspectives énergétiques à long terme de la Communauté européenne*, p. 196.

CHAPTER 3. FIXING THE CRUDE OIL PRICE STRUCTURE

1. The various formulae in effect at different times are discussed at length in the staff report to the FTC entitled the 'International Petroleum Cartel', p. 352 et. seq.

2. The U. S. Maritime Commission (USMC), a scale of freight rates at the time, along the same lines as today's Worldscale. Market freight rates were quoted in terms of a percentage above or below the flat scale rate for a given shipping route.

CHAPTER 4. THE GROWTH OF COMPETITION, 1950-1970

1. Notably by Exxon. According to Bennett H. Wall, Exxon's official historian, after the law's promulgation, Exxon praised it as 'a model Petroleum law', and one which Exxon helped frame with legal and technical advice. However, according to Wall, Exxon director Howard Page 'sought to have the Libyan law written so as to provide for taxes to be collected on the posted price of oil, rather than on the realized price. Walter Levy, a noted oil consultant, represented Libya in discussions, and he agreed with Page.' These assertions are undocumented, and I have been unable to find any reference to Walter Levy's role in representing Libya, nor the nature or time of the discussions referred to. However, they must be accorded *some* credence because in the event, when Exxon began exporting crude from Libya, it in fact initially paid taxes on the basis of postings rather than realized prices.

2. Hogenhuis, a retired Shell employee, is mentioned by Anis Qasim, the first Chairman of the Libyan Petroleum Commission, as being adviser, as well as C. Andrews, a British adviser at the Ministry of Justice.

CHAPTER 5. ENTER OPEC: THE EARLY YEARS, 1960-1968

1. Bennett H. Wall, *Growth in a Changing Environemt*, p. 601 et seq.

2. *OPEC Bulletin*, 14 September 1990. Interview with Dr. Fuad Rouhani, OPEC's first Secretary General.

CHAPTER 6. THE TEHRAN AND TRIPOLI AGREEMENTS, 1971

1. See MNC Report, p. 117, and Socal's forecast, "Free World Oil Consumption and Supply and Growth Prospects for Crude Oil Production in the Middle East."

2. *Petroleum Press Service* was a monthly publication, later renamed *Petroleum Economist,* originally sponsored by BP and Shell, and, though owned and run by an "independent" trust by 1969, it was still at the time effectively an industry mouthpiece.

3. "Financial Needs of the Oil Industry in the Seventies." Shell Briefing Service, April 1971.

4. "A Comparison of Energy Projections to 1985," International Energy Agency, January 1979.

5. "Participation Upstream and Downstream – A Preliminary Report." Joint Committee on Participation, appointed by the Eighteenth OPEC Conference. Vienna, November 1969. Unpublished.

6. Notably by George Henry Schuler [1974], Ian Seymour [1978], Pierre Terzian [1985], Ian Skeet [1988], and Professor M. A. Adelman [1990], each from a different point of view.

7. MNC Report, p. 129

8. Kissinger in his memoirs is scathing about the Irwin mission. "Under Secretary of State John N. Irwin II was dispatched to the Mideast [by Secretary of State William Rogers] on January 16, 1971, to urge moderation on the oil-producing nations. . . . Irwin proudly reported to the President on January 25 that in the three countries he had visited (Iran, Saudi Arabia and Kuwait), he had stressed that we would follow our tradition of not becoming involved in the details of commercial negotiations – neatly removing the one fear that might have moderated producer demands: the threat of US governmental intervention." See Kissinger, *Years of Upheaval,* pp. 863 & 864. It is not clear what Kissinger meant by "intervention", but it was singularly lacking during his tenure as Secretary of State coping with successive oil price increases.

CHAPTER 10. THE AFTERMATH OF '73

1. Note No. 785 dated November 9, 1976, from the US Embassy in Caracas to the Venezuelan Foreign Minister, transmitting a 'personal message' from President Ford to President Pérez.

2. Kissinger did ask King Faisal to reduce prices, during his and Nixon's 1974 visit to Saudi Arabia. But everything was contingent on Nixon bringing pressure on Iran to join in the price-cut, which he did not do. Simon came back from the Middle East thinking he had a commitment from Faisal and Yamani, but Kissinger knew that the "commitment" was contingent on Iran doing something; and he also knew that Iran would do nothing.

3. Gary Sick, *All Fall Down,* pp. 15 & 16

CHAPTER 11. THE CRISIS OF '79

1. *The Geopolitics of Energy,* p. 1, Executive Summary, "The Gathering Energy Crisis". Staff Report to the US Senate's Committee on Energy and Natural Resources. Washington DC, December 1980.

2. Ibid., p. 11.

3. Ibid., p. 69.

4. United States Congress. Senate. Committee on Foreign Relations. Subcommittee on International Economic Policy. Staff Report. *The Future of Saudi Arabian Oil Production.* Washington, April 1979.

5. The "Aramco Advantage" case, *Exxon Corporation and Affiliated Companies et al.,*

v. Commissioner of Internal Revenue, docket nos. 24855-89, 18432-90, 22 December 1993.

6. Ibid., p. 10. The "New Arrangements" were informally agreed between the four US Aramco participants and the Saudi Government (SAG) "in late 1976 or early 1977". "Under the New Arrangements, the SAG assumed 100 percent ownership of Aramco, and the (now former) shareholders provided services to the SAG's oil business in exchange for stated fees. Many of the financial aspects of the New Arrangements were implemented in a draft crude oil sales agreement (COSA), but the New Arrangements and the draft COSA were never signed."

7. US General Accounting Office. *The United States Exerts Limited Influence on the International Crude Oil Spot Market.* Report by the Comptroller General of the United States. EMD-80-98. Washington DC: GAO, 21 August 1980. p. 14.

8. Ibid., p. 7.

9. Exxon Corporation, *1980 First Quarter Plan. Presentation to Exxon's Petroleum Supply Coordination Committee,* December 1979 (Proprietary Document), p. 14.

10. Exxon Corporation, *1980 Second Quarter Plan. Presentation to Exxon's Petroleum Supply Coordination Committee,* March 1980 (Proprietary Document), see last (unnumbered) page of plan.

11. OPEC: *Official Resolutions and Press Releases, 1960-1990.* OPEC: Vienna 1990. (OPEC Consultative Meeting in Geneva - Press Release no. 2-79, Vienna 21 February 1979.)

12. OPEC: *Official Resolutions and Press Releases, 1960-1990.* OPEC: Vienna 1990. (Fifty-Fourth Meeting of the Conference, Press Release no. 5-79, Geneva, 28 June 1979.)

13. See 'COMMA - The EEC Register of Spot Transactions' a report prepared by Joe Roeber Associates, published by the Commission of the European Communities, Directorate General for Energy, Brussels 22 October 1980 (Ref. XVII/368/80).

14. US Defense Secretary Harold Brown said in a television interview on 25 February 1979 that the "protection of the oil flow from the Middle East is clearly a part of our vital interest . . . in protection of those vital interests we will take any action that is appropriate, including the use of military force". (See report in Middle East Economic Survey 5 March 1979, p. 13.)

15. For full text of the G-7 Tokyo communiqué, see Middle East Economic Survey 9 July 1979.

16. For example, studies by David Golub, William Quandt, Eliahu Kanovsky and the US GAO's *Critical Factors Affecting Saudi Arabia's Oil Decisions.* Except for Quandt, these deal with Saudi "price-moderation" during the period prior to 1979, but much of the analysis is equally applicable to the 1979-1981 period.

17. *Oil & Energy Trends,* May 1980.

18. *IEA Monograph: A Comparison of Energy Projections to 1985,* OECD: Paris, January 1979.

CHAPTER 12. BACKLASH: PRICES AND POLICIES

1. IEA, *Energy Policies and Programmes of IEA Countries,* 1980 Review, p. 325.
2. IEA *Energy Policies and Programmes of IEA Countries,* 1985 Review, p. 136.
3. Washington Post, 24 Sept 1985. "No More for Synfuels", an article by Mike Synar, Democratic representative from Oklahoma and chairman of a subcommittee on environment, energy and natural resources. Page A21.

CHAPTER 13. THE DEVELOPMENT OF NON-OPEC OIL SINCE 1970

1. *Middle East Economic Survey,* 7 March 1983, p. A4.
2. See *Petroleum Intelligence Weekly,* 30 May 1983, for text of full statement.

3. *Middle East Economic Survey*, 27 December 1993, p. A2.
4. Exxon *Annual Report* 1968, p. 6.

CHAPTER 14. OPEC AT BAY

1. U.S. Congress, Office of Technology Assessment, *U.S. Oil Production, the Effect of Low Oil Prices* (1987), p. 73.

CHAPTER 15. WAR IN THE GULF, 1990-1991

1. For an account of this and subsequent meetings, see Khadduri and Ghareeb, *War in the Gulf, 1990-1991*, p. 86 et seq.
2. *Middle East Economic Survey*, July 1990.
3. Khadduri and Ghareeb, op. cit., p. 110 et seq.
4. Colin Powell, *My American Journey*, pp. 461 & 462.
5. James A. Baker, *The Politics of Diplomacy*, p.273.
6. Colin Powell, *My American Journey*, p.498.
7. H. Norman Schwarzkopf, *It Doesn't Take a Hero*, p. 297.
8. Ibid., p. 316.
9. Khadduri and Ghareeb, *War in the Gulf 1990-1991*, p. 179.
10. James A. Baker, *Politics of Diplomacy*, p. 414
11. Colin Powell, *My American Journey*, p. 490.
12. Ibid., p. 531.
13. See Congressional Research Service Issue Brief (IB93113), *Saudi Arabia: Post-War Issues and U.S. Relations* dated 13 April 2001.

CHAPTER 16. OIL'S NEW WORLD

1. Jonathan Krim in *The Washington Post*, quoted in the *International Herald Tribune*, May 18, 2002.

CHAPTER 17. THE POLITICS OF PRICE AND THE PRICE OF DIVERSITY

1. In a speech to the Houston Forum in October 1999. See *Oil & Gas Journal*, 17 January 2000.
2. Quoted in *Middle East Economic Survey*, 28 August 2000.
3. Ibid.
4. In a press interview following the meeting of the International Energy Forum in Riyadh in November. Quoted in *Middle East Economic Survey*, 27 November 2000, p. D1.
5. But beware, we have been there before. In an article entitled "Moving Towards a Price Consensus", the *Petroleum Economist* said more than fifteen years ago (in its issue of November 1986, p. 398), "After the traumas of the past twelve months OPEC has adopted a moderate price target that will not immediately arouse the hostility of consuming interests. Some of the main importing countries have learned, for their part, that their best interests are not served by very cheap oil. So there is developing a consensus among importing and exporting countries that augurs well for the stability of the oil business."
6. Saudi Arabia sets its contract crude oil prices monthly, mainly by reference to Brent
7. Set aside the question of manipulation of the reference crudes, particularly Brent.

BIBLIOGRAPHY

Documents of Governments, International Organizations, Arbitrations, Tribunals

Cabinet Task Force on Oil Import Control. *The Oil Import Question.* Washington D.C. U.S. GPO, February 1970.

Communauté Européenne du Charbon et de l'Acier. *Etude sur les perspectives à long terme de la Communauté européenne.* Luxembourg, 1964.

Energy Message to Congress. *(1) Official Background Summary and Fact Sheet, issued by Office of the White House Press Secretary; (2) President Nixon's Message to Congress; (3) A Proclamation by the President of the United States of America, April 18, 1973, Modifying Proclamation 3279, Relating to Imports of Petroleum and Petroleum Products; (4) Executive Order Forming National Energy Office.* Washington, 18 April 1973. (Documents reproduced in *Petroleum Intelligence Weekly,* 23 April 1973.)

International Energy Agency (IEA). *Energy Policies and Programmes of IEA Countries.* (Annual). Various issues since 1978.

International Energy Agency (IEA). *A Comparison of Energy Projections to 1985.* IEA Monograph, by John R. Brodman and Richard E. Hamilton. Paris, OECD 1979.

International Law Reports (ed. Sir Hersch Lauterpacht). *Anglo-Iranian Oil Co. Case (No. 113), United Kingdom v. Iran. ICJ Order of July 5, 1951, p. 501 et seq.* and *Anglo-Iranian Oil Co. Case (No. 114), United Kingdom v. Iran. ICJ Judgment of July 22, 1952, p. 507 et seq.* Year 1952. Part X, Disputes. B - International Court of Justice. II. – Contentious Jurisdiction. London: Butterworth 1957.

International Law Reports (ed. E. Lauterpacht). Vol. 27. *Saudi Arabia v. Arabian American Oil Company (ARAMCO). Arbitration Tribunal. August 23, 1958. pp. 117-233.* (See Part V, State Responsibility. A. III. - For Revocation of, or Interference with, Concessions or Concessionary Contracts.) London: Butterworths, 1963.

International Law Reports (ed. E. Lauterpacht). *BP Exploration Company (Libya) Limited v. Government of the Libyan Arab Republic. 10 October 1973 and 1 August 1974, pp. 297-387.* (See Part V, State Responsibility. A.IV. - For Revocation of, or Interference with, Concessions or Concessionary Contracts.) Cambridge: Grotius Publications Limited, 1979.

Concession Agreement. *Agreement between the Government of IRAN and the Oil Companies of the Iranian Consortium,* 19-20 September 1954.

Organisation for Economic Co-operation and Development. *World Energy Outlook: A Reassessment of Long-Term Energy Developments and Related Policies.* Paris: OECD, 1977.

Organization of the Petroleum Exporting Countries. *Official Resolutions and Press Releases, 1960-1990.* Vienna: OPEC, 1990.

Organization of the Petroleum Exporting Countries. *General Information & Chronology 1960-1994.* Vienna: OPEC, 1994.

Organization of the Petroleum Exporting Countries. *Radical Changes in the International Oil Industry during the Past Decade.* Paper presented by F. R. Parra at the IVth Arab Petroleum Congress held in Beirut, November 5-12, 1963.

Organization of the Petroleum Exporting Countries. *Selected Documents of the International Petroleum Industry, 1967.* ed. *Nameer Ali Jawdat.* Vienna: OPEC, 1968 and subsequent volumes, published annually.

United Nations Economic Commission for Europe. *The Price of Oil in Western Europe.* ECE Secretariat. Geneva, March 1955.

United States Congress. Library of Congress, Congressional Research Service, Foreign Affairs and National Defense Division. *Saudi Arabia and the United States: The New Context in an Evolving 'Special Relationship.'* Report Prepared for the Subcommittee on Europe and the Middle East of the Committee on Foreign Affairs of the U.S. House of Representatives. Washington, 1981.

United States Congress. Senate. *The International Petroleum Cartel.* Staff Report to the Federal Trade Commission, submitted to the Subcommittee on Monopoly of the Select Committee on Small Business. Washington, 22 August 1952.

United States Congress. Senate. Subcommittees of the Committee on the Judiciary and Committee on Interior and Insular Affairs. Joint Hearings, February and March 1957. *Emergency Oil Lift Program and Related Oil Problems.* Washington 1957.

United States Congress. Senate. Committee on Foreign Relations. *Energy and Foreign Policy. The Implications of the Current Energy Problem for United States Foreign Policy.* (May 1973). Washington, 1974.

United States Congress. Senate. Committee on Foreign Relations. *The United States Oil Shortage and the Arab-Israeli Conflict.* Report of a Study Mission to the Middle East. from October 22 to November 3, 1973. Washington 1973.

United States Congress. Senate. Committee on Foreign Relations. Subcommittee on Multinational Corporations, ("Church" Committee) Report and Hearings, 1973 and 1974. *Multinational Corporations and United States Foreign Policy.* Washington 1975.

United States Congress. Senate. Committee on Foreign Relations. Subcommittee on Multinational Corporations. *The International Petroleum Cartel, the Iranian Consortium and U.S. National Security.* Washington 1974.

United States Congress. Senate. Committee on Interior and Insular Affairs. *United States-OPEC Relations.* Selected Materials. Prepared by the Congressional Research Service. Washington 1976.

United States Congress. Joint Economic Committee. Subcommittee on Energy. Hearings, January 12 & 13, 1977. *Energy Independence or Interdependence: the Agenda with OPEC.* Washington 1977.

United States Congress. Senate. Committee on Foreign Relations. Subcommittee on International Economic Policy. Staff Report. *The Future of Saudi Arabian Oil Production.* Washington, April 1979.

United States Congress. Office of Technology Assessment. *World Petroleum Availability 1980-2000. A Technical Memorandum.* October 1980.

U.S. General Accounting Office. *Critical Factors Affecting Saudi Arabia's Oil Decisions.* Report by the Comptroller General of the United States. ID-78-32. Washington DC: GAO, 12 May 1978.

Various Items from the 'Selected Documents' series published by the Organization of the Petroleum Exporting Countries:

Organization of the Petroleum Exporting Countries. *Iraq Petroleum Company's Concession Agreement, Convention of 14th March 1925, as Revised by Principal Agreement of 24th March 1931* in *Selected Documents of the International Petroleum Industry: Iraq and Kuwait, Pre-1966.* Vienna: OPEC, 1972.

Organization of the Petroleum Exporting Countries. *Iran Oil Nationalisation Act of 10th Ordibehesht 1330* in *Selected Documents of the International Petroleum Industry: Iran, Pre-1966.* Vienna: OPEC, 1972.

Organization of the Petroleum Exporting Countries. *Iran, Law Embodying Regulations for the Implementation of the Nationalisation of Oil Throughout Iran, May 1951* in *Selected Documents of the International Petroleum Industry: Iran, Pre-1966.* Vienna: OPEC, 1972.

Organization of the Petroleum Exporting Countries. *Iraq Law No. 80 of 1961 Defining the Exploitation Areas for the Oil Companies,* in *Selected Documents of the International Petroleum Industry: Iraq and Kuwait, Pre-1966.* Vienna: OPEC, 1972.

Studies and Monographs by International Organizations, Government Departments, Research Institutes, Companies, Consultants, etc.

Arthur D. Little, Inc. *Economic Aspects of the International Petroleum Industry.* Unpublished study prepared for OPEC, Cambridge, Mass., 1961.

Badger, Daniel and Robert Belgrave. *Oil Supply and Price: What Went Right in 1980?* Energy Paper No. 2. London: Royal Institute of International Affairs, 1982.

Exxon Corporation. *Middle East Oil and Gas.* Exxon Background Series, December 1984.

Gulf Trading and Transportation Company. Planning and Strategic Studies Department. *Short Term Market Outlook.* Gulf Trading and Transportation Co., 1981.

Kanovsky, Eliahu. *Saudi Arabia's Moderation in Oil Pricing - Political or Economic?* Tel Aviv: Shiloah Center for Middle Eastern and African Studies, Tel Aviv University, April 1977.

National Petroleum Council. *The Impact of Oil Exports from the Soviet Bloc. Supplement to the 1962 Report.* Washington, 1964.

Quandt, William B. *Saudi Arabia's Oil Policy.* Washington DC: The Brookings Institution, 1982.

Quandt, William B. *Saudi Arabia in the 1980s: Foreign Policy, Security and Oil.* Washington DC: The Brookings Institution, 1981.

Rockefeller Foundation. *Working Paper on International Energy Supply: A Perspective from the Industrial World.* New York: The Rockefeller Foundation, May 1978.

The Trilateral Commission. *Energy: Managing the Transition.* John C. Sawhill, Keichi Oshima, and Hanns W. Maull. New York, 1978.

Articles and Conference Papers

Adelman, M. A. "Is the Oil Shortage Real? Oil Companies as OPEC Tax Collectors." *Foreign Policy* (Winter 1972-73): 69-108

Adelman, M. A. "Security of Eastern Hemisphere Fuel Supply." Massachusetts Institute of Technology, Cambridge, Mass. December 1967.

Akins, James E. "The Oil Crisis: This Time the Wolf Is Here." *Foreign Affairs* 51 (April 1973): 462-490.

Akins, James E. "Projecting Oil Supply and Demand: A Science, an Art, or Just Politics?" Paper delivered at the Conference on World Energy Economics No. 4, held in London 26-28 February 1979. For full text, see Supplement to MEES, 12 March 1979.

Chalabi, Dr. Fadhil. "Middle East Crude Availabilities and World Oil Markets." *Middle East Economic Survey.* 5 March 1979.

Levy, Walter J. "The Past, Present and Likely Future Price Structure for the International Oil Trade." Paper presented at the *Third World Petroleum Congress, The Hague, May 28 - June 6, 1951.*

Moran, Theodore H. "Why Oil Prices Go Up. The Future: OPEC Wants Them." *Foreign Policy,* No. 25, Winter 1976-67.

Oppenheim, V. H. "Why Oil Prices Go Up. The Past: We Pushed Them." *Foreign Policy,* No. 25, Winter 1976-77.

Parra, Alirio A. "The Petroleum Industry and Its Fiscal Obligations in Venezuela." Paper presented on behalf of the Ministry of Mines and Hydrocarbons at *The First Venezuelan Petroleum Congress.* Caracas, March 1962.

Parra, Francisco R. "Venezuela's Changing Oil Policy." *World Petroleum.* December 1960.

Parra, Francisco R. "The Eastern Hemisphere – Oil Profits in Focus." *Middle East Economic Survey.* 1 November 1963.

Penrose, Professor Edith. "Vertical Integration with Joint Control of Raw Material Production: Crude Oil in the Middle East."

Yamani, Sheikh Ahmed Zaki. "Aspects of Oil Policy for the Arab Countries and the Relation of Arab Policy to that of OPEC." Talk given at the American University's annual seminar on the Economics of the International Petroleum Industry, Beirut 3 June 1968. Reported in MEES, 7 June 1968.

Yamani, Sheikh Ahmed Zaki. "Participation Versus Nationalization - A Better Means to Survive." Talk given at the American University's annual seminar on the Economics of the International Petroleum Industry, Beirut, 30 May 1969. Reported in MEES, 13 June 1969

Books

Acheson, Dean. *Present at the Creation: My Years in the State Department.* New York: W. W. Norton & Co., 1969.

Adelman, M. A. *The World Petroleum Market.* Baltimore: John Hopkins University Press, 1972.

Adelman, M. A. *The Genie Out of the Bottle: World Oil since 1970.* Cambridge: The MIT Press, 1995.

Adelman, M. A. *The Economics of Petroleum Supply 1962-1993.* Cambridge: The MIT Press, 1993.

Alam, Asadollah. *The Shah and I. The Confidential Diary of Iran's Royal Court, 1969-1977.* London: I. B. Tauris, 1991.

Anderson, Irvine H. *Aramco, the United States, and Saudi Arabia: A Study of the Dynamics of Foreign Oil Policy, 1933-1950.* Princeton: Princeton University Press, 1981.

Arthur Anderson & Co. and Cambridge Energy Research Associates. *The Future of Oil Prices: The Perils of Prophecy.* Houston: 1984.

Baker, James, with Thomas M. DeFrank. *The Politics of Diplomacy.* New York: G. P. Putnam's Sons, 1995.

Bamberg, J. H. *The History of the British Petroleum Company, Volume 2: The Anglo-Iranian Years, 1928-1954.* Cambridge: Cambridge University Press, 1994.

Betancourt, Rómulo. *Venezuela - Política y Petróleo.* Caracas: Editorial Senderos, 1967.

Bill, James A., and William Roger Louis, eds. *Mussadiq, Iranian Nationalism, and Oil.* London: I. B. Tauris, 1988.

Blair, John M. *The Control of Oil.* New York: Pantheon, 1976.

Bowie, Robert R. *Suez 1956.* London: Oxford University Press, 1974.

Cattan, Henry. *The Evolution of Oil Concessions in the Middle East and North Africa.* Dobbs Ferry, New York: Oceana Publications, 1967.

Cattan, Henry. *The Law of Oil Concessions in the Middle East and North Africa.* Dobbs Ferry, New York: Oceania Publications, 1967.

Al-Chalabi, Fadhil J. *OPEC and the International Oil Industry: A Changing Structure.* Oxford: Oxford University Press, 1980.

Al-Chalabi, Fadhil J. *OPEC at the Crossroads.* Oxford: Pergamon, 1989.

Daintith, Terence (Ed.) *The Legal Character of Petroleum Licences: A Comparative Study.* Centre for Petroleum and Mineral Law Studies, University of Dundee and Energy and Natural Resources Committee of the International Bar Association, 1981.

Drollas, Leo and Jon Greenman. *The Devil's Gold.* London: Duckworth, 1989.

Ebel, Robert E. *Communist Trade in Oil and Gas: An Evaluation of the Future Export Capability of the Soviet Bloc.* New York: Praeger, 1978.

Ebel, Robert E. *Energy Choices in Russia.* Washington DC: Center for Strategic and International Studies, 1994.

Eden, Anthony. *The Memoirs of Sir Anthony Eden: Full Circle.* London: Cassell & Company Ltd., 1960.

Elm, Mostafa. *Oil, Power and Principle: Iran's Oil Nationalization and Its Aftermath.* Syracuse, New York: Syracuse University Press, 1992.

Elwell-Sutton, L. P. *Persian Oil: A Study in Power Politics.* London: Lawrence and Wishart, 1955.

Epstein, Edward Jay. *Dossier. The Secret History of Armand Hammer.* New York: Random House, 1996.

Farmanfarmaian, Manucher and Roxane Farmanfarmaian. *Blood and Oil. Memoirs of a Persian Prince.* New York: Random House, 1997.

Farman-Farmaian, Sattareh (with Dona Munker). *Daughter of Persia. A Woman's Journey from her Father's Harem through the Islamic Revolution.* London: Bantam Press, 1992.

Ford, Alan W. *The Anglo-Iranian Oil Dispute of 1951-1952: A Study in the Role of Law in the Relations of States.* Berkeley: University of California Press, 1954.

Frank, Helmut J. *Crude Oil Prices in the Middle East.* New York: Praeger, 1966.

Frankel, Paul. *The Essentials of Petroleum: A Key to Oil Economics.* New ed. London: Frank Cass, 1969.

Golub, David B. *When Oil and Politics Mix: Saudi Oil Policy 1973-85.* Centre for Middle Eastern Studies, Harvard University, 1985.

Goodwin, Crauford D. *Energy Policy in Perspective: Today's Problems, Yesterday's Solutions.* Washington DC: Brookings Institution 1981.

Hartshorn, J. E. *Oil Companies and Governments.* London: Faber and Faber, 1962.

Hartshorn, J. E. *Oil Trade: Politics and Prospects.* Cambridge: Cambridge University Press, 1993.

Horsnell, Paul and Robert Mabro. *Oil Markets and Prices. The Brent Market and the Formation of World Oil Prices.* Oxford: Oxford University Press, for the Oxford Institute for Energy Studies, 1993.

Hoveyda, Fereydoun. *The Fall of the Shah.* New York: Wyndham Books, 1979. (Translated by Roger Liddell.)

Huyser, General Robert E. (Dutch). *Mission to Tehran.* New York: Harper & Row, 1986.

Jaidah, Ali M. *An Appraisal of OPEC Oil Policies.* London: Longman, 1983.

Khadduri, Majid and Edmund Ghareeb. *War in the Gulf, 1990-91.* Oxford: Oxford University Press, 1997.

Kissinger, Henry. *The White House Years.* Great Britain: George Weidenfeld & Nicolson, 1979.

Kissinger, Henry. *Years of Upheaval.* Great Britain: George Weidenfeld & Nicolson, 1982.

Lawson, Nigel. *The View from No. 11. Memoirs of a Tory Radical.* Great Britain: Bantam Press, 1992.

Leeman, Wayne A. *The Price of Middle East Oil.* Ithaca, NY: Cornell University Press, 1960.

Lieuwen, Edwin. *Petroleum in Venezuela: A History.* Berkeley: University of California Press, 1954.

Longrigg, Stephen Hemsley. *Oil in the Middle East: Its Discovery and Development.* London: Oxford University Press, 1954.

Mabro, Robert, Robert Bacon, Margaret Chadwick, Mark Halliwell and David Long. *The Market for North Sea Crude Oil.* Oxford: Oxford University Press, for the Oxford Institute for Energy Studies, 1986.

Mitchell, John (ed.) *Companies in a World of Conflict. NGOs, Sanctions and Corporate Responsibility.* London: The Royal Institute of International Affairs, 1998.

Mitchell, John, with Koji Morita, Norman Selley and Jonathan Stern. *The New Economy of Oil. Impacts on Business, Geopolitics and Society.* London: Earthscan Publications Ltd., for The Royal Institute of International Affairs (Energy and Environment Programme, 2001.

Mughraby, Muhamad A. *Permanent Sovereignty Over Oil Resources: A Study of Middle East Oil Concessions and Legal Change.* Beirut: Middle East Research and Publication Center, 1966.

Odell, Peter R. *An Economic Geography of Oil.* London: G. Bell and Sons, 1963.

Pahlavi, Shah Mohammad Reza, *Answer to History.* New York: Stein and Day, 1980.

Painter, David H. *Private Power and Public Policy. Multinational Oil Companies and U.S. Foreign Policy, 1941-1954.* London: I. B. Tauris & Co., 1986.

Parsons, Anthony. *The Pride and the Fall: Iran 1974-1979.* London: Jonathan Cape, 1984.

Penrose, Edith. *The Large International Firm in Developing Countries: The International Petroleum Industry.* London: George Allen and Unwin, 1968.

Penrose, Edith. *The Growth of Firms, Middle East Oil and Other Essays*. London: Frank Cass & Co., 1971.

Pérez Alfonzo, Juan Pablo. *El Pentágono Petrolero*. Caracas: Ediciones Revista Politica, 1967.

Powell, Colin, with Joseph E. Persico. *My American Journey*. New York: Random House, 1995.

Roeber, Joe. *The Evolution of Oil Markets: Trading Instruments and their Role in Oil Price Formation*. London: The Royal Institute of International Affairs (Energy and Environment Programme), 1993.

Roosevelt, Kermit. *Countercoup: The Struggle for the Control of Iran*. New York: McGraw Hill, 1979.

Rouhani, Fuad. *The History of OPEC*. New York: Praeger, 1971.

Salinger, Pierre and Eric Laurent. *Guerre du Golfe: Le Dossier Secret*. Paris: Olivier Orban, 1991.

Sampson, Anthony. *The Seven Sisters: The Great Oil Companies and the World They Made*. London, Hodder and Stoughton.

Schwarzkopf, General H. Norman, with Peter Petre. *It Doesn't Take a Hero*. New York: Linda Grey Bantam Books, 1992.

Seymour, Ian. *OPEC, Instrument of Change*. London: Macmillan, 1980.

Skeet, Ian. *OPEC, Twenty-Five Years of Prices and Politics*. Cambridge: Cambridge University Press, 1988.

Sullivan, William H. *Mission to Iran*. New York and London: W. W. Norton & Company, 1981.

Terzian, Pierre. *OPEC: The Inside Story*. ZED Books, 1985.

Thatcher, Margaret. *The Downing Street Years*. New York: Harper Collins Publishers, 1993.

Waddams, Frank C. *The Libyan Oil Industry*. Baltimore: The Johns Hopkins University Press, 1980.

Wall, Bennett H. *Growth in a Changing Environment: A History of SONJ 1950-72 and Exxon 1972-75*. New York: McGraw-Hill Book Company, 1988.

Warner, Rawleigh. *Mobil Oil: A View from the Second Century*. New York: Newcomen Society in North America, 1966.

Yergin, Daniel. *The Prize. The Epic Quest for Oil, Money and Power*. New York: Simon & Schuster, 1991.

Periodicals and Reference Works Consulted

Keesing's Contemporary Archives.

International Crude Oil & Product Prices. Parra, Ramos & Parra in co-operation with Middle East Economic Survey. Bi-Annual.

Middle East Economic Survey. Beirut and Cyprus. Weekly.

Oil & Energy Trends. Energy Economics Research Ltd. London. Monthly.

Oil & Gas Journal. Weekly.

Petroleum Press Service. London. Monthly.

Petroleum Economist. (Formerly *Petroleum Press Service*). London. Monthly.

Petroleum Argus. London

Petroleum Intelligence Weekly. New York. Weekly.
Platts Oilgram News Service. New York. Daily.

Annual Reports of Companies, 1950-2001

British Petroleum Company
Chevron Corporation
Exxon Corporation
Gulf Oil Corporation
Mobil Oil Corporation
Petróleos de Venezuela
Petróleos Mexicanos
Shell Transport and Trading Co.
Texaco Inc.
TotalFinaElf

INDEX

Abdesselam, Belaid 122, 150
Adelman, M. A. 49, 70, 143
Agreements
Achnacarry 'As Is' 89; Aramco 92, 103, 228, 284; crude sales 36, 228;
EEC International Energy Programs (1974) 191; Evian (1965) 150;
   Iraq: concession (1925) 12-13; fifty/fifty (1952) 20; posted prices (1971) 133; Syria (1998) 310
   Iran: Amoco (1958) 84; concession (1933) 22; consortium (1954) 28-30; ENI (1957) 84; Supplemental (1949) 21, 23-5; joint venture 155-6
   Kuwait: Aminoil (1948) 85; AOC (1958) 85; concession (1931) 20; Lagos (1971) 178; Libya (1970) 123-4; offtake 39, 69-74, 86
   OPEC: London (1983) 280-3; OPEC production program (1965) 105; participation, General Agreement (1972) 121, 158-9; 'Red Line' (1928) 7-8, 36; safety net (1971) 129; San Remo (1925) 152
   Saudi Arabia: Al-Yamamah (1986) 291; Concession (1933) 20; Getty (1949) 85; JPTC (1957) 85
   technical assistance 228;
   Tehran & Tripoli (1971) 110, 113, 118, 130, 133-5, 139-41, 147, 52, 155-6, 162, 164, 166, 168, 171-2, 175-80, 268, 336; Geneva I (1972) 121; Geneva II (1973) 121
   trade: bilateral 83, 185-6
   US-UK 11, 37-8; London (1945) 37; Washington (1944) 37
Ait Laoussine, Nordine 121, 150-1
Akins, James 124, 130, 140, 147-8, 172, 174, 202-4
Al-Sabah, Ali 107, 291
Alaska North Slope price 320-1; development 267, 269; discovery 142,

249; Exxon Valdez 333; pipeline 149, 169, 186, 252, 269; see also 40, 115, 144, 176, 223, 259, 265
Amuzegar, Jamshid 107, 178, 199, 291
Anbari, Abdul Amir 309
Arab Petroleum Congress 93-6, 107
Arabian American Oil Co. (Aramco) "advantage" 236-7; concession 8, 36-7, 104; crude sales 227; capacity expansion 153, 157-8, 181, 217, 224-5, 306; participation 119, 154, 177, 179-80, 194, 207-8; production ceilings 224, 226-7; Saudi taxes and 50/50 15, 17-19, 24, 92-3, 128, 133, 155
Arbitration Iran-AIOC 22; Iran Consortium 29; Libya 80, 82, 135, 154; Libya-Liamco 154; Libya-Shell 194; see also 9-11, 27, 31
Baker, James 300, 302-3
Barran, Sir David 123, 126, 136
Bin Laden, Osama 313, 343
British National Oil Corp. (BNOC) 260, 263, 270, 280, 319, 324
British Petroleum (BP) Alaska 269; concessions 71; crude sales 36, 42; diversification 212; embargo 188, 275; Iran - see AIOC; Iraq 194; Libya 86, 124; mergers & acquisitions 324-5, 327; Nigeria 227; North Sea 268; OPEC 103-4, 123-4, 136, 168; participation 193, prices 39, 95, 97; profits 222; rationalization 277; Tehran agreement 130, 134
Bush, George H. 291, 297-301
Bush, George W. 305, 312, 327, 341-3, 345-6
cartel anti-trust 10-11, 64; OPEC cartelized 182-3, 195-6, 213, 217; competition 263, 317; OPEC quotas 278-9; see also 37, 39, 70, 167, 202, 206, 222, 224, 239, 242, 337, 347
Carter, Jimmy 233, 240, 253-5

Chevron Corp. (Standard Oil Co. of California) Caltex 43; concessions 7-8, 10, 36; crude purchases 311 (Iraq), 289, 321 (Saudi Arabia); crude sales 73, 226-7, 236, 284; diversification 212-3; Iran 28; Libya 81, 86, 122-4, 154; mergers 325-7; participation 207

coal ECE Coal Committee 65-6 European 48-50; diversification 212-3; fuel-switching 242-6, 249; see also 44-5, 48-50, 52, 65-6, 137, 141, 161, 169-70, 212-3, 242-6, 249, 251-3, 255, 315-6, 323

Consortium, Iranian 22, 28-9

companies, independents competition from 2, 43, 74, 87; Iran 28; Libya 74-8, 81-2; Venezuela 47, 74-5; see also 47, 84, 88, 128, 230, 314, 319

companies, majors cartel 2-3, 10-11, 38-9; competition 42, 68-71, 73-5, 78, 85-8; concessions 7-9, 210-1; diversification 212-3, 323; earnings 159, 162; joint ventures downstream 42-3; mergers & acquisitions 324-3; offtake agreements 69-72; price structure 37-8, 55-61, 65-7; posted price reductions 96-7; security of supply 50-2, 167-8, 187; vertical integration 43, 155, 227-8, 275; see also 1, 7, 28-31, 44-5, 81-3, 115, 118, 123, 135-7, 146, 151-2

companies, national (state)oil 47, 50-1, 94, 107, 128, 131, 210, 227, 260, 263, 270-4, 280, 294, 319, 324, 326, 328, 330

concessions characteristics 8-10; conservation regulation 111-2; in 1950 32; Iran 22, 25, 30, 84-5; Iraq 12-13, 90; Kuwait 85; Libya 76-9, 81-2, 135; loss of 314-5; policy 270; Saudi Arabia 18, 36-7, 85; system 6-7, 93; Venezuela 14-15, 19-20, 74-5; see also 1, 2, 4, 6, 69, 88, 101-3, 137

corporate social responsibility 314, 331-2

Drake, Sir Eric 123, 136, 210

E c o n o m i c   C o o p e r a t i o n Administration (ECA) 60-1

Economic Commission for Europe (ECE) 65-7, 168

EEC 107-10

embargo Arab oil 139, 179-90, 205, 219, 239, 246; Iran 340; Iraq 299, 303-4, 307-8; Libya 340; see also 121, 131, 174, 246, 293-4

energy policy EEC 170-1; IEA 247-9, 251, 336; US 169, 197-8, 253-4, 341

environment 241, 246, 249-50, 314, 331-6

Exxon Corp. (Standard Oil Co. (New Jersey)) Alaska 269, 333; Aramco 8,36; diversification 212-3, 243, 323; Libya 75, 77-82, 86, 121-4, 133, 154; mergers and acquisitions 325-7; Occidental 122; outlook 117, 189, 315-6, 334; participation 156, 178, 207; posted price reductions 96-7; spot markets 230; Tehran agreement 130; Venezuela 42, 63, 70-1, 73, 75, 94

Fallah, Reza 101, 103

Farmanfarmaian, Manucher 16-17, 23, 95, 99

fifty/fifty 50/50 Iran 24-6, 29; Middle East 20-1; Saudi Arabia 17-20, 166; Venezuela 14-16, 137; see also 30, 62-3

Ford, Gerald 185, 199-200, 205, 253-4

Garvin, Clifton 189, 213, 246

Glaspie, April 297, 300

Gorbachov, Mikhail 299

Gulf Oil Corp. crude sales 36; Kuwait 8; Consortium 28; Libya 82; mergers & acquisitions 326-7; outlook 41; participation 153, 193, 197**Hearings, US Congress** Multinational Corporations (MNC) 124, 130, 134, 175, 188, 199-200

Heath, Edward 49, 275

Hussein, Saddam 238, 296-301, 305, 308, 311-3, 342-4, 346

Ickes, Harold 11, 37, 166

International Energy Agency (IEA) 190-1, 203, 218, 223-4, 226-7, 232, 242, 247-9, 251, 336

Iranian Consortium

Kissinger, Henry A 181, 184-5, 190, 197-205, 209, 223, 246, 340

Lawson, Nigel 274

Legislation Alberta Oil & Gas